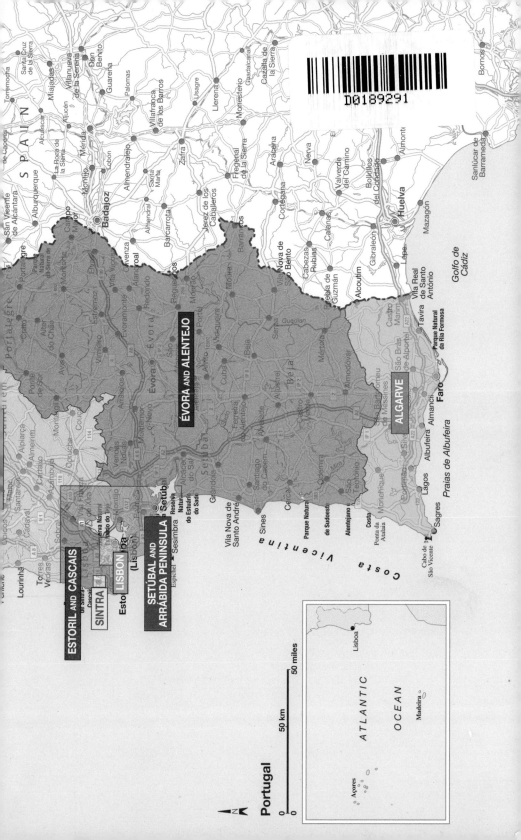

2014

-- 2014

INSIGHT GUIDES

PORTUGAL

The first Insight Guide pioneered the use of creative full-colour photography in travel guides in 1970. Since then, we have expanded our range to cater for our readers' need not only for reliable information about their chosen destination but also for a real understanding of the culture and workings of that destination. Now, when the internet can supply inexhaustible (but not always reliable) facts, our books marry text and pictures to provide those much more elusive qualities: knowledge and discernment. To achieve this, they rely heavily on the authority of locally based writers and photographers.

How to use this book

Insight Guide: Portugal is structured to convey an understanding of the country and its culture and to guide readers through its attractions:

The **Best of Portugal** section at the front of the guide helps you to prioritise what you want to do.

The **Features** section, indicated by a pink bar at the top of each page, covers Portugal's history, people and culture in lively, authoritative essays written by specialists.

The main **Places** section, indicated by a blue bar, provides full details of all the sights and areas worth seeing on your visit to Portugal. The chief places of interest are coordinated by number with specially drawn, full-colour maps.

The **Travel Tips** listings section, with a yellow bar, provides full information on transport, hotels, restaurants, activities from shopping to sports, an A–Z section of essential practical information, and a handy phrasebook with Portuguese words and expressions.

A special section of photographic features showcases what makes Portugal unique; from its religious festivals to *azulejos* and Port wine.

Photographs are chosen not only to illustrate geography and

buildings but also to convey the many moods of the country and its people.

The contributors

This new edition of *Insight Guide: Portugal* was managed by Insight Guides Series Editor **Carine Tracanelli** and copy-edited by **Stephanie Smith**.

Abigail Blasi, a lover of everything Portuguese, thoroughly updated the book throughout.

This edition builds on the original book put together by **Alison Friesinger Hill, Thomas Hill, Ruth Rosengarten, Jean Anderson, Scott Carney, Katherine Barrett Swett, Sharon Behn, Marvine Howe, Deborah Brammer, Jeremy Boultbee, Jenny Wittner, Nigel Tisdall, Brian and Eileen Anderson**.

Many of the stunning photographs are the output of **Lydia Evans**, with contributions by other talented photographers.

Map Legend	
▬ ▪ ▪	International Boundary
▬ ▬ ▬	Province Boundary
▬ ● ▬	National Park/Reserve
▬ ▬ ▬	Ferry Route
Ⓜ	Metro
✈ ✈	Airport: International/Regional
🚌	Bus Station
ℹ	Tourist Information
🏛 † ⛪	Church/Ruins
†	Monastery
☾	Mosque
✡	Synagogue
🏰 🏯	Castle/Ruins
∴	Archaeological Site
⌂	Cave
𝟏	Statue/Monument
★	Place of Interest
🏖	Beach

The main places of interest in the Places section are coordinated by number with a full-colour map (eg ❶), and a symbol at the top of every right-hand page tells you where to find the map.

Contents

THE BEST OF PORTUGAL: TOP ATTRACTIONS

From the gorgeous beaches and balmy waters of the Algarve to the intellectual buzz of medieval Coimbra, the pleasures of the Alentejo Wine Route, and Lisbon's sights, tastes and sounds.

△ **Algarve**. The region has the greatest choice of beaches and warmest waters, from the semi-wild beaches on the windy west coast, like Monte Clerigo, to the more sheltered stretches around Lagos with gorgeous rock-framed sandy coves nearby. See page 187.

△ **Sintra**. Once a cool summer residence for kings, Sintra is a magical place that has kept the character that was a lure for poets and rich foreigners alike. Its beautiful royal palace, splendid *quintas* (estates), the extraordinary Pena palace, and some good museums all add lustre. See page 171.

▽ **Évora**. Gleaming above the Alentejo plains, Évora traverses the ages with amazing megaliths nearby, a glorious Roman temple, spectacular churches, shops under ancient arcades, and great food and lodgings. See page 209.

△ **Vila Nova de Milfontes**. The most charming of the Alentejo seaside resorts, Vila Nova de Milfontes is a white-washed, laid-back town close to some lovely golden-sand beaches. See page 222.

◁ **The Convento do Cristo, Tomar**. This Unesco World Heritage Site is a dazzling Manueline maze of winding passageways, irregular cloisters and extraordinary carving, centred around the mystical octagonal Templar church. See page 233.

▷ **University town Coimbra**. Once Portugal's medieval capital, Coimbra combines beautiful ancient buildings and a sense of tradition with the buzz from the population of present-day students, dressed in their traditional black capes. See page 245.

△ **Lisbon**. The Portuguese capital is stunningly rich in historic sights, led by the great Jerónimos monastery at Belém. Picturesque neighbourhoods, like Moorish Alfama or the Beira Alta, are architecturally pleasing and full of colour, music and good places to eat. See page 139.

△ **The Alentejo Wine Route**. This route offers a chance to explore the ancient bleached landscape of the Alentejo. See page 207.

▷ **Reserva Natural das Berlenga**. This protected archipelago 10km (6 miles) offshore from Peniche on the west coast is characterised by a dramatic rocky terrain home to thousands of nesting sea birds, especially guillemots. See page 240.

◁ **Porto**. This glorious city has a beguilingly pretty river front, wonderful *azulejos*, a cutting-edge Casa da Musica and lots of lively places to eat, drink and sip port. See page 275.

THE BEST OF PORTUGAL: EDITOR'S CHOICE

Dramatic mountains, lively markets, a long stretch of coastline with some lovely beaches, fascinating museums, great food and wine and many family-orientated places… Here, at a glance, are our recommendations for a visit.

The high-perched Castelo de Almourol.

ONLY IN PORTUGAL

The Douro valley. The valley thrillingly evokes Portugal's famous port wines in vineyards that stripe the river's steep slopes. Start your tour at ancient Porto or the port-wine lodges of Vila Nova de Gaia opposite, and work your way through the valley. Or you can sit back and enjoy a cruise, from Porto's colourful Ribeira, lasting several hours or several days. See page 285.

Bullfighting. Portuguese-style bullfighting is different from Spain's to-the-death approach. A *cavaleiro*, a decoratively coated horseman,

demonstrates his skills and those of his horse. But as *banderillas* (sharp darts) are used, it is not for those against cruel sports. There are arenas in many cities but, for atmosphere, a Ribatejo fair is most colourful. See page 369.

Fado. Meaning fate or destiny, fado is Portugal's most renowned music – intense, soulful singing accompanied usually by a 12-stringed Portuguese guitar. In Lisbon you can hear it at its best in the Bairro Alto or Alfama. In Coimbra it is usually black-cloaked male students who sing fado. See page 79.

BEST CASTLES AND ANCIENT SITES

São Jorge (St George). With its long history and dominant hilltop position, Lisbon's São Jorge takes pride of place. The city views are spectacular, there's a citadel to explore, birds to spot, a restaurant, and quite often an exhibition or an event. See page 147.

Foz Côa. A Unesco heritage site, this **archaeological park** is to be found in the Douro valley region. With the largest area of palaeolithic engravings in Europe, it is one of the surprises in a country rich in historic treasures, and the area has been enhanced by a beautiful new museum. See page 290.

Guimarães. This 10th-century castle is the "cradle of Portugal" where the nation's first king, Afonso Henriques, was born in 1110. Restored castle walls and towers remain impressive. See page 307.

Almourol. Set on a river island, Almourol castle has an enchanting atmosphere. Built (or possibly rebuilt) by Gualdim Pais, the founder of the Templar city of Tomar, it is haunted by legends. See page 232.

Conímbriga. Near Coimbra, this the site of marvellous Roman ruins and mosaics and is complemented by an excellent museum. See page 255.

The Douro Valley.

BEST FESTAS AND SPECTACLES

An Easter procession in Lisbon.

Viana do Castelo's Festa. This three-day *festa* in August is queen of the folk fairs. Vivid embroidered costumes and "brides" in black adorned in gold jewellery are the highlight of a stunning festival of traditional music, dancing and parades. See page 303.

The Festas dos Santos Populares. This festival held in June celebrates Lisbon's favourite saints with parades, feasting and wine. The aroma of grilled sausages and sardines hangs over Alfama during this fun, friendly festival. See page 99.

Escola Portuguesa de Arte Equestre shows.

Parque Nacional Peneda-Gerês.

Classic displays of stylish horsemanship by the school's *equitadores* (horse riders) are a treat. For shows, the Alter Real horses are beribboned and the riders dressed in courtly costumes and tricorne hats. The *escola* performs at 11am every Wednesday (May–July, Sept and Oct) at the Queluz National Palace. See page 172.

The Colete Encarnada (Red Waistcoat). The Ribatejo's favourite *festa* takes place in July and October in Vila Franca de Xira, northeast of Lisbon. The red waistcoats are those of *campinos* or herdsmen who tend to the region's bulls, cattle and horses all year. You can bypass the bullfights and still be richly entertained by local colour, bullrunning, riding and herding contests. See page 231.

Carnival. The pre-Lenten celebration is practised each February in several towns, but most charmingly in Loulé in the Algarve. Children parade in costumes, adults on themed floats toss sweets – or bags of flour – into the crowds. See page 98.

BEST MOUNTAIN PARKS

The Serra da Estréla. There's enough snow for gentle skiing in winter and wonderful herb-scented pastures for shepherds' flocks in spring and summer – providing Portugal's finest *serra* cheese. See page 267.

Parque Nacional Peneda-Gerês. This national park is wild, grand and great for hiking. It covers 720 sq km (278 sq miles) with peaks up to Nervosa at 1,545 metres (5,070ft). The park includes tiny granite villages like Soajo. See page 305.

The Serra da Arrábida. Cliffs plunging into blue sea give this *serra* an extra dimension. Its great natural beauty is enhanced in spring by a dazzling array of wild flowers. The Arrábida area is also known for a savoury cheese, Azeitão. Best access is by car. See page 181.

Ilha de Tavira beach.

BEST BEACHES

Ilha de Tavira. Accessible by ferry from Tavira, this beached ringed island of the Algarve is unspoilt, beautiful, and rarely over-crowded. See page 193.

Praia Dona Ana. There are some wonderful beaches around Lagos in the Algarve, which has dramatically beautiful rock formations lining the coast, and this is one of the most attractive. See page 197.

Praia do Guincho. This long, white-sanded beach in Cascais is easy to access from the capital and a favourite of windsurfers. See page 169.

Praia da Rocha. Close to Portimao in the Algarve, this is backed by dramatic cliffs. See page 196.

Praia de Mira. Backed by the forested nature reserve Mata Nacional das Dunas de Mira, this is a pretty, white-sanded beach. See page 260.

Almograve. The Alentejan coast, edged by the Atlantic, is short but attractive, and Vila Nova da Milfontes is one of its loveliest spots. See page 222.

The unusual grain stores of Soajo.

Cais da Ribeira in Porto is a Unesco World Heritage Site.

WHERE LAND ENDS AND SEA BEGINS

Portugal's diverse landscapes as well as its history and culture set it apart from the rest of Europe.

Accordion player in traditional dress, Viana do Castelo.

Portugal is a land on the edge, "where land ends and sea begins", as the 16th-century epic poet Luís Vaz de Camões put it. At the western periphery of Europe, it is also caught between traditional ways of making a living – fishing and farming – and the technology that has made the world smaller, more integrated, more complex.

It is a small country, encompassing an area of 92,100 sq km (33,550 sq miles) – a bit bigger than Austria – but has a stunning diversity of lovely landscapes: long white beaches and pretty coves; ranges of rolling hills and mountains, the central Serra da Estrela (Mountains of the Stars) being the highest; numerous rivers; and, in the southern central area, Alentejo's broad plain, which is patched with cork oaks and olive plantations.

Crowning Portugal's natural beauty for much of the year are blue skies and a glowing light: an agreeable climate of hot summers and chilly but never freezing winters. It's a temperate country, in mood as in weather. The characteristics of its people (numbering about 10.8 million) tend towards gentleness, courteousness, hospitality and tolerance – with a pronounced streak of fatalism.

Portugal offers everything a visitor could want, from the clubs and bars of Lisbon, often open till long after a new day dawns, to the most obscure village in Trás-os-Montes, with its simple ways of baking, spinning and farming.

This guide describes Portugal's long and fascinating history, and provides an introduction to its people. The book's Features section will familiarise you with Portugal's foods and wines, its wonderful accommodation in *pousadas* (inns) and manor houses, and with its glorious art and architecture. Once you feel you know a little about the culture of Portugal, you are bound to be inspired to begin your tour of the country, and the Places section of this guide will help you to get the most out of it.

Barrels from the José Maria da Fonseca Winery.

Traditional folk dancing at Viana do Castelo.

THE PORTUGUESE

A passion for coffee and cakes is a national characteristic to which visitors can instantly relate. Other traits are a little more complex.

C haracterised as easy-going, smiling, patient, good-natured but imbued with an inner *saudade*, a tricky-to-define quality that equates to nostalgia or melancholy, the Portuguese tend to come across as a gentle, cordial people. They certainly offer a relaxed welcome to foreign visitors, whether they are seeking sunny beaches, medieval architecture, the beauties of the countryside, or the local food and wines. In addition, generations of international exploration, connections with former colonies, and immigration from abroad have made this a much more cosmopolitan country than you might expect – in Lisbon and the Algarve, at least.

Infinite variety

It remains that the Portuguese population is one of the most homogeneous in Europe; however the country displays surprising variations from region to region, and in particular between north and south. There are also some

A night out in Bairro Alto.

> Of its 10.8 million-strong population, around two-thirds of the Portuguese live in the coastal areas, with the north far less populated.

physical differences in the people: in the north the basic Iberian strain – dark, thick-set – has been leavened with Celtic blood, while in the south, Jewish, Moorish and African ancestors are evident. The more sparsely populated north is generally more conservative, both politically and culturally, and is the bastion of Portuguese Catholicism. The south has a tradition of liberalism and adaptation. The two different

temperaments – the warm Mediterranean and cool Atlantic – wash over each other. The people are as varied as their land. There is a saying that "Coimbra studies while Braga prays, Porto works while Lisbon plays".

Internal differences

There are other internal differences, too. Portugal had the fastest expanding economy in the European Union 10 years after joining, but in the last decade, it has been one of the least healthy economies in the EU sickroom. Like other countries in Europe, Portugal is attempting a tricky balancing act between decreasing the budget deficit, avoiding discontent, and promoting growth, and all while inflation and unemployment rise and wages fall. It seems that all the Portuguese have to look forward to at the moment is more austerity and an uncertain future.

There's a greater sense of certainty, however, in the bucolic backways of Trás-os-Montes and the Beiras, among the windmills, the cobbled roads, and horse-drawn farmers' carts. These rural communities remain almost defiantly untouched, with the men in their flat caps chatting in the town square. Venturing here you may well feel that you have stepped back in time. Rural people generally distrust Lisbon

that of their counterparts in other European countries, but despite legal equality, attitudes are slow to change, particularly in rural areas, where most people live.

If in many ways the rhythm of Portuguese life is slow and habits cautious, this is less to do with Latin temperament or the climate than with the effects of the Salazar era and its aftermath; many people returning from the colonies had a deeply traumatic time in the clashes between new left and old right.

However, there's a more forward-looking feel to Portugal's cities. Cutting-edge archi-

Fado in Tasca di Chico, Bairro Alto.

and all that it stands for: social turmoil, taxes, bureaucracy, centralised education. They would rather keep their distance. Able to sustain themselves by their harvests, they have little interest in inflation or trade deficits. They are self-reliant. Religious festivals are taken very seriously and can last for several days, especially in the Minho province and the Azores Islands, with celebrations including solemn processions, traditional dances and fireworks.

This was once an extremely patriarchal society, where women only gained the vote in 1975, and there has been great progress in terms of the position of women. Some urban women hold important jobs, and the lifestyle of many of the younger ones in the cities is similar to

tecture has changed the face of Lisbon and Porto, and the cities are also significantly multicultural. Portugal has long been notable for emigration, with Portuguese people living all over the world, in South America, Africa, India and China. More than four million Portuguese citizens still live abroad, most of whom emigrated in the early and mid-20th century, settling mainly in France, Germany, Switzerland, Luxembourg (curiously, 15 percent of the population there are of Portuguese descent), United States, Canada, Brazil, and Venezuela. The majority of the Portuguese population in the United States is from the Azores islands, as are the Portuguese who settled in Canada.

In the 1970s the tide turned, and there was an influx of people from the former Portuguese colonies, especially Brazil, Angola and Cape Verde, bringing their influence to bear, particularly in and around Lisbon and Algarve. Other minority communities include Goans from India and Chinese from Macau. The African clubs in Lisbon are some of the capital's funkiest venues; this is one of the best places in Europe to hear African music and experience its nightlife. Mariza, the current queen of *fado*, was born in Mozambique, and one of her most emotional songs is *O Gente da Minha* Terra (Oh

in the world, unemployment has been rising steadily over the last decade, and is at its highest among the under-24 age group. As people move to find work in the cities, and the birth rate remains low, villages are rapidly depopulating – some appear to be inhabited only by elderly widows. The urban population accounts for more than 50 percent of the national total, which is a considerable shift.

In industry and commerce there are a few conglomerates; the large majority of companies are small- and medium-sized businesses employing, for the most part, fewer than 10

Portuguese farmer tilling his field.

People of my Country) – which expresses a very Portuguese sentiment in a very bittersweet, Portuguese way: the love of this staunchly patriotic land, a place of poets and sailors.

With the economic crisis and biting austerity of recent years, once again the flow has turned outwards. Young Portuguese are heading abroad – in many cases reversing the trend and making their way to Portugal's former colonies in Angola and Brazil – in search of opportunities and a brighter future.

Work

Unfortunately for the entire Portuguese population, and in keeping with the slowdown of the global economy and conditions elsewhere

COMING HOME

Traditionally Portugal was a country of emigration, where the very young and the old were left behind while wage-earners went abroad to work and send money home. However, in the 1990s, as Portugal boomed and EU capital brought new life to the country, many professional workers arrived from Brazil and elsewhere, bringing with them their tastes and lifestyles. Portugal also received an influx of migrant workers from Eastern Europe in an interesting reversal of earlier times. But with the economic crisis the situation has reversed once again, with 2 percent of the population leaving in 2011–2013, mostly young graduates.

people; textiles and shoes are the top manufactured products and excellent value for tourists. There are no local huge shopping chains, and the biggest department stores in Lisbon, malls apart, are the French-owned Fnac and Spanish-owned El Corte Inglés.

With a long coastline, fishing remains strong but it is not a high-paying industry. Agriculture has never been more than basically productive, despite the country's rustic image. Portugal's olive oil production, for example, just meets its own needs. About 10 percent of the workforce is in agriculture, which produces less than 4

Shopping for hats.

percent of the GDP. Despite appalling annual fires, forestry is profitable, with cork still a major harvest. Port wine from the Douro valley is among Portugal's most famous products, but table wines from many newly designated areas are reaching new peaks of quality. Tourism contributes a high proportion of foreign earnings and around two-thirds of the workforce is in the service sector.

Family ties

The family unit is a bedrock of Portuguese society, but this is now also beginning to change, with a decline in the birth rate (1.5 is now the national average) resulting in an ageing population. However, the Portuguese adore babies and small children, as you will notice out and in restaurants.

Portugal is a predominantly Roman Catholic country (around 97 percent), with a few Protestant communities, and a few Jewish and Muslim ones as well. One interesting group is the so-called *Marranos*, Jews who converted during the 16th- and 17th-century persecutions, and who retain some Jewish rituals, sometimes in combination with a nominal Catholicism. Catholicism in Portugal tends towards the colourful and mystical, bound up with local superstitions, ancient traditions and pre-Christian practices. Popular beliefs involve the phases of the moon and the threat of the evil eye. It is the tradition that older rural women dress in black after the death of their husbands for about seven years, and many wear it for the rest of their lives.

A changing society

As you travel around Portugal, it becomes increasingly obvious that this is a country that hangs in the balance between the old ways and the new. You can go from the graceful formality and strict religious conformity of a traditional village, where life seems to have remained unchanged for hundreds of years, to a sleek modernist art gallery or a nightclub that flings its doors open at 5am so that punters can dance their way through to the following afternoon. You can wander from an ironic and arty bar in Lisbon's Bairro Alto, to a nearby hole-in-the-wall drinking den selling cherry brandy to gnarled old-timers.

This is a nation that is fiercely proud of its identity and traditions, but is not averse to change. Considering that Portugal was a country living under a dictatorship until 1973, it is extraordinary to think that it is one of the few places worldwide where the policy on illegal drugs is aimed at rehabilitation rather than retribution – drugs were decriminalised here in 2001, and the problem is regarded as a public health issue (those found in possession of less than 10 days supply are offered treatment rather than incarcerated).

These elements – of worldliness versus the parochial, of great exploration overseas versus the timelessness of life in a tiny whitewashed village – point to some of the contradictions in the Portuguese soul, contradictions that will remain part of the beguiling complexity of this mesmerising country.

Celebrating the Festa de São João.

1147

1227

1497

1762

1385

1834

DECISIVE DATES

A statue of the D. Fernando, the 2nd Duke of Braganca at Braganca

Early Days

9th–6th centuries BC
Phoenician and Greek traders establish settlements.

5th century BC
Carthaginians in control of the Iberian peninsula.

130 BC
Roman conquest.

4th century AD
Christianity spreads.

AD 419
The Germanic Suevi arrive; vanquished by the Visigoths over the next 50 years.

711
African Moors occupy Iberia.

718
Victory by the Christians over the Moors at Covadonga starts the reconquest.

11th–12th centuries
A complex round of civil wars between Henri of Burgundy and his cousin Raymond.

Reconquest and Nationhood

1143
Afonso Henriques is declared first king of Portugal, but is not recognised by Pope Lucius II.

1147
Henriques captures Lisbon.

1179
Afonso Henriques is finally recognised by Pope Alexander III as king.

1249
Moors expelled from Algarve.

1260
Afonso III transfers capital from Coimbra to Lisbon.

1279–1325
Reign of King Dinis.

1297
Treaty of Alcañices establishes Portugal's borders.

1348
Plague ravages Lisbon.

1373
First Anglo-Portuguese Alliance signed.

1385
Defeat of Castilians. João I becomes king, commencing the House of Avis.

Medieval map of Portugal.

The Age of Discoveries

1415
Ceuta, North Africa, is taken by Portuguese force. Madeira discovered.

1427
Azores discovered.

1434
Gil Eanes discovers parts of West Africa.

1481
João II ascends the throne.

1487
Bartolomeu Dias rounds Cape of Good Hope.

1492
Around 60,000 Jews expelled from Spain flee to Portugal.

1494
Treaty of Tordesillas: Portugal and Spain divide up New World.

1497–98
Explorer Vasco da Gama opens a sea route to India.

1500
Pedro Alvares Cabral discovers Brazil.

1510
Conquest of Goa.

1519–22
Ferdinand Magellan circumnavigates the globe.

1536
Holy Inquisition is introduced.

1557
Trading post opens in Macau.

1580
Portugal falls under Spanish rule.

1640
Spanish overthrown; Duke of Bragança becomes João IV.

1668
Treaty of Lisbon; Spain recognises Portugal's independence.

early 1700s
Gold is discovered in Brazil.

1755
The Great Earthquake devastates Lisbon.

1777
Maria I becomes queen.

1807
France invades; royal family leaves for Brazil.

1808
The Peninsular War. Portugal invokes the British Alliance.

1820
Liberal revolution.

1822
New liberal constitution ends the Inquisition. Brazil proclaims independence.

1829–34
Miguelist Wars between factions led by brothers Miguel and Pedro. The latter wins and becomes Pedro IV in 1834.

1834
Religious orders expelled from Portugal.

1834–1908
Rise of political parties, Septembrists (Liberals) and Chartists (Conservatives).

1908
King Carlos and crown prince are shot dead in Lisbon. Manuel II ascends the throne.

1910
Portugal becomes a republic; Manuel II exiled.

1910–26
Political turmoil, military coups and assassination.

Salazar and After

1926
Military coup overthrows democratic government and brings General Carmona to power.

1932
Salazar becomes PM and rules as dictator until 1968.

1939–1945
World War II: Portugal is neutral.

1955
Portugal allowed to join the UN.

1961
Angolan uprising brutally crushed. Goa lost to Indian control.

1970
Death of Salazar. Marcelo Caetano becomes prime minister.

1974
Young Captains' Revolution restores democracy. Armed Forces Movement governs until 1976. African colonies granted independence.

1976
Socialist Mario Soares becomes prime minister.

1979
Coalition of the right in power.

1986
Portugal joins the European Economic Community (EEC).

1999
Macau reverts to Chinese control.

2002
Euro becomes official currency. Centre-right government elected.

2005
Socialists sweep to victory in general elections. Jose Sócrates sworn in as PM.

2006
Former Social Democrat PM Cavaco Silva elected president.

2011
EU and IMF supply a 78bn-euro loan package, conditional on reducing the public deficit.

2013
Portugal's highest court strikes down some of the 2013 budget's austerity measures.

Portugal's President Anibal Cavaco Silva.

ANCIENT LUSITANIA

For centuries, successive waves of invaders swept over the peninsula. The Moors held on longest, even after Afonso Henriques became Portugal's first king.

Portugal, with borders already established by the 13th century, is one of the oldest nations in Europe. Despite its small size, its impact on global history has been powerful and its influences visible in many places across the world. Over the centuries it has discovered and lost an empire, relinquished and regained its cherished autonomy and, since the 1974 revolution that ended decades of dictatorship, has formed new ties with some of its former possessions.

Cultural diffusion

A rich prehistoric culture has left its traces throughout Portugal. There is evidence of the earliest stages of human evolution and a large number of megalithic sites. The variety and quantity of these finds have led many scholars to a theory that cultural diffusion came primarily from overseas. Opponents of this notion point out that this is unlikely, as most of the megalithic sites are far from the coastline. They think the population grew via natural land routes of settlement which, unsurprisingly, correspond to the paths invaders have taken

The ancient standing stones at Almendres, Évora, is the largest existing group of structured menhirs in the Iberian Peninsula.

Evidence of 2nd millennium BC Portuguese society can be seen in the form of the constructions that still stand, for example at the Citânia de Briteiros near Guimarães.

throughout Portugal's history: across the Rio Minho from the north and over the Alentejo flatlands from the south.

In any case, by the 2nd millennium BC, social organisation consisted of scattered *castros* – garrisoned hilltop villages that suggest warfare between tribes. The people subsisted on goat-herding and primitive agriculture, and clad themselves in woollen cloaks.

In the south, tribes came under the influence of Phoenician trade settlements in the 9th century BC, and Greek ones in the 6th century BC, both on the coast and inland, where metals were mined. Only at this late point is there evidence of a significant fishing economy among the indigenous people. Perhaps before then the rough-hewn and storm-beaten Atlantic coast was too intimidating for their small boats. During the 5th century BC, the Carthaginians wrested control of the Iberian peninsula from these earlier traders, but lost it to the Roman Empire in the Second Punic War.

Wars of conquests

The Romans called the peninsula Hispania Ulterior. Here, as elsewhere in the empire, they combined their economic exploitation with cultural upheaval. They were not traders, after all, but conquerors, who set about the business of founding cities, building roads and reorganising territories. They also implemented governmental and judicial systems.

The locals resisted. The largest and most intransigent group were the Lusitani, who lived north of the Rio Tejo (Tagus), and after whom the region was given its name, Lusita-

In 61 BC, Julius Caesar governed the province from Olisipo (as Lisbon was then called). Cities were established and colonised at Évora, Beja, Santarém and elsewhere. Roads linked the north and south, and Lisbon became an important administrative centre, at the hub of the Romans' local road network linking the major population centres. These centres and routes have waned in importance, but many – most notably the capital, Lisbon – are still geographic focal points.

Before their empire eventually fell, the Romans had infused the area with their language, legal system, currency, agriculture and,

A sculpture found in Lisbon's Roman theatre.

nia. Bitter guerrilla fighting was intermittent for two centuries. The most renowned rebel was a shepherd named Viriathus, who led uprisings until he was assassinated in 139 BC by three treacherous comrades who had been bribed by the Romans. It was during these wars of conquest that Roman troops are said to have refused to cross the Rio Lima, believing it to be the *Lethe*, the mythical River of Forgetfulness. Their commander, the story goes, had to cross the river alone, then call each soldier by name to prove that the dip had not affected his memory. The death of Viriathus took the heart out of the revolt, although the Lusitanian uprisings were not finally quelled until 72 BC.

eventually, with Christianity. The organisation of *latifundios* – great, landed estates – was particularly significant as it brought large-scale farming to the area for the first time.

With the conversion of the late Roman emperors (Constantine, who issued an Edict of Tolerance in AD 331, was the first Christian emperor), the tenets and organisation of Christianity spread throughout the fading empire. Bishoprics were established in a number of cities, Braga and Évora among them. As the church expanded, it usurped the administrative power that had been developed by the empire at the height of its strength.

Heretical Christian doctrines held sway in Portugal during the 3rd and 4th centuries. In the early 5th century various groups of barbarians occupied the land. The Alani and Vandals each settled for a short time, but by 419 the Suevi were in sole, if not steady, possession of Galicia, and from there they conquered Lusitania and most of the Iberian peninsula. The Suevi apparently assimilated easily with the existing Hispano-Roman population, but the tide turned with the fall of Rome and the arrival of the Visigoths.

For the next half century, military conquest inevitably meant religious conversion. In 448, Rechiarius, the king of a diminished Suevi empire, converted to Catholicism, perhaps hop-

The Temple of Diana at Évora.

ing to elicit aid from Rome in battling against the Visigoths, who were nominally Christian but clung to vestiges of heretical beliefs. When Rechiarius was killed in 457, the Suevi kingdom survived, led by his son, Masdra. The latter's son, Remismund, succeeded him and in 465 renounced Christianity, probably hoping to appease the Visigoths. But by 550, the growing power of the Catholic Church had produced a new round of conversions, led by St Martin of Dume. The remnants of the Suevi were politically extinguished in 585.

Invaders from the south

Visigoth rule, under an elective monarchy, was not seriously challenged until the Moors

– Muslims from North Africa – arrived on the south coast in 711 and began their expansion northwards. The Moors were following the instructions of their leader, the Prophet Mohammed (who died in 632), to wage a holy war *(jihad)* against non-believers. However, like the Christian Crusades that followed (see page 30), their advances were increasingly concerned with empire building.

The Visigoths were defeated at the Battle of Jerez, and Lisbon soon fell into Muslim hands. Southern Portugal became part of Muslim Spain, loosely organised under the Córdoba caliph – caliphs were successors of the Prophet, regional rulers created under the Umayyad dynasty (650–749).

To the Moors, this land was known as Al-Gharb (the West), from which was derived the modern name Algarve. The Moors soon ruled all Portugal, and Christianity was forced north of the Minho, where it lay gathering strength for the *reconquest* – the *Reconquista.*

A nation in prospect

Stirrings of the *Reconquista* were believed to have started as early as 718 at Covadonga. Here in Asturias, the Christians defeated a small force of Moors. Galicia became a battleground over the next century and a half. The kings of Asturias-León made ever-increasing excursions into Galicia and beyond. Slowly, towns fell before the Christian armies: Porto in 868, Coimbra in 878, and by 955 the King of León, Ordona III, had engineered a raid on Lisbon. Most of the victories below the Douro, however, were transient ones, amounting to nothing more than successful raids, as the territory was seldom held for more than a season or two. Under the Emir of Córdoba, Muslims in Portugal lived in relative peace, introducing irrigation systems and water mills as well as wheat, rice, oranges and saffron. Shipbuilding was active, copper and silver mines were exploited, Roman roads expanded and towns were planned. There was religious tolerance and the arts flourished. Muslim stuccowork and glazed tiles, called *azulejos*, were a lasting contribution to the nation's architectural style.

Although the local culture was strong, the authority of Córdoba began to wear thin and small kingdoms called *taifas* gained local control. Decentralisation led to internal dissent, partly caused by the rise of the Sufi religious sect. Sufism was considered a subversive and heretical kind of mysticism, but it gained popularity in reaction to the rationalism of conventional Islamic beliefs. These internal divisions allowed Christian forces to push the frontier lines down from the north, but they also permitted radical Muslim military groups such as the Almoravids and the Almohads to rise rapidly to power.

The Almoravids, who had built an empire in Africa, spread northwards. After helping the Islamic rulers in the peninsula to force the Christians back, they unified the *taifas* under their own rule. By 1095 they had succeeded in installing an austere military system and harsh government. They were soon followed by the still more fanatical Almohads and the simmering *Reconquista* took on the aspect of a Holy War for both Christians and Muslims.

The split with Spain

Portugal's separateness from Spain, with which it shares a border, has been attributed to various causes, from the original borders between indigenous tribes to the land held by the Suevi against the Visigothic advances. However, it

Afonso Henriques, first king of Portugal.

> The most famous Sufi poet was Omar Khayyám (1048–1120), whose Rubaiyat, in which women and wine are given mystical significance, was translated into English by the Victorian poet Edward Fitzgerald.

was during the Christian reconquest of Iberia that Portugal first truly asserted its independent stance and its leaders gained their sense of national destiny.

Late in the 9th century, the area between the Lima and Douro rivers, a territory which became known as Portucale, was divided under unstable feudal states, and came under the control of the Kingdom of León.

Fernando I of León was the great consolidating force in northern Spain during the 11th century. As part of his policy of centralising authority, he tried to diminish Portugal's power by dismantling it and dividing it into different provinces under separate governors. When Fernando's successor Alfonso VI took over the kingdoms of León, Castile, Galicia and Portugal, he declared himself "emperor", putting himself above kings. It may have been the lure of the title "king", which the emperor had unwittingly made available, that inspired Afonso Henriques, in the 12th century, to battle, deal and connive for the autonomy of his particular *terra*, Portugal.

Feuding cousins

Afonso Henriques was the son of Henri of Burgundy and his wife Teresa. Henri was among a number of French knights who had arrived in the late 11th century to fight the infidels. They were mostly second and third sons, who,

MILITARY ORDERS

The crusades produced an unusual kind of soldier – that is, those belonging to the military orders created by St Bernard of Clairvaux in 1128. The Knights Templar was the first such order, based in Jerusalem, which had been captured in the First Crusade (1096–99). They were followed by the Knights of St John (the Hospitallers), established in Rhodes, and by the Teutonic Order and the Spanish Knights of Calatrava. Originally, their role was to fight for the true faith while obeying monastic rules of poverty, chastity and obedience. Soon, however, the spoils of war became more important than the spread of Christianity.

under the prevailing system of male primogeniture – which meant that the eldest son inherited property and titles – were left with no real inheritance. If they wanted land and riches, they usually had to travel abroad to win them.

Henri's cousin Raymond, who, like Henri, was a fourth son, also came south. After proving his heroism in battle, Raymond married Alfonso VI's eldest daughter Urraca, and was granted the territories of Galicia and Coimbra. When Henri married Teresa, who was Alfonso's favourite (although illegitimate) daughter, he was given the territory of Portugal. With the

as a lover, displeasing some of the nobility as well as her son. Continuing her husband's policies, Teresa schemed successfully to maintain Portugal's independence, but in 1127 she submitted to Alfonso VII's dominion after her army's defeat. A year later 18-year-old Afonso Henriques led a rebellion against his mother, ending her rule at the battle of São Mamede, near their castle in Guimarães.

A king is crowned

Over the next decade, Afonso Henriques vied with his emperor cousin for ultimate control of

An 18th-century engraving showing Afonso rallying his troops at the conquest of Lisbon in 1147.

death of Raymond and Alfonso VI, Urraca inherited that crown, but her second marriage, to Alfonso I of Aragon, also set in motion a complex round of civil wars.

During this period, Henri of Burgundy made significant strides towards gaining autonomy for the state of Portugal. The most important of these was the support he offered to the archbishops of Braga in a dispute with those of Toledo, the principal see of Spain.

In 1126 Urraca died and her son, Alfonso Raimundez, became Emperor Alfonso VII. When Henri died, his widow, Teresa, ruled Portugal as regent for her son, Afonso Henriques. Without wasting much time in mourning, she took a Galician count, Fernão Peres,

Portugal. After a brilliant military victory over the Moors in the Battle of Ourique in 1139, he began to refer to himself as king. In 1143, the Treaty of Zamora was signed between the two cousins, wherein Alfonso VII gave Afonso Henriques the title of King of Portugal in exchange for feudal ties of military aid and loyalty.

Afonso Henriques sought to fix the title more firmly by seeking recognition from Rome. Pope Lucius II refused, keeping to a policy of supporting Iberian union in the hope of stemming the tide of Islam. It was only in 1179 that Pope Alexander III, in exchange for a yearly tribute and various other privileges, finally granted recognition of the Portuguese kingdom. By that late date, papal acceptance served only to formalise an entity that was not only well established but growing. Afonso Henriques had enlisted the aid of crusaders and beaten back the Moors, adding his conquests to the emerging nation. Santarém and Lisbon were both taken in 1147; the first by surprise attack, the second in a siege that was supported by French, English, Flemish and German crusaders who were passing through Portugal on their way to the Holy Land, to fight what we now know as the Second Crusade.

The inestimable assistance of these 164 shiploads of men was extremely fortuitous; it one batch of infidels was as good as another was crucial to the *Reconquista*. However, Afonso Henriques's confessor questioned the diversion of troops from the crusade, and the story is told that on the way to Santarém – with crusaders in tow – the king, believing his confessor to be right, was besieged by guilt. He was also, understandably, anxious because of the Moorish stronghold's reputation for impregnability.

To soothe his torment, he vowed that he would build an abbey at Alcobaça (some 90km/55 miles southwest of Coimbra) in hon-

> One result of the crusades – which began in 1096 and lasted for more than 150 years – was the founding of powerful military-religious organisations such as the Knights Templar and the Hospitallers (see page 30).

our of the Virgin if the attack was successful. The battle was won, and Afonso Henriques laid the foundation stone of the promised building the following year. The imposing abbey still stands (see page 237).

In 1170, Afonso Henriques fought his last battle, at Badajoz. The powerful Almohads had enlisted the aid of Fernando II of León, who felt that the Portuguese were recapturing not only the Moorish-held land, but territory that was by right a part of León.

Azulejo in the Sala dos Reis (King's Hall), Alcobaça Abbey.

very nearly fell through when Afonso Henriques pronounced that he expected them to fight only for Christianity and not for earthly rewards. This was not the way the crusaders believed holy wars should be fought. The English and Germans walked out, and the king quickly compromised, offering loot and land in exchange for military service.

The western crusade

The Bishop of Braga also offered aid in recruiting foreign crusaders, providing theological assurance that their enemies in the south would be heathens, and therefore no different from those they would be fighting in the Holy Land – convincing crusaders that

The most renowned of Afonso Henriques' military cohorts was Geraldo Geraldes, a local adventurer dubbed O Sem Pavor (The Fearless) for his brilliant raids into Muslim territory. This popular hero had won a string of epic victories, but at Badajoz the combination of Moorish and Leonese forces was too much for both Geraldes and his king. The ageing Afonso Henriques broke his leg and was captured. His release came only after he had surrendered hard-won castles and territories to enemy parties. His retreat allowed the Moors to entrench their forces along the battle zone.

The founding king of Portugal's days of victory were over, with the *Reconquista* still a century away. Yet, with Henriques' monarchy, a country was born. Whether it was through an act of political will or not, the independence and individuality of the Portuguese nation was forever determined.

CASTRO VERDE

King Dinis, depicted in a
17th-century screen.

A NATION IS BORN

With the final expulsion of the Moors, Portugal
steadily established a kingdom under the
House of Burgundy.

For a century after the death of Afonso Henriques in 1185, the first order of business was the slow riddance of the remaining, and still feisty, Moors. The *Reconquista*, now virtually sanctioned by the Church with various papal bulls and indulgences as a "western crusade", was still very much under way.

The Knights Templar had arrived in Portugal when they stopped on their way to Palestine in 1128. They were soon followed by other military-religious orders – the Hospitallers and the Knights of Calatrava and Santiago – who all clung to the religious justification for their warmongering and for their massive accumulation of land and loot.

However, the western crusade remained controversial. In Palestine the dividing line between Christians and infidels was clearly drawn, but southern Iberia had intermingled Muslim, Christian and Jewish people in economic, cultural and political spheres. In 1197, papal indulgences were even promised in a war against Alfonso IX of León, a Christian, though at that time an ally of the Muslims.

The war proceeded steadily, if slowly. The first kings of the Burgundian line after Afonso Henriques continued to press the borders southwards. Under Sancho II, the eastern Algarve and Alentejo were incorporated in the burgeoning nation. By 1249, during the reign of Afonso III, the western Algarve and Faro had fallen. By 1260 Afonso had moved the capital south from Coimbra to Lisbon. These boundaries – much like today's – were finally recognised by Castile in the Treaty of Alcañices in 1297.

Social transformation

The *Reconquista* brought Portugal fundamental social transformation. The lands of the south,

The 13th-century cross of Sancho I.

having been reclaimed, now had to be populated. In order to do this, the Burgundian kings needed to balance their centralised, essentially military power with popular and financial support. The need for such support forced successive kings to consult the cortes, local assemblies of nobles, clergy and, later, mercantile classes. At the *cortes* of Leiria (1254), Afonso III conceded the right of municipal representation in taxation and other economic issues. For the most part, the cortes were gathered whenever the king needed to raise money. When later monarchs used trade and their own military orders to reap independent profits, the *cortes* fell into disuse.

Another result of the *Reconquista*, with the expansion of properties and the need for labourers, was an increase in social mobility among the lower classes. Distinctions fell away among various levels of serfs as farm workers became a scarcer and more valuable commodity. Another effect was the early amalgamation of the divergent cultures of north and south. The south was a culture of tolerance, marked by refinement and urbanity, while the northern culture had a certain arrogance, the attitude of invaders. Differences between the two remain today.

The Church rode the *Reconquista* to riches. The various military-monastic orders were

granted vast areas of land in return for military assistance. Furthermore, Church and clergy were free from taxation, and were granted the right to collect tithes from the population. Their power was such that it soon threatened the monarchy. Afonso II was the first ruler to defy the Church by attempting to curb its acquisition of property. His efforts generally failed, as did those of

In his role of "farmer king" Dinis reformed the agricultural system and initiated programmes that encouraged the export of olive oil, grain, wine and other foodstuffs.

his successor, Sancho II, who was finally excommunicated and dethroned in 1245 for his insistence on royal prerogatives.

The poet king

It was the reign of Dinis, known both as "the farmer king" and "the poet king", that truly cemented Portuguese independence and the power of the monarchy. After briefly joining Aragon in war against Castile, Dinis ushered in a long period of peace and progress. He encouraged learning and literature, establishing the first university in 1288, initially in Lisbon, then transferred to Coimbra. Portuguese, having distinguished itself from its Latin roots and from Castilian (which became Spanish), was established as the language of the troubadour culture, and the official language of law and state.

The troubadour culture – poetry and music spread by peripatetic minstrels – was greatly

Tomar's Convento do Cristo.

THE STORY OF PEDRO AND INÊS

Betrothed to Constanza, a Spanish princess, Pedro, son of Afonso IV, fell in love with her lady-in-waiting, Inês de Castro, from a powerful Castilian family. She was banished in 1340, but returned upon the princess' death in 1345. The threat of a Castilian heir was intolerable to Afonso, so, under pressure from his noblemen, he agreed to her assassination, then immediately withdrew consent. In 1355, taking matters into their own hands, the nobles murdered Inês in the grounds of what is now Quinta da Lágrimas (House of Tears) in Coimbra (see page 250). Pedro was inconsolable. Two years later, when he assumed the throne on his father's death, he tracked down his lover's assassins, caught two of them,

and had their hearts torn out. He then ordered the exhumation of Inês, whose body was dressed in royal robes and placed next to him on the throne. Each member of the court was forced to pay homage by kissing her decomposed hand. She was finally entombed in Alcobaça Monastery along with Pedro, who insisted their tombs were placed foot to foot so that, on the Day of Judgement, the first thing they would see would be each other. Both tombs carry the same inscription *Até o Fim do Mundo* – "Until the End of the World".

This dramatic and touching story of love and revenge has been an inspiration to generations of Portuguese writers and poets.

influential. Drawing on French tradition and Moorish influences, Portuguese troubadours created a native literature. These song-poems of love and satire were often written by nobles, among them, of course, Dinis himself. Other forms of literary expression lagged far behind.

Dinis's rule also brought political progress. Landmark agreements were made to seal peace with Castile (the Treaty of Alcañices, 1297) and the clergy (the Concordat of 1289). The latter agreement was a major victory for royal jurisdiction in matters of property. Dinis also fortified the frontier, building some 50 castles.

the idea of corporations. Craftsmen tended to work on their own, and thus confined themselves to local markets and limited quantities, although some goldsmithing, shipbuilding, and pottery was done in commercial quantities.

Perhaps the most significant of Dinis's accomplishments was the disbanding of the Knights Templar in 1312. The order was under fire throughout Europe, and its demise was imminent. Dinis's triumph was to retain its wealth within the country and prevent the Church from appropriating it. In 1317 he founded the Order of Our Lord Jesus Christ,

The tomb of Pedro I in the monastery at Alcobaça.

Economic advances

By now a monetary economy was well established, internally as well as for international trade. Agricultural production was more and more geared towards markets, although self-sufficient farming did not disappear. Dinis encouraged the expansion of the economic system with large fairs, trading centres that encouraged internal trade – he chartered 48 such fairs, more than all the other Portuguese kings combined. This concentration of trade also, not coincidentally, allowed for more systematic taxation.

The only section of the economy to lag behind was industrial production. Dinis, and later kings, were counter-productive in resisting

which was granted all the former possessions of the Knights Templar, under royal control.

Plagues and crises

Afonso IV succeeded Dinis. His administration was less secure and hostilities with Castile waxed and waned. More significantly, his reign was burdened with the Black Death. The first bout devastated the country, particularly the urban centres, in 1348–9. Throughout the next century the pestilence returned again and again, causing depopulation and despondency. Concurrently, various demographic and economic crises were undermining the nation. The attraction of urban centres left the interior underpopulated, causing inflation in food prices. Successive monarchs tried to regulate population movements but were ineffectual. Economic stagnation, whose dreary influence extended to literature, religion, and every element of daily life, dragged on until the coming of the maritime empire.

The reign of Pedro I was marked by peaceful coexistence with Castile. Social and political growth flourished as the country recovered from the convulsions of the Black Death. However, the increasing power of the nobles, the clergy and the emergent bourgeoisie, all represented in the *cortes*, would later break loose

The carved figures of Batalha Abbey.

in active social discontent during the reign of his son, Fernando I. It was this social unrest, coupled with Portuguese commitment to total independence from Castile, that would finally bring down the House of Burgundy.

Fernando tried to unite Portugal and Castile, engaging the country in a series of unpopular and unsuccessful wars. France and England joined the turmoil, using the Iberian peninsula as a theatre for the Hundred Years' War. In 1373, Fernando signed an Anglo-Portuguese alliance with John of Gaunt, who had married a Spanish princess (see page 40). The same year, Enrique II of Castile attacked Lisbon, burning and pillaging the city. To add to the confusion, the "Great Schism" divided the Catholic Church

under opposing popes from 1378, and Fernando changed loyalties frequently. Wars ravaged the country, leaving the populace tired and angry.

Fernando further alienated his subjects with his unpopular marriage to Leonor Teles, who was perceived to represent the landed gentry. Riots broke out at the wedding and again in 1383 when Fernando died, leaving his widow (aided by her lover, the Galician count João Fernandez Andeiro) to rule as queen mother.

Andeiro was assassinated within weeks by João, illegitimate son of Pedro I. In the ensuing civil war, Leonor had the support of most of the nobles and clergy, while João relied upon that of the middle class. He depended upon the deepening resentment the people felt towards Castile – where Leonor had fled after Andeiro's death – and rode this growing wave to victory. The final military conflict was the Battle of Aljubarrota (1385), a decisive victory for João's troops, despite being outnumbered.

The subsequent rule of João I, founder of the House of Avis, one of the military-religious orders, represented a new political beginning. The disputes with Castile continued, but they were winding down. The unsteady Anglo-Portuguese alliance was cemented by the Treaty of Windsor in 1386, a document cited as recently as World War II, when Britain invoked it to gain fuelling stations in the Azores. João I brought stability, but the change of order was not a social revolution. New political representation was established by the mercantile class, but it soon became clear that only the names had changed. The landed aristocracy still held the real power, and the new dynasty was much like the old.

THE BATTLE OF ALJUBARROTA

Many stories surround the Battle of Aljubarrota. Nuno Alvares Pereira, captain of João's army, was ravaged by thirst when leading his forces into battle, and swore no traveller would ever go thirsty there again. Since 1385 a pitcher of water has been placed daily in a niche of the Aljubarrota chapel of São Jorge. João, too, made a vow: to build a church in the Virgin's honour if his outnumbered army was victorious. As the enemy fled, João hurled his lance into the air to pick the spot where the monastery of Batalha would be built. He must have had a very strong arm, because the battlefield is 16km (10 miles) from the monastery.

Castles in the Air

It is said that there are 101 castles in Portugal. In fact there are many more.

Most of Portugal's many castles were either built or rebuilt between the 12th and 14th centuries. King Dinis (1279–1325) alone began the construction or expansion of more than 50 fortresses. Perhaps he should have been called "the king of the castle" along with his other titles: "the poet king" and "the farmer king". His labours can be seen throughout Portugal, but he concentrated his efforts along the eastern boundary. He strengthened the towns of Guarda, Penedo, Penamacor, Castelo Mendo, Pinhel and others, attempting to secure the area from the threat posed by Castile. He was well rewarded: the Treaty of Alcañices, signed in 1297, initiated a period of peace and stability between the two countries.

Dinis provided the money for the castles, and even specified the exact measurements of walls and towers. They were of a particularly fine construction, with designs not found on other buildings. Some of the towers were slender and elegant; many balconies were elaborate, with detailed machicolations. Dinis often gave a specific character and grandeur to the structures, as in the 15 towers he had built at Numão, or the Torre do Galo (Cockerel Tower) at Freixo de Espada à Cinta, with its beautiful seven faces.

Preparing for war

Many castles were on the sites of earlier forts: Moorish, Visigothic, Roman, or even earlier. It is interesting to note the developments in warfare as they are reflected in physical features of Portugal's castles. Long wooden verandahs, for example, were attached to the castles' walls in early days. Later these verandahs were covered with animal hides to prevent, or at least inhibit, them being burned by flaming arrows, but these too were abandoned at the end of the 13th century.

By this time, the carved stone balconies were being used for defensive purposes, with machicolations which allowed the defending forces to repel attackers as they attempted to scale the castle walls. (Machicolation is the name given to a space between corbels, or in the floor of a balcony, from which boiling oil or other substances could be poured or dropped onto the enemy.)

The most significant change came with the advent of gunpowder and artillery. The heavy cannons required thicker walls, sloped to resist the more powerful projectiles. Thicker walls also meant that the ramparts, running along the tops of the walls, could be wider, and enabled the heavy artillery to be perched on top. Arrow slits, a common feature in castles, were rounded to accommodate the new artillery, then abandoned as impractical.

All Portugal's castles – many still sound, some in semi-ruin – are dramatically sited. Among the best are Lamego, in the Douro Valley (see page 288);

Almourol Castle stands on Almourol island.

Almourol, perhaps the most romantic of all, set on its own tiny island in the Rio Tejo (Tagus) and the subject of many myths (see page 232); and, of course, Guimarães, the birthplace (c. 1110) of Portugal's first king, Afonso Henriques. Guimarães is one of Portugal's oldest castles, having been built in the 10th century, and restored many times since. Early in the 19th century the castle was used as a debtors' prison. It underwent extensive renovation in the 1940s (see page 307).

Most castles are open to visitors; some have been converted to hotels, while others stand ignored in empty fields. Solid though their construction may have been, do be careful when visiting the semi-ruined ones; it wouldn't do to end your visit under a piece of falling masonry.

THE ENGLISH CONNECTION

A much-loved English queen for Portugal, firm
military alliances, and mutually beneficial trade
have all helped cement the Anglo-Portuguese
relationship over the centuries.

In 1147 a band of crusaders – English, German, French and Flemish – broke their journey in Porto en route to the Holy Land (some by choice, while others may have been shipwrecked). They were persuaded by the new king of Portugal, Afonso Henriques, to join him in an expedition to seize Lisbon from the Moors. Chronicles of the time praised the beauties of Lisbon as seen by the English crusaders. Its fertile countryside, lush with figs and vines, epitomised the seductive pleasures of the south, and encouraged many Englishmen to settle there. The first Bishop of Lisbon, Gilbert of Hastings, was English.

The 17-week siege of the city ended in victory for the Christian forces, and was much celebrated. Much later it became the subject of a poem by William Mickle, the 18th-century translator of Luís de Camões (see page 51), who is considered Portugal's greatest poet:
The hills and lawns to English valour given
What time the Arab Moors from Spain were
driven,
Before the banners of the cross subdued,
When Lisbon's towers were bathed in Moorish
blood
By Gloster's Lance – Romantic days that yield
Of gallant deeds a wide luxuriant field
Dear to the Muse that loves the fairy plains
Where ancient honour wild and ardent reigns.

The Portuguese themselves had less happy memories of the crusaders from the north, whom they considered a loud and drunken lot, given more to piracy than to piety. But the English, with their superior numbers and martial skills, would long feel a condescending pride in their Portuguese achievement, expecting gratitude and deference from their southern allies.

John I, King of Portugal marries Philippa of Lancaster.

Treaties and alliances

Kingdoms were there for the taking. In 1371, John of Gaunt, Duke of Lancaster, hoped to ensure one for himself by marrying the ex-Infanta Constance, the elder of two surviving daughters of the murdered King Pedro the Cruel of Castile. Gaunt then firmly believed himself to be the rightful king of Castile. To double the family's claim, his brother married Constance's sister. But one problem remained: the incumbent king of Castile needed to be convinced. John of Gaunt enlisted the help of Fernando of Portugal, and after rounds of courtship, lavish entertaining and the bestowal of favours, an alliance was signed in 1373 by which the two nations agreed to help one another against all enemies.

In 1385, the youthful Dom João ascended the Portuguese throne with English help, and John of Gaunt felt the time was right to go to Castile to establish his royal claims. Along with his wife Constance and two daughters – 26-year-old Philippa from his first marriage, and Katherine – a couple of his illegitimate children and an army, John of Gaunt set up court in the north, in Santiago de Compostela. He met the king and the earlier alliance was formalised as the Treaty of Windsor. In return King João was offered the hand of the devout and virtuous Philippa. They married in Porto and the city celebrated lavishly.

The English queen

Philippa was a remarkable queen. By surrounding herself in court with an English retinue, she encouraged merchants from England to come in pursuit of trade. Children were born of the marriage at regular intervals, six in all, alternately named after their English and Portuguese families. All five princes were highly gifted and excelled during their lifetimes. Henry, known later as Henry the Navigator, became the most famous of them all through his contribution to Portuguese exploration of the world. Philippa died of the plague in 1415, at the age of 51, and was mourned throughout the country.

> Admired by the Portuguese, generous, kind, high-minded Philippa slowly transformed the king. João, a notorious womaniser, strayed no more and ended his days translating religious books.

Wellington rides in

Contact between these two Atlantic nations remained close. Following the period of Spanish domination of Portugal, the old alliance with England was reinstated, with Charles I (1642), Oliver Cromwell (1654) and finally by the Treaty of 1661, by which Charles II married Catherine of Bragança. Combined Anglo-Portuguese armies were not unusual: they were in action on a number of occasions, fighting each other's battles. The most heavily recorded is the Peninsular War in the Napoleonic era. Sir Arthur Wellesley, who became the Duke of Wellington, commanded the British troops and built the famous defensive Lines of Torres

Vedras, which effectively repelled the French and won the war for Portugal.

The wine trade

Throughout the history of trade between these two countries, textiles made their way to Lisbon and Porto, but there was usually wine in the hold on the return trip. During the second half of the 17th century, increasing factors of British firms settled in Viana do Castelo, Monção and Porto, and selected the wines for shipping home. Porto soon became the centre of the wine trade (see page 275). Names like Taylor, Croft, Cockburn,

Wellington and Sir William Carr Beresford at Salamanca in July of 1812.

Symington, Sandeman and Graham became established, and by the 19th century these families were busy buying their own *quintas* (manor houses) along the banks of the Douro.

The trade in port wine flourished through wars, civil dissent and fierce regulation, and the British made a valuable contribution, especially through people like Baron Joseph James Forrester, who helped improve port safety standards, and also mapped the Rio Douro, in which he eventually drowned in 1862.

Born out of mutual need, the Anglo-Portuguese friendship has been touched by romance, passion, piety, greed, hope and despair, and yet has endured intact for almost a millennium.

A Japanese screen commemorates the arrival of Portuguese traders.

EMPIRE BUILDING

Under the House of Avis, Portugal matured as a
nation. The golden age of discoveries began,
bringing untold wealth to the Church and the Crown.

João I ruled from 1385 to 1433, fending
off the demands of a resurgent nobility
by installing his legitimate sons Duarte,
Pedro, Henry, Fernão and João in powerful
positions as the leaders of military-religious
orders – Henry the Navigator, for example,
headed the wealthy Order of Christ. It was
under João I that Portugal first began to look
across the seas for solutions to internal economic and political problems.

João's successor, Duarte, initially continued
with overseas expansion, but drew back after a
disastrous failed attack on Tangiers in 1437. The
following year Duarte died, precipitating a brief
civil war to determine who would act as regent
to his young son, who became Afonso V.

Two of Afonso's uncles were particularly
trusted advisers: Henry the Navigator, who was
in the forefront of exploration and conquest,
and yet another Afonso, the Duke of Bragança,
leader of the newly strengthened nobility.

Henry the Navigator, son of John I of Portugal.

> Trade and exploration, it was then thought,
> would serve both to occupy the nobility and
> to boost commerce.

Each was granted a large share of independent
power. King Afonso himself remained above
the administrative fray. He was not particularly
inept, but he was a chivalric leader in an era
where politics had been sullied by the growing power of mercantiles and low nobility, and
he was out of tune with the times. Afonso concerned himself largely with martial glory, which
he found crusading in North Africa. In 1471 he
took Tangiers. Another of his accomplishments
was the minting of the first *cruzado,* the gold
coin that became a symbol of the wealth flowing in from the voyages.

In 1475 dispute over the crown of Castile
led to civil discord. Afonso married his niece,
Joana, one of the claimants, and thus united
Portugal and Castile under his monarchy. He
invaded in support of his wife's claims, and
occupied León, but failed to hold his ground.
Defeated by the forces of Ferdinand of Aragón
and Isabela of Castile, he tried to enlist the
aid of French king Louis XI in support of his
claims to the Castilian throne, travelling to
France to make a personal plea. He arrived in
the midst of Louis XI's tumultuous rivalry with
the Duke of Burgundy and proved a hapless
diplomat, alienating both sides.

Frustrated, he announced his intention of abdicating his throne to go on a pilgrimage to the Holy Land, but even this quixotic voyage was thwarted. Louis prevented him from embarking, and the despondent Afonso was sent back to his homeland. His son, the future João II, allowed Afonso to resume his nominal position, and rule was shared until the older man's death in 1481.

Overseas expansion

The 15th century was the era when overseas expansion began in earnest, but no one had any

Lisbon's Padrao dos Descobrimentos celebrates Portuguese explorers from the Age of Discovery

idea of the empire that was to come. The existing policy was a strange mixture of crusading ideals, romantic curiosity and, of course, profit. Charting the world was a secondary matter to João II – less important, for example, than the acquisition of spices, or the search for the odd figure who was known as Prester John.

A mythical priest and king, Prester John was supposed to have been the leader of a vast and powerful Christian empire located somewhere in the African interior. His legend was elaborated with tales of a kingdom that was an earthly paradise peopled with a bizarre menagerie of chimeras and mythical characters. Strange as it seems, this tale had an enormous

influence on early exploration of Africa. In fact, in 1455, after the Portuguese had established their dominance all along the northern coast, a papal bull granted them the sole right to discovery and conquest of all Africa except those parts ruled by Prester John. It was only later, by the early 16th century, that Portugal's explorers began to realise that spices and gold were more tangible goals, and the voyages in and around Ethiopia were replaced by more profitable itineraries.

Another goal of the seafarers was the still-popular slaughter of the infidel. Attacking Muslims wherever they could be found gave the voyages all the benefits of a crusade: the effort was legitimised, and the Church lent its financial resources along with spiritual support. The sanctions of Rome, like the papal bull of 1455, would become an important factor when maritime competition intensified.

Economic and social needs undoubtedly motivated the voyages. There was a shortage of gold all over Europe, and without it, coinage was severely debased and the growth of commerce retarded. Gold from Africa, America and India eventually did find its way into the coffers of Lisbon, but it also proved to be a debilitating obsession, diverting attention from surer if less spectacular sources of profit. These lesser goals were nevertheless an impetus for exploration from the start. Fishing boats had circled further and further out in search of more richly stocked waters. Moroccan grain, sugar, dyestuffs and slaves were all highly prized. These commodities were eventually joined by the pungent spices and rare woods of India and the Orient.

Henry the Navigator

Before any exploration could begin, of course, the technical aspects of navigation had to be mastered and improved. Navigators familiar with the Pole Star, dead reckoning and the compass began to establish their position with the quadrant, the astrolabe adapted for sea use, and a simple cross-staff from which they calculated latitude. Celestial tables and so-called *portolano* charts, basic maps, became ever more detailed. Ships, too, radically changed – neatest of all was the nimble caravel, derived from the heftier cargo-carrying *caravela* of the Rio Douro. Prince Henry, who was born in Porto, would have known it well.

The prince was dubbed Henry the Navigator and is credited with masterminding the discoveries from a centre of navigation in Sagres at Cabo de São Vicente in Algarve, where he surrounded himself with astronomers and shipbuilders. His sponsorship and enthusiasm were profoundly influential, and the research material he assembled was unrivalled (much of it contributed by his brother, Pedro, a true wanderer who sent Henry every relevant map and book he could find). But discovering the world – the Portuguese were the first Europeans to find two-thirds of it – was beyond the scope of any one man, and there must be other, unsung, heroes.

With many hands at the tillers, the enterprise was not always well coordinated. The main goal was to press the crusade forward and to advance knowledge of navigation and the oceans. Maps were accurate enough to suggest that there were islands in the unknown Sea of Darkness, and land beyond it, but it needed courage and determination to sail into oceans that legend had filled with fearsome monsters. (For more on Henry, see the panel below.)

Pedro Alvares Cabral lands in Brazil.

HENRY THE HERO?

Prince Henry the Navigator's primary goal, rather than to discover uncharted territory, was the taming of the North African coast. He never travelled farther than Morocco, where he had taken Ceuta in 1415, and gained his lifelong interest in discovery and conquest. Contemporary chronicles portray Henry devoting most of his time to squeezing profits out of his various tithes, monopolies and privileges. However, the riches uncovered by his expeditions were undeniable, whatever his motivation. It was an expedition initiated by Henry the Navigator that, quite accidentally, discovered Madeira and the Azores. In 1415, two ships were blown off course and landed on the uninhabited island, which they named Madeira (meaning "wood") because it was thickly forested. The first of the nine Azores (Açores) islands was discovered a dozen years later, the others over a period of 25 years. Henry proved to be an efficient and able coloniser, introducing wheat, vines and sugar cane to Madeira, and organising the settlement of the Azores, which later became recognised ports of call for sailors en route to and from the New World.

Later in life increasing reports of wondrous and far-off places inspired Henry to give the discoveries his full attention. Yet throughout his life he ploughed much of his profits back into the enterprises, which were a costly business, and died in debt.

Epic voyages

It is easy to see why popular history might accord undue credit to an individual like Henry. The Age of Discoveries was a time for heroes and adventurers, and also a time for the rebirth of chivalric ideals. Fearless mariners sailed off into unknown realms. Their voyages were imbued with noble intentions: the greater glory of the Church, the advancement of knowledge, and the benefit of their nation.

Popular history also makes unverifiable, but plausible, claims that Portuguese mariners were the first Europeans in America.

A statue of Vasco de Gama.

Among explorers who sailed from the Azores were members of the Corte Real family, who explored the North American coast in the 1470s. One of them, Miguel, may have been marooned there.

The first hero of the discoveries was Gil Eanes. Madeira and the Azores, along with the north of Africa, had been charted. The islands had begun to be colonised. The fabulous tales of the edge of the world and the various horrors of the southern seas were soon connected with the stormy promontory of Cape Bojador, on the west coast of Africa. It became the boundary. Finally, in 1434, Gil Eanes, a pilot commissioned by Henry the Navigator, broke the barrier. He found more coastline and safe

waters, and returned to Portugal triumphant, bringing wild plants plucked from the land beyond. The next year he led voyages further down Africa's coast, and the way was opened for the many who followed. They searched primarily for the legendary Rio do Ouro (River of Gold). Eventually some of the precious ore was found.

In 1482, Portuguese ships explored the mouth of the Congo. Five years later, Bartolomeu Dias rounded the Cape of Good Hope. So intense did the competition between Spain and Portugal become that in 1494 papal inter-

> The Portuguese began fishing for cod (bacalhau) in Newfoundland's Grand Banks shortly after Columbus's voyage of discovery. It soon became a very popular dish.

vention resulted in the famous Treaty of Tordesillas, which divided the newly discovered and the still unknown lands between the two countries. It granted Portugal the lands east of a line of demarcation 592km (370 miles) west of the Azores, which put Brazil (then unknown, but discovered by Pedro Alvares Cabral in 1500) within Portugal's sphere.

In 1497–9, Vasco da Gama sailed to Calicut (Calcutta) in India and back – with great loss of life – immediately throwing Portugal into competition with Muslim and Venetian spice traders. In 1519–22, Fernão de Magalhães (anglicised to Ferdinand Magellan), a Portuguese serving Spain, led the first voyage to circumnavigate the globe, although he died before it was completed.

The expeditions opened the seaways, but there were battles to be fought to establish trading posts in Africa and the Indies. Arabs, protecting their own trade interests, fought the Portuguese wherever they could. The Portuguese, of course, were still intent on eradicating such infidels from the face of the earth. So although Portugal originally had no intentions of land conquest, by simply striving to establish and maintain a monopoly of the high seas, they were constantly at war.

Colonies

The leader of these voyages of eastern exploration was Governor Afonso de Albuquerque, a brilliant strategist and, in essence, the founding father of the empire in Asia. His victories allowed garrisoned ports and fortresses to be built in key locations. Goa, in India, conquered in 1510, became the centre for all operations. Malacca (now in Malaysia) fell in 1511 and served as the East Indies hub, while Ormuz came under Portuguese control in 1515, proving the ideal seat from which to dominate the Persian Gulf. Later, in 1557, Macau was established on a kind of permanent lease with China, extending Portugal's reach to the Far East.

administered these new holdings under a basic policy of colonisation rather than exploitation. All the major cities, Goa in particular, were converted by architecture and government into European towns. Interracial marriages were encouraged and Catholic missions established.

The growth of Goa was extraordinary. By 1540, there were 10,000 households of European descent and the town was the seat of a bishopric. However, these few much-changed cities and the battles of the Indies were in marked contrast to the general policy of peaceful coexistence that Portugal adopted wherever it could. In Africa, Brazil, and the various islands and archipelagos, they tried to set up trading stations without interfering with local customs or politics.

It is, however, the exceptions that proved the most interesting. In the Congo, for example, where a number of missions were established, the people were quite taken with their European visitors, though they could provide little of interest to the traders. The Portuguese had begun by overestimating the political and cultural sophistication of these people, and once the Congolese were exposed to certain Western practices, they embraced them rapidly. They took to Christianity, and imitated the manners and fashions of the Portuguese. Their first Christian monarch dropped the title "Nzinga a Nkuwu" and renamed himself João I. His son took the name Afonso, and from that point until the 17th century the land was ruled by a succession of native Henriques, Pedros and Franciscos.

Although it provided both ivory and slaves, the Congo was not of central economic importance to the Portuguese, who were too busy reaping bounty elsewhere: spices were carried from the east, gold was found in Ghana and other parts of Africa, sugar and wine were brought from Madeira, while sugar and dyestuffs came from Brazil.

The wealth reaped overseas made for a stable economy, but it did not make Portugal rich. Enterprising individuals and the monarchy – taking its royal fifth of all trade revenues – flourished, but even they eventually found it difficult to build or hold on to their fortunes.

At its beginning, the "empire" demanded little from its diminutive fatherland. Like other small trading centres in Italy and the

Afonso de Albuquerque, painted by an unknown artist, c.1509.

later Dutch empire, organisation and central authority were more important than mere size. Furthermore, the early expeditions required little manpower. It was only later, when they found themselves trying to enforce the worldwide trade monopoly, that the sparseness of Portugal's population began to tell. It has also been suggested that a crucial deficiency was Portugal's lack of a middle class. Quashed by royal and noble dominance of commerce, it might have provided qualified and educated planners, pilots and administrators.

In explaining the empire's failure, some have pointed to widespread corruption or to the foreign control of profits garnered from Portuguese expeditions. How great an effect they had is arguable. Certainly the religious efforts that went hand in hand with Portuguese voyages did not make the wheels of commerce spin any more freely. Whether fighting Muslims, or trying to force Christianity down the throats of local populations, the Portuguese wasted time and diverted their focus from the business at hand.

Whatever the causes, potential benefits of the burgeoning overseas trade were not being reaped. Deflation in Europe stifled trade.

Azulejo of a Portuguese expedition ship.

Domestic agricultural production, hampered by a lack of manpower, lagged, occasionally causing serious shortages of meat and grain. Even the Crown was in debt, as the cost of the trading empire rose higher than its revenues. It was, of course, many years before these flaws and inadequacies truly sank the empire. Trade was to continue for several centuries, although it steadily deteriorated.

Domestic life

Before the slide began, the lucrative age of empire brought sufficient peace and prosperity for Portugal to sustain great eras of artistic and humanist achievement. João II had taken over from his father, the unreliable Afonso V, in 1481. Revitalising the throne, he managed to take up where Henry the Navigator, who died in 1460, left off. João turned away from the nobility, minimising their rights and calling on the *cortes* for support. A conspiracy soon gathered against him, but he learned of the central traitors soon enough to strike back. In 1484, the Duke of Bragança was tried and beheaded. When other members of the nobility fled the country, their titles and holdings reverted to the Crown.

The Duke of Viseu, who was both cousin and brother-in-law to the king, unwisely mounted a second plot, and was stabbed by the king himself. Another group fled the country, and João II was left in full command. The prestige and authority that these tactics bestowed on the monarchy would stand undiminished for centuries. However, João's successor, Manuel I, who came to the throne

---

THE JEWS IN PORTUGAL

As moneylenders, tax collectors, bankers, physicians and astronomers, the Jews had, by the 15th century, lived peaceably in Portugal for a thousand years or more. In 1492, Spain, having rid itself of the Moors, was equally determined to expel the Jews from its soil. Some 60,000 were allowed to settle in Portugal.

The contribution of the Jews to the economy and progress of the country was already invaluable, and their influence was increasing. It was the Jews who opened Portugal's first printing presses, and the first 11 books published were in Hebrew. Abraham Zacuto, astronomer and mathematician, published the *Almanach Perpetuum*, which contained tables enabling mariners to determine

latitude by declination of the sun. The *Almanach* was translated into Latin and became the basis of a system used by the Portuguese for many years.

When King Manuel married Princess Isabella of Spain in 1497, he was forced, as a condition of marriage, to act against the Jews. Realising their value to the country, he was reluctant to expel them so he offered them the option of baptism as "New Christians", with a 20-year period of grace before their faith would be tested. Many refused outright, and those who accepted soon found that they were not treated as equals. Prejudice and intolerance were quick to burgeon into full-scale repression as the Inquisition took hold.

in 1495, had to find a balance between the ferocity of his predecessor and the confused idealism of Afonso V.

This he accomplished through diplomatic and far-sighted administration. The estates of the noble families were largely restored, though this did not restore their political power. Judicial and tax reforms worked to bring authority to government on both the national and local levels. A postal system was instituted. Public services such as hospitals were centralised. Essentially, Manuel lifted the power of the monarchy above both the nobles and the *cortes*, launching the first era of enlightened absolutism.

The importance of education

Manuel also fostered contacts with proponents of Renaissance humanism, which was then spreading throughout Europe. There were many trading, religious and cultural contacts with Italy in particular, and young Portuguese men began to seek education abroad, at universities in France or Spain.

Manuel tried to buy Paris's renowned St Barbara College, and, although he failed, it became a centre for Portuguese students. By 1487 a printing press had been established in Lisbon. Portugal entered the 16th century with a rush of new cultural currents and ideas.

New colleges and educational reforms were basic elements of the new century's progress. Teaching methods were modernised and the curriculum expanded. The students were drawn from a larger pool, including aristocrats and members of the wealthy bourgeoisie, in addition to young men from the religious orders.

These changes were not without crises. The University of Lisbon had a cultural and political influence that threatened the Crown. It was difficult to impinge on its traditional autonomy, but Manuel, as part of his process of centralisation, tried to force change through economic and legal pressure.

Finding great resistance, he turned to the idea of founding a new university elsewhere, without success. João III, who came to the throne in 1521, on his father's death, continued these efforts, later giving control of national education to the Jesuits and moving the university to Coimbra, where its permanent home was established. It was a victory for

the monarchy. There would be no university in Lisbon until 1911.

Nonetheless, the century inspired a broad-ranging intellectual vigour. Some of the works produced were directly attributable to the expeditions of discovery. Travel books, with both scientific and cultural themes, were a rich vein: Tomé Pires, for example, wrote *Suma Oriental* in 1550, describing his voyages to the East.

Portugal's main contributions to the intellectual ferment of the Renaissance were in science, particularly navigation, astronomy,

João III, in a portrait by Cristovão Lopes.

mathematics and geography. This was not the mere accumulation of facts from foreign places: they amounted to a kind of sceptical empiricism, a science based on experience. Having disproved a dozen theories about the shape, limits and contours of the earth, Portuguese intellectuals felt free to question the other dogmas of antiquity.

New writers and new sciences were emerging but there was no real Reformation in Portugal, where there was an antipathy towards Germanic philosophies. Nevertheless, the Counter-Reformation cast a pall of religious conformism over learning and creativity. In addition, the political threat to Portuguese autonomy – the future union with Spain was already an undercurrent – hung over all these academic achievements.

Portuguese Inquisition

João III ruled from 1521 to 1557. The Inquisition had by now become established in Spain, where it had been enforced with vigour after the Moors had been expelled in 1492 by the "Catholic Monarchs", Isabel and Ferdinand. The papacy knew there was no real need for it, no menaces to the unity of faith, so resisted its introduction. But João III was more fanatical than the pope and he used every diplomatic

Heretics are led to their death by fire in an auto-da-fe procession.

intrigue at his disposal to get his way. Finally, in 1536, he won approval for a limited version of the Inquisition, but within a dozen years these limitations had been lifted and its full force arrived.

João III had turned away from the current humanist influences of Europe towards religious fanaticism, and the power and the bureaucracy of the Inquisition expanded rapidly. Its main target was the converted Jews known as New Christians. What had been intended as a tool of the monarchy soon took on a direction and authority of its own. The Inquisitor-Generals, who took their orders from Rome, had the right of excommunication and, utilising the

spectacular *autos-da-fe*, the public burning of heretics, soon wielded an influence far beyond their legal authority.

The impact of the Inquisition, with its rigid orthodoxy, vengeful judiciary and general intolerance, was deadening to both culture and commerce. Many of the bourgeois leaders of trade were targets. In those uncertain times, epic poet Luís de Camões and the great 16th-century playwright Gil Vicente became renowned for their works in the Portuguese language.

The Inquisition's power continued under King Sebastião, who came to the throne in

> João III continued Manuel's expansion of the trading empire and of royal authority, but his most significant act was the establishment of the Inquisition in Portugal.

1568, when he was 14 years old. An unstable and idealistic king, with a dangerous streak of misplaced chivalry, Sebastião took upon himself a crusade against the Moors of North Africa. A lack of funds prevented him from undertaking the task for many years. In the meantime he surrounded himself with cohorts no older and no more sensible than himself, dismissing the warnings of older, more prudent statesmen. Finally sensing that the time was right, he spent every *cruzado* he could raise on mercenaries and outfitting his troops. He set sail for Morocco in 1578, appointing his great-uncle, Cardinal Henrique, regent in his absence.

Sebastião was as bad a military leader as he was an administrator, dismissing stratagem and planning as cowardice. He refused to consider the possibility of retreat, and therefore had no plan for it. Outnumbered and outmanoeuvred at the Battle of Alcácer-Quibir, his army of 18,000 men was destroyed. Some 8,000, including Sebastião and most of Portugal's young nobility, were slaughtered. Only 100 or so escaped.

In the wake of this debilitating disaster, the way was open for Spain to step in. From 1578 to 1580, Cardinal Henrique ruled the country, occupied primarily with raising the ruinous ransoms for the captured soldiers of Alcácer-Quibir. In 1580, Felipe II of Spain invaded and within a year was installed as Felipe I of Portugal.

Luís de Camões

Portugal's greatest poet never reaped fame or riches in his lifetime, but his life and his works still entrance the Portuguese today

Luís Vaz de Camões (1524–80), Portugal's greatest poet, was born poor, and he died poor, but the life he led – of passion and adventure – enthrals the Portuguese almost as much as the epic, eloquent phrases in his works, which many people can quote at length even today.

After attending the University at Coimbra, his prospects were good. But many twists of fate lay ahead. An affair with one of the queen's ladies-in-waiting caused his banishment to North Africa, where he lost an eye in military service. Returning to Lisbon, Camões was involved in a skirmish that wounded a magistrate. He ended up in prison and then was banished again, in 1553, this time to the colony of Goa in India.

It was 1570 before he returned to Lisbon. Having written poetry and plays for many years with some success, he published Os Lusíadas in 1572. The poem's worth was recognised immediately, and Camões received a small royal pension. His final illness, however, was spent in a public hospital, and he was buried in a common grave.

The title Os Lusíadas means "The Sons of Lusus", the mythical founder of Portugal: symbolically, then, it means "the Portuguese". Echoing classical models, the poem chronicled the voyages of Vasco da Gama, before a panorama of strangely mixed Christian and pagan images.

Os Lusíadas has been hailed throughout Europe (Lope de Vega and Montesquieu were among early admirers), sometimes to the detriment of the rest of Portugal's extensive literature. Under Salazar (see page 62), Os Lusíadas became an icon of Portuguese nationalism. Speeches and propaganda were peppered with quotes from it, providing a mythology for imperialism that failed to differentiate between the 16th and 20th centuries.

The 18th-century verse translation by W.J. Mickle, quoted below, though tinged with the lyrical romanticism and chauvinism of that era, captures the proud spirit of the poem from the opening lines:

Arms and the heroes, who from Lisbon's shore,/ Thro' seas where sail was never spread before,/

Beyond where Ceylon lifts her spicy breast,/And waves her woods above the watery waste,/With prowess more than human forc'd their way/ To the fair kingdoms of the rising day.

In the second canto the Moors prepare to attack:

On shore the truthless monarch arms his bands,/ And for the fleet's approach impatient stands:/ That soon as anchor'd in the port they rode/ Brave Gama's decks might reek with Lusian blood:/.

In the world of the Portuguese discoverers, enemy forces take their strength from the netherworld:

As when the whirlwinds, sudden bursting, bear/

Luís de Camões.

Th' autumnal leaves high floating through the air;/ So rose the legions of th' infernal state,/ Dark Fraud, base Art, fierce Rage, and burning Hate:/ Wing'd by the Furies to the Indian strand/ They bend; the Demon leads the dreadful band,/ And in the bosoms of the raging Moors/ All their collected living strength he pours.

At Vasco da Gama's request, his ship's chronicler recounts the "glad assistance" brought by the crusaders who helped take Lisbon from the Moors:

Their vows were holy, and the cause the same,/ To blot from Europe's shores the Moorish name./ In Sancho's cause the gallant navy joins,/ And royal Sylves to their force resigns./ Thus sent by heaven a foreign naval band/ Gave Lisboa's ramparts to the Sire's command.

Engraving of the fall of Lisbon into Spanish rule (1580).

THE CONQUERORS ARE CONQUERED

Portugal was under Spanish rule for 60 years, until a popular uprising against the Habsburgs put the country back in charge of its own destiny.

Throughout their rule over Portugal, the Spanish Habsburg kings faced many challenges to their authority. Not the least of their problems was that Sebastião kept rising from the grave. After the massacre at Alcácer-Quibir in 1578, a devastating blow to national pride, there arose a popular belief, known as *sebastianismo*, that the lost Portuguese king would rise again. Consequently, a number of false Sebastiãos tried and failed to reclaim the throne.

At the root of the Iberian Union was the support it provided for merchants and traders. The Netherlands and France were strongly challenging Portuguese shipping, slicing into vital profits. In any case, there were few options: in 1560 the Casa da India, the national trade corporation, had gone bankrupt and Portugal's treasury was empty.

The three Filipes

After Alcácer-Quibir, a number of candidates had aspirations to the Portuguese throne. Though the genealogical claim of Felipe II of Spain was more tenuous than those of his

Antão de Almada, one of the movers and shakers of the Restoration.

It was supposed by the bourgeoisie that by combining Spanish and Portuguese interests, the maritime empire could be reclaimed, while the "alliance" would also open up inland trade.

competitors, he was the grandson of Manuel I and a far more viable ruler than his rivals. The majority of the populace was opposed to the Spanish king, but the relatively impoverished nobles, clergy and upper bourgeoisie saw that Felipe could provide fiscal and military stability. Ironically, the most powerful group to resist the union was the Spanish ruling classes, who

saw the danger of untrammelled Portuguese trading within their traditional markets.

Part of Felipe's appeal was that he promised to maintain Portugal's autonomy: no Spanish representation in Portuguese legislative and judicial bodies; no change in the official language; the overseas empire would still be ruled by Portugal; no grants of Portuguese assets to non-Portuguese; and so on and so forth. Felipe took up residence in Lisbon. In 1581 he summoned the *cortes* to declare him King Filipe I.

After the years of mismanaged government, the efficient bureaucracy of the union was a relief. However, with the succession of Felipe II (Felipe III of Spain) in 1598, the Spanish began to press their powers too far. The new king lacked his predecessor's diplomatic savvy, relations between the two countries were bungled, and the Spanish tried to correct their mistakes through force. Resistance grew. Under Filipe III (IV of Spain), who succeeded to the throne in 1619, the union continued to erode. Spain was weakened by the Thirty Years' War with France. Portuguese troops were forced into battle and taxes increased.

The 60 years of union with Spain did nothing to protect Portugal's empire. Between 1620 and 1640, Ormuz, Baia, São Jorge da Mina and many more trade centres fell. In 1630 the Dutch

Pedro II, a more effective king than his brother.

established themselves in Brazil; in 1638 they took Ceylon. There were still ports and territories controlled by Portuguese traders, but the monopoly of the seas was an era quickly fading from memory. What's more, to a country that had once been intent upon ridding the earth of the last vestige of the infidels, it was devastating to surrender their missions to the Dutch, purveyors of heretical Protestantism.

For the Portuguese, each of the three Filipes was worse than his predecessor. Filipe II did not even deign to visit the country for years after his coronation. Filipe III systematically breached all the guarantees put in place by his grandfather. The incipient revolution was aided by secret diplomatic agents sent by the French,

who were still embroiled with Spain in the Thirty Years' War.

The Bragança regime

On 1 December 1640, a coup in Lisbon reflected the growing revolutionary fervour. The palace was attacked, and the reigning Spanish governor, the duchess of Mantua, was deposed and arrested, while her strongman, Miguel de Vasconcelos, was defenestrated. Though reluctant to lead the revolt, the Duke of Bragança was declared King João IV. So began Portugal's final royal period: the House of Bragança would hold power until the 20th century.

Most of João IV's 16-year reign was occupied in hapless efforts to form diplomatic ties in Europe. France, England, Holland and the pope all refused to confirm Portuguese independence. Only Spain's preoccupation with other battles, some heroic Portuguese military stands along the frontier, and a well-organised national administration enabled the country to retain its restored independence.

When he ascended the throne in 1656, Afonso VI (João's son), who suffered both physical and mental handicaps, was still a minor. Later, married off to a French princess, he associated with criminal elements and, worst of all, proved to be impotent, a fact elicited from the public inquiry needed to annul his marriage. He was eventually usurped by his brother, who ruled as Pedro II.

War with Spain waxed and waned from 1640 until 1665. In 1654, a treaty of friendship and cooperation was signed with England, a useful link, but also the first step down a path that guaranteed Portugal's economic subservience to Britain for centuries to come. The alliance was sealed by the marriage of Princess Catherine to the English king, Charles II, in 1662. Included in her dowry gifts were Tangiers and Bombay. In 1661 a treaty was signed with Holland. These moves sparked a new round of battles with Spain. In 1665 a decisive Portuguese victory at Montes Claros ended the fighting and three years later, in the Treaty of Lisbon, Spain offically recognised Portugal's independence.

Pedro II became prince regent to his brother in 1668 and ruled from 1673 until 1706. His long reign, although stable, was deeply marked by an unrelenting economic depression. The spice trade had slipped almost entirely out of Portuguese hands, while trade in sugar and slaves went through periods of competition and crisis at a time when Portugal could ill afford such instability.

On the mainland, olive groves and vineyards offered good profits, but they were largely controlled by English interests. The Treaty of Methuen (1703) established English dominance of the wine industry and served to stifle industrialisation in Portugal. Grain shortages were common throughout the era – perhaps because investment went into vines instead of wheat.

Two of Pedro's finance ministers, the Count of Ericeira and the Marquês of Fronteira, helped plan numerous factories. Glass, textile, iron, tile

> *Restoration Day on 1 December is still celebrated in Portugal as a national holiday to commemorate the 1640 coup in Lisbon.*

and pottery industries were all supported by the state in an effort to balance trade deficits.

Going for gold

The mercantilist approach made some headway, but what finally dispelled the economic gloom was the discovery of gold in Brazil. But the constant stream pouring in from across the Atlantic was not invested in the infant industries, which spluttered and halted. The Count of Ericeira committed suicide, while Fronteira renounced his previous economic philosophy.

Even before gold, Brazil had offered a number of valuable commodities: sugar, cotton and tobacco, as well as some spices and dye-stuffs. The husbandry of cattle started slowly, but by the end of the 17th century was providing lucrative exports of meat and leather.

The Jesuit missionaries were extremely influential in Brazil, as both explorers and settlers. Among other things they held the brazilwood monopoly for over two decades (1625–49). More importantly, they were successful in winning over the native populace to Christianity, and in large part preventing their enslavement. But the abundant colonial economy naturally had a great need for native labour, and the Jesuits were pressured to step aside, even though they had the clear support of Rome in the form of a papal bull (1639) that threatened excommunication for the trading of natives.

João V, who succeeded Pedro II in 1706, spent the Brazilian gold with a vengeance. Taking his

cue from the French court of Louis XIV, he quickly earned the nickname "The Magnanimous". Palaces, churches and monasteries were erected, and support was granted to the arts and to education. Along with this extravagance came a moral profligacy. Convents around Lisbon were converted from religious houses into aristocratic brothels. Among the royal constructions were palaces to house João's numerous bastard sons, born of various nuns.

When João died in 1750 he was succeeded by his son José, who proved to be more interested in opera than in matters of state. The full

A scene in Lisbon harbour during the Great Earthquake of 1755.

power of the crown was entrusted to a diplomat, Sebastião José de Carvalho e Melo, who eventually earned the title by which he is better known: the Marquês de Pombal.

Enlightened absolutism, as typified by the ministry of Pombal, represented both a beginning and an end. The Enlightenment ideal of rationalism meant a leap towards modernity, while the concomitant republican ideal of social equality meant royal absolutism was on its last legs. Pombal's insistence on exercising royal prerogative sounded a death knell for the political power of nobles and clergy alike, and allowed the bourgeoisie to take over administrative and economic control. His was an oppressive, dictatorial rule, though he was careful never to claim any personal power.

The great earthquake

In 1755, on All Saints' Day – just as Mass was beginning – Lisbon was destroyed by a massive earthquake. At least 5,000 people were killed in the initial impact, many while attending morning services. Many more died later. Fallen church candles quickly ignited the wreckage around them. Survivors rushed towards the safety of the Tejo, only to be met by a huge tsunami.

In the subsequent weeks infected wounds,

The Marquês de Pombal, an enlightened despot.

epidemics and famine increased the death toll, which may have been as high as 40,000. The Jesuits tried to fix the blame for what they saw as divine retribution upon Pombal's wayward and "atheistic" policies. He weathered both their criticism and their plot to assassinate him. The Jesuits' power throughout Europe was dissolving, and in 1759 they were officially disbanded and exiled from Portugal.

The catastrophe that shook the country's faith allowed Pombal's policies of secularisation and rational government to take firm hold. He took absolute control, and with the order to "close the ports, bury the dead, feed the living", began reconstruction. José granted his minister emergency powers (which were not rescinded

for some 20 years) and Pombal used them to rebuild Lisbon according to a neoclassical plan, both neatly geometric and functionally sound. The social and legal distinction between "Old" and "New" Christians (the latter being Jews who had converted at the end of the 15th century) was abolished. Pombal's economic reforms helped Portugal remain stable when Brazilian gold production waned in the middle of the century and he managed to rebuild Lisbon without depleting the treasury.

As Pombal's sponsor-king, José, neared the end of his reign, the Marquês plotted to force the crown princess Maria to renounce her rights so that her son, another José, and a disciple of Pombal, could continue the policy of despotism. These efforts failed and Maria, a pious but unbalanced woman with no sympathy for Pombal's methods of rule, took over in 1777. She immediately had Pombal tried for crimes against the state and, when convicted, confined him to his estate rather than prison, out of deference to his age.

Though she revived religious elements in a government and culture that had become increasingly secular, Maria allowed most of Pombal's essential economic and administrative reforms to stay in place. Her reign was a conservative one, with steady, if slow, economic progress. Both her political and personal health were badly shaken by news of the French Revolution. In 1798, long after her behaviour had become an embarrassment, she was declared insane. Her son João, an awkward, nervous man, took over as regent, becoming king after Maria died in 1816.

POMBAL'S LEGACY

Anyone visiting Lisbon should know a little about the Marquês de Pombal, to better appreciate the city. Under his direction, the whole of the devastated Baixa area was rebuilt in neoclassical style, laid out in an orderly grid system. The upper parts of the city – the Bairro Alta and Alfama – had been spared the worst effects of the tremors. In the centre of the great Praça do Comercio he erected a statue of his king, José, astride his horse. Pombal's own statue was erected much later, on a column in the square that bears his name, and looking out over the new city which, under his guidance, rose like a phoenix from the ashes.

The Peninsular War

The Portuguese monarchy and nobility feared that the fervour behind the French Revolution of 1789, and, to a lesser extent, the American one the previous decade, might be contagious. They were particularly wary about possible insurgency in Brazil. In 1793, Portugal sent troops to fight revolutionary France, further aligning itself with Britain and against French-controlled Spain. In 1801, Spain invaded in the War of the Oranges. Portugal ceded various political concessions, and lost forever the town of Olivença.

In 1807, Napoleon delivered an ultimatum to Portugal, in which he demanded that Portugal declare war on Britain and close its ports to British shipping. But Portugal could not turn on its long-term allies, and Napoleon was defied. While the royal family speedily sailed to the safety of Brazil, the French General Junot marched into Lisbon. Initially, the Portuguese Government offered no resistance.

In July 1808, Britain came galloping to the rescue under the leadership of the master military tactician, Sir Arthur Wellesley (1769–1852), who became the Duke of Wellington. The Peninsular War, sometimes called the War of National Liberation, lasted two years, expelling the French but devastating the country. Three waves of attacks were halted by Portuguese victories at Roliça, Vimeiro, Buçaco and the famous Lines at Torres Vedras. The wars left the country in a rocky state. Since the flight of the royal family, Portugal's capital was effectively located across the ocean in Rio de Janeiro and the nation's general weakness fostered Brazil's claims for autonomy. In 1822 Brazil was declared a kingdom on an equal footing with Portugal.

The regency in Lisbon showed very little political intelligence or common sense, governing with uncoordinated despotism and completely ignoring the burgeoning democratic groundswell. The monarchy's blindness to contemporary political ideas fostered the revolution that would break out in 1820.

The British military occupation, under the leadership of Marshal William Carr Beresford (1768–1854), although necessary and sometimes appreciated, further undermined Portuguese self-determination. British control had been growing throughout the 18th century. In the 19th, it became stronger. In 1810, Portugal was forced to cede to Britain the right to trade directly with Brazil, eliminating its own role as middleman. Portugal was taking on the aspects of a British protectorate, with William Beresford wielding dictatorial control.

The liberal revolution

The roots of the liberal uprising of 1820 lay in the French Revolution, its influences disseminated by military and secret societies, especially a Masonic lodge called Sinédrio. A plot against British rule by one of these clandestine groups proved to be a catalyst. A dozen conspirators accused of plotting to assassinate Marshal Beresford in 1817 were summarily tried and

British and Portuguese troops commanded by the Duke of Wellington repulse Napoleon's army.

executed, a brutal reprisal that heated Portuguese resentment and fostered support for the liberal movement.

In 1820, the Spanish liberal movement won control of their government, providing further inspiration, as well as political support, for Portuguese liberal forces. When Beresford left for Brazil on a diplomatic mission to discuss the growing problem, his absence sparked the Portuguese military into revolt. The uprising began in Porto, and eventually forced João VI to return from Brazil. By the time he arrived, the new constitutional ideology had gained ground. A constitution was adopted in 1822. The document was ahead of its time, with broad guarantees of individual liberties and no special prerogatives for nobles or clergy. It lasted only two years, but succeeded in ending the Inquisition.

Conspiracy and confusion

Portugal's profoundly conservative streak made the revolution a simple split between republicans and absolutists. New charters and new efforts to restore full-bodied monarchy kept the country unsettled throughout the first half of the century. In 1824, João VI resisted a conspiracy of royalist extremists led by his own wife Carlotta and his son Miguel.

had other ideas. Upon his return he abolished the constitution and invoked a counter-revolutionary *cortes* to name him king. There was considerable popular support for these moves, but enough sympathy for constitutional ideas remained for Pedro, who had abdicated power in Brazil, to return and eventually defeat his brother in the Miguelist Wars.

Pedro IV reigned until his death in 1834, when his daughter, then aged 15, finally took the throne as Maria II. She reigned until 1853, during which time the first political parties developed. The liberals, victorious over abso-

Citizens rallied in the streets for the liberal revolution of 1820.

João's queen was the Spanish princess Carlotta Joaquina, who epitomised the old regime. Her flamboyant leadership of the absolutist cause made her popular, but the failure of her conspiracy to dethrone her husband in favour of her son Miguel – who was then banished to live in Brazil – marked the end of her influence.

The politics of the next 50 years were endlessly complex. In 1826 João VI died, leaving the throne to Pedro, his eldest son, who was still in Brazil. After failing to unite the two kingdoms, Pedro chose to stay in Brazil, abdicating the Portuguese throne to his seven-year-old daughter, Maria. Pedro intended her to marry her uncle, the exiled Miguel, who would rule as regent under a moderate constitution. Miguel

lutism, divided into conservatives and progressives. The Septembrists, named after their revolutionary victory in September 1836, came into power first. They initially restored the constitution of 1822, but then adopted a more moderate one. They were opposed by Chartists who took their stand, and name, from the conservative charter of 1826.

The Chartists came to the fore in 1839, when, supported by the queen and led by António da Costa Cabral, they took power. Costa Cabral's government was authoritarian, and, though it provided stability, became more and more corrupt and autocratic. In 1846 a popular uprising demanded his downfall. Maria II tried to replace him with the equally conservative Duke of Saldanha, a grandson of Pombal, and the country stood on the brink of civil war. English and Spanish intervention prevented mass violence, but resulted in Costa Cabral being returned to power. In 1851 he was (peacefully) ousted for good and Saldanha took his place.

The early period of Saldanha's rule was a period of transformation out of which came the political divisions that would exist throughout the century. Saldanha introduced a compromise that allowed his new party, Regeneração, to encompass both the old Chartists and the moderate progressives. The amendments to the

Carlotta Joaquina tried her best to make a Versailles of her palace at Queluz, surrounding herself with absolutists and, outrageously, decadently producing children by various lovers.

constitution allowed for direct elections and an expanded electorate. A still more radical faction, initially a small group, became known first as the Históricos, and then the Progressistas.

In 1853 Maria II died in childbirth. Her husband, the German duke Ferdinand of Saxe-Coburg-Gotha, ruled as regent until their son, Pedro V, came of age in 1855. Pedro died six years later and was succeeded by his brother, who became Luís I.

Literary Luís

The best constitutional monarchs are those who avoid politics, and the change from the meddling Maria to the literary Luís was a clear victory for the republican government. Among his other accomplishments, King Luís translated Shakespeare into Portuguese.

Arts and literature were greatly influenced by politics during this period. The energies of both liberal and conservative intellectuals were focused on rebuilding their nation. The best Portuguese prose was in essay form, the best poetry and drama was in satire, and historical writing flourished. Among the celebrated literati of the era were Alexandre Herculano (1810–77), who wrote historical fiction and a monumental history of Portugal; and the brilliantly versatile Almeida Garrett (1799–1854), best known for his drama, but also the author of poetry, novels and essays.

The reign of Luís lasted until 1889 and was a period of relative peace. Conservatives and liberals alternated in controlling the legislature. Portugal's external affairs were more or less dictated by Britain, their protector under the Congress of Vienna's partitioning of small countries under major powers, in 1814–15. But Portugal was tenacious in holding on to many of its colonial claims and territories in Africa. The high expense of maintaining those colonies was a burden on the rickety national economy, but it would stand the country in good stead when the holdings finally did pay off during the 20th century.

Lisbon's Queluz Palàcio.

CULTURAL QUESTIONS

The influence of the rest of Europe on Portugal's cultural development in the 19th century was strongly felt. Intellectual conflicts were encapsulated in the "Coimbra question". Two groups of university scholars stood divided: the older group advocated the virtues of the status quo, while the "Generation of 1870", as they became known, called for revision of intellectual and spiritual values. Like their European counterparts, they were rationalist, anti-clerical and anti-monarchist. In their writing could be heard the first strains of emerging socialism. Their daring critiques, however, were suppressed by the government in 1871.

A sailor of the revolution troops in Necessidades Palace Emmanuel II in 1910.

REVOLUTION AND EVOLUTION

Republicanism failed to restore Portugal's former glory. Political turmoil followed by dictatorship hindered growth and modernisation until the 1980s.

The end of the 19th century saw Portugal's finances in complete disarray. The havoc wrought by the Peninsular and Miguelist wars, on top of the loss of Brazil, was insurmountable. In 1889, Carlos I became king, setting African expansion as his primary goal, but his efforts were unsuccessful. In 1892, Portugal declared bankruptcy.

Still dreaming of restoring the empire, Carlos could do little to defuse the growing anti-monarchical sentiment. Socialism and trade unionism were growing influences. The legislative *cortes* had degenerated into a powerless assembly full of obstructive and self-promoting debate. Corruption and inefficiency were rampant.

In 1906, struggling to maintain some form of control, Carlos appointed João Franco as prime minister, endowing him with dictatorial powers. He quickly dissolved the useless legislature. In 1908 unknown parties, either members of a republican secret society or isolated anti-monarchical fanatics, assassinated Carlos and his son, Luís Filipe, heir to the throne. In the assault on the royal carriage, Manuel, the king's second son, was wounded but survived.

Over the next two years Manuel II tried to save the monarchy, offering various concessions, but the assassination had fortified the republican movement. The long-decrepit House of Bragança finally crumbled to dust.

The rise of republicanism

The rising tide of republicanism could not be stopped. The democratic ideal was combined with a nationalistic vision, a shift it was hoped would return Portugal to its long-lost glory. The national anthem adopted in 1910 echoed the theme: "Oh sea heroes, oh noble people... raise again the splendour of Portugal... may

An allegory of the 1908 elections.

Europe claim to all the world that Portugal is not dead!"

The assassination of Carlos sealed the victory of republicanism, but it took time for the various parties and coalitions to sort themselves into a workable government – practically speaking, they never did. Between 1910 and 1926 there were 45 different governments, with most of the changes brought about by military intervention rather than parliamentary procedures. The early leadership pressed their radical anti-Church and social reforms too hard, causing a reaction that revived the influence of the Catholic Church. Labour movements sprang up with the best intentions, but often paralysed industry. First and foremost, the republicans were unable to deliver promised financial reforms and stability, both through their own ineptitude and, later, because of the international depression of the 1920s. It was their economic failure that most significantly eroded their popular support.

Afonso Costa rose to leadership of the republican factions, but the hard stance of his anti-clericalism caused too much ill feeling to allow stability. Coups became standard. General Pimenta de Castro grabbed control briefly, but democratic forces deposed him.

Portugal, initially neutral, joined the Allies under Britain's influence in 1916. The causes

General Oscar Carmona, Portugal's president until 1951.

behind World War I meant little to the nation but cost thousands of lives, in Europe and Africa, and brought further financial upheaval and political unrest. Sidónio Pais formed a dictatorial government in 1917, but was assassinated in Lisbon the following year. Three years later, António Machado Santos suffered the same fate. In 1926, the democratic government of Bernardino Machado was overthrown by military forces and the constitution suspended. Leadership passed through various hands and finally to General Oscar Carmona. He remained president until 1951, but it was not his leadership but that of his most influential appointee that made stability possible. In 1928, Carmona appointed António de Oliveira

Salazar to the post of finance minister, with wide-ranging powers. By 1932, Salazar was effectively prime minister.

Salazar's New State

Salazar immediately set about reorganising the country's disastrous financial morass, mostly through the narrow-minded austerity which reflected his own character. Having achieved what no leader had been able to do for a century, Salazar used his political capital to form a dictatorship, taking Mussolini's Italy as his model for national order and discipline.

The "New State", though nominally a corporative economic system under a republican government, was a fascist regime, with the National Union its only political party. It was authoritarian, pro-Catholic and imperialist. A state police organisation, the PIDE, was notorious in its suppression of subversion. A rigid and effective censorship settled like a thick fog over art, literature and free speech. Nothing negative or critical could find its way into print. A formerly lively journalism withered away. In blatant doublespeak, the government often referred to itself as a dictatorship without a dictator.

There was some resistance. In reaction to the powerful militaristic control there were numerous attempted coups and an underground Communist party that grew in power, leading the clandestine opposition. However, Salazar's leadership was never strongly challenged.

Putting self-preservation ahead of ideology, Salazar pretended to adhere to the League of Nations' non-intervention policy during the Spanish Civil War (1936–9) because he could not afford international censure, but actually sent a legion of some 20,000 soldiers to aid General Franco's Nationalist forces. Franco's victory served to validate the authority of Salazar's own regime.

The republican era had seen a minor cultural resurgence, when democratic ideals encouraged efforts at mass education, a proliferation of journalism, and a few writers of modern fiction and poetry. But this was slowed by political upheavals, and effectively quelled by the New State. The greatest writer of the period, the poet Fernando Pessoa (1888–1935), had one major work, *Mensagem*, published in 1934, but it was not until after World War II that most of his works were in print. Few others transcended the romantic nationalism of the era, as formidable barriers to the larger currents of European culture were created. The censorship of the New State slowed original thinking to a trickle, and most of that was devoted to political subversion rather than artistic endeavour.

After World War II

During World War II, the New State concentrated on self-preservation. Though Salazar admired Hitler, Portugal's traditional political and economic ties with Britain demanded neutrality, at least. However, Portugal did supply the Axis with much-needed wolfram (the ingredient necessary to alloy tungsten steel), almost until the end of the war. On the other hand, the Allies were granted strategic bases in the Azores. In fact, the war's main effect – though it was not widely advertised – was to replenish Portugal's coffers, as the government did business with both sides.

The defeat of the fascists should have given a signal to Salazar, a warning to mute his totalitarianism, but he was by now firmly entrenched. The changes over the next decade served primarily to protect the dictatorship still further from democratic insurgency.

In the 1950s, opposition to the New State solidified into two blocs. The legal bloc took advantage of the relaxed censorship in the

> Censorship was nothing new to a country dominated for so long by the Inquisition. In the 500-year history of publishing in Portugal, little more than 80 years have been free of censorship.

month preceding the 1951 elections (the state's way of giving the impression of some democratic freedom) to run independent candidates. Members of the other, furtive, bloc organised various protest actions and engaged in what propaganda they could. These means kept resistance alive, forcing Salazar's hand and provoking new rounds of repression, deceit and constitutional changes, which eroded both Salazar's authority and popularity.

In 1958, General Humberto Delgado, a disenchanted member of the regime, stood for president, announcing that he would use the constitutional power of that position to dismiss Salazar. Despite mass demonstrations in his support, the official count declared that

Admiral Américo Tomás, a Salazar loyalist, had been elected. Afterwards, constitutional decrees were enacted to prevent the repetition of such an event. The president was to be elected not by popular vote, but by an electoral college of the National Assembly, which was Salazar-controlled. Delgado was assassinated in 1965 by state police, while attempting to cross the Spanish border back into Portugal.

The empire strikes back

Portugal's entry into the United Nations was prevented by the Soviet bloc and by oppo-

General Craveiro Lopes, Portugal's twelfth president (1951–58), before the crowds.

nents of Salazar's imperial colonialism, until 1955. Membership was finally granted not because of any real change, but by a successful diplomatic effort to whitewash his despotism. Salazar would not change his policies because, despite the increasing cost of maintaining military rule in the colonies, they were very profitable for the homeland. Subsistence crops were increasingly neglected in favour of products like cotton, which fed the mills of Portugal while the Africans went hungry. The policy of *assimilado* – claiming that the goal was to assimilate the ethnic culture into the Portuguese one – allowed Portugal to exploit these "citizens" as virtually free labour.

Salazar's imperial intransigence led to serious consequences in the post-war world, where old empires were rapidly crumbling. The violent 1961 Angolan uprising, brutally crushed by the Portuguese, ignited an explosion of African nationalism. Throughout the 1960s, the government became more and more involved in maintaining the colonies, which were renamed "provinces" in a 1951 decree that underscored the insistence on a permanent Portuguese settlement.

As many young men were conscripted for the wars in Africa, popular support waned rapidly.

relatively smooth. Salazar lived his final years in seclusion and died in 1970.

Caetano, once a protégé of Salazar, had resigned seven years earlier over conflicts with his superior. Called upon to resolve the national crisis, he saw the need for balanced change and stability, but was not bold enough. Many of the gravest injustices of the old regime were righted, but other changes were superficial, and the colonial issue was not confronted. When his early efforts at liberalisation failed to appease opposition unrest, Caetano returned to oppressive hostility.

Salazar reviewing the Portuguese troops in 1940.

Angola continued to be an economic boon, but the other colonies were a drain. Salazar trusted ever fewer members of his regime, taking on more direct responsibilities himself for continuing the wars. He also relaxed his policy of fiscal austerity, and increasingly relied on foreign credit to finance the overseas operations.

The end of an era

In 1968, the 79-year-old dictator suffered an incapacitating stroke; the long-awaited succession had arrived. Because Salazar – who was unwilling to face his own mortality – had made no provision for a successor, major upheavals were expected. But the transition to power of "Acting Prime Minister" Marcelo Caetano was

AN UNWILLING RETREAT

Despite international pressure, and increasing agitation within the colonies, Salazar's regime fiercely resisted any incursions on its colonial outposts. In 1961, the territory of São João da Ajuda, a tiny enclave surrounded by the country of Dahomey, consisted only of a decrepit fortress and the governor's estate. When Dahomey became independent from France, and delivered an ultimatum to Lisbon to return Ajuda, the Portuguese governor was forced to comply, but he waited until the last possible moment to surrender, then spitefully burned down the buildings before departing.

Discontent among all ranks of the military over the continued ineffective colonial wars led to the formation of the Armed Forces Movement (MFA) in 1973. The following year, General António de Spínola published *Portugal and the Future*, a stinging critique of the current situation, which recommended a military takeover to save the country. The book's messages had been voiced before but never by so powerful a source. Many factors built towards the revolution, but this publication, whose importance Caetano himself said he had profoundly felt, lit the fuse.

The initial government was a National Salvation group of military men, designed to give way to a constituent assembly as soon as it was practical. A provisional government was soon in place, and negotiations with African liberation movements went ahead. There were divisions about overseas policies, and an odd coup-within-a-coup developed, with Spínola attempting to wrest control from his opponents. It was unsuccessful and liberal forces continued to divest Portugal of its colonies. Guinea-Bissau, Mozambique, the Cape Verde Islands, São Tomé and finally Angola were granted independence. One result of de-colonial-

General Antonio Spínola exits Queluz Palace after being nominated President of the Republic, 15 May 1974.

Bloodless coup

Two months later, on 25 April 1974, after a handful of premature uprisings, a near-bloodless coup began in Lisbon. Involving General Spínola and his fellow General Costa Gomes, it was conducted by angry "young captains" who commanded the 27 rebel units that seized key points throughout the city. Caetano and other government officials took refuge in the barracks of the National Republican Guard. The formal surrender came after a young officer threatened to crash a tank through the gates. The rebel takeover was quickly accepted throughout the country. The revolution, taking the red carnation as its symbol, sparked nationwide celebration culminating in joyful demonstrations on 1 May.

isation was a mass return of Portuguese nationals to their homeland – as many as 500,000 people. Angola and Mozambique were abandoned to civil wars, East Timor devoured by Indonesia.

As the economy careered into an abyss, the political pendulum swung the other way, and there was huge social unrest. In 1976 the socialist leader Mário Soares became prime minister, but over the following decade governments frequently came and went. Socialist experiments were attempted as an antidote to years of Salazar. Land reforms were initiated, breaking up *látifundios*, the vast and long-established agricultural estates, particularly in the Alentejo, but these reforms have not proved successful.

In 1982, a long-awaited revision of the new

constitution arrived. The democratic alliance and the far right were determined to rid the document of its Marxist taint. They were partially successful, but only after a period of nationwide demonstrations, strikes and resignations. The Council of the Revolution was eliminated, and the hope for a truly classless society remained an unrealised goal.

In the next few years, the country witnessed a shift away from socialism towards capitalism. Although the veteran socialist leader Mário Soares was elected president in 1986 (the first civilian to hold the post in over 60 years) and

Ex-Portuguese president José Manuel Barroso is now president of the European Commission.

re-elected by a landslide in 1991, the capitalistic social democrats, under youthful economist Aníbal Cavaco Silva, won an overall majority in July 1987. In 1991, after a campaign based largely on his own forceful personality and his claims that his government had wrought nothing less than an economic miracle, Cavaco Silva won another resounding electoral victory.

Joining the EU

Such stability allowed Portugal to emerge from being the most backward economy in Europe to becoming, by the early 1990s, one of the most buoyant. In 1986, it joined the European Community and in 1992 took its turn at assuming

presidency of the EEC. Among Cavaco Silva's most successful programmes was the re-privatisation of many companies and industries nationalised by the Communists after the revolution.

In 1997, the Portuguese economy, then one of the fastest growing in Europe, met the requirements for the country to join the single currency, along with 10 other qualifying European Union states. Major public works projects such as a second bridge over the Tejo in Lisbon had already culminated in the successful hosting of Expo '98, and this, even more than monetary union, was seen by many Portuguese as the

> The Portuguese continue to seek their fortunes abroad. Around 4.3 million Portuguese live abroad, 10 times the number of foreigners living in Portugal. Their remittances make up 10 percent of the GDP.

final confirmation of their country's arrival as a modern, thriving European economy, poised to meet the challenges of the new millennium.

However, a slowing down of the economy had wrong-footed the socialist government elected in 1995, and in 2002 Durão Barroso became prime minister of a centre-right government. In July 2004, he accepted the post of European Commission president. Former Lisbon mayor Pedro Santana Lopes became prime minister. In February 2005 a displeased electorate voted in the Socialist Party, now led by little-known José Sócrates, with its first ever overall majority. Restoring balance, the presidential election in January 2006 was won by a familiar social democrat, former prime minister Cavaco Silva. In 2007 the Portuguese experienced their most significant social change in years when they voted to legalise abortion. The same year, Prime Minister Sócrates assumed the EU presidency. In 2009, as leader of the re-elected Socialist Party, he formed a minority government.

Hit by the global recession, Portugal's economic problems are profound. Like Greece, it suffers feeble growth, hampered by debt, low productivity and an ageing population, although its funding requirements are not as severe. In 2010, the government implemented austerity measures in an attempt to reduce the budget deficit; now comes the task of meeting the needs of its people while improving its economic outlook.

Salazar

António de Oliveira Salazar, who led the country for 40 years, was the dominant figure of 20th-century Portugal

António de Oliveira Salazar was a country boy, born in 1889, who took the strict conservative values of his father far beyond the small rural world that formed them, ultimately transforming the whole nation into his image of what it should be. As a professor of economics at Coimbra, Salazar was an active polemicist for the right. He made his first political impact as the youthful leader of the Centro Académico da Democracia Cristã (Academic Centre for Christian Democracy), a Catholic intellectual group that opposed the anti-clerical and individualistic philosophy of the republic. He made a brief foray into national politics but only accepted a political position when he could be assured of complete control.

This came in 1928, when the prime minister, General Carmona, offered Salazar the role of finance minister with absolute power over national finance. In 1932, he was appointed president of the Council of Ministers – another name for prime minister. Although there was opposition, dissent, and various plots against his life, Salazar's pervasive influence on Portugal would not truly lift until the April revolution of 1974, six years after a disabling stroke, and four years after his death.

Salazar's Portugal

Salazar imposed his own character upon the nation. He was austere, introverted, and seldom travelled outside Portugal. He steered his country through international affairs with as much neutrality as possible. Portugal accepted Salazar's fascism as a kind of defensive posture in the face of the worldwide technological explosion of the 20th century. His conservative and at times reactionary attitudes towards industrialisation, agricultural reform, education and religion kept Portugal apart from the turbulence of the age. His attitude that Portugal was a naturally poor country – good for living in but not for producing anything – was widely held. Catholic cults, like that of Our Lady of Fátima, were encouraged and turned into propaganda.

Salazar also drew upon the romanticised history of Portuguese exploration and trade, inculcating a generation of schoolchildren with the self-aggrandising idea of Portugal's manifest destiny as an empire. The country turned inwards, though still holding on to its colonies for as long as possible, and tried to ignore the changing face of world politics. It was a comforting but debilitating attitude.

Salazar lived quietly, taking modest vacations by the sea or in his beloved Beira countryside. He remained unmarried, though he had a close but apparently celibate relationship with his lifelong housekeeper, Dona Maria de Jesus Caetano.

Salazar in 1958.

On 3 August 1968, in his fortress sanctuary in Estoril, Salazar suffered a stroke that left him an invalid. He left no designated heir, but with surprisingly little turmoil, Marcelo Caetano, a brilliant lecturer but a rather weak politician, was made prime minister. For the remaining two years of Salazar's life, he received few visitors and was given very little public attention. Those close to him chose not to tell him the truth about the succession of Caetano. Instead, they fabricated an image of Portugal still led by the old dictator.

When Dona Maria tried to convince him to retire, he refused and, in a last pathetic boast, claimed that he had no choice but to remain, because there was no one else. He died, aged 81, believing that he was still in control.

The shrine of Fátima draws thousands of pilgrims and worshippers.

SAINTS, MIRACLES AND SHRINES

Religion in Portugal touches all aspects of life.
Every town and village has its own saint, which is a
cause for celebration at least once a year.

I n the middle of the 6th century a young monk named Martin arrived in Mondoñedo, in northwest Spain, where he founded the abbey of Dume. His mission then took him to Braga, the former Roman city that had become the political and religious stronghold of the Suevi, a barbarian tribe that had adopted Arianism, a heretical form of Christianity. Martin, who had been inspired at the shrine of St Martin at Tours, was determined to convert their leaders to true Christianity.

In 559, he converted the Suevi king, Theodomirus. Within a decade, Martin was appointed archbishop of Braga. He found a further challenge, however, among the general population. Catholics since their conversion under the Roman Empire, they had incorporated many local beliefs and customs into their religion. To Martin, this was unacceptable, and in a written sermon entitled *De*

Watching the Easter procession.

> Many unorthodox elements linger to this day as an obstinate strain within Catholic traditions – naturally, there is much wrestling over the issues between the Church hierarchy and the parishes.

Correctione Rusticorum (On the Correction of Peasants), he called for an end to the use of charms, auguries and divination, of the invocation of the devil, and of the cults of the dead, of fountains and stars.

St Martin did not succeed, nor have 14 centuries of similarly inclined zealots and reformers. Yet, though frowned upon by the orthodox Church, spontaneous, independent Catholicism should not be seen as a form of

superstition or magic; rather, it is evidence of a vigorous religious tradition.

In the past, when a newborn child proved healthy, it was said that it was conceived when the moon was waxing. The states of the moon were believed to be very influential in the way all living things grow: vegetables, animals and human beings. Similarly, certain fountains were reputed to have particular healing powers. And under many of these, Moorish princesses were said to be hiding, watching over treasures.

Around midnight

One of the more dramatic folk practices was the midnight baptism. This developed during the 17th century, and occurred when a pregnant woman was prone to miscarriages or when her previous child was stillborn. The "baptism" used to take place at midnight in the middle of a bridge that divides two municipalities – a powerful spot that is neither one place nor another, at the moment that is neither one day nor the next. Certain bridges, such as the Ponte da Barca in the Minho, were famous for this.

When everything was ready, the child's father and a friend, armed with sticks, used to stand guard at the ends of the bridge. They are there to ward off cats and dogs – potentially witches or the devil in disguise. The first person who

to the church, it is a symbol of the new life shared by the whole community.

Similarly, on All Saints' Day and All Souls' Day (1 and 2 November), the celebrations at the parish cemetery are attended by everyone. Lamps are lit, tombs are cleaned and decorated with flowers. The whole parish celebrates this strongly felt sense of continuity with the past, praying together for their dead.

Perhaps the strongest evidence that the feeling of community extends beyond this life is the common belief in the "procession of the dead". Certain people claim that they have the

Street party during the Festas dos Santos Populares.

passes after the church bells strike midnight was charged with performing the rite. He or she would pour river water over the expectant mother's belly and baptise the child "in the name of the Father, the Son and the Holy Ghost" but the final "Amen" would not be uttered; this would wait until the child was born and properly baptised by a priest in church.

Such practices may now be consigned to history, but religious passion still governs behaviour in Portugal, and the church is the central meeting place of the whole parish. At Easter, the cross that represents the resurrection of Christ is taken from the church and carried to all the households. It is kissed as it enters each house, and when it is returned

power to hear or see a procession of the ghosts of those parishioners who have recently died. This procession is seen leaving the cemetery, with a coffin in its centre. When it returns, the ghost of the parishioner who will be the next to die will be in the coffin. Thus, it is said, these seers can predict how many people are going to die imminently – but they cannot reveal the names to anybody if they themselves want to remain alive.

Patron saints

The use of religion to establish a communal identity is most clearly shown by the celebrations for the local patron saint. An organising committee busies itself all year collecting money, planning decorations, arranging events. The importance of these celebrations is immense. They represent and solidify local pride. The *festa* is a joyful occasion heralded by firecrackers and by music blaring from loudspeakers placed on the church tower. The pivotal event is the procession after Mass, when the image of the patron saint is carried with great pomp on a brightly decorated stand in a traditional, roughly circular path.

After that, the secular celebrations begin. These usually involve dancing to traditional brass bands, folk-dance groups and, nowadays, rock and pop bands as well. A great deal of wine is consumed and the festivities are a popular social focus for young people. Not surprisingly, it is this aspect of the celebration that some priests oppose.

Popular attitudes to saints differ from church doctrine not so much in content as in emphasis. The people place great importance on material benefits and personal, reciprocal relationships with saints. They pray to specific saints for specific problems – St Lawrence if they have a toothache, St Brás if suffering from a sore throat, St Christopher when going on a journey. Our Lady of the Conception, natu-

> The notion of the miracle in popular religion is more loosely interpreted than in the Church. Essentially, a miracle is considered to have taken place every time a specific prayer is answered.

rally, helps with problems of infertility, and the Holy Family is asked to intervene in family problems, and so on. People will also address personal prayers to particular saints. If the believer's prayer is answered, this proves that the particular image is a singularly sacred one, a favoured line of communication. In this way shrines develop, whether individual, family, or even national, with images famous for their miraculous powers.

Wax offerings

When a prayer to St Anthony asks for a specific favour – that a loved one, or even a pig or sheep, recover from a bout of ill health, or an offer of marriage be accepted – a promise is made to give the saint something in return. A wax heart might

be given for a successful engagement, or a wax pig if the animal has fully recovered. But if the promise is not fulfilled, punishment may follow.

If you visit churches in northern Portugal, you will often see these *ex voto* offerings hanging on the walls alongside other gifts such as bridal dresses, photographs, written testimonies or braids of women's hair. Shrines of great importance such as Bom Jesus and Sameiro, near Braga, have large displays. At Fátima (see box page 74), the best-known shrine in the country, wax gifts accumulate so quickly that special furnaces have been installed to burn them.

Easter procession in Obidos.

There is also another kind of gift: a personal sacrifice. The church has been strongly critical of this, but until the late 1960s, it was firmly encouraged. If you visit the shrine of São Bento da Porta Aberta (St Benedict of the Open Door), in the beautiful mountain landscape of Gerês near the dam of Caniçada on 13 August, you will find men and women laboriously circumambulating the church on their knees.

This scene is even more striking because these people are surrounded by others celebrating the day with singing, dancing, eating and drinking. But those on their knees are celebrating, too – because the saint has answered their prayers – you will see the same scene at the Fátima shrine at any time of year.

Another kind of payment to patron saints has all but disappeared, due to strong Church opposition. In the parish of Senhora da Aparecida in Lousada, for example, before the main procession leaves the church there is another one in which 20 or more open coffins – containing living people, their faces covered with white handkerchiefs – are carried through the streets. Those who ride in the coffins are offering a false burial to the saint who saved them from having to participate in a real one. The occasion, therefore, is a joyful one, although it sounds macabre. There is plenty of light-hearted banter, and the "dead"

Shrine outside Ferraguda church in the Algarve.

participants mingle with the other parishioners afterwards, drinking and dancing.

Surviving cults

The cult of the dead, another morbid religious tradition and one of the targets of St Martin during the 6th century, remains an object of popular fascination in the north. Very occasionally, a body is buried but does not undergo the normal process of decay. Such people are often considered to be saints and there are a number of grim shrines where the corpses are exposed. The Church nearly always opposes these cults at first, but eventually tolerates them as they grow in popularity: three such shrines are the Infanta Santa Mafalda in Arouca, the São Torcato near

Guimarães, and the Santinha de Arcozelo near Porto. Even in an unlikely spot like the small urban cemetery of the elegant Foz neighbourhood in Porto, a shrine to one of these "saints" can be found.

Along rural roads one will frequently find pretty little shrines, but these are intended to protect travellers, and are not connected with the cult of the dead. They contain images of Christ or the Virgin or a popular saint. At the base, little moulded flames surround figures that represent the souls of sinners suspended in Purgatory.

Compromise and coexistence

Portuguese history is full of examples of the continuing conflict between the spontaneous and all-embracing religiosity of the less educated classes, and the more restrictive attitudes of the theologically minded – and the ways in which the two have learned to coexist. From the early days of the Western Crusade in the 12th century, and the power of military-religious orders like the Knights Templar and the Hospitallers, to the dark days of the Inquisition, religious and secular authorities have vied with each other for power, and used each other to the best advantage. In more recent years imperialism, like the early exploration and discoveries, was seen as a form of religious crusade: each victory along the way was considered a miracle. And Salazar's regime actively encouraged the cult of Our Lady of Fátima, even managing to present its policy of neutrality during World War II as being based on the soothsayings of the Virgin.

OUR LADY OF FÁTIMA

Fátima, near the town of Leiria, is one of the largest shrines in Western Europe (see page 234). On 13 May 1917, the Virgin is supposed to have appeared to three children. The event is said to have been repeated on the 13th of the subsequent five months, and each time the Virgin spoke about peace in the world. Fátima became a rallying point for the revival of Catholicism in the 1930s and 1940s. Today, from May to October the roads around Leiria are lined with pilgrims, many of whom have come great distances on foot to "pay" the Virgin for her favours.

TRAVELLERS' TALES

There were some distinguished names among early
visitors to Portugal, and they left with strong
impressions. Some fell in love with the country,
while others were more critical.

English visitors to Portugal long believed
themselves to be discoverers of the
one exotic land left in well-visited,
well-described Europe. In 1845, Dorothy
Quillinan, daughter of William Wordsworth,
wrote, "There is, I believe, no country in
Europe that is less thoroughly familiar to me."
A century later, Evelyn Waugh thought it was
still a well-kept secret, and wrote: "There is no
European capital of antiquity about which
one hears so little." But English travellers had
been going to Portugal, and writing about it,
for some time.

Eighteenth-century opinions

The most flamboyant of the 18th-century visitors to Portugal was William Beckford, who
set up a sumptuous house in Ramalhoa near
Sintra in 1787. He inspired Byron's *Childe
Harold*, whose first stop on his pilgrimage to
Portugal was to wander through Sintra conjuring Beckford's ghost and meditating on
the brevity of life and pleasure.

The flamboyant William Beckford.

Beckford first visited the peninsula in 1787,
shortly after the publication of his Gothic
novel *Vathek*. The unorthodox Englishman,
who had left England in the wake of a homosexual scandal, caught the fancy of the pious
Marquis of Marialva, who hoped to convert
him to Catholicism. But Beckford, as we learn
from his diary, was desperate not for the salvation of his soul but for an introduction to the
court of Queen Maria. England's ambassador
Sir Hugh Walpole refused to perform this service for his disgraced countryman. The marquis guaranteed an introduction if Beckford
would convert, but the writer had no such
intention and he left, petulant and thwarted.
By the time he was finally presented at court

in 1794, poor Maria had long been insane.

Beckford's *Sketches of Spain and Portugal*
give an idiosyncratic, bitchy but sensitive
view of Portugal's art, music, nature and society. His is a land of the senses: he described
the *modinha*, a haunting, erotic song, and the
luxuriant beauty of the vegetation. His journals provide a brilliant, if haphazard, guide to
Portugal's art and climate.

On his first visit to Portugal in 1796, Robert
Southey, a Romantic and the future English
Poet Laureate, expressed disapproval of the
filth of Lisbon, the discomfort of the country inns, and the corruption and superstition
of the priests. But on a subsequent visit, four
years later, although he still mourned the lack

of "genial company", he fell in love with the country, and delighted in the sensual orange groves, long lazy days and lush, fertile fields.

William Mickle, the 18th-century poet and translator of Luís Camões' works, was a great admirer of Portugal's "genial clime" and contrasted the "gloomy mists" of England to the "sun-basked scenes… where orange bowers invite".

Lord Byron

Lord Byron was a little more ambivalent. He wrote to his mother in 1809: "except the view from the Tagus, which is beautiful, and some fine churches and convents, it contains little but filthy streets and more filthy inhabitants". But he was far more enamoured of Sintra: "To make amends for this, the village of Cintra, about fifteen miles from the capital, is, perhaps in every respect, the most delightful in Europe; it contains beauties of every description, natural and artificial. Palaces and gardens rising in the midst of rocks, cataracts, and precipices; convents on stupendous heights… It unites in itself all the wildness of the western highlands, with the verdure of the south of France."

Byron's view of Lisbon also resonates in his poetry, where he painted the city as a faithless harlot of a town, a siren who glitters beautifully from the water but who reveals, on closer contact, only filth and treachery:
But whoso entereth within this town,
That, sheening far, celestial seems to be,
Disconsolate will wander up and down,
Mid many things unsightly to strange see;
For hut and palace show like filthily…
Poor paltry slaves! yet born midst noblest scenes.

Borrow's travels

The ingratitude of the Portuguese towards the British for their help in expelling Napoleon was a cause of resentment for another Englishman, George Borrow. Travelling in 1835, on a mission for the Bible Society, he complained that the English "who have never been at war with Portugal, who have fought for its independence on land and sea, and always with success, who have forced themselves by a treaty of commerce to drink its coarse and filthy wines… are the most unpopular people who visit Portugal."

Borrow's account of Portugal, although less famous than Byron's stanzas, is an original, entertaining and evocative description. He was a great reporter of human eccentricity, and was also enthusiastic about the beauties of Portugal. Lisbon, he claimed, "is quite as much deserving the attention of the artist as even Rome itself". Sintra, so lavishly praised by Byron, captivated all travellers and was "a mingled scene of fairy beauty, artificial elegance, savage grandeur, domes, turrets, enormous trees, flowers, and waterfalls, such as is met with nowhere else under the sun". It is truly, Borrow wrote, "Portuguese Paradise".

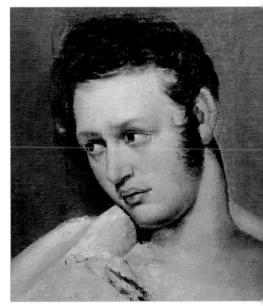

Portrait of Lord Byron.

SPEAKING TO THE NATIVES

George Borrow was a wonderfully comic traveller, erratic and egoistical. His self-confidence was typified by his belief that after just two weeks he could speak fluent Portuguese. He refused to accept that much of the time people could not understand what he was saying, and his advice to novices speaking a foreign language offered the sort of wrong-headed lesson that some tourists seem to take to heart even today. "Those who wish to make themselves understood by a foreigner in his own language should speak with much noise and vociferation, opening their mouths wide."

Portuguese fado singer, Katia Guerreiro, performs at The Bahrain International Music Festival in Manama.

FADO

The Portuguese blues, fado (which comes from the Latin *fatum*, meaning fate), presents elegiac songs about love, loss, the sea, poverty and beauty.

The unique musical tradition of fado has grown out of Portugal's cocktail of culture – a result of the country's early exploration and connections with places overseas. Like the blues, flamenco and tango, it was a music that grew out of hardship and poverty, but became the soundtrack to a nation.

Fado's sad, distinctively Portuguese songs are thought to have developed from the music of the Moors, who influenced the country in many ways, and the Lundum music of the Brazilian slaves, who would arrive in Portugal after long sea voyages in the early 19th century. One famous fado song, called *The Black Boat*, talks specifically of a *senzala* (place where the slaves were kept). Many early songs are related to the sea, to faraway lands, and longing for home – subjects unsurprising in such a seafaring nation.

The other major source for the songs is believed to have been the verses of the minstrels and jesters in the middle ages, which share similar themes to those of fado. These included the *cantigas de amigo* (songs about a boyfriend), love songs that are sung solely by women, and satirical songs making jibes about the government and politicians.

Fado seems to have first taken off in the working-class districts of Alfama and Mouraria in Lisbon, and, rapidly gaining in popularity, later spread to the university of Coimbra, where it took on a quite different character. The fado in Coimbra is sung only by men, praising the beauty of women, and often takes the form of serenades.

Fadistas at first came from the working class – this was not the music of the bourgeoisie. Its musicians and singers mixed with the edgier elements of society – the criminals and prostitutes.

Historic entertainment in a café.

The most famous *fadista* of the 19th century, Maria Severa, was a prostitute, who sang in her mother's tavern in Alfama. She attracted the attention of the aristocratic Conde di Vimioso with her singing, and they embarked on a scandalous love affair which crossed class barriers in a hitherto unacceptable way.

The conde's influence saw fado reach the court, but Maria Severa died aged just 26, either from tuberculosis or suicide. She always sang wrapped in a black shawl, which female fado singers still do today in her memory.

During the mid-20th century, the dictator Salazar (in power from 1932 to 1968) insisted that fado singers become professional and only sing in specially designated fado houses.

This was the "golden age" of fado. During this period the famous names were Alfredo Marceneiro and Maria Teresa de Noronha, and the guitar players Armandinho and Jaime Santos, but most famous of all was Amália Rodrigues (see panel page 80), whose rise to international superstardom saw the status of fado change forever.

The singers and the song

The *fadista*, a powerfully voiced singer, is usually backed by a guitar – the twelve-stringed Portuguese version – and a classic guitar,

> *The Portuguese say that it takes more than a good voice to become a true fadista – it takes soul.*

fado of Coimbra is usually taken even more seriously than that of Lisbon, which means it is very serious indeed.

For a while after the 1974 Carnation Revolution, fado lost some currency in Portugal, as it was associated with the old regime. However, it crept back, becoming even more widely sung

Fado singer, Mariza, performs during a concert in homage to legendary singer Amália.

Portuguese fado singer and former judge Fernando Machado Soares.

which is called a viola in Portugal. The male fado singer usually wears a black suit; he sings about love affairs, the city, life's misery, bullfighting, politicians, and about the past. The female singer will also wear black, and sings heart-rendingly about love and death, love lost, and tragic romance.

All fado is linked with the concept of *saudade*. This difficult-to-translate term is a kind of nostalgic longing and yearning for something that is lost. It is an emotion that has a peculiar resonance in the Portuguese make-up.

Fado is a performance, not a sing-song, and you are expected to be quiet and listen. The

AMÁLIA RODRIGUES

Portugal's most famous *fadista*, Amália, was born in 1920 into a poor family, and as a child sold fruit on the Lisbon docks. Her remarkable voice was noted by local people, who often asked her to sing for them, and after years of amateur performances she had her first professional engagement aged 19. Her career quickly took off, and she became Portugal's most revered star. Amália appeared in films and became an international icon and a national treasure, continuing to perform in public until 1990. When she died in 1999 there were more than three days' mourning in Alfama. Her house in Lisbon now houses the Museu de Amália Rodrigues.

than before. Modern *fadistas* have brought the sound up to date (see panel, page 81).

Where to find it

There are plenty of places where visitors can experience fado for themselves. It is best to hear it sung at its source, in Alfama, Bairro Alto and Mouraria in Lisbon or in Coimbra, although there are fado houses in other towns across Portugal. Finding true, earthy fado has some similarities with seeking out authentic Spanish flamenco. There are smart and formal venues, with famous singers, but these tend to work out very expensive when you combine admission charges and the accompanying drinks and meals, and they don't have the same intimate atmosphere.

Alternatively, there are scruffier backstreet bars where the experience feels more spontaneous and earthy. These offer *fado vadio* (street fado), which means anyone can stand up and have a go, and some local people come back to do so week after week. The singers might not be of quite the same quality, but the immediacy of the passion and atmosphere may far exceed the more refined version.

Singers in the Barrio Alto.

MODERN FADISTAS

The new wave of *fadistas* is still dominated by women: Mariza, Mizia, Ana Moura, Katia Guerreiro and Cristina Branco. Of the male new guard, there is Pedro Moutinho, born into a well-known family of *fadistas* in Oeiras. The most natural successor to Amália is Mariza, instantly recognisable with her bleached blonde hair. She was born Marisa dos Reis Nunes in Mozambique, then a Portuguese colony, in 1973, of Portuguese-African parentage. At the age of three, the family moved to Mouraria in Lisbon, and she began singing at the age of five in her parents' restaurant.

Mariza moved away from fado in her teens, experimenting with other types of music, and travelling in Brazil when she was in her twenties, but she came back to fado, and her powerful, theatrical, yet emotional performances make her a natural star. Her background, with elements of German, Spanish, French, African and Indian ancestry, in some ways represents the story of Portugal, and a particularly emotional song of hers is *Oh Gente do Minho Terra* (Oh People of my Country).

Mariza performs in sell-out concerts all over the world, in venues such as the Carnegie Hall in New York and the Royal Festival Hall in London, and has twice received Latin Grammy nominations. In 2002 she sang the Portuguese national anthem at the FIFA World Cup, when Portugal played against the hosts South Korea.

Chestnut street seller, Lisbon.

PORTUGUESE FOOD

If you like fresh fish, succulent pork and hearty soups, laced with plenty of garlic, you will find Portuguese food to your taste.

To dine in Portugal is to taste the presence of other countries, other cuisines. It is to conjure up images of empire: Brazil, Angola, Mozambique, Goa and Macau. These and others all "belonged" to Portugal once and, in a manner of speaking, foods from four continents helped to stir the pot.

The period of Portuguese empire, when this small nation reached out across the terrifying "Green Sea of Darkness", as the Atlantic was called, has long passed. Yet Portugal, left with only the Azores and Madeira, has preserved the flavours of other cultures in its cooking.

Prince Henry the Navigator, less than 30 years old when he began to promote exploration, was a true scientist in an age of superstition. He ordered his explorers to bring back from new lands not only riches and wild tales, but also fruits, nuts and plants. In 1420 he sent settlers to colonise the newly discovered island of Madeira. With them went plants he believed would thrive in Madeira's volcanic soil and subtropical climate, including grape vines from Crete and sugar cane from Sicily. Even more significant for Portuguese cooking was Vasco da Gama's discovery of the sea route to the east in 1497–8, only five years after Christopher Columbus's discovery of the West Indies.

Portuguese sardines are plump and succulent.

The Portuguese word for tea – chá – is almost identical to the Cantonese one – ch'a – from which is derived the colloquial English term "char".

Spices of the Orient

Black pepper was what Vasco da Gama sought, but cinnamon, which he also found in Calcutta, would soon become equally precious to Portuguese cooks. Indeed, one boatload of cinnamon sticks fetched enough money to pay for an entire expedition to India. Cinnamon is perhaps the most beloved spice in Portugal today, certainly for the famous egg sweets (*doces de ovos*, see page 91). Spaniards, on the other hand, prefer vanilla for their puddings and flans. There is a good historical reason for this: it was the Spaniards who found Montezuma sipping vanilla-spiked hot chocolate in Mexico and learned the trick of curing vanilla beans, the seed pods of a wild orchid. Perhaps this is why chocolate, too, is more popular in Spain than in Portugal.

The spiciest Portuguese dishes, incidentally, are not found on the mainland but in the

Azores and Madeira. These islands were ports of call for the early navigators, who would barter with the native people, offering spices in exchange for fresh fruits, vegetables, meat and the local brew.

New food for old

During Portugal's lavish Age of Empire, its navigators became couriers, bringing New World foods to the Old and vice versa. Mediterranean sugar cane, for example, was cultivated in Brazil. Brazilian pineapples were introduced to the Azores, a colony established

(an oil and vinegar mixture strewn with minced chillies) is as popular a table condiment in mainland Portugal as salt and pepper.

Other exchanges were African coffee, transplanted to Brazil, which today produces about half of the world's supply; Brazilian cashews, which landed in Africa and India; and Oriental tea plants, which were taken to the Azores.

All this transporting of seeds, leaves, barks, roots, stalks and cuttings by Portuguese explorers across oceans and continents dramatically affected Portuguese cooking. New World tomatoes and potatoes came to Portugal about

Portuguese food is rustic.

under Prince Henry. They still flourish there in hothouses, ripening under wafting wood smoke. Azorean pineapples, chunky, honey-sweet and tender to the core, are teamed today with rosettes of Portugal's mahogany-hued, air-cured *presunto* (prosciutto-like ham) and served as an elegant appetiser in fashionable Lisbon restaurants.

Tiny, incendiary Brazilian chilli peppers took root in Angola, another important Portuguese colony, early on, and became so essential to cooks there that today they're known by their African name, *piri-piri*. Since Angola ceased to be a Portuguese colony in the mid-1970s, the subsequent influx to Lisbon of thousands of Angolan refugees has meant that *piri-piri* sauce

the same time as they did to Spain, in the 16th century. Portuguese cooks might drop a few garlic cloves into the soup or stew along with the tomatoes and potatoes, or tuck in a stick of cinnamon.

A la Portugaise

It is unlikely that anyone grows nuttier, earthier potatoes today than the Portuguese. Indeed, along the New England coast in the United States, where so many Portuguese families have settled, there is an old saying: "If you want your potatoes to grow, you must speak to them in Portuguese." Tomatoes respond to the Portuguese touch, too, and those harvested in the vast Alentejo province, east of

Lisbon, are as juicy, red and tasty as any on earth. Not for nothing does the phrase found on French menus, *"à la Portugaise"*, mean a dish that is richly sauced with tomatoes.

Onions and garlic, indispensable to any respectable Portuguese cook, were probably introduced by the Romans, who are believed to have brought wheat here, too. They aimed to make the Iberian peninsula the granary of Rome. They also probably introduced olives (a major source of income today) and grapes. From shards found in Alentejo, it is known that the Romans were making wine there as early as the 2nd century AD.

The Moors, who occupied a large chunk of Portugal from the early 8th to the mid-13th centuries, enriched the pot even more than the Romans. The southern provinces were the Moorish stronghold – the Algarve and Alentejo, in particular – and many traces of North Africa can still be seen.

It was the Arabs who dug irrigation ditches, who first planted rice (it now grows up and down the west coast), and who also covered the Algarve slopes with almond trees. The Algarve's almonds were ground into paste, sweetened, and shaped into delicate miniature fruits, birds

> *Most supposedly vegetable dishes include meat fat or stock; even a salad is not considered complete without a sprinkling of tuna. Vegetarians may prefer self-catering, shopping at markets for fruit, vegetables and bread.*

and flowers displaying intricate detail that are still produced today.

The Moors also introduced figs and apricots to the Algarve, together with the trick of drying them in the sun. They planted groves of lemons and oranges and, as was their custom, they combined fish with fruit and fruit with meat.

It was the Arabs who invented the *cataplana*, a hinged metal pan, a sort of primitive pressure cooker shaped like an oversize clam shell that can be clamped shut and set on a quick fire. The food inside – fish, shellfish, chicken, vegetables or a medley of all – steams to supreme succulence. What goes into a *cataplana* depends on the whim of the cook (and on what is available), but the most famous recipe is *amêijoas na cataplana*, clams tossed

with rounds of sausage and cubes of ham in an intensely garlicky tomato sauce. This unlikely pork and shellfish combination was supposedly created at the time of the Inquisition as a test of true Christianity. Pork and shellfish, of course, were forbidden to Jews and Muslims alike.

There is no shortage of examples of Portugal's culinary ingenuity. Thrifty Portuguese cooks with an eye on their wallets made bread a main course by layering yeast dough into a pan with snippets of chicken and sausage and two kinds of ham – a classic from the remote

Shopping at Casa Oriental, Porto.

northern Trás-os-Montes which is called *folar*. And when times were particularly hard they would crumble yesterday's bread into shrimp cooking water and come up with the Estremadura favourite known as *açorda de mariscos*.

Less economical but equally inventive is the Serra da Estrela recipe, which involves braising duck with bacon and rice; or smothering red mullet the Setúbal way, with tiny tart oranges; or scrambling flakes of salt cod with eggs and shoestring potatoes (thinly cut and crisply fried), as is done all over the country.

Cod country

Dried salt cod, or *bacalhau* (pronounced buckle-yow), is a purely Portuguese invention.

António M. Bello, first president of Portugal's gastronomic society, wrote in his *Culinária Portuguesa*, published in Lisbon in 1936, that the Portuguese were fishing Newfoundland's Grand Banks for cod within just a few years of Columbus's discovery of America.

New fishing rules impose restraints and quotas, and cod fishing especially is much altered. Yet Portuguese poems, stories, folk sayings and fado songs still maintain a bittersweet seafaring tradition:

O waves from the salty sea,
From whence comes your salt?

The best and most famous dishes are *bacalhau à Gomes de sá* (cod cooked in a casserole with thinly sliced potatoes and onions, garnished with hard-boiled eggs and black olives), *bacalhau à brás* and *bacalhau dourado* (two similar recipes composed of scrambled eggs, onions and shoestring potatoes), *bacalhau à Conde de Guarda* (salt cod creamed with mashed potatoes) and *bolinhos de bacalhau* (cod fish balls, a very popular hors d'oeuvre). All these once-humble recipes are served today in the most expensive restaurants. Prepared properly, they are delicious, but if too little care is taken they can be very salty.

Classic cod dish.

From the tears shed on the
Beaches of Portugal.

It was in the 16th century that Portuguese fishermen learned to salt cod at sea to make it last the long voyage home, and to sun-dry it into board-stiff slabs that could be kept for months then soaked in cool water before cooking.

Fish is still sun-dried on racks in the old way on the beach at Nazaré, although much less cod is available now. The Grand Banks have become so over-fished that the Portuguese have taken to importing *bacalhau* from Norway, just to be able to meet their annual demands. This, of course, prices salt cod – once an inexpensive staple of the national diet – beyond the reach of the very people it sustained for centuries.

SARDINE SEASON

Nearly as popular as salt cod are the sardines netted off the Atlantic coast. These are what the fishermen of Nazaré go out looking for day after day – although the men are less likely now to wear their traditional tartan, and the flat-bottomed boats have mostly given way to motorised craft. Portuguese sardines are considered the sweetest and fattest in the world, and local women grill them right on the streets, using little terracotta braziers. But you will only see this going on in spring, summer and early autumn, the "sardine season". As every right-minded Portuguese knows, sardines are too bony to eat from November to April.

King carne

If salt cod and sardines share top billing as the favourite fish, pork reigns supreme as the king of *carne* (meat). Portuguese pork is incomparably sweet and tender because of the pigs' agreeable diet and life of leisure. In the northerly Trás-os-Montes province, they say that if you want good pork in the autumn you must feed your pigs twice a day in August. Some farm women even go so far as to cook potatoes for their animals.

Small wonder the hams (*presunto* and *fiambre*) and sausages (*salsichas*) are so highly prized here (the best of all are said to come from Chaves). Small wonder, too, that charcuterie figures so prominently in the regional soups and stews. Cooks here will wrap freshly caught brook trout in slices of *presunto*, then bounce them in and out of a skillet so hot the ham is transformed to a crisp, deeply smoky sort of pastry.

But Portugal's most famous pork dish comes from the Alentejo. It is *porco à alentejana*, for

> Someone once said that the Portuguese live on dreams and subsist on salt cod. They do claim to know 365 ways to prepare it, one for each day of the year.

which cubes of pork are marinated in a paste of sweet red peppers and garlic, browned in the fruity local olive oil, then covered and braised with baby clams, still in the shell. The clams open slowly under the gentle heat, spilling their briny juices into the ambrosial red mixture. The secret behind achieving the distinctive nut-like flavour of Alentejo pork is that the pigs are turned loose each autumn to forage among the cork oaks. Here they nibble on acorns and wild herbs, as well as the occasional truffle.

Sausage-making is also highly prized in the Alentejo, and this region's garlicky *chouriços*, *linguiças*, *farinheiras* (sausages plumped up with cereal) and chunky, smoky *paios* are without peers. As one of Portugal's food authorities, Maria de Lourdes Modesto, writes in *Cozinha Tradicional Portuguesa*, "The grand destiny of the pig in the Alentejo is to become sausage."

Here, every part of the pig is used – ears, snout, tail, feet – even, it would seem, the squeal. At carnival time, for example, the centrepiece of

each banquet *festa* is *pezinhos de porco de coentrada*, dainty pigs' feet braised with onions, garlic and fresh coriander.

Another province famous for its pork is the coastal Beira Litoral, particularly the little town of Mealhada, which is not much more than a wide place in the road about 20km (12 miles) north of Coimbra. Here both sides of the highway are lined with restaurants that make suckling pig (*leitão assado*) a speciality. The piglets are rubbed with secret blends of oil and herbs, skewered from head to tail, then spit-roasted over white-hot hardwood

Caracóis (snails) are popular in Portugal.

coals until their skin is as crisply brittle as an onion's and their milk-white flesh so meltingly tender it falls from the bones at the touch of a fork.

Cabbage patch

The Portuguese national dish is built neither upon salt cod nor pork. Its key ingredient is cabbage, specifically a richly emerald, tenderleafed variety (*couve galega*). The dish itself is called *caldo verde*, a bracing, jade-green soup which is brimming with potatoes, onions, garlic and filament-thin shreds of green cabbage. Sometimes the soup may be fortified with slices of *chouriço* or *linguiça*, although in the humblest Minho versions (it is here that the recipe originated) it often contains nothing more than water, potatoes, onions, garlic, cabbage and perhaps a tablespoon or two of robust *azeite* (olive oil).

The preparation of *couve galega*, the minutely shredded vegetables that go into the soup, is something passed on from generation to generation in the countryside. The trick is to shred it with the speed of light: the leaves are stacked, perhaps five or six deep, rolled into a fat cigar, then literally shaved as a razor-sharp knife is whisked back and forth across the end of the cabbage roll so fast the

eggs (a Madeira speciality), of pumpkins and onions (a Trás-os-Montes staple), or of dried white beans and sausages (the universally beloved *feijoadas*) – are frugal and filling, nourishing and soul-satisfying. To make a meal, all they need for accompaniment are a glass of wine, a chunk of cheese and a crust of bread.

Bread and cheese

Portugal's simple country breads usually contain only the usual four ingredients – flour milled from hard wheat, water, yeast and

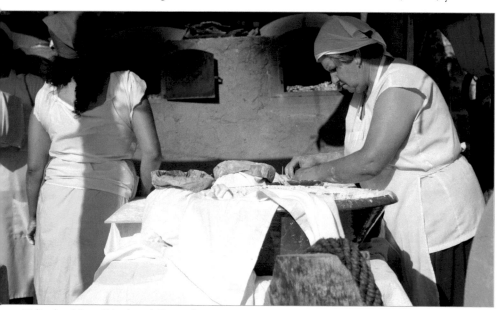

Making bread the traditional way in Estremadura.

movements are scarcely visible. The fineness of the cut is what makes a bowl of *caldo verde* resemble molten jade; also the cabbage is tossed into the pot just minutes before serving so that its colour intensifies rather than turning to a paler shade.

Soups and stews

Next to *caldo verde*, Portugal's most famous soup is probably *açorda à alentejana*, a coriander-strewn, bread-thickened, egg-drop soup seasoned, as someone once remarked, "with enough garlic to blow a safe".

The soups and stews of Portugal – whether they're made of chickpeas and spinach (another Alentejo classic), of tomatoes and

salt – but they are kneaded until their dough fairly springs to life. And because they are baked in wood-stoked brick or stone ovens, they have a faintly smoky flavour. There are fancier breads, to be sure, notably the sweet festival breads, the *pão doce* of Easter and the fruit-studded *bolo rei* of Christmas. There are huskier breads, too, the rough round barley breads and, most famous of all, the *broas* – yeast-raised corn breads of the Minho that are sold by the truckload at the market in the river town of Barcelos.

Cheeses can be bought at country markets everywhere. The queen of them all is the ivory-hued *queijo da serra*, a cheese so strictly demarcated it can be made only from the milk of sheep grazing on the wild mountain herbs of the Serra da Estrela. At the peak of its season – winter – a properly ripened *serra* is as biting, buttery and runny as the finest Brie.

Portugal also produces a number of other delectable cheeses: the nutty, semi-dry *serpa* from the Alentejo town of the same name, which is cured in caves and brushed regularly with paprika-laced olive oil; *beja*, a buttery semi-hard cheese from Beja, near Serpa; *azeitão*, lovely little rounds of gold cheese, tangy and creamy, that come from the village of Azeitão on the Arrábida Peninsula just across the Tejo from Lisbon. Finally, there are the *queijos frescos*, snowy, uncured cheese much like cottage cheese, which calorie-conscious Portuguese sprinkle with cinnamon.

Egg desserts

The Moors are thought to have introduced egg sweets and tarts to Portugal during their 500-year occupation. But it was the 17th- and 18th-century nuns of Portugal who glorified them (see panel, page 91). This is one reason, no doubt, why so many egg desserts bear such names as "bacon from heaven" *(toucinho do céu)*, "nuns' tummies" *(barriga-da-freira)* and "angels' cheeks" *(papos d'anjo)*.

Regardless of their names, what the dozens of different egg sweets have in common is a prodigious use of egg yolk and sugar. Many are flavoured with cinnamon, others with lemon or orange or almonds, and each is shaped in its own traditional way: like little bundles of straw, for example, miniature haystacks, or even lamprey eel. The Portuguese so love this ugly river fish they make golden egg effigies of it for festive occasions.

For dessert, you might encounter sunny little hillocks bathed in clear sugar syrup, flans decorated with cinnamon, individual goblets of rice pudding *(arroz doce)* as radiant as molten gold, flat yellow sponge cakes twirled around orange or lemon custard fillings, tiny translucent tarts *(queijadas)* and a snowy, poached meringue ring known as *pudim molotov* (one of the few egg desserts that is made out of the whites rather than the yolks).

The Portuguese find that nothing complements – or follows – an egg sweet so well as a silky, syrupy wine, usually a vintage port, or a Madeira, but better still will be a good, strong cup of coffee to cut the sweetness.

Coffee

Coffee houses are a Portuguese institution, a gathering place morning, noon and night, where people meet to talk and read newspapers while they drink coffee. This is not surprising in a country whose former colonies – Brazil and Angola – still produce some of the finest coffee beans in the world. The choice may be a *bica*, a powerful espresso-type brew, or a *café*, which is closer to percolated or filter coffee. Or you can order *carioca*, which is half *café*, half hot water (it is also the colloquial name for a resident of Rio de Janeiro); it will still be pretty strong and very good indeed.

Freshly baked pastéis de Belém.

PASTÉIS DE BELÉM

Constant queues testify to the success of Casa Pastéis de Belém in Lisbon. The light-as-air custard tarts on sale here, *pastéis de Belém*, were first created nearby by nuns at the Mosteiro dos Jeronimous, who used the egg whites to starch their habits and so began making the tarts to use up the excess yolks (handily there was a sugar-cane refinery next door). When the liberal revolution in 1820 saw all the convents and monasteries shut down, the monastery began to sell pastries in a bid for survival. Obviously God was on their side: these are some of the finest custard tarts in Portugal, still made to the original secret recipe.

Casks must be tended with skill and care.

WINES OF PORTUGAL

Wine-making is moving into an exciting phase. New favourites are supplementing old reliables, and many smaller *quintas* are producing quality wines.

For many years port and Madeira were the only wines that people associated with Portugal. But things are changing: the country's *vinhos verdes* have a well-deserved reputation, and besides classic Bairrada or Dão varieties, wine-lovers can explore the exhilarating wines of the Douro, of Tomar in the Ribatejo, and the rich reds of the Alentejo.

Port wine

Port wine begins life in the Upper Douro, a demarcated region whose boundaries cling to the banks of the Douro and its tributaries. A wide variety of grapes grow here: preferred reds include Tinta Roriz, Tinta Francesa (a descendant of the French Pinot Noir), Touriga Nacional and Bastardo; among the whites are Malvasia, Esgana Cão and Rabigato.

The regions producing the finest ports presently centre around Pinhão, some 20km (14 miles) east of Régua, and extend to the Spanish border. The famous shipping firms all have their *quintas* (manor houses) in the hills of the Douro. It is here that the fermentation process takes place in autumn, interrupted by the addition of grape brandy, to create the raw, fortified wine. Young port then spends the winter at the *quinta*. In springtime, it is transported to the port lodges (many of which are open to the public) in Vila Nova de Gaia, where it is blended and matured into a variety of styles. It is here that you can learn about and taste the basic differences between ports.

Vintage port

The most famous and most expensive of the ports is the vintage variety. It is produced from the grapes of a single harvest and is "declared" only in years when the quality is deemed

Tawny port is aged in wood for seven years.

One good place to sample various port wines is at the Solar do Vinho do Porto (near Palácio Cristal in Porto).

extraordinary. Vintage port is bottled after just two or three years in wood. This is what distinguishes vintage from all other ports: the majority of the ageing process takes place in glass, rather than wood. From a legal standpoint, vintage port must identify itself as such – stating the name of its producer and the year of the vintage – and must carry the governmental seal. For example, the great 1963 vintage must, by law, have been bottled between 1 July 1965 and 30 June 1966.

Vintage port may be drunk 10 years after its vintage date, but most wines hit their stride after about 15–20 years. Classic wines were produced in 1963, 1977 and 1994; 2000, 2003 and 2007 are particularly good years. Taylor, Graham, Croft, Noval and Ferreira are some of the best-known among a host of eminent port-wine makers.

Crusted port

Crusted port differs from vintage port in that its grapes need not come from a single year, or vintage, but is mostly created from two or

Vintage port wine Pintas by Jorge Borges and Sandra Tavares.

three different harvests. Crusted port spends extra time in wood, accelerating the maturation process. This extended ageing makes for a lighter-bodied wine. Like vintage port, however, it throws a sediment and needs to be decanted.

Late-bottled port

Late-bottled vintage (LBV) sees even more time in wood – from four to six years. As its name implies, the wine comes from a single year's harvest, but is much lighter in colour than vintage port and need not be decanted. Both the date of the vintage and the date of bottling must appear on the label. When buying, it is worth remembering that shippers generally do not offer late bottled vintage in the same years as they offer real vintage port.

Wood ports

Wood ports are blended wines – using grapes from several harvests – that are matured in casks until they are ready for drinking. Because they are blended, it is the goal of the shipper to define his style through this wine so that year after year the customer can confidently expect a consistent product. The three main types are ruby, white and tawny.

Ruby is young and hearty and inexpensive. To a port drinker, it is the staple wine, attractive for its full, overt flavour. It is aged for two or three years in cask before bottling. One off-shoot of ruby port is called "Vintage Character" port. It will have the same general features but will be of a higher quality, usually older, and more expensive.

White ports are also matured in wood. They can come from either red or white grapes: a clear wine can be obtained from red grapes by separating the juice from the skins during fermentation before the colour has been extracted. Wine-makers have tried to popularise whites by fermenting out the sugar, adding brandy, and marketing them as dry aperitif wines.

Then there is tawny port, a special blend of port wine from different vintages which sees many years in cask. Through the more rapid oxidisation process within the barrel, this wine matures rather more quickly. Tawny port is thus more mellow in style than the "vintage-dated" ports, but it is refined, with a rich tawny colour and fabulously scented bouquet.

CONFUSING COLHEITAS

There is a confusing offshoot of the vintage-dated wines, called "Port of the Vintage" or "Port with Date of Vintage". These wines come from a single year, but will have been aged in wood for no less than seven years. The bottle will often say *Colheitas* (vintage) and give the year; it will show the date of bottling and some indication that the wine has been aged in wood. The house of Nierport has a wonderful stock of these *Colheitas*. They are the first step into tawny ports, but the fact that they are from a single vintage prevents them legally being so titled under the strict regulations on port making and marketing.

Old tawnies are expensive, priced in correlation to the longer ageing period. They should not be confused with the cheap tawny port available abroad, which owes its existence to the demand for a less concentrated but drinkable port wine, which the port shippers have answered by concocting a blend of ruby and white port. The product is a simple wine of pinkish hue, in contrast to the fading russet and complexity of a true tawny. Since the name "tawny" can apply to either wine, the consumer must rely on colour and price to distinguish between the two. Among a wide choice, Ferreira, Noval and Taylor 10-, 20- and 30-year-olds are fine examples of tawny port. Only the "real thing" will reveal why this is the wine which many port houses most prize and which many blenders enjoy as an all-day drink (and have even been seen to add ice cubes to).

Vinho verde country

The lush, green Minho is the country's oldest and most intensively cultivated wine area, the region of *vinho verde*. The vine seems to be everywhere – along narrow roads, framing houses with pretty bowers called *ramadas*, across new, neat plantations of *cruzetas*, crosses with wire supports a tractor operator can reach.

Not green, as its name suggests, *vinho verde* is made from fully matured grapes from varieties that include Azal, Trajadura, Alvarinho and Loureiro for the whites, and Brancelho, Pedral and Tinto Cão for the reds. The taste is dry, with many subtle shadings; it is light and refreshing, with an alcohol content of only 8 to 11 percent. The fizz – known as *pétillance* to wine connoisseurs, *agulha* to the Portuguese – is not added, but appears naturally during the making.

First, the grapes are fermented to convert their natural sugars into alcohol. Then a secondary fermentation, called the malolactic, takes place. Induced by naturally occurring bacteria, this converts malic acid to lactic; a harsher, rather unpleasant acid into a milder, more palatable one.

While this secondary fermentation is common to wines made in many countries, the *vinhos verdes* are distinguished by their retention of the fermentation's by-product: carbon dioxide. From this comes that characteristic sparkle in the wine, which can vary, depending upon age,

technique and storage, from a light tingle on the tongue to a spritely carbonation, the hallmark of *vinhos verdes*.

Notable estate-made *vinhos verdes* come from more than 50 members of the Association of Producers and Bottlers of Vinho Verde, who must produce wine only from their own grapes (not buy them, as bulk producers do). The result is a range of wines produced in small quantities but with individual characteristics.

Much admired among single-estate wines is the Palácio da Brejoeira *vinho verde* produced

A vineyard in the Alentejo.

from a single grape variety, Alvarinho, in Monção. It is also the most expensive. You can, though, taste a good, and cheaper, Alvarinho made by the Adega Cooperativa of Monção.

Wine regions

Truly superb wines, a few eccentric and many sublime, are to be found in Portugal. From the once-cherished Dão area, which in recent years has tumbled from its pedestal, comes Caves São João's good red Porto dos Cavaleiros (its Reserva among the very best Dão wines) or the Sogrape Dão Reserva; and, from Sogrape's technologically advanced winery, the old favourites Grão Vasco and Terras Altas. Bairrada, a small area north of Coimbra, has held its reputation for classic wines, more than 80 percent red, mainly from the Baga grape. The whites include a pleasant *espumante*, or sparkling wine. Good Bairrada wines are made by Sogrape, Messias and Caves Aliança.

For something really special, head for the bizarre and extravagant neo-Manueline Palace Hotel do Buçaco (see page 256), which has a stupendous cellar of its own Buçaco wines, dating from the 1920s.

You can also taste perfectly good Bairrada wines at the cluster of down-to-earth roadside restaurants that can be found in nearby Meal-

Processing the grapes.

hada, all offering the local speciality, *leitão*, suckling pig.

The Douro is the source of many of Portugal's finest table wines (even in the port region only 40 percent of the grapes go into port). Ferreira, a distinguished port-wine producer, also makes the renowned Barca Velha, probably the finest of all Portugal's red wines. Other Ferreira reds include their Reserva Especial or the more accessible Esteva. Top-ranking Douro wines include those under the Quinta do Cotto label – Grande Escolha is one. As in other areas, Sogrape are conspicuous – Planalto is just one of their good Douro wines. Adriano Ramos Pinto produce the really excellent Duas Quintas red.

Closer to the capital

From nearer to Lisbon comes a variety of good wines – the white from Bucelas is a consistent favourite. Pleasant wines, too, come from the Colares area, just beyond Sintra.

To the south of Lisbon two major wineries, confusingly with very similar names, are in Azeitão, near Setúbal (both are open to the public). One, José Maria da Fonseca, makes a very popular red, Periquita, and the excellent dry Branco Seco. If you care for sweet muscatel dessert wines, you might like to try the Moscatel de Setúbal. The second, more modern winery is J.M. Fonseca International, widely known for its very successful Lancer's red, white and rosé, sold in their distinctive clay jars.

Two eminent wines from the Setúbal area are João Pires, and the deep red from the Quinta de Bacalhoa, both developed by the skills of Australian oenologist, Peter Bright, who has lived in Portugal since 1982, and founded the Terras de Alter winery in the Alentejo in 2004.

Wines from Portugal's southernmost province, Algarve, are largely table wines, consumed on the spot, but they should not be dismissed and many are improving.

A range of good-quality wines is made in the eastern Alentejo in such towns as Borba, Reguengos and Vidigueira, which produce a very good white *reserva*. Look, too, for the deep-red and distinctive Esporão. In many good Lisbon restaurants you are very likely to be recommended an Alentejo red, rather than the more usual white, if you choose any variety of *bacalhau* (salt cod).

"GREEN WINE"

No one knows for sure where the eloquent phrase *vinho verde* (green wine) originated. One explanation is that it derived from the Minho region's green landscape, which receives up to 200cm (78ins) of rain a year. Another equally likely explanation is that the name simply refers to the youth or "greenness" of the wine, because it is not allowed to mature in the same way as normal table wines. The fact that *vinho verde* can be either white or red, and called *verde branco* (white) or *verde tinto* (red), introduces an even more colourful note. Whatever the origin of the name, the connotation of a cool, refreshing liquid is appealing.

Port Dynasties

In a technological age there are few trades where heritage and family ties are a matter of pride, but port is one of them

Port has its roots in the wild upper reaches of northern Portugal's Douro valley, a wine region that has had virtually the same frontiers since the Marquês de Pombal defined them in 1756. At the time, the reforming Pombal, who felt a hearty dislike for the British and their leading role in Portuguese trade, was determined to restrict the hold they had had on the area ever since the Methuen Treaty of 1703 had established their dominance of the industry. In subsequent centuries, port has improved immeasurably in quality and the profits are more evenly spread. But although snobbish exclusivity is long gone, the British are still very much part of the port scene.

The British affinity with port

The British association with port is long and eventful – although these days the French buy more. British buyers enthusiastically explored the Douro valley in the 17th century. George Sandeman instructed the Duke of Wellington's troops on the finer points of port. One of the pioneers, cartographer Joseph James Forrester, a Scot, fought tirelessly for high standards and mapped every centimetre of the river. He was made a baron in 1855 for his efforts. It was regarded as a national tragedy when, in May 1862, Forrester's boat overturned and he drowned in the Douro. He was travelling between various wine-growing *quintas*, paying the farmers in gold coins, and it is said that it was his money belt, heavy with gold, which helped to drag him down.

A survivor of the tragedy was another personality in the saga of port: Dona Antónia Adelaide Ferreira, whose vineyards covered huge areas of the Douro.

These and other colourful characters are familiar to everyone in the business. The founders of the port-wine trade are ever-present, their faces and names on port-wine labels. Many rival companies have inter-family links. Their names, however, can be deceptive: for all its English ring, Cockburn Smithes has had a Portuguese managing director for many years.

Generations of family firms are at the core of the port-wine business and their names provide lustre

to superb wines. But in the nature of business, companies change. The Taylor, Fladgate & Yeatman group, including the much-esteemed Guimaraens, became the Fladgate Partnership. The historic Casa Ferreirinha is owned by multi-armed Sogrape. Cockburn Smithes in 2006 entered the embrace of the renowned family firm of Symington.

The name of Symington has been inescapable since the 1800s. The family owns and manages a distinguished list: Warre's (founded in the 1670s), Silva & Cosens (whose brand is Dow), Quarles Harris, Smith Woodhouse, and Graham's. In the 1990s two generations and eight members of the

Mateus Estate, near Vila Real, Douro area.

Symington family were still involved in management, production, sales and marketing of the fine ports made by these independent companies. The family has, more recently, become prominent in promoting the re-emergence of much underrated Madeira wine.

The wine shippers still meet at lunch on Wednesdays in the Feitoria Inglesa or "English Factory House" in Porto to discuss business and sample a good vintage following the meal.

Efficient modern methods are used in the wine industry these days, but technology blends smoothly with tradition. Even the Symingtons' Gaia offices hold echoes of port's memorable past: they are in Travessa do Barão Forrester, in the very house where Baron Forrester once lived.

FESTIVALS FOR ALL SEASONS

You can't go far in Portugal without stumbling across a festival – colourful occasions that demonstrate a national talent for celebration.

On almost every weekend throughout the year there will be a festival taking place somewhere in Portugal. Saints' days are the biggest single stimulus for holding a *festa*, and every village and town in the country enjoys the protection of a patron saint. *Romarias* are generally more sober affairs with a greater religious dimension. Plenty of these take place too, especially at Easter time.

Good festivals to catch wherever you are in the country include the semi-pagan carnival, the last party before Lent, in February or March; and the solemn celebrations of Semana Santa, the week before Easter, which are particularly awe-inspiring in Braga, in the north. Twice annually (May and October) there is the Fátima Romaria, when thousands of pilgrims pay tribute at the Fátima shrine, founded on the spot where three children are believed to have seen an apparition of the Virgin in 1917.

But Portuguese festivals are not just about religion. In June it's worth going to Lisbon's Festas da Lisboa (www.egeac.pt), with live fado, street parties, music, theatre and more. The Festa do Sudoeste in August is Portugal's answer to Glastonbury, with lots of international names and a laid-back beach vibe (it takes place in pretty Zambujeira do Mar, in Alentejo). Also in August, you can celebrate the delights of Portuguese shellfish at the Festival do Marisco (www.festivaldo marisco.com) in Olhão.

The annual October pilgrimage to the Fátima Sanctuary.

Festa da Flor in Funchal.

Medieval festival in Lamago.

Festival decorations in Tavira.

Ikloric decorations in Braga.

Biscuit-eating competition is popular with children.

REGIONAL CELEBRATIONS

Portugal has many festivals that are unique to a particular region. At Miranda do Douro, Trás-os-Montes, stick dances are performed to the music of bagpipes, cymbals and drums (15 August); in Amarante (early June) young men offer phallus-shaped cakes as tokens of love to the young ladies in celebration of São Gonçalo, the patron saint of love and marriage; at the Festas de São João in Braga, townsfolk bash each other on the heads with squeaky plastic hammers; and in Lisbon street parties celebrate the matchmaking Santo António (June), and men present a sprouting basil plant with a love poem hidden in it to the girl they hope to marry. Others are simpler affairs, where the fringe activities, such as biscuit-eating competitions are as popular as the main attraction.

Lisbon hosts several lively festivals: one of the biggest is Festas dos Santos Populares in June, which celebrates saints Anthony, John and Peter, and takes place in Alfama. The liveliest night is 12 June, when thousands gather to eat sardines, drink vast amounts of wine and join in the singing and dancing until late.

Medieval festivals inspire re-enactors to dress up in the garb of the times.

Exquisite ceiling in the Igreja dos Paulistas, Bairro Alto, Lisbon.

Lisbon's cathedral.

PORTUGUESE ARCHITECTURE

Some of Portugal's finest architecture is found in its
religious buildings, but the wealth from the Age of
Discoveries also left a legacy of fine palaces.

Portugal's unusual geographical position,
cut off from Europe by Spain on one
side, facing the New World on the other,
is reflected in its architecture. The country's
architects have always looked outside for influence and affirmation, and local traditions have
blended harmoniously with imported ideas.

Romanesque

The story of Portuguese architecture really
begins in the Romanesque period of the 12th
century, when nearly all buildings of any
importance were religious ones. This was the
time when the kingdom was founded, when
Portugal was (largely) reconquered from the
Moors, and Christianity was strongly felt.

In the north, Romanesque-style churches
continued to be built well into the 14th century,
when the Gothic style was already spreading
throughout the rest of the country. Portuguese
Romanesque is an architecture of simple, often
dramatically stark forms, whose sturdiness is
frequently explained by the need for fortification against the continued threat of Moorish
or Castilian invasion. This fortified appearance
is enhanced in the cathedrals of Lisbon and
Coimbra by the crenellated facade towers.

Most of these buildings are of granite. The
hardness of this material renders detailed carving impossible, thus favouring a simplicity
of form. In areas where the softer limestone
abounds, such as the central belt of the country

The Old Cathedral in Coimbra.

(including Coimbra, Tomar and Lisbon), carved
decorations are more common.

These Romanesque churches share a certain
robustness; a method of construction based on
semicircular arches and barrel vaults; a cruci-
form plan; and a solid, almost sculptural sense
of form in the interior which allows for a play
of light and shade. This sobriety is accentu-
ated by the paucity of decoration, which is frequently reduced to the capitals of columns and
the archivolts surrounding the portals. When
the tympana are not bare, the simplified carvings are usually stylised depictions of Christ in
Majesty, or the *Agnus Dei* (Lamb of God), or
simply of a cross. In some cases, animals and
serpents climb the granite columns, as in the Sé

> *The Romanesque period saw the construction
> of cathedrals follow the path of reconquest
> from Braga to Porto, southwards to Coimbra,
> Lamego, Lisbon and Évora.*

Velha (Old Cathedral) of Coimbra or the richly decorated principal portal of the early 13th-century São Salvador, in Bravães in the Minho.

Gothic

In France, new methods of construction involving pointed arches and ribbed vaults allowed for lighter, taller architectural forms. As the main weight of the building was now borne outside at fixed points by flying buttresses, the walls could be pierced at frequent intervals. The light filtering into these Gothic interiors became a metaphor for Divine Light, replacing

A portal in the lovely Gothic abbey at Alcobaça.

the Romanesque emphasis on Mystery.

The first building in Portugal to use these new construction methods was the majestic church of the abbey of Alcobaça, commissioned by Afonso Henriques. With its great height and elegant, unadorned white interior bathed in a milky light, Alcobaça is one of the most serene and beautiful churches in Portugal. Begun in 1178 and consecrated in 1222, it is almost purely French in inspiration: its plan echoes that of Clairvaux, the seat of the Cistercian Order in Burgundy – a nave and two side aisles of almost the same height, a two-aisled transept, and an apse whose ambulatory fans out into chapels.

The apogee of the national Gothic style came after the Portuguese armies defeated the

invading Castilians at the Battle of Aljubarrota. In fulfilment of a religious vow João I commissioned the construction in 1388 of the Dominican Monastery of Santa Maria da Vitória (St Mary of the Victory), better known as Batalha, which simply means battle.

The stylistic influence of Batalha is seen in various churches throughout the country, such as the cathedral at Guarda and the now-ruined Carmo church in Lisbon, which were both begun at the end of the 14th century.

Generally speaking, Portuguese Gothic leaned towards temperance rather than flamboyance, a reflection of the austerity imposed by the mendicant orders and, perhaps, the sombre streak in the national character.

The Manueline style

The exhilaration of Portugal's overseas discoveries had a marked effect on art, architecture and literature. The term "Manueline" was first used in the 19th century to refer to the reign of Manuel I (1495–1521), during which Vasco da Gama reached the coast of India (1498), and Afonso de Albuquerque conquered the Indian city of Goa (1510). The term is now used more often to refer to certain stylistic features predominant during the Avis dynasty (1383–1580), especially in architecture.

Manueline architecture does not have major innovative structural features – the twisted columns, such as those at the Church of Jesus in Setúbal, perform the same function as do plain ones. Rather, Manueline can be seen as heterogeneous late Gothic, its real innovation lying in its stone decoration, the exuberance of which

BUILDING BATALHA

Batalha's construction can be divided into three distinct stages.

1. During the first phase (1388–1438) the central nave, with simple ribbing supporting the vault, was built. The Founder's Chapel and the chapterhouse vault have a greater refinement and elegance, influenced by English Gothic. Contact with England was close at this time as João I's wife, Philippa of Lancaster, was the daughter of John of Gaunt.

2. During the second stage, which lasted until 1481, a second cloister was built.

3. The Manueline phase culminated in the Arcade of the Unfinished Chapels and the Royal Cloister.

reflects the optimism and wealth of the period. Inspired by the voyages to the New World, it is ornate and imposing, uniting naturalistic maritime themes with Moorish elements and heraldic motifs: during the reign of Manuel I, the king's own emblems are usually included – as they were in the churches built in the newly discovered overseas territories.

The Monastery of Santa Maria de Belém in Lisbon, better known as Jerónimos, is one of the great hall churches of the period – that is, a church whose aisles are as high as its nave. Perhaps the most notable feature of Manueline architecture

modified certain Moorish (*morisco*) features. At the Palácio Nacional at Sintra, restored during Manuel's reign, *morisco* features include the use of tiles, merlons, and windows divided in two by columns. Another important *morisco* feature is the horseshoe arch, as in the chapterhouse of the Convent of Lóios in Évora. In Alentejo, many provincial palaces have *morisco* decoration, including latticework ceilings and chimneys.

Renaissance and Mannerism

The Renaissance has been described as a narrow bridge crossed the moment it was reached.

The graceful cloister of Jerónimos Monastery.

is the copious carving that surrounds portals and semicircular windows. The imposing southern portal of Jerónimos, together with the window of the chapterhouse at the Convent of Christ in Tomar, well deserve the acclaim they both receive. Construction on the Tomar window began much earlier, in the 12th century, along with the Templar Charola – a chapel with a circular floor plan. During the 16th century, the convent buildings, including four cloisters, were added. The lavish Manueline decoration of the church culminates in the famous window, designed with two great ship's masts on either side, covered with carvings, topped, like the southern portal at Jerónimos, by the cross of the Order of Christ.

Manueline architecture also adopted and

This was certainly the case in Portugal. In their art and architecture, the Portuguese shied away from Renaissance rationalism, instead inclining towards naturalism or the drama of the Baroque.

The Renaissance in Portugal, then, was best represented by foreign artists. Foreign sculptors were frequently invited to decorate the portals and facades of Manueline buildings, introducing elements of Renaissance harmony and order within the general flamboyance of the Manueline decorative scheme. The coincidence of Manueline and Renaissance influences, and later of Renaissance and Mannerist forms, explains the hybrid style prevalent during this period. Mannerism uses elements of Renaissance classicism but the sense of an ordered, harmonious whole gives way to an exaggeration of these elements.

The Spaniard Diogo de Torralva is thought to have been responsible for one of the finest examples of Renaissance design in the Iberian peninsula – the Chapel of Nossa Senhora da Conceição (Our Lady of the Conception) in Tomar (*c.* 1530–40), with its simple exterior and diffusely lit, barrel-vaulted interior. Also in Tomar, Torralva's Great Cloister at the Convent of Christ evokes the balance and harmony of Palladian classicism. Many years after Torralva's death in 1566, this majestic cloister was completed by the prestigious Italian architect

Azulejos adorn a facade in Alfama, Lisbon.

Filippo Terzi, a specialist in military architecture who had been invited by Felipe II of Spain (who became king of Portugal in 1581).

Baroque

The Baroque is considered to be the stylistic range which, although it uses a basic classical vocabulary, strives for dissolution of form rather than definition. Emphasis is given to motion, to the state of becoming rather than being. This obliteration of clear contours – whether by brushstrokes in painting or as an optical illusion in sculpture and architecture – is further enhanced by a preference for depth over plane. These features all stress the grand, the dynamic and the dramatic.

The first truly Baroque Portuguese church is Santa Engrácia in Lisbon, with its dome and undulating interior walls. This building, begun in 1682, was not completed until 1966. The richness of the coloured marble lining the walls and floor, the dynamic interior space, and the general sumptuousness of the edifice are typical of construction during the reign of João V (1706–50), known as João o Magnânimo.

The wealth from Brazil and the extravagance of João V made the early 18th century a period of great opulence. He was the king who commissioned the Chapel of St John the Baptist at the Church of São Roque in Lisbon. The entire chapel was built in Rome, blessed by the Pope, shipped to Lisbon and reassembled in the church, where it shines with bronzes, mosaics, rare marble and precious stones.

In the north of the country the major centres for the development of the Baroque were Porto and Braga. Here, the influence of the Tuscan

> Painted ceramic tiles called *azulejos* are a major feature of Portuguese architecture, with their use reaching its apex in the 17th century (for more information, see page 160).

architect-decorator Nicolau Nasoni, who came to Portugal in 1725, predominated. He introduced a greater buoyancy and elegance, and rich contrasts of light and shade, and incorporated local characteristics as well. His elliptical-naved Church of Clérigos in Porto had no successor but his secular buildings, such as the Freixo Palace in the same city, with their interplay of whitewash and granite, established a large following.

The gleaming Basilica da Estrêla in Lisbon, dating from the 1780s and commissioned by Maria I, was the last church to be built in the Baroque Grand Style. By then, architectural styles had moved on and, with the dissolution of the monastic orders in 1834, religious architecture lost its privileged position in Portugal.

Rococo

In the rococo style, drama was replaced by fantasy, and an emphasis on flourish, sensuality and ornamentation. The chapel of Santa Madalena in Falperra is a good early example of the style. Rococo was also marked by a growing interest in landscaping. The type of church represented by Bom Jesus in Braga became popular: surrounded by gardens, it sits on the top of a hill and is reached by a sweeping succession of stairways which from a distance seem to cascade downward.

In Lisbon the rococo was more sober than in the north. After the earthquake of 1755, Carlos Mardel designed many of the city's public fountains in a toned-down version of rococo, including those of Rua do Século and Largo da Esperança. Mardel was also responsible for part of the Aguas Livres Aqueduct, which withstood the earthquake, and is still a familiar landmark.

of the 19th century was the Theatre of Dona Maria II (1843), with its white Greco-Roman facade. The dissolution of the monasteries had a negative effect on the development of public buildings, as well as on religious architecture.

The middle-class ambience of Porto proved fertile ground for conservative neoclassicism. It was favoured by the English community connected with the port industry, perhaps because of affinities with the work of Scottish architect Robert Adam (1728–92). British consul Sir John Whitehead commissioned the Feitoria Inglesa in Porto and the Hospital of Santo

The entrance to Bom Jesus de Braga.

Neoclassicism

Although it took place at much the same time, the Pombaline style of the reconstruction of Lisbon (see box) is closer in many respects to classical models than to the rococo constructions in the north. The neoclassical style proper, with its emphasis on Greco-Roman colonnades and porticoes, was introduced to Lisbon in the last decade of the 18th century. It received court approval when used for the Royal Palace of Ajuda (begun in 1802 and never completed), after a fire destroyed the wooden building that had been the temporary royal residence since the earthquake.

After this, perhaps the only noteworthy public building to be built in Lisbon in the first half

POMBAL'S PROJECT

The reconstruction of Baixa, the lower city of Lisbon, which the Marquês de Pombal embarked on after the devastating earthquake of 1755, was the most ambitious urban planning scheme ever seen in Europe, and serves as the statesman's lasting memorial. "Pombaline Lisbon", as it is known, is built on a grid system, with clean, uncluttered lines. The area is epitomised by the Praça do Comércio, the huge square bounded on three sides by neoclassical arcades. In the centre stands a large equestrian statue to José I, erected in 1755. The majestic triumphal arch, however, was not completed until the 1870s, long after Pombal's death.

António, perhaps the finest neoclassical buildings in the country.

Romanticism

If neoclassical art and architecture represented an escape from the turmoils of the present into a restrained, harmonious classical ideal, another form of escapism was an important ingredient of Romanticism. It was typified by flights into medievalism and orientalism, or into altered states of dreams and madness.

The most extraordinary architectural manifestation of this was the Pena Palace in Sintra

Grand arch in the Baixa of "Pombaline Lisbon".

(commissioned around 1840 by Prince Ferdinand of Saxe-Coburg-Gotha, the consort of Maria II). The building is a strange mix of medieval and oriental forms, including Manueline, Moorish, Renaissance and Baroque, and incorporating parts of the site's original structure – a 16th-century monastery. The result is a pastiche of English Gothic revivalism.

Modern styles

One of the best examples of Portuguese architecture from the first half of the 20th century is the Art Deco Casa Serralves in Porto (now a museum), but there are also many gorgeous Art Nouveau cafés in Lisbon and Porto. Under Salazar, the fashion was for brutalist

Soviet-style blocks, with exceptions such as the pared-down aesthetic of the Gulbenkian Museum. More recently, Porto architects such as Fernando Távora and Alvaro Siza Viera have established solid reputations: the rebuilding of the Chiado district after Lisbon's 1988 fire was entrusted to the latter, who also designed Porto's beautiful Museu de Arte Contemporânea (see page 280).

The postmodernist work of Tomás Taveira is also notable in Lisbon, particularly his office towers at the Amoreiras (see page 151). And Expo '98 was a launching pad not only for

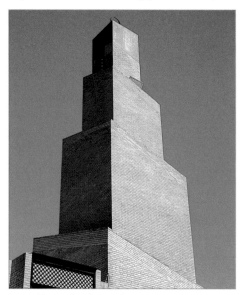

Portugal has modern landmarks, too, such as the mosque in Lisbon's Avenidas Novas.

some stunning modern pavilions and Europe's longest bridge, the Ponte Vasco da Gama (see page 140), but also a clear, uncluttered building style across Portugal. A prime example is Rem Koolhaas' Casa da Música in Porto, which mixes minimalist Modernism with traditional elements, such as *azulejos*. Close to Obídos, the spectacular Bom Sucesso development is a collection of villas and leisure facilities designed by star architects including Alvaro Siza Viera. The most breathtaking new addition to the contemporary architecture landscape is the Museu do Côa, in the Douro, a monolithic triangular block, all concrete walls and sharp angles, designed by Porto architects Pedro Tiago Pimentel and Camilo Rebelo.

PORTUGUESE ART THROUGH THE AGES

From rock paintings via neoclassicism to Modernist masterpieces, the country's museums, galleries and churches cover the artistic spectrum.

Portugal has a rich collection of artworks spanning the centuries, from prehistory to modern times. In terms of masterpieces from more recent times, the 15th century was the first great age of Portuguese painting. Almost no works from the 12th to the 14th centuries have survived, although frescoes were certainly painted in churches. One interesting, rare example of an early 15th-century fresco is a surviving fragment from a secular painting – the allegory of justice entitled *O Bom e o Mau Juiz* (The Good and the Bad Judge), in a Gothic house in the town of Monsaráz.

The most notable surviving religious fresco of the same period is the *Senhora da Rosa* in the sumptuous church of São Francisco in Porto. It has been attributed to an Italian painter, António Florentino, who, it is thought, may also have painted the portrait of João I now at the Museu Nacional de Arte Antiga in Lisbon.

> Portugal is also home to Europe's largest collection of palaeolithic rock paintings, discovered only in the 1990s, and now in a protected site close to Museu do Côa in the Douro (see page 290).

By far the most brilliant contribution to painting during this period was the introduction of Flemish-influenced painted altarpieces called retables (*retábulos* in Portuguese). In 1428, the Flemish master Jan van Eyck was invited to the court of João I to paint a portrait of the Infanta Dona Isabel, future wife of Philip the Good (Philippe le Bon, 1396–1467), Duke of Burgundy. The Netherlands were, at the time, under the control of the dukes

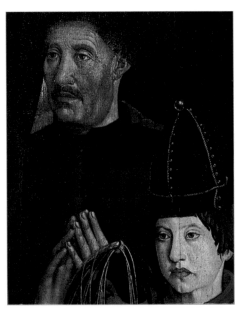

Detail from Nuno Gonçalves' The Adoration of St Vincent polyptych, showing Henry the Navigator and the future João II.

of Burgundy, who were renowned for their excellent taste in art. When the Flemish artists turned from illumination to the painting of altarpieces, they added to their own love of realistic detail the Burgundian passion for gemlike decoration.

The polyptych of St Vincent

The most outstanding *retábulo* of the 15th-century Portuguese School is the polyptych of St Vincent attributed to Nuno Gonçalves, in Lisbon's Museu Nacional de Arte Antiga. The mystery that enshrouds this work has increased its aura. The panels were lost for centuries, and there are conflicting accounts of their reappearance at the end of the 19th century. No sooner were they cleaned and hung publicly than an angry controversy arose as to the identity of their creator as well as of the figures depicted. A touch of drama was added when one eminent scholar committed suicide after a dispute concerning two documents that radically altered the direction of the research. The documents were later proved false.

The theme of the polyptych has also given rise to dispute. Some see in it the veneration of the Infante Santo Fernando, uncle of Afonso V, who died at the hands of the Moors. But nowadays it is generally thought to represent the adoration of St Vincent, patron saint of the kingdom and of the city of Lisbon. The important point of departure was the identification of the Infante Henrique (Henry the Navigator) to the left of the saint in the third panel from the left.

The panels, from left to right, are known as the Panel of the Monks (of the Cistercian Order), the Fishermen, the Infante, the Archbishop, the Calvary and finally, the Relic Panel.

The real genius and originality of the work lie in the exquisiteness of the portraiture: the masterful attention to realistic detail as well as the psychological dimension. It appears to be the visual representation of King Afonso's dreams of conquest and of the magical world of Prince Henry's navigations, blessed by the patron saint of the kingdom.

The Flemish influence

During the reign of João II (1481–95), when voyages of discovery occupied the energies of the nation, there was a lull in painting activity. However, with the discovery of the sea route to India and the consequent prosperity, painted *retábulos* again became a dominant form of expression. At the end of the 15th century, Portugal was one of the largest importers of Flemish paintings. Many of the altarpieces in Portuguese churches were Flemish, and some can still be seen today, such as the *Fons Vitae* at the Misericórdia church in Porto.

Nevertheless, Portuguese painting maintained local features, giving rise to the "Luso-Flemish" style. Manueline painting evolved during the reign of Manuel I (1495–1521), although the style is more closely associated with architecture (see page 104). It has been

characterised by features such as monumentality, a fine sense of portraiture, brilliant gem-like colours, a growing interest in the naturalistic depiction of both architectural and landscape backgrounds, and an increasing preoccupation with expressive detail. Sculpture exploded in a frenzy of detail during this period, celebrating the sea and covering buildings in a barnacle-like frenzy of exuberant detail.

During this period painting was not the expression of an individual sensibility, but more often the collaborative effort of a master and his assistants. Attribution, then, is extremely

Another detail from the polyptych, showing St Vincent and the members of the Regnant House.

PEDRO AND INÊS'S TOMBS

While little surviving painting predates the 15th century, some lovely pieces of sculpture do. The crowning glory of 14th-century funerary sculpture is the tombs of King Pedro and his lover, Inês de Castro at Alcobaça (see page 36 for their dramatic story). The sarcophogi do justice to the tale: the sculptor is unknown and the influences are hybrid, but the naturalistic detail and rich symbolism are unsurpassed. Inês, surrounded by angels, is crowned queen in death as she never was in life. Pedro's tomb displays a superb rosette, believed to symbolise a wheel of fortune, representing life's vicissitudes.

difficult, and often paintings are known as the products of particular workshops rather than artists. The two principal workshops were those of Jorge Afonso in Lisbon, and of Vasco Fernandes in Viseu.

Afonso was appointed royal painter in 1508: documents identify various projects with which

> The altarpiece and the panels for the chapels in Viseu Cathedral, painted by Grão Vasco, are now in the museum that bears his name.

town), dated 1506–11, as well as the one for the Viseu Cathedral of a slightly earlier date.

The pronounced stylistic differences between the two works confused scholars for some time, but it is now assumed that Flemish assistants at Lamego account for the differences. The panels for the chapels of Viseu Cathedral, of which those of the Calvary and St Peter are the most renowned, are also attributed to Grão Vasco, but these date from his mature phase (1530–42).

Noteworthy for their emotional strength and drama, these works are also characterised by a denser application of paint than that used by

Detail from the sepulchre of Inês de Castro.

he and his workshop were involved, but none shows his direct responsibility, although he is believed to have painted some of the panels in the rotunda of the Convento de Cristo in Tomar.

Grão Vasco

Vasco Fernandes, better known as Grão (the Great) Vasco, is undoubtedly the most celebrated regional Manueline painter. For many years, the myth of Grão Vasco obscured his real work in a plethora of attributions – he was thought to be the author of Gothic and Renaissance paintings, although a single lifetime would not have sufficed for so large an output. But he was responsible for the altarpiece originally in Lamego Cathedral (now in the Museu Regional in that

the Flemish masters. Furthermore, the faces of the Portuguese works tend to be less stylised, more expressive, and, it would seem, often drawn from specific local models, just as the landscape backgrounds are drawn from the Beja region rather than being imaginary or purely symbolic.

The 16th and 17th centuries

As in architecture, the Renaissance, the "rebirth" of art based on classical models, was resisted by Portuguese artists and mainly represented by those from abroad. Mannerism employed many elements of Renaissance classicism but the sense of an ordered, harmonious whole gives way to an exaggeration of those defining elements. The most characteristic feature of this style is a certain elongation, together with unexpected highlighting of seemingly incidental sections of a work.

The 17th century saw the flourishing of portrait painting in Portugal as elsewhere in Europe. Perhaps the most celebrated portraitist of the period was Domingos Vieira (1600–78), known as "the Dark" to distinguish him from his contemporary Domingos Vieira Serrão. His nickname stemmed from his predilection, in works such as the portrait of Isabel de Moura (in the Museu Nacional de Arte Antiga in Lis-

rare example of a single life encapsulating two eras. He was nominated court painter in 1802 by João VI, and was commissioned to provide paintings for the rebuilt Ajuda Palace. Political turbulence forced Sequeira to emigrate to France, and then to Italy, where he died.

His work can be divided into three stages: the first, largely academic and neoclassical in inspiration, corresponds to the first period he spent in Rome, and to his work as a court painter. The second stage (1807–23), which includes the *Alegoria de Junot* (in the Soares dos Reis Museum, Porto), is stylistically freer and more individu-

King Sebastian, by Cristovão de Morais.

A detail from Calvário by Gregório Lopes.

bon), to make dramatic contrasts between the deep, velvety backgrounds and the rich, creamy whites of ruffs and headgear.

Neoclassicism

During the 18th century, two outstanding painters emerged: Francisco Vieira, known as Vieira Portuense (1765–1805), and Domingos António Sequeira (1768–1837). The two met in Rome, which was the essential venue for any serious artist. Vieira Portuense also spent some time in London, where the classicising Roman influence was tempered by that of Sir Joshua Reynolds (1723–92).

The work of Sequeira is a study in the transition from neoclassicism to Romanticism, a

alistic, with Goyaesque contrasts of dark and light, rapid brushstrokes and sudden bursts of luminous white.

The final phase of Sequeira's work corresponds to his visits to Paris and Rome. These late works show great painterliness and luminosity. The four cartoons for paintings in the Palmela collections, now in the Museu Nacional de Arte Antiga in Lisbon, are some of his most inspired, mystical works.

Romanticism

Romanticism was a form of escapism into medieval, oriental and mystical realms. Heroic, religious and ceremonial works gave way to more intimate and personal pieces. The mid-19th century also corresponded to the rise of the middle class. Courtly art had breathed its last. The liberal revolutions questioned the long-upheld notion of history as the unfolding of a predetermined order, in favour of a relativism which heralded modern times. Similarly, the idea that art expresses timelessly valid principles gradually gave way to the subjectivist and individualist notions which continue to hold sway in art today. Sequeira represented the mystical, religious side of early Romanticism. With his death, the movement in Portugal underwent a change: nature became the new religion.

An early nineteenth-century portrait of entrepreneur Joaquim Pedro Quintela by Domingos António Sequeira.

The humbling of man before the larger, inscrutable forces of nature was already a contemporaneous theme elsewhere. Lisbon-born Tomás José da Anunciação (1818–79) became the foremost romantic landscapist of his generation, along with Luís Cristino da Silva (1829–77).

Not surprisingly, portraiture not only became the art form of the bourgeoisie *par excellence*, but it also gave increasing emphasis to the sitter's inner life. In Miguel Lupi's *Sousa Martins' Mother*, painted in 1878 and now in the Museu Nacional de Arte Contemporânea in Lisbon, the illumination of the hands and face, the most expressive parts of the body, conveys a sense of pensive dignity.

At the end of the 19th century, Romanticism began to give way to naturalism in both landscapes and portraits – although the difference between the two styles was largely one of emphasis, and António Silva Porto and José Malhoa were the foremost naturalist painters. But in stark contrast to their luminous outdoor scenes, Columbano Bordalo Pinheiro (1857–1929) continued in the tradition of studio painting. Columbano, as he is known, is considered the Grand Master of Portuguese 19th-century art. He studied under Miguel Lupi at the Academy of Fine Arts (founded

Admiring a painting in Lisbon's Fado Museum.

in 1836), and then spent three years in Paris.

His brother, Rafael Bordalo Pinheiro, was perhaps even more popular in his day. A celebrated ceramicist, he was also known for his biting political caricatures.

Modernism

The artistic ferment that gripped much of Europe and America in the first decades of the 20th century arrived late, or in a very diluted form, in Portugal. The political turmoil that ended the monarchy in 1910 did not provide a propitious context for an artistic revolution, and there was then a window of only some 20 years before Salazar's authoritarian regime closed the door to all external cultural influences.

But some ideas took root. In 1911, the Museu Nacional de Arte Contemporânea was founded in Lisbon, and the first Salon of Humorists represented a move away from conventional salon painting. One of the most daring and interesting of this generation of painters was the Cubist Amadeo Souza-Cardoso, whose premature death in 1918 was a great loss. Many of his works are now in the Centro de Arte Moderno at the Fundação Calouste Gulbenkian in Lisbon, and some can be seen in a museum in his home town of Amarante. Another star was José Almada

necessary to keep the arts alive had to be clandestine during these years. The return to democracy in 1974 (six years after Salazar's death) breathed new energy into the arts and an outburst of fervent activity echoed the sense of exhilaration after long years of repression and censorship.

Among contemporary artists, Paula Rego is one of the brightest stars (see box page 115). Another is Helen Almeida, the conceptual artist daughter of Portuguese sculptor Leopoldo de Almeida (whose works include Lisbon's Monument to the Discoveries).

Paula Rego in her London studio.

Negreiros (1893–1970), one of the most charismatic and energetic cultural figures in Portugal. His early caricatures drew the attention of the poet Fernando Pessoa, who became his friend, and whose posthumously painted portrait now hangs in the poet's old home, with a replica in the Fundação Calouste Gulbenkian. One of Negreiros' most important commissions was for the frescoes at the port of Lisbon, in 1943–8. His last major project was the mural for the lobby of the Gulbenkian Foundation.

The military regime, initiated in 1926 and led by António de Oliveira Salazar from 1932–68, prevented contact with outside stimulus, so all the artistic and intellectual exchange

PAULA REGO

Paula Rego's art calls to mind grotesque fairy tales, psychoanalytic images, and the mysteries of childhood. Her paintings present a kind of magical realism that is uniquely recognisable, presenting a narrative and providing unsettling, intriguing subjects, such as apparently dysfunctional family relationships. Rego was born in Portugal, and grew up there during the Salazar years, but was later sent to a finishing school in England, then went on to study at the Slade. Despite having lived in London since 1976, where her work is widely exhibited, in her paintings she always seems to return to the place of her childhood.

POUSADAS AND MANOR HOUSES

Pousadas and manor houses offer something different from ordinary hotels. Above all, they give visitors a chance to experience local life and colour, usually in extremely comfortable surroundings.

Converted castles, palaces, monasteries, *quintas*, manor houses, water mills: there is no other country in Europe that offers good-quality accommodation in such variety. If taking a stroll around the castle walls before retiring to a grand bedroom once used by royalty, or waking to the tinkling sound of a stream beneath a miller's cottage sounds appealing, Portugal could be just the right place.

Pousadas

Unlike some other accommodation, *pousadas* have a clear identity. They are nationwide establishments, now under the management of the Pestana hotel group. Usually they are historic buildings, national monuments or notable regional houses, and are found in both urban and rural areas throughout the country.

Architecturally and historically fascinating, *pousadas* have earned a reputation for quality and service. Lofty rooms and heavy stone walls do not always lend themselves to luxury – in fact, some are extremely simple – but the style of decor is always sympathetic to the character of the building. Some *pousadas* also provide air conditioning and a swimming pool. They pride themselves, too, on the high standard of their restaurants, which are open to non-residents, and serve dishes based on regional recipes. A relaxed and distinctly Portuguese ambience is perhaps the one thing that they all have in common. There is now a choice of more than 40 *pousadas*, although many offer only a limited number of rooms, some as few as six.

For travellers in the lush green northwestern corner of Portugal, there is a good choice. To mention just a few: in the medieval town of Valença do Minho you will find the **Pousada** de Valença do Minho, **São Teotónio**. It sits on

An elegant corridor in the Pousada dos Lóios, in Évora.

a high point inside the ancient walled city with a spectacular view of the Rio Minho across to Spain and the Galician mountains. It is also perfectly located for walks through the winding city streets.

Further east is the **Pousada do Gerês-Caniçada, São Bento**, a chalet-style building on a hill just south of the Parque Nacional Peneda-Gerês. Its floor-to-ceiling windows overlook the Caniçada Dam and a forest. It has its own pool and tennis court.

Be the king of the castle

If you fancy staying in a castle, try the **Pousada do Óbidos**, in the delightful old walled town of Óbidos, north of Lisbon. Built into a section of the 12th-century castle, the *pousada* is very small, with only nine rooms, and very popular, so advance reservations are essential. **Palmela**, with 26 rooms, is another castle *pousada* that is much in demand. Originally a fortress, it became a monastery in the 15th century and was severely damaged in the 1755 earthquake. Now the refectory is the dining room and the cloisters are used on festive occasions for gala dinners.

Manor houses

The manor house scheme, to which numerous gracious old houses belong, began in the

Casas Antigas: elegant manor houses or estates originating from the 17th and 18th centuries. Furnished according to the period, they are sometimes full of antiques and artworks.

Quintas and Herdades: both are agricultural farms, but a *quinta* differs in being a walled estate. Although mostly located in rural settings, some are handily situated for towns.

Casas Rústicas: usually located in the heart of villages or on farms, and often quite isolated. Their architecture has a rustic feel , but they maintain a good level of comfort and amenities.

The Pousada Palacio de Estoi.

north of the country. The scheme, run by Turihab and called Solares de Portugal, was created to conserve some of the country's most beautiful manor houses and palaces. The owners of these magnificent homes can no longer afford the maintenance and have opened them up to tourists, who are quite often treated as guests of the family. The term "manor houses" has broadened to encompass an extremely wide range of accommodation, which is available throughout the country. Privately owned manor houses are also known as *solares*. Stately manor houses, elegant country homes, farmhouses and rustic cottages are all included in this one general description. They are often listed under three categories:

WHERE TO BOOK

Although reservations can be made directly, there is a central agency in Lisbon that handles bookings for all *pousadas*. There is no minimum-stay requirement. Contact Pousadas de Portugal, Rua Soares de Passos 3, Alto de Santo Amaro, 2300-314 Lisbon; tel: 218 442 001; www.pousadas.pt. For Turihab properties contact Praça da República, 4990-062 Ponte de Lima; tel: 258 741 672; www.turihab.pt or www.solaresdeportugal.pt. Several other agencies handle bookings for manor houses, including Manor Houses of Portugal, Apartado 596, 4901-908 Viana do Castelo; tel: 258 835 065; www.manorhouses.com (also see page 349).

Winding road in the Serra da Estrela mountains, central Portugal.

Beach and cliffs near Lagos on the Algarve.

NATURAL PORTUGAL

This is a land where complex forces of nature have created diverse environments andopportunities for different lifestyles.

For a country no more than 565km (350 miles) long and 220km (137 miles) wide, at best, and edged by the Atlantic Ocean, Portugal enjoys a surprising diversity of topography, geography and climate. Half a day's journey in almost any direction leads through climatic zones, from wet to dry, hot to cool, through mountains to plains, from rich pastures to poor, from large estates to small farms, and from affluence to poverty. Adaptation, community by community and region by region, to the heterogeneous forces of nature has fashioned a country set apart from its neighbours and unique in Europe.

Portugal is home to Europe's largest artificial lake, formed by stemming the Guadiana river with the Alqueva dam, at a cost of $1.7bn (see page 216 for details).

Olive grove.

Climate

Portugal is the mixing pot for three powerful climatic regimes. It is attacked from the west by moist westerlies from the Atlantic, carrying rain deep into the country. These are arrested by a dry continental climate giving hot dry summers and cold dry winters in the interior. From the south a Mediterranean climate invades, bringing hot dry summers and cooler, moist winters.

The high landmass of Serra da Estrela acts as a fulcrum point for all these climatic types. Descend from the mountain at any point and you will find a different country on the other side. The biggest contrast is from the wet northwest to the drier southeast.

Rain patterns vary from north to south, with the north receiving the highest rainfall, especially between November and March. Summer conditions are not too dissimilar, with all regions generally enjoying high temperatures tempered in coastal regions by Atlantic influences. Inland regions, particularly in the port-wine areas and Alentejo, suffer very high temperatures in summer.

One of the most useful indicators of a Mediterranean climate is the olive tree. This grows happily throughout most of Portugal with the exception of the mountainous regions and the most northerly part of Trás-os-Montes.

However, only Algarve enjoys anything approaching a truly Mediterranean-type climate and this has allowed its development as a year-round destination for holiday-makers.

Even Algarve is not immune from Atlantic westerlies which sometimes bring spells of wet weather in winter.

Mountain life

Rolling granite mountains, safe refuges in ancient times, dominate the north. Many settlements from those early days remain even today. Here residents eke out an existence in a harsh environment using tools (adapted for their own needs) which have hardly changed over the centuries.

Although most of the mountain areas are lightly populated, there is an area of near-wil-

peak of all. This distinction is reserved for the Serra da Estrela (Mountain of the Stars), an isolated, majestic mountain range in the centre of the country, which rises from the plains of Alentejo. Here, Torre, at 1,993 metres (6,539ft), marks the summit of Portugal. This area, too, enjoys protection but as a natural, not a national, park.

Geology

Considering its size, Portugal has remarkably diverse geology. Ancient crystalline rocks of granite and gneiss predominate in the moun-

Waterfall in the Peneda-Gerês National Park.

derness tucked away on the northern border of the country. Recognised as a sanctuary for wildlife and valued for the traditional way of life that persists in the villages on the fringes, the Parque Nacional Peneda-Gerês area, covering 720 sq km (278 sq miles), was opened in 1971. It is the country's only *national* park although other areas of natural beauty have been designated *natural* parks and are also protected, but by less stringent regulations.

Most of the highest peaks in the northern mountains lie within the park. Many of these exceed 1,300 metres (4,265ft), with Nervosa reaching a height of 1,545 metres (5,070ft). But although this region is the most mountainous in the country, it is not home to the highest

tainous regions, often presenting a landscape of grey rounded hills and steep valleys. For many inhabitants, it is the only natural building material available and they have perfected the tools and ways to work this material to an art form. Granite is a hard material but it has just enough malleability to make it workable. The evidence is all around, especially in the north. Farms, churches, water mills and fencing posts for the vines are all solidly constructed from granite.

Limestone and marble are found in the central region, especially near Évora, where it is mined commercially, and near Coimbra. The latter is particularly valued by sculptors, who have used it extensively. There is another significant limestone region, now protected as the

Parque Natural das Serras de Aire e Candeeiros (see page 235), an area riddled with deep caves, three of them open to the public.

River communities

Many of the rivers arising in the mountainous interior on the western side of the Iberian peninsula flow to the Atlantic through Portugal. In fact, only one, the Mondego, is truly Portuguese, rising in the region of Serra da Estrela and flowing into the sea at Coimbra. Some of these rivers were once navigable, allowing boats access deep into the countryside. Early

roads now penetrate the area but at the height of the port trade, all the wine had to be shipped down this difficult and dangerous river.

Perhaps the largest remaining river community is Lisbon itself, on the shores of the Rio Tejo (Tagus). The mouth of the Tejo proved a natural harbour offering safe anchorage to early traders. The prosperity of Lisbon has barely faltered throughout the ages.

Coastal life

With 832km (516 miles) of coastline, it is not surprising that the Portuguese are people of

The Douro River plays a major part in Porto's port industry.

settlers were not slow to use the Rio Guadiana in this way to penetrate inland in search of metal ores. Mértola in Alentejo developed as a port under the Romans, to ship ores down the Guadiana from nearby São Domingos, and there are significant remains of the port area to be seen.

The Romans were overwhelmed by the beauty of the Rio Lima in the north. This, for them, was the Lethe, the mythical River of Forgetfulness. This meandering river has created a fertile valley as beautiful as any you'll see in Portugal, where productive farming has been practised for centuries. In modern times, the Rio Douro has played a significant role in the development of the port-wine trade. Good

THE STORY OF MAIZE

The introduction of maize in the 16th century proved a lifeline for the people of the hill villages, for here was a crop they could adapt to their own situation. Land around the villages was pressed into use for maize and animals were moved to still higher pastures for the summer. More changes were demanded to store the crop and grind the corn. This resulted in granite-built stores perched on mushroom-shaped legs, *espigueiros*, as seen at Soajo. Water provided the power for grinding the corn. Water mills, again built of granite, were erected in profusion, often with the water of a single stream powering a succession of mills.

the sea. Fishing has sustained them over the centuries, providing an industry which has grown large, especially through cod fishing, yet also remained a small local activity. The coast is still littered with villages that rely heavily on reaping the sea's harvest, and especially on the sardine, which keeps many small fishermen in business. Tuna fishing is another sector that grew to massive proportions. Shoals of tuna migrate along the southern shoreline towards spawning grounds in the Mediterranean. Floating traps were used to catch the fish and fishermen were on

Flora

With so many different habitats, climates and microclimates in this hugely diverse country, the flora responds with equal diversity. Many species simply reflect the climatic influence of the region. Certain erica heaths, green lavender (*Lavendula viridis*), and ulex species (gorse) typify western Atlantic plants and are found almost exclusively in the far west of the country. They can coexist with Mediterranean cistus species. Algarve offers the best display of Mediterranean flora, including wild orchids, like the bumblebee orchid (*Ophrys*

Beach flora.

hand to complete the job, but over-fishing led to a decline in numbers and the industry collapsed.

Fish (there is reckoned to be more than 200 species off these shores) is not the only commercial product. Algarve has produced salt from ancient times; the Romans salted fish here to export back to Rome, and there are still salt-pans in operation. Seaweed for fertiliser is now less of an industry at Aveiro than it once was. Here, specially shaped boats, *moliceiros*, were used to collect seaweed from the extensive system of lagoons in the area.

The magnificent beaches adorning much of the coastline are now the basis for another important industry: tourism.

bombyliflora) and the yellow bee orchid (*Ophrys lutea*).

Narcissus is associated with the Iberian peninsula and many are endemic, although some are found throughout the Mediterranean. Portugal has its fair share, from the diminutive jonquil, *Narcissus gaditanus*, to more popular garden species like *N. bulbocodium* and *N. triandrus*.

Fauna

Wild boars are one of the largest mammals roaming Portugal. Their foraging marks can be seen in many parts of the country, from the golf courses of Algarve – much to the fury of the green keepers – to the inland forests. Boar hunting is a form of tourism Alentejo is keen to develop. The best wildlife sanctuary is the Parque Nacional Peneda-Gerês, in the north (see page 306). Brown bears have not been seen for centuries but there are still some wolves, and plenty of beech martens, deer, badgers and otters.

Birdlife is particularly rich in some areas, especially around the saltpans in Algarve, where some 300 species have been recorded. Around Lisbon 200 sq km (77 sq miles) of the Tejo estuary are protected as one of the most important wetland areas in Europe. The west coast estuaries and wetlands are situated on some of the major migratory routes, so spring and autumn

future is now in the balance. Environmentalists and farmers both oppose further plantations on the grounds of its destructive influence. Not only are eucalyptus rapacious in their demand for water, but they provide poor natural habitats and their litter is so slow to decompose that it further inhibits naturally occurring cycles within the soil.

The almond and the carob are indigenous to Algarve, the latter bearing long wizened beans that yield a fine variety of oil.

One major problem is forest fires, which cause widespread devastation annually, ruining huge tracts of forest land.

Cork bark drying in the sun.

are particularly rewarding for ornithologists. Sadly, in some areas years of uncontrolled hunting have significantly reduced wildlife.

Trees of life

Forestry in Portugal is big business, with over one-third of the country, some 3 million hectares (7.5 million acres), under forest. Pine, said to be of use from cradle to grave, is used to produce timber for furniture and construction as well as resin for pitch and turpentine. Pine accounts for around 40 percent of the country's wooded land. Pulp, used to manufacture paper and cardboard, is economically the most important woodland product. The Australian eucalyptus was introduced in 1856 for the paper industry, but its

THE CORK INDUSTRY

About half the cork in the world comes from Alentejo. The cultivation of cork is not for the impatient: there's a wait of 25 years before the first crop is stripped from the trunk, and a further decade before the next harvest. Cork is a labour-intensive industry, as machines cannot duplicate the expertise of the men who strip bark from the trees, although the punching out of corks and stoppers is increasingly mechanised. Although plastic corks and screwtops are becoming popular for wine bottling, these artificial products have yet to make any significant impact on the Portuguese cork industry.

A seed shop in Figueira.

The stairway to the church of Bom Jesus do Monte, Braga.

Street decorations in Tavira.

INTRODUCTION

A detailed guide to the entire country, with principal
sites clearly cross-referenced by number to the maps.

There isn't a wrong way to explore Portugal – except to make too many plans in advance. Train services here are efficient and the buses adequate, and slow travel has a charm of its own, but a car will allow you flexibility and make it easier to access the more remote places.

Belém's Aviation Memorial.

The roads are good and a motorway links Lisbon with Porto in the north, two hours' drive away, and goes on to Galicia in Spain. The roads south from Lisbon cross the Tejo and head for Alentejo and Algarve. Away from the national highways, east–west motorways help you leap distances but north–south roads tend to be narrower, more winding.

Lisbon and its environs are the best starting point for a first taste of Portugal. From there, if the weather is fine, you may want simply to head south, to the glorious beaches of Algarve. After relaxing for a few days, you could start exploring the countryside. Begin by meandering through the expanse of Alentejo, which largely consists of spectacular plains, with the entrancing ancient town of Évora in their midst.

Bite-size sweets, or doces.

Cutting back towards the Atlantic, still heading north, you could visit the old university town of Coimbra and the surrounding sights. Look in on some of the traditional fishing communities along the coast: to the north is Porto on the Rio Douro and the wine districts of Douro and Minho. Here, world-famous port, delicious *vinhos verdes* and other wines are produced.

The far interior north of Portugal is called Trás-os-Montes, a remote and hauntingly beautiful area. South of here, and still ruggedly hilly, is the Beira Alta; below that, the plains of Alentejo creep up into the province of Beira Baixa. And if you have time to visit Madeira and the Azores, you will discover lush, mountainous islands, rich in dramatic landscapes and subtropical flora.

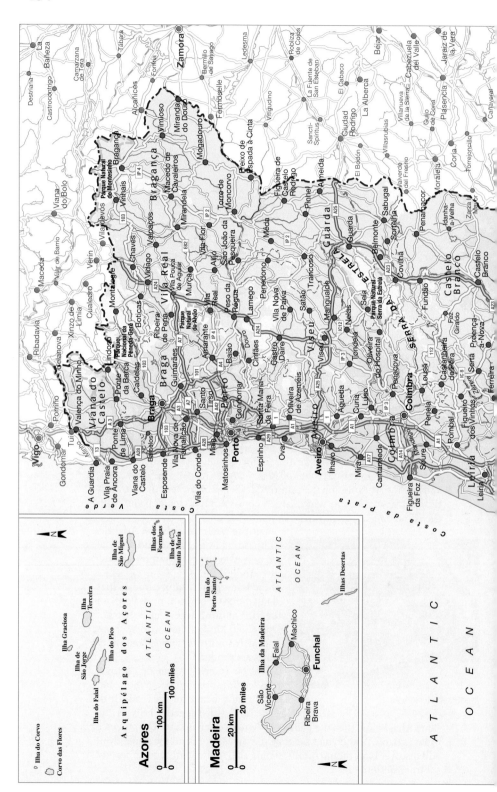

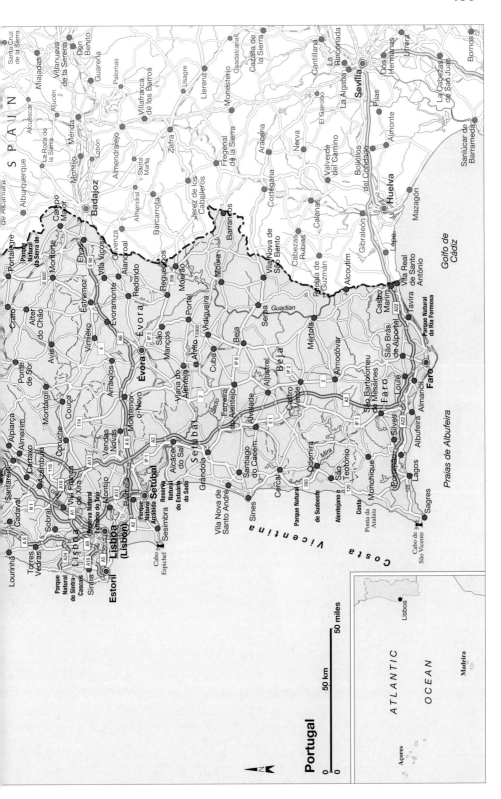

The lovely view from the Miradouro de Santa Luzia.

Climbing the hills of Lisbon on the Elevador da Bica.

LISBON

With cafés, culture and a castle, Lisbon is a vibrant city, mixing old-world charm, local colour and modern amenities. A good local transport system will help you discover the best of it.

isbon (Lisboa) is a bewitching city. It is remarkably picturesque, draped across its seven hills and overlooking the wide blue expanse of the River Tagus (Tejo), with wonderful *miradouros* (viewpoints). It is not only a cultural feast, with more than 30 museums, but has a thriving nightlife, with the charismatic districts of Alfama and Bairro Alto coming alive after dark, with buzzing restaurants, fado houses, and, later, bars and clubs to keep you going until daylight if you are so inclined.

A flavour of what Lisbon has to offer can be sampled in a crowded one-day visit, but that is barely enough to scratch the surface of the city's complexities. Three days allows time to absorb the atmosphere, and city lovers will probably find a week too short. Lisbon's climate of hot summers and mild winters makes it an ideal place to visit for most of the year, although spring and autumn are good times to enjoy the city at its best.

Many of the highlights of a visit to Lisbon are conveniently concentrated in three main areas, the heart of the city centred around the Baixa, and a significant cluster out along the riverside at Belém. Baixa is the hub of the city centre, watched over by Castelo São Jorge, below which cling the narrow streets and alleys of Alfama. To the west lies the hill

of Bairro Alto, entered through the Chiado area. North, beyond Rossio, the main thoroughfare, Avenida da Liberdade, leads to Praça Marquês de Pombal and Parque Eduardo VII. East is the new neighbourhood of Parque das Nações with many pleasures of its own to offer.

Building Bridges

Most architecture in the city is post-1755, after the great earthquake, except for Alfama and Belém, which escaped virtually unscathed. There

Main Attractions
Sé
Castelo de São Jorge
Museu Nacional do Azulejo
Elevador de Santa Justa
Igreja São Roque
Museu Nacional de Arte Antiga
Mosteiro dos Jerónimos
Museu Calouste Gulbenkian

Café life, commemorated.

A bunch of flowers for sale in a Lisbon market.

View of Alfama from Largo das Portas do Sol.

has been an upsurge in the restoration of old buildings and many dilapidated palaces and mansions have been tastefully renovated. Many have become elegant restaurants, fashionable boutiques, art galleries and even discotheques. Crumbling houses in the old quarters are also being restored, and in outlying neighbourhoods there are new hotels, vast and popular shopping malls, office complexes, cinemas and museums.

Visitors usually arrive by air and enter the city from the northeast, but a spectacular entrance is over the Ponte 25 de Abril from the south. Completed in 1966, the Ponte de Salazar was renamed in 1974 when democracy was restored to Portugal. A second bridge, Ponte Vasco da Gama, further up the river, was built for Expo '98, which was sited on the river front nearby and has become the Parque das Nações.

A touch of history

The mythical founding of the city on seven hills is attributed to Ulysses (Odysseus) and his encounter with the nymph Calypso. Left behind when he departed, the heartbroken nymph turned herself into a snake whose coils became the seven hills. In reality, there has been a settlement on the site at least since prehistoric times. Its advantageous geographical position caught the attention of Phoenician traders in search of safe anchorage who developed a port, Alis Ubbo (Serene Port), around 1200 BC. The Greeks, then the Carthaginians, subsequently laid claim to the site. In 205 BC Olisipo (as it was then known) was incorporated into the Roman province of Lusitania. Julius Caesar elevated the status of the city to a *municipium* in 60 BC and renamed it Felicitas Julia. What little remains of the Roman occupation today is from this period of relative prosperity and growth. As the Roman Empire crumbled, the city was left unprotected and vulnerable to attacks by a succession of barbaric Germanic tribes.

After the arrival of the Moors in the 8th century, the city enjoyed 400 years of stability and increasing prosperity, which came to an end in 1147, when the first king of the newly formed nation of Portugal, Dom Afonso Henriques, captured Lisbon. Around 1260 the Moors were finally vanquished and the capital moved here from Coimbra. A university was established in 1290 by King Dinis but transferred to Coimbra in 1308. A power struggle between the Church and the Crown over the next 200 years saw the university shunted between the two cities. In the end, Coimbra won that particular battle and Lisbon was left without a university until 1911.

The dawn of the "Age of Discoveries" at the end of the 15th century turned Lisbon into an important trading centre. Wealth from the opening up of the sea route to India by Vasco da Gama flowed into the country and the city entered a golden age that lasted for a century. A 60-year period of Spanish rule then saw a decline in fortunes, and for a while after the Spanish were ousted Lisbon suffered economically as maritime trade declined. The discovery of gold in Brazil ensured a return to former prosperity but most of this fortune was squandered by Dom João V on lavish building projects that were destroyed in the massive earthquake of 1755. The Marquês de Pombal was on hand to oversee the rebuilding of the city (see page 56).

Since then, Lisbon has witnessed the end of the monarchy, gunned down in its main square, and endured a long period of dictatorship under Salazar, which kept the city free of modern development, perhaps the only thing we can thank him for.

Baixa and the city centre

Baixa (the lower quarter) covers the level area in between the hills of Alfama and Bairro Alto. It slopes gently to the banks of the Rio Tejo (Tagus) from Rossio and down through Pombal's famous grid system of streets. City life centres around the vast expanse of the **Praça do Comércio ❶** by the riverside. The earlier name of the square, Terreiro do Paço,

TIP

Walking is the best way to see the city, but there is a good transport system of trams (*eléctricos*), buses, taxis, lifts (*elevadores*) and the metro. You can buy a 24-hour pass (€6), that covers buses, trams, funiculars and the metro, or invest in a Viva Viagem card (€0.50), which you charge up as you go; a single journey costs €1.25, compared with a normal price of €1.40.

The vast Praça do Comércio.

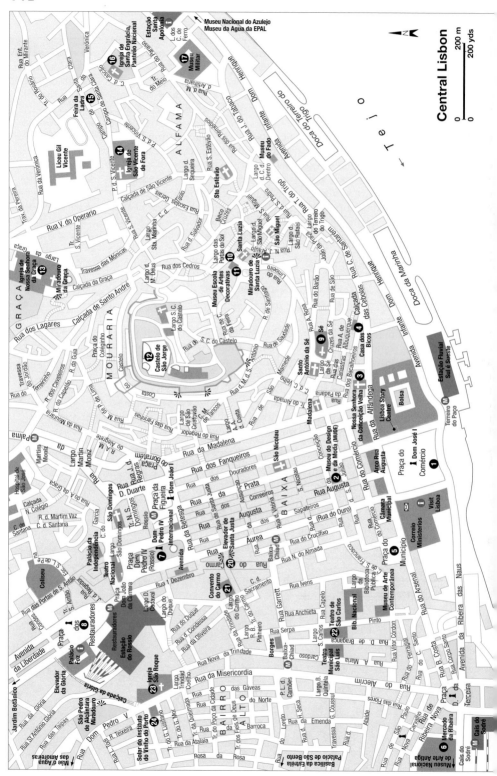

Museu Nacional do Azulejo
Museu da Agua da EPAL

Central Lisbon

0 ___ 200 m
0 ___ 200 yds

is still used and dates back to the time before the earthquake when the 16th-century royal palace stood on the site. Behind the elegant Pombaline neoclassical arcades are municipal and judicial offices, and on the west side of the square is the city tourist office, the **Lisboa Welcome Centre**. You can also visit the new Lisboa Story Centre (www.lisboastorycentre.pt; daily 10am–8pm) here, a playful audiovisual exhibition that vividly immerses the visitor in the city's history, and includes a dramatic cinematic recreation of the 1755 earthquake. Lisbon's former Stock Exchange is to the east. In splendid isolation in the middle of the square stands a bronze statue of the ruler at the time of the earthquake, Dom José I, which gave rise to the English name of Black Horse Square. The riverside serves as a quay for ferry boats along the Tagus and across to the *Outra Banda*, the communities on the southern shore of the river. Completely overshadowing the delicacy of the arcaded buildings is the impressive triumphal **Arco Rua Augusta**. The arch is a late

19th-century addition to the square. Near here, the former colonial bank headquarters has been turned into the colossal eight-storey **Museu do Design e da Moda** ❷ (Rua Augusta 24; www.mude.pt; Tue–Thur and Sun 10am–8pm, Fri–Sat 10am–10pm), which opened in 2009 (see box page 143).

A short walk along the road, from the northeast corner of the square, is the notable Manueline doorway of the church of **Nossa Senhora da Conceição Velha** ❸. Further along, the unusual pyramidal stone facade of the 16th-century **Casa dos Bicos** ❹ (House of the Pointed Stones) seems almost modernistic. There is a clear distinction between the lower storeys, which survived the 1755 earthquake, and the top two storeys, which were faithfully reproduced from old engravings during the 1980s. A short distance further along the road lies the little-noticed 13th-century fountain **Chafariz do Rei**, once the major source of the city's water supply.

Walking down Rua Augusta.

The neo-Manueline Rossio Station.

MUDE

MUDE (Museu do Design e da Moda; www.mude.pt) means "change" in Portuguese. This fantastic museum combines Lisbon's former Design Museum – perhaps the world's best collection of modern design – with works from the priceless collection of art mogul Francisco Capelo. The Design Museum collection is a roll call of modern design classics, featuring furniture and household objects by anyone who's anyone in design: Charles Eames, Frank Gehry, Verner Panton, Philippe Starck, and many more. Ex-stockbroker Capelo's contribution is a breathtaking collection of fashion, which includes 1,200 couture pieces, such as a Jean Dessé's gown that Renée Zellweger wore to the 2001 Oscars, and Christian Dior's landmark 1947 New Look.

St Anthony is the unofficial patron saint of Lisbon.

The grand artifice of the Teatro Nacional in Lisbon.

Leaving the square from the northwest corner you pass the spot where, in 1908, Carlos I and his heir, Luís Felipe, were assassinated. Close by is the **Praça do Municipio** ❺, with an 18th-century *pelourinho* (pillory) and the **Câmara Municipal** (Town Hall), where Portugal was declared a republic in 1910. Further west, trains arrive from Estoril and Cascais at the Cais do Sodré railway station close to the city's main market, **Mercado da Ribeira** ❻. This is a colourful place selling an amazing array of fresh produce, including fish landed at the nearby Ribeira dock.

Back in the Praça do Comércio, make a grand entrance through the Arco Rua Augusta into the neat grid of streets which form the main area of Baixa, the lower town. Pedestrianised Rua Augusta provides plenty of diversions along the way as it sweeps up towards Rossio. Shops are definitely the main attraction but, at busy times, street entertainers and balloon sellers lend a carnival atmosphere and pavement cafés bring a relaxed but buzzy feel to the scene. At one time, the streets of the grid represented various crafts, hence names such as Rua da Prata (silver), Rua do Ouro (gold) and Rua dos Franqueiros (haberdashers). Today, many of these streets are home to banks and offices as well as shops.

Rua Augusta opens into **Praça Dom Pedro IV** ❼, better known by its common name of **Rossio**, and the focus of major city events for 500 years, until the 18th century. This was where citizens gathered to enjoy carnivals and bullfights or to witness public executions, particularly the autos-da-fe of the Inquisition. Now, cafés, flower sellers, shops, kiosks and traffic create a swirl of activity and colour in a square, which is a great place for a coffee or early evening drink, at rooftop bars such as the eponymous Rossio.

At the northern end of the square, the **Teatro Nacional** (Dona Maria II Theatre), built in the 1840s, overlooks the two fountains brought from Paris in 1890, which flank the statue of Dom Pedro IV. They are rather more authentic than the statue, which is a cobbled version of a statue of Emperor

Maximilian of Mexico. A ship carrying it from Marseilles to Mexico docked in Lisbon just as news came of the emperor's assassination. Pressed for cash, the city council snapped it up as the bargain of the day and attempted some remodelling in the hope that no one would notice.

Paço dos Condes de Almada (Palace of the Counts of Almada), just to the east of the theatre, is where the *Restauradores* (Restorers) conspired in 1640 to wrest power back from the occupying Spaniards. The Igreja de São Domingos nearby oversaw the sentencing of victims of the Inquisition, who had been tried in the palace that once stood on the Teatro Nacional site. South of the church the **Praça da Figueira** (Fig Tree Square), with its statue of João I, has a quieter ambience.

To the northwest of Rossio is the **Estação do Rossio** (Rossio Station), with its lovely neo-Manueline facade. Trains from Sintra arrive on the fourth floor, at the level of Bairro Alto (the upper part of town), from where an escalator takes passengers down

to Baixo level. They emerge not far from **Praça dos Restauradores** ❽, named in honour of the Restorers. In this square stands the 18th-century **Palácio Foz**, now used by Turismo de Lisboa as the Ask Me Lisboa tourist information centre. Until 1821, access to the square was closed off to keep out the rabble inhabiting Rossio Square and thereby create a peaceful haven for the gentry. After that it was opened up to the general public and used for celebrations and dances.

East to Alfama

Alfama is the oldest part of the city, and clings tenaciously around the feet of the Castelo de São Jorge. The steep, narrow streets and alleys of this old Moorish quarter spill down to the riverside, and a succession of conquerors over the millennia has left vestiges of their occupation. A tapestry of life unfolds around every corner: drink it all in, but keep a tight hold on your valuables. The area really comes alive on 12 and 13 June for the feast of St Anthony of Padua (1195–1231), the unofficial patron saint of Lisbon, who

TIP

Head to Rua dos Bacalhoeiros in Alfama, to find a wonderful shop full of stuck-in-time design, the Conserveira de Lisboa, which specialises in canned fish.

The canons and view from Castelo São Jorge.

The knife grinder is a familiar figure in the streets of Lisbon, as in any Portuguese town.

The Museu Escola de Artes Decorativas.

was born in the area (he acquired his title after a sojourn in Italy).

Head up from Baixa past the Igreja de Madalena, dating from the late 18th century but preserving a Manueline porch from an earlier church. On the left, as the Romanesque facade of the Sé comes into view, is the small church of **Santo António da Sé**, built on the alleged site of St Anthony's birthplace.

Seeing the Sé

Dom Afonso Henriques, the first king of Portugal, ordered the **Sé** ❾ (Cathedral; Tue–Sat 9am–7pm, Mon & Sun 10am–5pm; free) to be built soon after banishing the Moors from Lisbon. The first incumbent was an Englishman, Gilbert of Hastings, who fared rather better than the 14th-century Bishop Martinho Anes, who was flung from the north tower for harbouring Spanish sympathies. Today the cathedral's fortress-like facade stands testament to the turbulent times in which it was constructed. There has been much restoration over

the centuries but the two original crenellated towers, softened by the large rose window in between, remain the most striking feature.

Inside, the barrel-vaulted ceiling leads to a low lantern, and to the left on entry, is the baptismal font where St Anthony was christened in 1195. Further along, in the first chapel on the left, is a beautifully detailed crèche – Nativity scene – by the sculptor Joaquim Machado de Castro. The chancel is 18th century and the ambulatory was remodelled in the 14th century. In the third chapel from the south side of the ambulatory are the tombs of Lopo Fernandes Pacheco and his wife. He was a companion in arms to Afonso IV (1325–57), and responsible for much of the cathedral's remodelling during those years.

The ruined **cloisters** are worth the modest entrance fee to view the excavations in what were once the gardens. Vestiges of Moorish buildings overlay Roman remains, and beneath those is evidence of an Iron Age settlement.

In the sacristy is the cathedral **treasury** (Mon–Sat 10am–5pm) where numerous sacred objects are on view. Of most importance is the casket containing the remains of St Vincent, the official patron saint of Lisbon, which were brought here by the order of Afonso Henriques from Sagres in Algarve. Legend relates how ravens accompanied the boat that carried his remains from Spain and again on the journey from Algarve to Lisbon. To this day, the raven is a feature of Lisbon's coat of arms.

Still heading uphill, you will reach the **Miradouro de Santa Luzia** which is a good vantage point to look down over Alfama. The church of the same name is decorated externally with some interesting *azulejo* panels, one showing the heroic soldier Martim Moniz, who died keeping the city gate open – an act that enabled Afonso Henriques to capture Lisbon.

A little further up is **Largo da Portas do Sol** ❿ (Sun Gate), where

one of the original city gates once stood. A statue of St Vincent looks out over the city from this popular viewpoint. Terrace cafés provide an excuse to linger, and the 17th-century palace of the counts of Azurara, now the **Museu Escola de Artes Decorativas** ⑪ (Museum of Decorative Arts; Wed–Mon 10am–5pm), is certainly worth a visit. The museum is a showcase for the work of Portugal's master craftsmen.

The Castelo de São Jorge

Perhaps the most beautiful view of the city is from the ramparts of **Castelo de São Jorge** ⑫ (daily Mar–Oct 9am–9pm, Nov–Feb 9am–6pm), which crowns the first hill east of the city centre. If you want to take the hard work out of the climb up to the castle, you could take a taxi or catch the No. 28 Graça tram to Portas do Sol, then visit the Sé and surrounding sites on the walk down. The castle can be seen from nearly anywhere in Lisbon, serving as an apt and romantic reminder of the capital's ancient roots. Many of the castle walls and towers are from

the Moorish stronghold, although there were earlier fortifications on this site.

After the Portuguese drove out the Moors in 1147, the residence of the Moorish governor, Paço de Alcáçova, became the royal palace of Dom Dinis (1279–1325). It remained a royal residence until Dom Manuel (1495–1521) decided to build a more comfortable abode down by the river. Except for a short period, when Dom Sebastião preferred the military fortification of the castle to the graceful splendour of the palace, it served its time as a barracks and prison until 1939, when it was freed from any official duties.

All that is left now are walls, 10 towers and the remnants of the palace, but shaded gardens, fountains, cafés and a restaurant, presided over by a statue of Afonso Henriques, make it an ideal spot to escape the heat of summer. The *miradouro* (lookout spot) provides a marvellous panorama of the city, and from here it is possible to pick out many of the city's landmarks. Further good viewpoints lie to the north at the Baroque **Igreja de Nossa Senhora da**

The mighty walls of Lisbon's Castelo São Jorge.

TIP

Save money at Parque das Nacões (www. portaldasnacoes.pt) by buying the Cartão do Parque, which offers admission to the key attractions here, plus 20 percent off bike and audioguide rental.

The Aqueduto das Aguas Livres.

Graça and, beyond that, the even higher Senhora do Monte.

Back down the hill, the **Museu do Fado** (Largo do Chafariz de Dentro; Tue–Sun 10am–6pm) tracks the development of Portugal's saudade-charged musical soul.

Outside the city walls

A short walk from the castle leads to the **Igreja de São Vicente de Fora** ⑭ (Tue–Sun 10am–6pm; free). *De fora* describes the church's position outside the city walls. It was built on the site of a 12th-century monastery dedicated to St Vincent to commemorate the battle fought by the crusaders to capture Lisbon. The white limestone building, with short twin towers, was designed by Italian architect Filippo Terzi; construction began in 1582, and took more than 40 years.

Of more interest than the church interior are the cloisters (daily; charge), which are covered with 18th-century *azulejos* depicting La Fontaine's *Fables*. The former refectory, off the cloisters, has served as the Pantheon of the Royal House of Bragança since the mid-19th century. Portuguese kings, queens, princes and princesses, the earliest being João IV (who died in 1656), are entombed here.

A flea market, **Feira da Ladra** ⑮ – literally, the Thieves' Market – takes place on Tuesday and Sunday morning in the Campo de Santa Clara. You must cross this square to reach the Baroque **Igreja de Santa Engrácia** ⑯, now the **Panteão Nacional** (National Pantheon; Tue–Sun 10am–5pm), containing monuments to many of Portugal's non-royal heroes. Work on this church started in 1682 but was not completed until 1966, giving rise to the Portuguese idiom for a project that is never finished: *"obras* [works] *de Santa Engrácia"*. Although the building is in the compact, satisfying shape of a Greek cross, with a central dome, the stamp of Salazar on its eventual completion has left it a somewhat sterile monument.

Back down towards the riverside, opposite **Estação Santa Apolónia**, the station for international arrivals, is the **Museu Militar** ⑰ (Tue–Sun 10am–5pm). This museum charts

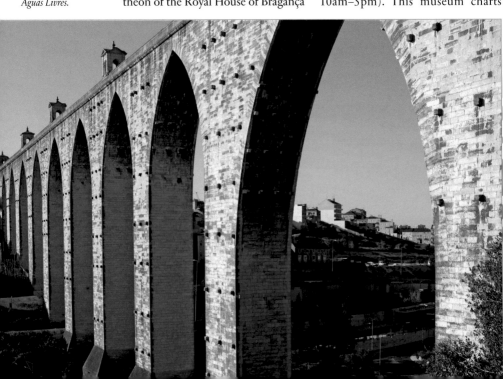

Portugal's military history in paintings and extensive collections of armour and weapons in a building which was, until 1851, the national arsenal.

Head eastward, along the coastal route, paralleling the railway lines, then turn left up Calçada dos Barbadinhos to the **Museu da Agua da EPAL** ⑱ (Water Museum; Mon–Sat 10am–5.30pm; free). Named after the engineer of the Aqueduto das Aguas Livres (see page 152), it was the first steam pumping station of its kind in Portugal. The building, in a surprisingly tranquil oasis, records the history of Lisbon's water supply from Roman times and includes the story of the aqueduct.

Further east stands the tile museum, the **Museu Nacional do Azulejo** ⑲ (Tue–Sun 10am–6pm). Again, the easiest route runs parallel to the railway track, but you may find it worth taking a taxi. The building was originally part of the Convento da Madre de Deus, founded in 1509 by the widow of João II, Dona Leonor of Lancaster. All that remains of the original exterior is the Manueline doorway, but the 18th-century interior of the main church provides the perfect foil for the national collection of *azulejos*, in a breathtaking combination of gilded woodwork, blue-and-white Dutch *azulejos* and superbly painted walls and ceilings. One of the most outstanding tile scenes is a 1730 panorama of Lisbon, some 37 metres (120ft) long. Besides tiles and architecture, there are paintings to admire, a bookshop in which to browse, and a very pleasant café/restaurant.

Heading east out of the city, 5km (3 miles) upriver, beside the Oriente Metro station, is the **Parque das Nacões**, the Expo '98 site, stretching along 2km (1.25 miles) of waterfront. Its attractions include one of the largest sea-life centres in Europe, the **Oceanário de Lisboa** (daily summer 10am–8pm, winter 10am–7pm), the huge Atlantic Pavilion, the Camões Theatre, a waterside cable-car ride, the **Pavilhão do Conhecimento** (Tue–Fri 10am–6pm, Sat–Sun 11am–7pm) interactive science museum (lots of fun for children),

The tram is the most pleasant way to get around in Lisbon – No. 28 from Chiado to the castle has the most scenic route.

Looking down from the Elevador de Santa Justa.

Many different trees grow in the Jardim Botanico.

Looking up at the Elevador de Santa Justa.

and the **Vasco da Gama Tower**, which has a viewing platform with amazing views, and also houses a luxury hotel.

Through Bairro Alto

Bairro Alto (the upper quarter) rises to the west of Baixa. This area is renowned for its shops and restaurants. Shoppers can approach via the fashionable **Chiado** district, looking in at the popular French-owned FNAC department store, built after the 1988 Chiado fire; or have a great coffee in A Brasileira in Rua Garrett, a café favoured by generations of artists and politicians, now rather more by tourists.

The walkway into the Chiado from the top of Raoul Mesnier de Ponsard's **Elevador de Santa Justa ⑳** is accessible, and you can take the lift to the top of the tower to the café and viewing platform (daily 7am–9pm, till 11pm in summer).

The walkway, alongside the roofless **Convento do Carmo ㉑**, used to connect the lift with the Largo do Carmo and entrance to the **Museu Arqueológico do Carmo** (Tue–Sun June–Sept 10am–7pm, Oct–May 10am–6pm). This remarkable ruin is one of Lisbon's most poignant sights. It was built by Nuno Alvares Pereira, João I's young general at the Battle of Aljubarrota (1385), who spent the last eight years of his life here. Left unrestored after the 1755 earthquake, the remains of the nave give the most eloquent reminder of that tumultuous event. Gothic arches soar skywards over a grassy nave, a venue for occasional concerts, while the part that survived serves as an archaeological museum with some curious tombs and an eclectic mixture of exhibits from as far afield as South America and England.

From the convent, turn right on Rua Garrett, then left on Rua Serpa Pinto, to reach Lisbon's opera house, the **Teatro de São Carlos ㉒**. La Scala in Milan and the San Carlos theatre in Naples were the inspiration behind the theatre's construction in 1792, and the Italian influence is obvious.

RETRO RECIPES

Try retro Portuguese drinks at Lisbon's ultra-cool, renovated kiosks. These were operational originally in the 19th century, but had gradually closed down, only to be reopened, complete with vintage-style tipples and snacks in 2004. The lovely, ornate wrought-iron, circular kiosks are to be found in central locations such as Camões Square, Jardim do Principe Real and Praça das Flores. They don't serve fizzy drinks or beer, but traditional drinks such as *orchata* (a chilled almond concoction), lemonade, iced tea, port wine, and some with long-forgotten recipes, such as sweet, refreshing *capilé*, made with spleenwort (a type of fern) and orange blossom, along with traditional Portuguese snacks, such as cod-fish or olive sandwiches.

A short walk to the northwest, along Rua Nova da Trindade, brings you to **Igreja São Roque** ㉓ (St Rock Church; Mon 2–6pm, Thu 9am–9pm, Tue–Wed, Fri–Sun 9am–6pm; free). Behind an unremarkable post-1755 facade lies an opulent interior. The ceiling has been painted to give a beautiful trompe l'oeil effect, and the eight chapels are all individual works of art. There are notable *azulejos* by Francisco de Matos and an excellent canvas, *Vision of St Rock*, painted by Gaspar Dias around 1584.

The main draw is the **Capela de São João Baptista**, said to be the costliest chapel in the world and commissioned in 1742 by João V. Luigi Vanvitelli and Niccolo Salvi designed and built it in Rome, where it was blessed by the Pope, then dismantled and transported to Lisbon. Gold, silver and bronze decorate the extravagant confection of lapis lazuli, alabaster, marble and ivory, central to which is a mosaic of St John. Adjoining the church is the **Museu de Arte Sacra**, a small but impressive collection of vestments and ecclesiastical furnishings in rich Baroque designs.

Wine and water

If you continue up Rua Dom Pedro V, you will reach the **Solar do Instituto do Vinho do Porto** ㉔ (Port Wine Institute; Mon–Fri 11am–midnight, Sat 2pm–midnight; free). A vast selection of ports can be sampled in the cosy bar of this former 18th-century palace. Virtually opposite is the shady São Pedro de Alcântara *miradouro* (viewpoint), which offers an admirable panorama of the city.

The Portuguese delight in gardens, so naturally Lisbon is laced with green spaces. Perhaps the finest of them all is the **Jardim Botânico** ㉕ (daily summer 9am–8pm, winter 9am–6pm), to the right of the Praça do Príncipe Real, one of the richest such gardens in Europe. Created in 1873, it has a magnificent wall of 100-year-old palm trees, banana trees, bamboo and water lilies, and many tropical plants.

Northwest, up the Rua das Amoreiras, beyond Largo do Rato, is a large, simple building, the **Mãe d'Agua das Amoreiras** ㉖ (Mon–Sat 10am–6pm), which once stored the city's water supply, brought in along the

FACT

The towerblock Amoreiras Shopping Centre (daily 10am–11pm) is a popular destination in Lisbon, centrally located and with more than 300 shops covering every category from haute couture to pet supplies. There are also numerous food outlets, a play centre, cinemas, post office and a church.

The atmospheric ruins of the Convento do Carmo.

TIP

The giant Centro Comercial Colombo – with more than 360 shops, including a hypermarket – is opposite the Benfica Football Stadium (Estadio da Luz), the site of the 2004 Euro Final. It is open daily 9am–midnight. Colegio Militar Metro.

The Basilica da Estrela.

Aqueduto das Aguas Livres (enquire at the water museum, page 149, about visits).

South from Amoreiras (head down Rua Ferreira Borges into Domingo Sequeira) are the attractive Jardim da Estréla and the splendid late 18th-century **Basílica da Estrela** ㉗, with its great dome and multi-hued marble interior. Close by is the British Hospital, the little English Church of St George, and the adjacent **Cemité-rio dos Ingleses** (English Cemetery) where Henry Fielding (1707–54), the author of *Tom Jones*, was buried, after a trip to the warmer climes of Lisbon failed to cure his gout or asthma.

Special permission is required to visit nearby **Palácio de São Bento** ㉘ (east along Calçada da Estréla), now the Portuguese Houses of Parliament. Originally built as a monastery, the palace was transformed into the parliament building at the end of the 19th century and was renovated in 1935.

On the docks at Alcãntara, the **Museu do Oriente** (Doca de Alcãntara; Tue–Sun 10am–6pm, Fri 10am–10pm), housed in a former fish warehouse, has an interesting collection examining Portugal's historical links with Asia.

Down by the river is the **Museu Nacional de Arte Antiga** ㉙ (Museum of Ancient Art; http://mnaa.imc-ip.pt Wed–Sun 10am–6pm, Tue 2–6pm). This, one of Lisbon's most important museums, is located in a fine 17th-century palace (property of the Counts of Alvor), with a tasteful modern extension. The term "ancient" may be misleading, as most of the exhibits are only a few centuries old, but there are fine displays of 16th-century porcelain brought back by Portuguese sailors from India, Japan and Macau, and displays of furniture, sculpture and glass.

Perhaps of most interest, the museum's galleries also hold a wide selection of paintings by Nuno Gonçalves and other artists of the 15th–16th-century Portuguese School (see page 110), as well as works by Hieronymus Bosch, Brueghel the Younger, Hans Memling, Giambattista Tiepolo, José de Ribera and other great masters.

Belém

In a green spacious zone by the river, on the western side of town beyond the **Ponte 25 de Abril** ③ and the restaurants and nightclubs around the renovated dock at **Alcântara**, a number of monumental buildings stand as testimony to Portugal's maritime past. Belém means Bethlehem, and reflects the country's involvement with the crusades.

It is here that you will find arguably Lisbon's most glorious monument, the **Mosteiro dos Jerónimos** ③ (www.mosteirojeronimos.pt; Tue–Sun May–Sept 10am–6.30pm, Oct–Apr 10am–5.30pm), built to honour Vasco da Gama and his successful journey to India in 1498, and now a Unesco World Heritage Site. This vast, opulent limestone building, a masterpiece of Manueline (or late Gothic) architecture (see page 104), took 70 years to complete.

The main body of the church is breathtakingly high-ceilinged and elegant. Ribbed vaulting, supported by polygonal columns, becomes an eye-catching star-shaped feature where the transepts cross, and elephant-supported tombs are a reminder of India. The delicacy of the sculpting makes the double-storey cloisters well worth a visit.

Built on the western side of the monastery, in the latter part of the 19th century, is a wing that houses the **Museu Nacional de Arqueologia** ② (National Museum of Archaeology; Tue–Sun 10am–6pm), with an interesting collection of folk art dating from the Stone and Bronze ages. Part of the same wing, the **Museu da Marinha** ③ (Maritime Museum; Tue–Sun Apr–Sept 10am–6pm, Oct–Mar until 5pm) tells the story of Portugal's seafaring discoveries, with redundant royal barges and fishing vessels on display in a separate building.

The **Planetário Calouste Gulbenkian** ③ (Planetarium; http://planetario.marinha.pt) behind it gives regular presentations, two or three times a day, mainly in Portuguese, but with some shows in English, Spanish or French.

Nearby stands the huge **Centro Cultural de Belém** ③, (www.ccb.pt) opened in 1992; exhibitions and events here are usually excellent. It also contains the ultra-minimalist Museu Colecção Berardo (www.museuberardo.com; Tue–Sun 10am–7pm; free), which contains a dazzling array of modern art, with works by Picasso, Magritte, Warhol, Bacon, Pollock and many more, along with sculpture, photography and installations.

On the bank of the Rio Tejo, on the far side of the broad Avenida da India and a small park, stands the **Torre de Belém** ③ (daily May–Sept 10am–6.30pm, Oct–May 10am–5.30pm), on the site where Vasco da Gama and other navigators set out on their explorations. This exquisite little 16th-century fortress is another fine example of the Manueline style, with its richly carved niches, towers and shields bearing the Templar cross.

On the waterfront a short distance

A colourful kiosk in the Avenida da Liberdade.

Guarding the Palácio de São Bento.

Sculpture in the park of the Gulbenkian complex.

The doorway to the Mosteiro dos Jerónimos.

away, you can't miss the impressive **Padrão dos Descobrimentos** ③⑦ (Monument of the Discoveries; May–Sept daily 10am–7pm, Oct–Apr Tue–Sun 10am–6pm). Erected in 1960, the monument is a stylised caravel, with Prince Henry the Navigator at the fore gazing seawards and other leading figures of the age behind him.

East of the monument, on the Calçada da Ajuda, rises the ornate rose-coloured **Palácio de Belém**, which once served as a royal retreat but is now the official residence of the president of the Republic. Adjacent, in what was once the royal riding school, is the **Museu Nacional dos Coches** ③⑧ (Coach Museum; Tue–Sun 10am–6pm), which houses one of the finest collections of coaches in Europe.

Up the hill to the side of the palace is the magnificent **Palácio Nacional da Ajuda** ③⑨ (Thu–Tue 10am–7pm, Sat 10am–9pm), built after the great earthquake as a royal palace but never completed. It is now used for exhibitions and concerts, and numerous rooms are open to the public.

The northern hills

Travelling northeast and crossing the Avenida da Ponte again (all but the most hardy will do this by public transport or taxi), you will find that the **Parque Eduardo VII** ④⓪ provides an immediate escape from the clamour of the city and offers magnificent views back down to the Tejo. The park was named to mark the state visit of King Edward VII of England in 1903, which was the first he made to a foreign country after his coronation. In the top left-hand corner of the park, but reached from Rua Castilho, are two greenhouses, the **Estufa Quente** (Hothouse), originally built to house exotic orchids, and the better-known **Estufa Fria** (Cold house).

At the southeast corner of the park is the **Praça Marquês de Pombal** ④①, or the Rotunda, as it is more commonly known. From his lofty perch in the centre, a statue of the Marquês looks out over the city he rebuilt. From here, the **Avenida da Liberdade** sweeps southwards, linking the Rotunda with the Baixa area.

The *avenida* was developed as a dual carriageway in 1879 and became the epitome of style, with palm trees and water features lining the route. It's now the best place in Lisbon to shop for big name labels, such as Gucci and Prada. The little **Parque Mayer**, about two-thirds of the way down, is an enclave of restaurants and theatres, the latter specialising in popular comedy known as *revistas*, satirical variety shows commenting on current political events.

Gulbenkian's legacy

Instead of returning to Baixa, leave the Parque Eduardo VII by the northern exit and walk northeast for a short way to a large landscaped complex containing the **Museu Calouste Gulbenkian ㊷** (Avenida de Berna 45; www.museu.gulbenkian.pt; Tue–Sun 10am–5.45pm). The Calouste Gulbenkian Foundation was set up by the Turkish-Armenian oil magnate, who was born in Istanbul in 1869 and became very attached to Portugal after being harassed and hounded by the Allies in World War II, and seeking refuge in neutral Portugal. The foundation is the most important funding source for the arts in the country, and there are Gulbenkian libraries and museums throughout the country. When Calouste Gulbenkian died in 1955 his collection, one of the richest private collections in the world, was bequeathed to the nation.

The museum's contents include displays of Middle Eastern and Islamic art, Chinese porcelain, Japanese prints and gold and silver Greek coins. Among magnificent exhibits from the West are paintings by 17th-century masters like Rubens and Rembrandt, and by Impressionists such as Renoir, Manet and Monet. There are also rich Italian tapestries, and a whole room dedicated to the Art Nouveau creations of René Lalique.

A pleasant walk through the park-like complex leads to the **Centro de**

The Museu Calouste Gulbenkian is surrounded by a sculpture park.

The manicured gardens of Parque Eduardo VII.

Arte Moderna (Tue–Sun 10am–6pm), which displays the work of 20th-century Portuguese artists, including Paula Rego (see panel page 115).

For a rather different form of entertainment, you can take the Metro one stop northwest to the zoo, or **Jardim Zoológico de Lisboa** ㊸ (www.zoo.pt; daily summer 10am–8pm, winter 10am–6pm), which is set in the attractive Parque das Laranjeiras (Orange Tree Park).

Just southwest of the zoo, on the edge of the Parque Florestal de Monsanto, you will find an unexpected gem in the form of the glorious, pink-washed **Palácio dos Marquêses de Fronteira** ㊹ (guided tours Mon–Sat 10.30am, 11am, 11.30am, noon), built as a hunting villa for the first Marquês de Fronteira in 1640. The house and beautiful formal gardens are decorated with some unusual and captivating *azulejos*.

Campo Grande: north and south

On Campo Grande you will find the group of pleasant modern buildings that make up the **Cidade Universitária** (University), although the nearby **Arquivo Nacional da Torre do Tombo** ㊻, a fort-like building that holds the national archives, is architecturally more striking. In an 18th-century palace at the end of Campo Grande is the **Museu da Cidade** ㊼ a (City Museum; Tue–Sun 10am–1pm, 2–6pm), with an interesting collection of archaeological pieces and engravings that trace the history of the city, housed in the charming Palácio Pimenta.

Heading south along Avenida da República, the large 19th-century bullring, **Campo Pequeno**, is hard to miss, and is not a bad place to witness one of Portugal's relatively animal-friendly bullfights.

If you head in the opposite direction, north from Campo Grande up Avenida Padre Cruz, you will reach **Parque do Monteiro-Mór**. Located in old manor houses in these gardens is the **Museu do Trajo e da Moda** (Costume and Fashion Museum; www.museudotraje.imc-ip.pt; Tue 2–6pm, Wed–Sun 10am–6pm).

The bullring at Campo Pequeno.

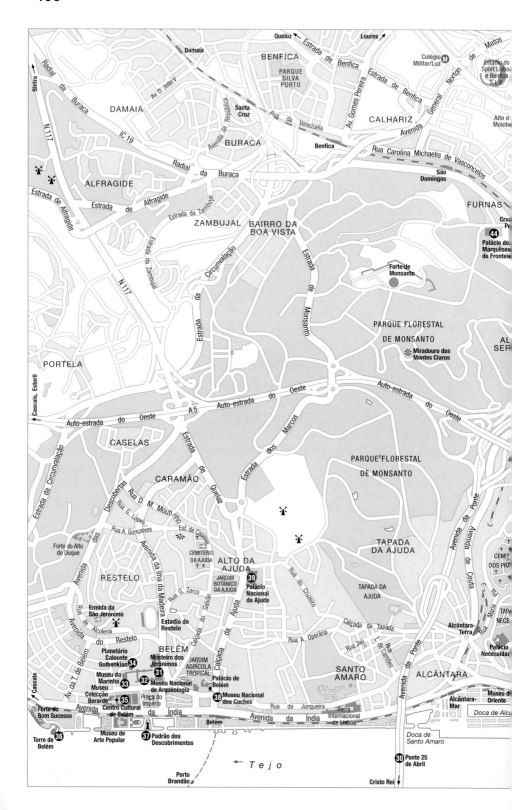

Lisbon

0   500 m
0   500 yds

← *T e j o*

Cacilhas   Seixal   Barreiro, Montijo

AZULEJOS: A NATIONAL EMBLEM

Featuring in everything from cathedral cupolas to beer houses, *azulejos* are an integral part of Portugal's architectural heritage.

The Portuguese have had a lasting love affair with *azulejos* – painted ceramic tiles – ever since they first set eyes on those imported from Seville in the 15th century. *Azulejos* are not unique to Portugal, but they have become almost a national emblem.

Local production of tiles began soon after the arrival of the geometric Sevillian prototypes. Early ones, used mostly in church interiors, were mainly in shades of blue, with patterns established during the course of firing by separating the colours using rivulets of linseed oil or ridges of clay. Quality improved with the introduction of the Italian *majolica* technique, in which the tile was covered with white enamel onto which paint could be applied directly. This greater freedom permitted more artistic expression. Tapestry designs, based on Moorish patterns, began to appear, founded on a module of four tiles, in blue, yellow, green and white.

Tiles along the Miradouro Santa Luzia in Lisbon.

The next leap was the introduction of tin-glazing techniques used in the production of Delftware from Holland. It dominated tile production for a period, but by the mid-18th century there was a return to polychrome tiles. During the rebuilding of Lisbon after the great earthquake of 1755, the demand for tiles escalated. They were used for internal and external decoration in every aspect of architecture: churches, private homes, public buildings and even on park benches. New factories opened to supply the demand but, inevitably, artistic standards fell and many tiles had to be imported. The best place to trace the development of the tiles is in the Museu Nacional do Azulejo, in Lisbon (see page 149).

Azulejo tiles are employed for useful purposes as well as decorative ones.

Used tiles can be found for sale at Feira da Ladra, Lisbon's legendary flea market, displaying secular motifs as well as sacred designs.

The 17th-century Palácio dos Marquêses de Fronteira in Lisbon is decorated with unusual azulejos.

MASTERPIECES OF DECORATIVE ART

Towards the end of the 17th century, tile painting became a recognised art form in Portugal. One of the earliest masters to find fame in this field was António de Oliveira Bernardes. Together with his son, Policarpo, he set up a school of painters in Lisbon which rapidly became influential. Many beautiful works produced by this school in the first half of the 18th century found their way into churches, monasteries and palaces.

The interior of the Capela de São Lourenço in Algarve is covered with *azulejos* depicting the life of the saint; many believe it to be the work of Policarpo. Art historians also greatly admire the work of Policarpo in Setúbal's São Filipe chapel.

A letter box set into a wall in Obidos is tiled with a floral motif. Once azulejos were no longer confined to churches and palaces, they cropped up everywhere.

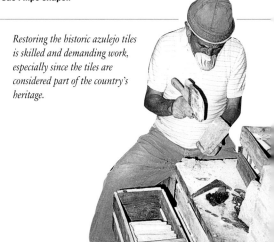

Restoring the historic azulejo tiles is skilled and demanding work, especially since the tiles are considered part of the country's heritage.

...on's Igreja de São Vincente de For cloisters are covered with ...-century azulejos depicting La Fontaine's Fables.

Surfing on Guincho beach.

ESTORIL AND CASCAIS

Close to Lisbon, these neighbouring resorts are well connected to the city, convenient for exploring as far north as Sintra, and also a delight for windsurfers and golfers.

andily located for **Lisbon ❶**, south-facing Estoril and Cascais are the most significant coastal resorts outside Algarve, although neither is especially large. They grew to prominence as a playground for Lisboetas, but modern times have witnessed a role reversal: these resorts and their environs are now dormitories for wealthy Lisbon commuters, and are the preferred places to stay for many visitors who like a tranquil base from which to explore the capital.

West along the coast

The electric train offers the quickest and most convenient way of travelling the 29km (18-mile) distance between Cascais, Estoril and Lisbon. It arrives in Cais do Sodré station on the west side of the city, close to the riverside, where the green (Verde) Metro line begins. Some of the mainline trains also stop at Belém, which is convenient for visiting one of the capital's most interesting areas. The train service between Lisbon and Estoril and Cascais is frequent, and the journey only takes about half an hour.

Driving, you can take the inland A5 route, which is faster, or the slower but more scenic *Marginal* (N6) route along the riverside out of Lisbon, which leads through Belém to the elegant hillside neighbourhood of Restelo, the location of many

embassies and diplomatic residences. **Alges** is the first town outside the city limits.

A string of small riverside towns follows. **Dafundo** has several splendid old mansions standing in rather sad contrast alongside dilapidated rent-controlled housing. It also has the **Aquário Vasco da Gama** (http://aquariovgama.marinha.pt; daily 10am–6pm), a fascinating world of sea turtles, eels, barnacles and all kinds of fish; it has been open since 1898, although it is now rather eclipsed

The sands of Tamariz Beach.

by the Oceanarium in the Parque das Nações. **Cruz Quebrada** is the site of a stone-seated soccer stadium, while **Caxias** is known for its flower-decked villas, 18th-century gazebos and an infamous coastal prison-fort. In **Oeiras** you will find a fine 18th-century Baroque church, a lovely park, modern apartment blocks and an austere 16th-century fort and vintage car museum.

Just beyond lies the 17th-century fortress of **São Julião da Barra**, marking the point where the Tejo meets the Atlantic. **Carcavelos** has several moderate hotels and a broad sandy beach.

Elegant Estoril

And so to **Estoril** ❷, the first point of what has frequently been referred to as the Golden Triangle, and which includes Cascais and Sintra. A flowering, palm-lined, pastel-coloured resort, it first gained fame at the turn of the 20th century for its therapeutic spring waters. During World War II, Estoril became well known as the low-key haunt of international spies. Later, this corner of the Atlantic, with its mild weather and gracious lifestyle, became a home from home for dispossessed European royalty and for refugees fleeing the political upheavals after the war. Among the Triangle's illustrious residents were former kings Simeon of Bulgaria and Umberto of Italy, and Bolivia's ex-leader, Antenor Patiño.

With changing times, local aristocrats are selling or renting out their

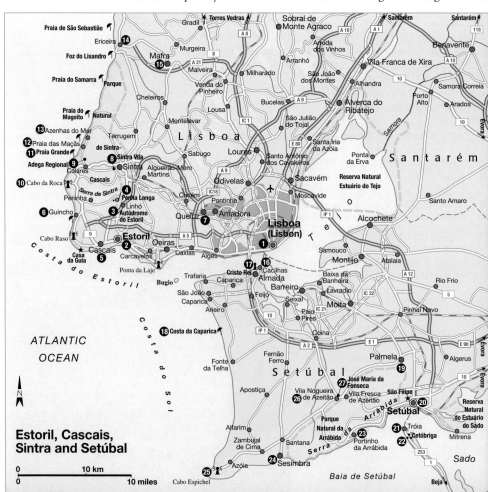

Estoril, Cascais, Sintra and Setúbal

villas. More and more Portuguese and foreigners come to the Triangle to live, retire or keep summer homes. Estoril now has the atmosphere of a rather staid, if attractive, resort – a kind of up-market, rather more glitzy version of Eastbourne.

Estoril's fine sandy **Tamariz** beach is attractively set with a touch of the picturesque, added by a castellated private house surrounded by palms at the eastern end. This Atlantic location been awarded a Blue Flag for cleanliness, as have Duquesa and Conceição nearby.

The **casino** in the heart of the town is a low, white modern building with immaculately kept gardens. In order to gamble here, you need to show a passport, driver's licence or identity card to get in, and the minimum age limit is 18. Some people come to the casino just to see the show, usually a colourful international extravaganza, but it's fun to keep an eye on the betting. As in all crowded venues, keep your valuables hidden. There is also an elegant dining room, an art gallery, a cinema and a bar.

Festivals and rallies

The **Estoril Music Festival** takes place in July. Concerts and recitals are held in Estoril Cathedral, Cascais Cidadela (fort) and other impressive settings. The **International Craft Fair** has become a major production, lasting throughout the months of July and August. Located near the railway station, the fair features arts and crafts, food, wine, and folk music performances from all over the country.

Casino Estoril was the inspiration for Ian Fleming's 007 novel Casino Royale.

There is a lot to do in the way of sports in the Triangle. The **Autódromo do Estoril ❸**, the automobile race track located inland on the road to Sintra, used to draw large crowds for the Grand Prix Formula One races but the track fails to meet current safety requirements for Formula One racing. However, it now hosts the Portuguese motorcycle Grand Prix and the Superleague Formula, both of which are popular events.

Mild winters and summers tempered by cool westerlies provide ideal weather conditions for golf all year

Golfing in Oitavos.

GOLF IN THE GOLDEN TRIANGLE

The Estoril Golf Club's course, on the outskirts of town, is one of the loveliest in Europe. It was laid out by McKenzie Ross on a hillside dotted with pine and eucalyptus groves. The smaller 9-hole Estoril-Sol Golf Course is located in a pine wood at Linhó near Sintra. Overlooking the Atlantic coast just west of Cascais is the Quinta da Marinha hotel and golf club. Designed by Robert Trent Jones, this attractive course, in a private 110-hectare (270-acre) estate, weaves through umbrella pines, water features and wind-blown sand dunes. Quinta da Beloura, designed by William Roquemore and opened in 1993, lies beneath the hills of Serra de Sintra. Six lakes provide golfers with plenty of watery challenges.

Penha Longa, built with Japanese finance, is more than a golf course; it is a country club with a whole range of sporting activities, and includes a five-star hotel. The 18-hole and 9-hole courses designed by Robert Trent Jones II embrace natural woodland and rocky outcrops. The complex is located between Serra de Sintra and the Atlantic. The Praia d'El Rey lies about an hour's drive from Lisbon on the A8 motorway. It is a championship links course right by the sea, and here too there is luxury accommodation, tennis and other activities on offer, and a spa. (See Travel Tips, page 368, for golf course contact details.)

Sailboats on the Praia dos Pescadores near Cascais.

round. There are several courses on the north side of the Tejo and four within easy reach on the south. **Penha Longa Atlantic**  (see box page 167) is one of the best.

Cascais: resort of kings

Once a royal resort, the attractive little town of **Cascais** is much livelier than its more sedate neighbour, although it still retains the laid-back atmosphere of a wealthy seaside suburb. In 1870, King Luís I established his summer residence in the 17th-century citadel on the Bay of Cascais. Before that, it was known only as a fishing port. Local people claim that it was a fisherman from Cascais, Afonso Sanches, who actually discovered America in 1482, and Christopher Columbus merely repeated the trip 10 years later and got all the glory. In 1580, the Duke of Alba attacked Cascais when Spain was laying claim to Portugal, and in 1589 the English arrived here to retaliate for the Spanish Armada's 1588 foray. The fishing port still remains, with the comings and goings of the

colourful fishing boats in the bay, the noisy nightly auction at the central fish market, and good shopping and restaurants.

Around the port has grown a resort with all the vibrancy that Estoril lacks, and yet it has managed to avoid spilling beyond its original boundaries. Pedestrianised streets are paved with traditional black-and-white *calçada* blocks, re-creating dynamic wave patterns – you will spot the same paving in former Portuguese colonies such as Macau. A busy Wednesday market, where you can buy fresh fruit and vegetables as well as handicrafts, is repeated on a smaller scale on Saturday morning.

There are several old churches and chapels in Cascais, including the 17th-century **Nossa Senhora da Assunção** with its plain facade, lovely tiles and marble nave. It contains several paintings by the 17th-century artist, Josefa de Obidos.

On the outskirts of town, in an exotic garden, is the **Museu-Biblioteca Condes de Castro Guimarães** (Mon–Fri 10am–5pm, Sat–Sun 10am–1pm and 2–5pm). Housed in a candyfloss-pale, fairy-tale mansion – the former residence of the Conde de Castro Guimarães, who donated it to the people of Cascais on his death in 1927 – this museum displays 17th-century Portuguese silver, tiles and furniture, and some good 19th-century paintings, as well as prehistoric finds.

The **Museu do Mar Dom Carlos** (Tue–Sun 10am–5pm) is the best place to get a glimpse of the community's past. It tells the lives of the fishermen and has many photographs of King Carlos, a keen oceanographer, who started the bathing season with his arrival here each September during the 1890s. The penultimate king of Portugal, Carlos was assassinated in Lisbon in 1908.

Dedicated to the renowned Portuguese artist Paula Rego, the Casa das Histórias Paula Rego (daily summer 10am–7pm, winter 10am–6pm; free) has a fine collection of her paintings, drawings and etchings.

There are also opportunities for horse riding around Cascais, at the Centro Hípico da Quinta de Marinha,

inland from the beach at Guincho (see page 169).

Close to Cascais, the clifftop Casa da Guia has incredible views, some excellent restaurants, shops and more.

The beaches

The main beaches lie between Cascais and Estoril; there is a small beach to the west, **Praia de Santa Marta**, but it is barely big enough for a game of volleyball. Take a short walk beyond, along the main road, and you will come to the **Boca do Inferno** (Mouth of Hell), a narrow inlet with arches and caverns. Waves crash into the inlet with some ferocity, especially when the Atlantic swell is running high.

Beyond here lies the rocky Atlantic coast. Lisboetas flock here at weekends to enjoy seafood lunches at several popular restaurants. Some also come to swim at the broad, clean beach of **Praia do Guincho ⑥**, where the waves can be wild and the undertow fierce. Windsurfers love it. Some people, however, simply like to take the road to Sintra (see page 171), through the pines and along the open coast.

Kayaks for rent on Praia dos Pescadores near Cascais.

The cliffs of Boca do Inferno.

Architectural excess at Palácio da Pena.

SINTRA

Known by the Romans as the Mountains of the Moon, the Serra da Sintra holds a delightful confection of palaces and monuments, along with some splendid beaches.

With its lush forests and gentle surrounding plain, beautiful, fantastical Sintra has long been a favourite summer resort for Portuguese and foreign visitors. The area, a mix of lush wooded hills and extraordinary pleasure palaces, was declared a World Heritage Site by Unesco in 1995. Lord Byron was enamoured of Sintra and likened it to "Elysium's gates". In *Childe Harold*, he wrote: "Lo! Cintra's glorious Eden intervenes in variegated maze of mount and glen."

Some 32km (20 miles) to the northwest of Lisbon, Sintra is another world, with its own climate – a clash of warm southerlies and moist westerlies over the Serra da Sintra. The most practical way to go is by train from Rossio station. Trains run regularly, taking 35 minutes and stopping at Queluz-Belas, for the palace, after 20 minutes. If you drive, try to avoid rush hour. The road to Sintra from Lisbon starts at the Praça Marquês de Pombal and is well marked. Avenida Duarte Pacheco runs into the *auto-estrada* or super highway that leads out of town, past the Aqueduto das Aguas Livres, up the hill through Parque de Monsanto, turning right to join the highway to Sintra.

Queluz Palace

A slight detour to visit **Queluz** ⑦ is worthwhile. The town has become a rather drab Lisbon dormitory, but its rose-coloured palace is anything but. The **palácio** (daily 9.45am–7pm) was built as a simple manor for King Pedro II in the mid-1600s and was enlarged when the court moved there. Most of the palace, including its magnificent facade, is Baroque, but the courtyard and formal gardens were modelled after Versailles. In summer, concerts are sometimes held in the Music Room. At other times, the public may visit the lavishly decorated Throne Room with its fine painted wood ceiling, the Hall

Main Attractions
Palácio Nacional de Queluz
Palácio Nacional de Sintra
Palácio Nacional da Pena
Convento dos Capuchos
Quinta da Regaleira
Mafra

Palace and gardens at Queluz.

Making use of the high winds.

The Palácio Nacional at Sintra, with its distinctive chimney cones.

of Mirrors, the Ambassador's Room, and others. The kitchen, with a stone chimney and copperware, has been turned into a luxury restaurant, **Cozinha Velha**. The palace and gardens are a spectacular stage during August and September for **Noites de Queluz**, enchanting musical re-creations of 18th-century court life. The Alter Real horses of Escola Portuguesa de Arte Equestre, with the riders in full courtly regalia, also perform outside the palace at 11am every Wednesday (May–July, September and October).

Sintra Vila

Back on the main road continue along rolling hills, past modest whitewashed villages and rich *quintas* (manors) to arrive at the Serra de Sintra. At the base of the mountain lies the village of **São Pedro de Sintra**, where, on the second and fourth Sunday of each month, a wonderful country fair and flea and book market takes place. São

Pedro is also known for its popular tavernas, with spicy sausages, hearty codfish and heady wines. The road now climbs slightly and curves around the mountain to reach **Sintra Vila ⑧**, the historic centre of Sintra, where you will find the tourist office, off Praça de República. The road to the left, Rua Gil Vicente, leads down to **Museu Ferreira de Castro Ⓐ** (Tue–Fri 10am–6pm, Sat–Sun noon–6pm), dedicated to the works of the great Portuguese novelist Ferreira de Castro (1898–1974). A little further on is **Hotel Lawrence Ⓑ**, formerly Estalagem dos Cavaleiros, where Lord Byron stayed in 1809, and now restored as an inn under its original name.

The centrepiece of Sintra is the royal palace, the Paço Real, now called the **Palácio Nacional de Sintra Ⓒ** (Thu–Tue 9.30am–5.30pm), parts of which date from the 14th century. Broad stairs lead up to the stately building with Gothic arches, Moorish windows and two extraordinary chimney cones above enormous kitchens. Of special interest are the Sala dos Brasões, with remarkable ceiling panels painted in

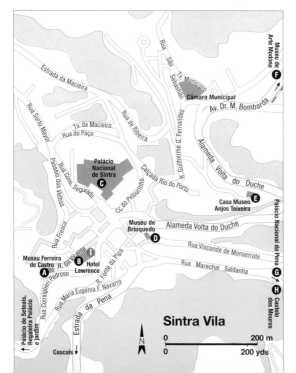

Sintra Vila

0   200 m
0   200 yds

1515, which show the coat of arms of 71 Portuguese noble families (that of the Távoras was removed after the conspiracy against King José in 1758); the Sala dos Arabes, with marble fountain and 15th-century Moorish tiles; the Sala dos Cisnes, an enormous reception hall with swans painted on the panelled ceiling; and the Sala das Pegas, its ceiling covered with magpies brandishing banners reading "Por Bem". It is said that when Queen Philippa caught João I dallying with a lady-in-waiting he claimed it was an innocent kiss. "Por Bem", he said, which loosely translated means: "It's all for the best". Philippa's response is not recorded.

The other Sintra

Estefânia, the third district of Sintra, is where you go to catch the train or a local bus to Lisbon. Walking in that direction from the historic centre, you will reach the **Museu de Brinquedo** **D** (Tue–Sun 10am–6pm), a charming toy museum full of vintage play things; and then come to the **Casa Museu Anjos Teixeira** **E** (Tue–Fri 10am–6pm,

Sat–Sun 2–6pm), which houses an important collection of sculptures.

Shortly after this, on the left and before the bus and railway stations, is Sintra's handsome Town Hall. It has a square castellated tower with a steeple in an exuberant Gothic style. Housed in a grand building, in Avenida Heliodoro Salqado, is the **Museu de Arte Moderna** **F** (Tue–Sun 10am–6pm), containing works by Hockney, Lichtenstein and many other 20th-century artists.

Mountain retreats

Sintra's other palace-museum, the **Palácio Nacional da Pena** **G** (Tue–Sun, May–Sept 9.45am–7pm, Oct–Apr 10am–6pm), dominates the town from the top of the mountain. The road winds up steep rocky slopes through thick woods to the castle, built on the site of a 16th-century monastery: you can walk up, drive or take a quaint bus.

Across the way, reached by the bus to Palácio Nacional da Pena, are the ruins of another mountain-top castle, the **Castelo dos Mouros** **H** (daily May–Sept 9.30am–8pm, Oct–Apr

A winged sculpture.

HOTCH-POTCH PALACE

The Palácio Nacional da Pena is entered through **Parque da Pena,** where there are lakes with black swans, myriad flora and tiled fountains. Some think the palace is better viewed from afar. Close up, the castle is an architectural potpourri: Arabic minarets, Renaissance cupolas, Gothic towers, Manueline windows. But its interior of cosy domesticity is appealing, with rooms furnished in early 20th-century style. It was commissioned by Prince Ferdinand of Saxe-Coburg-Gotha, husband of Queen Maria II, and built by German architect Baron von Eschwege around 1840. At the entrance to the castle a tunnel leads to the ruins of the original monastery. The old chapel walls are decorated with fine 17th-century tiles and there is a splendid altar of alabaster and black marble by 16th-century French sculptor Nicolas Chanterène.

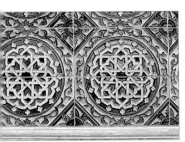

Tile detail on an outside wall at the Quinta de Monserrate.

Looking out from the Palácio Nacional da Pena.

10am–6pm), dating from about the 11th century. The fortifications visible along the mountain ridge were restored in the middle of the 19th century. To the southwest rises the highest peak, **Cruz Alta**, at 540 metres (1,772ft), marked by a stone cross. The mountainside is a luxuriant mass – subtropical plants, mossy boulders, giant ferns, walnut, chestnut and pine trees, and rhododendron bushes. One of the strangest sights on the mountain is the **Convento dos Capuchos** (daily Apr–Sept 9.30am–8pm, Oct–Mar 10am–6pm), a 16th-century monastery built entirely of rocks and cork. Some say the monks lined their cells with cork to obtain absolute silence, but there is little noise here other than bird sounds. More likely, the cork helped insulate them from the long bitter winters.

Palatial accommodation

On the outskirts of Sintra Vila (on the way to Colares) stands the **Palácio de Seteais**, an obscure name said to mean "the seven sighs". This was where the Convention of Sintra was signed in 1809, after the defeat of Napoleon by British and Portuguese forces. It is said that the terms of the treaty upset the Portuguese so much that the palace became known for their sighs of despair. Seteais was restored and turned into a luxury hotel in 1955 and should be visited, if only for tea or a drink. The elegant rooms contain crystal chandeliers, wall hangings, murals and antique furnishings. From the gardens you have a magnificent view of the surrounding countryside.

Almost opposite is the remarkable **Quinta da Regaleira** (daily Apr–Sept 10am–8pm, Feb–Mar and Oct until 6.30pm, Nov–Jan until 5.30pm), built at the close of the 19th century as an assembly of Gothic, Manueline and Renaissance styles that would be out of place anywhere but here. This is one of Sintra's most spectacular sights, with magical gardens filled with follies, which culminate in the initiation well, reached via a mysterious descending spiral staircase.

Nearby is the **Palácio de Monserrate** (daily 9.30am–7pm), a strange Moorish-type villa built in the 19th century. The exotic garden (daily 9.30am–8pm) and greenhouse are worth seeing for the trees and plants from all over the world: palms, bamboos, cedars, magnolias, cork oaks, pines and giant ferns. Once part of the Monserrate gardens, the **Quinta de São Thiago** is a 16th-century manor with a fine chapel, splendid kitchen, cell-like bedrooms, gardens, and its own swimming pool. The owners found taxes and other expenses prohibitive and opened the *quinta* to paying guests. You can also stay in the nearby **Quinta da Capela**.

Coastal excursions

For a delightful excursion, the road to **Colares** leads through vineyards, whitewashed hamlets and stone wall

to the sea. En route you could visit the **Adega Regional ❾** (Mon–Fri 9am–1pm, 2–6pm, Sat 9am–1pm; free), a traditional winery. Colares grapes grow in sandy soil in a humid maritime climate. The wines are dark ruby and very smooth.

Cabo da Roca ❿ is a wild desolate cape, the westernmost point of continental Europe, and visitors receive a certificate to mark their visit. Heading north, there are several beaches frequented mainly by the Portuguese: broad, sandy **Praia Grande ⓫** and **Praia das Maçãs ⓬**. The attractive fishing village of **Azenhas do Mar ⓭** has a natural rock swimming pool.

Magnificent Mafra

Heading north towards the coast you reach **Ericeira ⓮**, a beach resort and fishing village. From here, an easy 10km (6-mile) drive inland takes you to **Mafra ⓯**, a name shared by a modest village and a vast palace-convent (Wed–Mon 10am–5.30pm) that rises like a dark mirage across the plain. The complex of buildings, almost as large as Spain's Escorial, was erected by João V in fulfilment of a vow. Work began in 1717 and took 18 years, drawing so many artists from so many countries that João founded the School of Mafra, making these talented men masters to local apprentices. The most famous teacher was Joaquim Machado de Castro, who also worked on Lisbon's Basílica da Estrela (see page 152).

The limestone facade is 220 metres (720ft) long. At its centre is the **church**, with two tall towers and an Italianate portico. The interior is decorated with the finest Portuguese marble, while the 14 large statues of saints in the vestibule were carved from Carrara marble by Italian sculptors. The church also contains six organs. Most impressive is the **library**, full of Baroque magnificence and light. Among its 35,000 volumes are first editions of *Os Lusíadas* by Camões, and the earliest edition of Homer in Greek. Other areas open to the public include the hospital, the pharmacy, the audience room and the chapterhouse.

The great library at Mafra.

The bay at Parque natural da Arrábida.

Cristo Rei monument.

SETÚBAL AND THE ARRÁBIDA PENINSULA

A mixture of industrial sprawl, nature reserves, ancient sites and huge sandy beaches, the Arrábida peninsula is little known to visitors but is the preferred place to live for many Lisboetas.

Main Attractions
Cristo Rei
Costa da Caparica
Igreja de Jesus
Parque Natural da Arrábida
José Maria da Fonseca Winery

Lisboetas call it *Outra Banda*, the other shore, meaning the southern bank of the Tejo, long neglected because of the inconvenience of getting there. This changed after 1966 with the completion of what was then Europe's longest suspension bridge, the Ponte 25 de Abril, and an even longer bridge, the Vasco da Gama, in 1998.

The region between the Tejo and Sado rivers, known as the Arrábida peninsula, has developed rapidly and not always wisely. Directly across the Tejo is the unassuming ferry-boat port of **Cacilhas** ⓰. Its main charm is a string of river-front fish restaurants with grand views of Lisbon. About 5km (3 miles) west of Ponte 25 de Abril is Trafaria; the whole town was burned to the ground on the orders of Pombal in 1777 as punishment for resisting press gangs, but was later rebuilt.

Most visitors tend to drive through the neighbouring industrial town of Almada without stopping, except those who want to see the **Cristo Rei monument** ⓱ (Christ the King; daily 9.30am–6.30pm). A lift takes you to the top of the 82-metre (276ft) pedestal – so high it seems to dwarf the 28-metre (91ft) figure on top – for a magnificent view of Lisbon.

Most people avoid the *Outra Banda* dormitory district by taking the A2 highway directly from the bridge. After a few kilometres, a turn-off leads

to **Costa da Caparica** ⓲ (see box on page 181).

On to Palmela

Continuing south on the highway, the road marked **Palmela** ⓳ leads to a small town with a great medieval castle. This has been restored and converted into a luxury *pousada* (see page 352) with a lounge in the cloisters and an elegant dining room in the old refectory. The church is a beautiful Romanesque structure, its walls covered with 18th-century tiles.

Ponte 25 de Abril.

Built by the Moors, the castle was reconstructed in 1147 as a monastery and the seat of the Knights of the Order of St James. In 1484, the bishop of Évora was imprisoned in the dungeon for his role in the conspiracy against João II. He died a few days later, probably poisoned. The castle was badly damaged by the 1755 earthquake, but was rebuilt and monks remained there until the abolition of religious orders in 1834.

Just outside Setúbal rises another great castle turned *pousada*, **São Filipe**, with a magnificent view of the Sado estuary. Felipe II of Spain ordered its construction in 1590, to keep a watch over the area – Portugal was under Spanish rule at the time. The chapel is decorated with tiles that recount the life of the king's namesake, St Philip, signed by the master painter Policarpo de Oliveira Bernardes and dated 1736.

Setúbal and the Tróia peninsula

According to local legend, **Setúbal** ❷⓿ was founded by Tubal, the son of Cain. It is said that the Phoenicians and Greeks, finding the climate and soil similar to those of their homelands, planted vineyards here. Setúbal is known to have been an important fishing port since Roman times. Today it is an industrial town, a centre of shipbuilding, fish-canning, and the production of fertilisers, cement, salt and muscatel wine.

Setúbal's pride is the **Igreja de Jesus** (Tue–Sat 9am–12.30pm, 2–5.30pm), a spectacular monument dating back to 1491. The church was designed by Diogo Boytac, one of the founding fathers of the Manueline style of architecture. The narrow building has a high arched ceiling supported by six great stone pillars that look like coils of rope; its apse is etched with stone and lined with tiles. Arrábida marble was used, and the pebbled, multicoloured stone gives it a distinctive appearance. There are also lovely tiled panels along the walls. The cloister houses a museum, the **Museu de Setúbal** (same hours as the church), which contains religious art from the 15th to the 17th centuries.

Cooling fountains at the Praça do Bocage.

Palmela's castle-pousada.

Nearby is the **Praça do Bocage**, with palm trees and a statue honouring one of Setúbal's illustrious sons, 18th-century sonneteer, Manuel Barbosa du Bocage. Off the square stands the church of **São Julião** with a handsome Manueline doorway, built in 1513. The inside walls are decorated with 18th-century tiles showing fishing scenes and depicting the life of the saint.

Also of interest is the **Museu de Arqueologia e Etnografia** (Tue–Sat 9am–12.30pm, 2–5.30pm) with models depicting the main industries: fishing, farming and textiles.

Setúbal's harbour is fascinating, especially in the early morning, when brightly painted trawlers arrive loaded with fish. There is a continual show, as fishermen mend nets and work on their boats. Best of all is the lively fish auction.

Setúbal is the main point of departure for the peninsula of **Tróia** ㉑, a long, narrow spit jutting out into the Sado estuary. Ferry boats make the 20-minute crossing frequently in season. On the northern end of the peninsula there are apartment blocks, houses and a glamorous new resort. The Tróia Golf Club has an 18-hole course designed by Robert Trent Jones. On the southern end of the peninsula, however, there are still many kilometres of pine forest and glorious empty beaches and dunes. Tróia is said to be the site of the Roman town of **Cetóbriga** ㉒, destroyed by a tidal wave in the 5th century. Substantial ruins have been found at the nearby site but little has been excavated except for a temple and some tombs. Underwater, you may see remains of the walls of Roman houses.

Serra da Arrábida

A delightful excursion from Setúbal goes west through the **Parque Natural da Arrábida**, along the ridge of the Serra da Arrábida, which rises to 600 metres (2,000ft). As you leave the city, the only sight that mars the natural beauty of the coast is the cement factory, usually spitting black smoke. A road descends to **Portinho da Arrábida** ㉓, a popular bathing beach with transparent waters, white sand and the splendid **Gruta da Santa Margarida**. Hans Christian Andersen,

Enjoying the waves at Costa da Caparica.

COSTA DA CAPARICA

South of Lisbon is the city's playground: 8km (5 miles) of broad, sandy Atlantic beaches lined by acacia and eucalyptus trees, moderately priced hotels and cheerful fish restaurants. This popular stretch is cleaner than the Estoril/Cascais coast, and the currents are safer than those of the Atlantic north of the Tejo. The farther south you go, the less built-up the coastline becomes, lined with shady pine forests and dotted with ramshackle little cafés. Nude bathing is popular at the southern end.

During the summer a narrow-gauge railway service runs to the beaches. There are regular buses from Lisbon to Costa da Caparica town, or you can take the ferry to Cacilhas (from where there are buses to the town) from Cais do Sodré in Lisbon.

TIP

From Cetóbriga you could choose to return to Setúbal via Alcácar do Sal, a drive of some 120km (75 miles), though of course it is much quicker to take the inexpensive car ferry from Tróia; the downside is you may have to wait in a long queue in peak season.

who visited the region in 1834, marvelled in his diaries at this cave, with its imposing stalactites. But it was the poet and historian of the Peninsular War, Robert Southey (1774–1843), who consecrated Arrábida for English readers, calling it "a glorious spot". He tells of going swimming at the base of the mountain and writes: "I have no idea of sublimity exceeding it". Today, scuba diving is also popular here.

Regaining the ridge, continue along the skyline drive. The next turn-off leads to **Sesimbra ㉔**, a fine resort with a nearby port and a long fishing tradition. The **castle** (daily, daylight hours; free) above the village, although known as Moorish, has been entirely rebuilt since the time of the Moors. Afonso Henriques captured it in 1165, but the Moors utterly razed the structure in 1191. King Dinis almost certainly helped with the rebuilding, and King João IV again enlarged, enhanced and repaired it in the 17th century. Inside the walls are ruins of a Romanesque church.

João IV also ordered the fort of São Teodosio to be built, to protect the port from pirates. A newer fort, the

Sesimbra.

Nova Fortaleza on the seafront, now occupied by the police station, is at the heart of the town. Small bars and restaurants fill the streets around it and they are always full of appreciative customers at weekends. Swordfish is the local speciality.

Going westward about 11km (7 miles) the road ends at **Cabo Espichel ㉕**. This promontory, and the shrine of **Nossa Senhora do Cabo**, used to be an important pilgrimage site, as shown by the long rows of dilapidated pilgrims' quarters on either side of the church. There is still a fishermen's festival here each October, and on the edge of the high cliff is the small fishermen's chapel of Senhor de Bomfim, with a breathtaking view; the cliffs are wonderful for walking.

Olive tree village

The road back to Lisbon goes through **Vila Nogueira de Azeitão ㉖**, sometimes simply called Azeitão, which means "large olive tree". In the centre of this attractive village is the stately Palácio Távora, where the Duke of Aveiro and his friends are said to have

plotted to overthrow King José. They were burned at the stake in Belém in 1759. Lovely Baroque fountains border the town's main street. The Igreja São Lourenço has been restored and has beautiful 18th-century altars, paintings and tile panels.

The Azeitão fair, held in the central square on the first Sunday of the month, became so popular that it caused havoc and had to be moved to the outskirts of town. Less picturesque now, it is still a major attraction, offering everything from shoes and pottery to furniture, plus a large section devoted to livestock.

In the village is the original **José Maria da Fonseca Winery** ㉗ (tel: 212 197 500; www.jmf.pt; admission via pre-arranged tours), founded in 1834. The old family residence, which now houses a small museum, stands nearby. The winery still produces one of Portugal's best red table wines, the soft rich Periquita, as well as Setúbal's popular muscatel wines. Reservations should be made by calling the telephone number above to tour the factory and see its assembly-line production.

Not far from town stands one of the oldest inhabited manor houses in the country, the **Quinta da Bacalhoa**, built in 1480. It had fallen into ruins and was saved by an American woman from Connecticut, Mrs Herbert Scoville, who bought it in 1936. The **gardens** are admirable, with their clipped boxwood hedges in geometric design, orange and lemon groves, and a pavilion with beautiful tile panels. One of these tile scenes, showing Susanna and the Elders, is dated 1565, and is said to be the earliest known dated panel in Portugal.

The beautiful estate is now owned by the renowned Bacalhoa winery, and may be visited on an hourly pre-booked guided tour with tasting (Mon–Thu 9.30am–4.30pm, Fri 9am–11.30pm). Another attractive manor house, the **Quinta das Torres**, stands just outside the neighbouring village of **Vila Fresca de Azeitão**. This 16th-century *quinta*, decorated with tile panels and set in a romantic garden, has been converted into a cosy inn and restaurant. In the village, there is yet another lovely church, São Simão, with more ancient tiled walls and polychrome panels.

A local olive farmer.

The small town of Vila Nogueira de Azeitão.

Festival decorations in Tavira.

ALGARVE

Moorish arches drenched in sunshine and spectacular coves of golden sand: Algarve offers a touch of the exotic that attracts visitors by the million.

• Porto

Lisbon

I
f one region of Portugal stands alone, it is Algarve. Its history under long Moorish control, its climate – more typically Mediterranean – and its abundance of fine sandy beaches endow Algarve with a character so different that it could easily be taken as a separate country. In the minds of many visitors, it is.

Separated from the rest of Portugal by rolling hills, Algarve, the southernmost province, seduced the ancient Phoenicians with its abundance of sardines and tuna, which they salt-cured for export almost 3,000 years ago. Four centuries later, around 600 BC, the Carthaginians and Celts arrived, followed in turn by the Romans, who adopted the Phoenician practice of curing and exporting fish – the precursor of Portugal's large sardine tinning industry. They built roads, bridges and spas, such as that in Milreu.

But Algarve really blossomed under Moorish rule, which began in the early 8th century. The province's name comes from the Moorish *Al-Gharb*, meaning "The West". The Moorish period was one of vibrant culture and great scientific advances. Moorish poets sang of the beauty of Silves, its principal city, while the more practical settlers introduced orange crops, and perfected the technique of extracting olive oil, which is

still an important Portuguese product. The blossoming almond trees in January and February are one of the most beautiful sights of Algarve thanks, according to folklore, to the passion a Moorish king once felt for a northern princess.

Legend has it that the princess, pining for the snows of her homeland, slowly began to waste away. Distraught, the king ordered thousands of almond trees to be planted across the region, then one February morning carried her to the window

Main Attractions
Parque Natural da Ria Formosa
Ilha de Tavira
Praia da Rocha
Fortaleza de Sagres
Serra de Monchique
Castelo de Silves
Loulé market

Praia da Rocha.

where she saw swirling white "snow flakes" carpeting the ground – the white almond blossoms. She quickly recuperated, and the two lived happily ever after.

Moorish legacy

King Afonso Henriques led the Portuguese conquest southwards in the 12th century, and later his son, Sancho I, with the help of a band of crusaders, was to spearhead the siege of Silves and its estimated population of 20,000 people. It took 49 days before the Moors of Silves were forced to surrender. But in 1192 they reconquered the city and remained there for another 47 years. It was Sancho II, supported by military-religious orders under Paio Peres Correia, who finally crushed them. The last major city to fall was Faro, in January 1249.

The Arabic influence is visible even today: in many of the town names, in words beginning with the "al" prefix, in the so-called "North African blue" used for trimming the whitewashed houses, in the roof terraces used for the drying of fruit, and the

white-domed buildings still popular in many towns. Algarvian sweets made of figs, almonds, eggs and sugar called *morgados* or *Dom Rodrigos* are yet another reminder of the area's ancient heritage.

For centuries almond, fig, olive and carob trees represented a major part of Algarve's agriculture, as they are suited to dry inland areas. The carob, whose beans are now fed to cattle but which also produce a variety of oil, are said to have sustained the Duke of Wellington's cavalry during the Peninsular War. Thanks to the gentle climate, Algarve also produces pears, apples, quinces, loquats, damask plums, pomegranates, tomatoes, melons, strawberries, avocados and grapes.

Regional specialities

Wine critics regard all Algarve wines as undistinguished, and even in quite modest restaurants the house wine is usually from the better Alentejo range or perhaps from even further to the north. But many local wines are quite palatable and should not be written off completely.

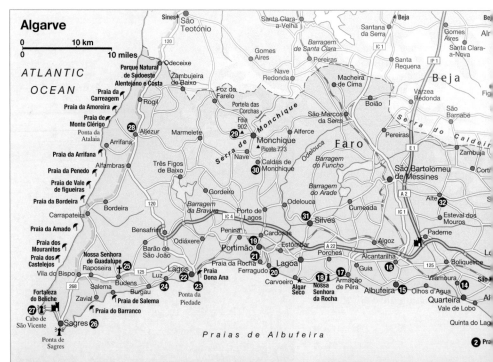

You will find good beer, the preference of most young Algarvios, widely available. Older men passing the time in tavernas and *tascas* drink *medronho*, a clear firewater with the kick of a mule, distilled from the fruit of the strawberry tree, *Arbutus unedo*. Another individual drink in Algarve is *Brandymel,* a type of honey brandy.

The pleasant market town of Loulé (see page 201), with its central tree-shaded walkway, is the crafts centre of Algarve, but local handicrafts are widely sold everywhere. Among them are baskets, hats, mats and hampers of rush or straw, which are made by local women who pick and dry the esparto grass in spring, then shred it into thin strips before they weave and plait it. You will see mats of grass, and of cotton and wool (although some of those on sale come from Alentejo). Cane basketry is almost always the work of men in the eastern towns of Odeleite, Alcoutim and Castro Marim. Despite the modern prevalence of cardboard boxes, baskets are still used to carry eggs, to display golden smoked sardines, and as fish traps.

Lagos, Loulé and Tavira – as well as numerous stores along the main N125 highway – are good places to find pottery, from big pitchers, plant pots, hand-painted plates and tiles, to the distinctive, lace-like chimney tops that embellish Algarve's skyline. You will find a considerable range of copper pots and bowls – one such shop is on a street corner beside the market in Loulé. If you walk down the avenue you will see – and hear – coppersmiths at work in tiny workshops.

Woodwork is also a regional craft, from spoons made in Aljezur, to the brightly coloured mule-drawn carts you still see on the roads. Handmade lace is a skill that is being kept alive in such places as Azinhal. Up in the hills of Monchique (where a small craft shop has grown to an extensive display) you will find wooden furniture and woollen weaves.

Faro, the capital city of the Algarve region is a popular destination.

Ilha de Tavira rescue equipment.

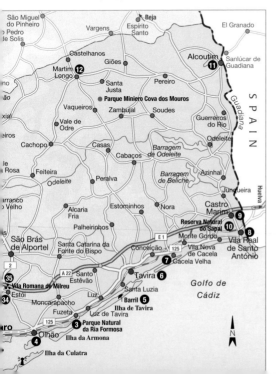

Key routes and places

The southern coastline, so richly endowed with golden sandy beaches in spectacular settings, is the region's prime asset. At the onset of mass tourism in the 1960s it attracted developers, and much of the central region, around Albufeira, is now well developed. Those looking for smaller, quieter coastal resorts can still find them by travelling out to the west beyond Lagos and, to a lesser extent, east of Faro. Inland Algarve has its share of pretty villages and remains largely unspoilt countryside, although it is rapidly becoming the preferred dormitory area for expatriate settlers.

Driving around Algarve is not difficult. The N125 travels the length of the coast, while the A22 motorway (tolls payable) shadows it just inland. It is possible to drive from Spain in the east to Sagres in the west in a little over two hours.

Faro: the hub of Algarve

An old building in the town of Faro is lit up at night.

The roots of **Faro ❶**, the capital of Algarve, are ancient but not well documented, although it is certain that it was used by Greeks and Romans as a trading post before it became a flourishing Moorish town. Largely devastated by the 1755 earthquake, the city now has an architectural hotchpotch of styles and eras.

The centre of Faro is walkable, its character changing as you wander through streets of tiny houses, 19th-century mansions, modern villas and shops. It's a bustling capital and has considerable charm. The main pedestrianised street, Rua de Santo António, is in the middle of the Moorish quarter (Mouraria), which lies between the old city (Vila-Adentro) and the 19th-century Bairro Ribeirinho, all of which lead from the port.

On the south side of the little harbour, through the 18th-century Arco da Vila that penetrates the old city walls, lies a peaceful and historic inner town, the Vila Adentro. At its centre is the Renaissance **Sé** (Cathedral; Apr–Sept Mon–Fri 10am–6pm Oct–Mar Mon–Fri 10am–5pm, Sat all year-round 10am–1pm) with its 13th-century tower. Eighteenth-century polychrome tiles are an impressive

feature in its chapels as well as in the body of the church. The red chinoiserie organ is also 18th century, and the choir stalls are a notable trophy from Silves Cathedral, installed when the seat of the diocese was moved to Faro in the 16th century.

In the square behind the cathedral a former convent with strikingly beautiful Renaissance cloisters is now the **Museu Municipal** (Apr–Sept Tue–Fri 10am–7pm, Sat–Sun 11.30am–6pm, Oct–Mar Tue–Fri 10am–6pm, Sat–Sun 10.30am–5pm), with a selection of Roman mosaics and stonework from Faro and from the important Roman site at Milreu, 12km (7 miles) to the north (see page 201).

On Praça da Liberdade, the **Museu Regional do Algarve** (Mon–Fri 10am–1.30pm, 2.30–6pm) displays some interesting relics of Algarve peasant life.

Beside the harbour, in the Port Authority building in the Bairro Ribeirinho, the **Museu Marítimo** (Maritime Museum; Mon–Fri 2.30–4.30pm) is worth a visit to see the broad range of Algarve fishing methods. Among the exhibits are model boats and a vivid depiction of the old way of trapping tuna in the bloody "bullfight of the sea".

Faro's most bizarre and macabre sight is the **Capela dos Ossos** (Chapel of Bones), reached through the Baroque Igreja do Carmo with its impressive facade and twin towers. The little chapel was built in 1816, its walls entirely covered with bones and skulls (allegedly 1,245 of them) from the church cemetery. Some find this grim display of mortality less depressing than the high-rises that contrast with the church's fine facade.

Lighthouse and lagoon

Faro is protected on the seaward side by a huge lagoon dotted with sandbanks, with the airport on the western edge. Some of the sandbanks are large, especially the outer barrier islands, and the southernmost point is marked by the Cabo de Santa

Maria lighthouse (*faro* means lighthouse in Portuguese).

The sand spit that starts near the airport and extends out as a long crescent, Ilha de Faro, can be reached by car and is the location of **Praia de Faro ❷**, a sandy resort much loved by the local people. Ilha da Culatra is the only other inhabited sand spit and can only be reached by ferry from Olhão. The whole of this natural lagoon and the adjacent area, stretching some 50km (30 miles) from Ancão in the west to Cacela in the east, has been protected since 1987 as the **Parque Natural da Ria Formosa ❸** (see margin tip for visitor centre details). This lagoon system provides 90 percent of Portugal's harvest of clams and oysters. It is also an important bird sanctuary, especially for waders such as egrets and oystercatchers, and some rare species, including the purple gallinule.

East of Faro

Travelling eastwards out of Faro takes you to the busy 17th-century town of **Olhão ❹**, built in the Moorish style, with a large fishing port. On the

TIP

Get a taste of the Parque Natural da Ria Formosa at the park headquarters (Centro de Educação Ambiental de Marim) at Quelfes, 3km (2 miles) east of Olhão (tel: 289 704 134; www.icnf.pt/portal). The park combines lagoons, marsh and islands and is great for birdwatching, as well as harbouring other rare creatures such as the European chameleon.

The exterior of Faro's Igreja do Carmo.

Fishing boats prepare in the early morning in the port town of Tavira.

Tavira garden.

seafront by the leisure boats' pontoons are the town's modern (1998) market halls. Arrive at the fish market early and be prepared to use your elbows to reach the slithery hills of fish that the women hawk at the tops of their voices, poking them to prove their freshness. The best buys are gilt-head bream *(dourada)*, bass *(robalo)* and sole *(linguado)*. The other halls sell fruit and vegetables.

If you are not catching the ferry out to beautiful Culatra beach, move on to **Fuzeta**, where there is a sandy beach and a boat that can take you out to uninhabited **Ilha da Armona** (summer ferries also run here from Olhão) for a spot of sunbathing. Almost next door to Fuzeta is Pedras del Rei, the starting point for an exciting little journey by train over to the beach of **Barril ⑤** on the Tavira sandbank, the Ilha de Tavira. There is a footpath by the track, should the train be full.

A café or restaurant along the broad palm-lined promenade of **Santa Luzia,** a colourful fishing village overlooking the lagoon, is the place to sit and watch the fishermen stacking up encrusted octopus pots *(alcatruzes)* after removing their catch.

Tempting Tavira

One of the larger towns on the eastern side, **Tavira ⑥** is a delightful spot that has avoided the excesses of development and lost none of its grace. It elegantly borders both sides of the Rio Sequa, which becomes the Gilão as it slides under the seven-arched Roman-style bridge, the Ponte Romana, towards the sea. With its estuary and outlying island, Tavira flourished in the 16th century. But trade dwindled as the fish disappeared, and this lovely town, composed of narrow streets, pastel-coloured patricians' houses, miniature towers, domes, unusual four-sided roofs and minarets, today leads a quieter life.

There are more than two dozen churches and chapels in Tavira, of which the most interesting are the **Igreja da Misericórdia**, built in 1541 but remodelled after the 1755

earthquake, with some lovely *azulejo* decorations; and the church of **Santa Maria**, rebuilt on the site of the town's old mosque. Many of the churches are closed, but information about access to the major ones, as well as maps of the area, is available from the tourist office, to be found up the steps from the town hall in the main square.

A short ferry journey from the town will take you to the long white beaches of **Ilha de Tavira**, an unspoilt paradise (see box page 193).

Atmospheric fortified hamlets where time appears to have stood still are not what you expect to find along the southern coast of Algarve, but there is one at **Cacela Velha** ❼. It has a miniature 18th-century fortress and a gleaming white church. The whole village clings tightly to a perch looking over a lagoon.

The border with Spain is reached at the Rio Guadiana. Facing Spain is **Vila Real de Santo António** ❽, its grid of geometric streets bearing the stamp of the Marquês de Pombal – the man who was responsible for redesigning old Lisbon in the 18th

century. Pombal intended this town to be a model administrative, industrial and fishing centre, and he founded the Royal Fisheries Company here, but he lost favour with the court, and his plans never really took off. All the same, fishing remains an important activity.

Just west of Vila Real is the largest touristic development this side of Faro, **Monte Gordo**. The clutch of high-rise buildings lining broad tree-lined streets and overlooking a vast flat beach as yet remains fairly compact.

Moors, mines and marshlands

Further inland along the Guadiana lies the architecturally appealing **Castro Marim** ❾. This little town is also one of the oldest and historically most important areas of Algarve. Once a major Phoenician settlement, it also played host to the Greeks and Carthaginians before the Moors and Romans invaded. Portugal's kings

Locals and visitors alike enjoy the beach at Ilha de Tavira.

Castro Marim.

later used it as a natural point from which to fight the infidel to the east.

The huge castle built by King Afonso III after he dispelled the Moors in 1249 is still standing, overlooking the surrounding valley. In 1319, it was the first headquarters of the Order of Christ. The fort on the hill opposite dates from 1641.

Surrounding the town is the Castro Marim fen or marsh, wetland home of many migratory birds including storks, cranes and flamingos, and a hundred different species of plant life. An area of 2,000 hectares (5,000 acres) is now protected as the **Reserva Natural do Sapal** .

Among the least-travelled routes in Algarve is the peaceful road along the Rio Guadiana. It is a soothing meander through golden, furze-covered hills dotted with corks, olive and fig trees. (Road numbers are N122 and 1063 for the riverside drive.) **Alcoutim** ⓫ is the northernmost Algarve town, and here it often seems as if time has stood still. Sunning dogs in the only square in town have priority, so you will have to park around them.

From the promenade that extends along the edge of the Guadiana River you can see the nearby Spanish town of **Sanlucar de Guadiana** reflected in the slow-moving water. Signs to the "castle" are a little misleading, as they lead to an empty shell of walls – but the view from here is worth the short walk.

An inland return route will take you through **Martim Longo** ⓬, where it is possible to make a diversion to the open-air copper mine at Vaqueiros, now transformed into the **Parque Cova dos Mouros** (http://minacova mouros.sitepac.pt; possible to join visiting groups if you call ahead), with a Neolithic settlement, gold prospecting and donkey rides. Continue through Cachopo to reach Faro.

West of Faro

The coastal route out to the west heads towards the main area of tourist development and to some of the most picturesque beaches. First stop outside Faro is at **São Lourenço** ⓭ for the small 18th-century church of the same name. Inside it is tiled, from top

The beach at Albufeira.

to bottom, in beautiful blue *azulejos* (tiles) depicting the life and martyrdom of São Lourenço himself.

Nearly all the well-known golf courses, more than 30 of them, lie west of Faro, each one an exclusive development with luxury accommodation (see page 368). Among them are Quinta do Lago, Vale do Lobo, which has a 16th hole, originally a famous seventh, above a coastal ravine, and Vila Sol at **Vilamoura** ⓮. They take up a huge area on the edge of the Ria Formosa reserve, presenting a neat face of colourful flowerbeds and well-manicured lawns.

Just to the west of Vilamoura is the small resort and fishing village of **Olhos d'Agua**. The bonus here is that it is too small to attract the large tour operators. Tucked into a small cleft, the fishing village is as picturesque as any in Algarve, with sculptured rock stacks decorating the beach.

Albufeira

Once a small fishing village favoured by the Romans and the Moors, **Albufeira** ⓯ today is enduringly pretty,

but also overwhelmingly touristy – rather like the Algarve version of the Costa del Sol in Spain – but has retained its character slightly better than some other Algarve resorts. It has a lively nightlife, scores of noisy bars, plenty of restaurants ranging from pizza joints to those serving more typical regional fare, and late-night discos. The steep streets descending into the old part of town are still very attractive, as are the rock-protected beaches where the fishermen keep their boats, traditionally painted with large eyes to ward off evil, as well as with stars and animals.

There is a bustling fish market near the Pescadores (fishermen's) beach and a fruit, meat and vegetable market in the main square. Although development has been intense in this region, the coast westwards is a delightful symphony of eroded cliffs, stacks, gullies, grottoes and arches reaching a crescendo at Lagos. It is still possible to follow your nose and divert off to quiet beaches.

Whichever route you take towards the west, it is likely you will end

Albufeira beach rock formations.

A street corner in Lagos.

Albufeira slopes down to the sea.

up in **Alcantarilha** . It's worth a stop here if only to look in on the parish church, and especially the Capela de Ossos around the corner, which is packed with a chilling array of skulls. For family fun, visit nearby **Aqualand** (www.aqualand.pt; daily June 10am–5pm, July–6 Sept 10am–6pm; advance tickets can be purchased online), a large water park, with chutes and slides aplenty. Head south from here into **Armação de Pêra** . This mundane resort is rescued by an attractive promenade and beach, and it is a good place to eat fish.

All the grandeur and cragginess return to the coastline here and it is quite a descent to reach the beach at **Rocha da Pena**. Sitting on a bluff between two sandy coves is the simple white church of **Nossa Senhora da Rocha** , dedicated to fishermen. Inland from here is **Porches**, which is famous for its painted pottery.

At the next roundabout on the N125 is **Lagoa**, increasingly commercial and with a lively morning market. This is also where farmers bring their grapes to the central cooperative wine cellar. A left turn at this roundabout leads down to Carvoeiro, a craggy coastline of isolated beaches, like that of Algar Seco. **Praia de Carvoeiro** which is a lively tourist spot itself, ha a pleasant little beach framed by cliff studded with villas.

Portimão (once a Roman harbour, Portus Magnus) lies west of Carvoeiro. An important fishing port, it is also one of the best shopping towns on the coast. Built on the west bank of the Arade estuary Portimão is famous for its grilled sardines – have lunch beside the river to try some – and for its pastry shops. Facing it is the pretty fishing village of **Ferragudo** , with cobbled streets, pavement cafés and a good fish market. Close by is ocean fronted **Praia da Rocha** , which has a superb, much-photographed beach characterised by strange towering rock formations standing in the blue-green sea. The town itself however, is a bit of a concrete jungle although it does have all the facilities that visitors could ask for.

Lagos

Moving west from here you will come to **Lagos** ㉒, with a fine maritime tradition and a safe harbour beside a river estuary. Founded by the Carthaginians, it was taken by the Romans in the 5th century BC, when it was called *Lacobriga* (Fortified Lake). The Moors took it over in the 8th century and renamed it *Zawaia* (Lake). The city finally fell to the Portuguese during the reign of Afonso III. In 1434 Gil Eanes left from Lagos and became the first sea captain to round Cape Bojador, off northwest Africa, south of the Canary Islands – which was then the limit of the known world.

Most of Lagos was rebuilt in the 18th century, but some evidence of its darker past still stands in the columns and semicircular arches of Portugal's first slave market in the **Praça da República**. Nearby stands a statue of Henry the Navigator, who sent ships from here off into the unknown. Note, too, the modern monument by João Cutileiro recording King Sebastião's departure to the disastrous battle of Alcácer-Quibir in 1578.

A walk through the city's attractive streets will lead you to the **Igreja de Santo António**, on the outside a sober-looking church, but inside an extraordinarily beautiful example of gilded carving. The nave has an impressive painted wooden barrel vault and Baroque paintings on the walls.

The church can only be visited through the **Museu Municipal** (Tue–Sun 10am–6pm), which has a delightful collection of exhibits on local life in Algarve. Its eclectic collection of local finds, dating from the Bronze Age and Roman times, is layered over with fascinating glimpses of local life, and though the layout may at first seem old-fashioned, it is one of the most intriguing museums in the country.

Lagos has several pretty coves and beaches, especially **Praia Dona Ana**. Don't miss the rock formations at **Ponta da Piedade** ㉓. From the foot of the cliffs you might also hire a boat from a local fisherman to explore the grottoes, with their cathedral-like natural skylights.

Beyond Lagos lie three relatively unspoilt fishing villages, each of a different character and each worth a visit. **Luz** ㉔ is the first of these, and perhaps the most developed, and is followed by **Burgau** and **Salema**. The countryside changes drastically, particularly after Salema, to a rockier and more undulating landscape. The trees look smaller and squatter, permanently bent from the unrelenting wind. Improved roads make driving in this area easier than it once was, but the new road actually bypasses the Knights Templar church of **Nossa Senhora de Guadalupe** ㉕, where Henry the Navigator is said to have worshipped. It is easier to spot it when travelling west and to visit it on the return.

Sagres

Sagres ㉖ is a small fishing town, with Baleeira Bay as its port. The

FACT

It was to Sagres that seafarers returned in 1419 with the news that they had discovered an uninhabited island they called Porto Santo, which was later found to be part of the Madeiran archipelago.

The lighthouse guards the coast at Cape São Vincente.

The Serra de Monchique.

attraction to visitors is **Fortaleza de Sagres**, the fortress at **Ponta de Sagres**, used by Henry the Navigator early in the 15th century. He invited the most renowned cartographers, astronomers and mariners of his day to work here, and thus formed a fund of knowledge unsurpassed at the time, although modern historians believe he did not found a formal School of Navigation. Nothing that Prince Henry built is left, so it is hard to be sure. But you can see clues – notably a huge, 43-metre (140ft) compass rose on the stone ground of the fortress. There is a modern exhibition hall and tourist facilities in the fort, and a 1km (0.5-mile) walk along the top of the cliff.

All that remains now is to continue driving through this windswept terrain passing the small Fortaleza de Beliche, now a small *pousada* and restaurant, to reach **Cabo de São Vicente** ㉗, known to ancient mariners as *O Fim do Mundo*, the End of the World. From within the walls enclosing the lighthouse you can look down upon St Vincent's rocky throne.

Legend has it that in medieval times Christian followers of the martyred St Vincent defied the Moors and buried his body on the cape, with a shrine to honour him. Sacred ravens were said to have maintained vigil over the spot and over the ship that carried the bones of the saint to Lisbon. Here, even on a calm day, waves crash against the cliffs with spray-tossing violence. In spring, the smell of the sea competes with the scent of cistus, the rock-rose bush whose perfumed leaves were once supposedly used by the Egyptians for embalming.

The wild west coast

Algarve's west coast is virtually a continuous vista of cliff and sand, frequently pounded by a restless ocean and almost constantly under surf and spray. Although there are endless beaches, there are few towns of significance. **Odeceixe**, the most northerly town on this stretch of Algarvian coastline, is a small Moorish-style, windmill-topped village. A road follows the river for 3km (2 miles) to a beautiful sandy beach beneath towering cliffs at Praia de Odeceixe.

The most popular west coast circuit starts from Cabo de São Vicente and continues north through the vast, dune-backed Carrapateira to the attractive village of **Aljezur** ㉘. The 10th-century castle was the last to be taken from the Moors. Directly to the west are the great sweeps of the **Monte Clérigo** and **Arrifana** beaches, the best on this coast. Heading inland from Aljezur towards Monchique leads back into the heart of Algarve.

Mountains and springs

Towering above rolling hills, the granite mountains of **Serra de Monchique** attract streams of visitors to enjoy the views from the summit. In spring, Monchique is covered in flowering mimosa, and wild flowers bloom in the valleys between the Fóia and Picota peaks. **Fóia** ㉙ is the highest point of Algarve, reaching 902 metres (2,960ft) above sea level. It is easily accessible along a winding road lined with cheerful restaurants selling roast chicken. The summit is heavily forested with transmitter aerials and the promised views are revealed only on clear days. Picota (774 metres/2,539ft) presents a different challenge and can be reached only on foot.

The town of Monchique is rather disappointing if you merely drive through, but park the car and walk the steep streets and you get a better feel for the place. Worth visiting is **Caldas de Monchique** ㉚, off to the right heading south, hidden in a deep valley and surrounded by chestnut, cork, pine, orange and eucalyptus trees. The spa has been in use since Roman times and the waters are believed to cure a number of ailments, from convulsions to rheumatism. The springs pour out an estimated 20 million litres (4 million gallons) of water a year.

Rural villages

Descending from the heights, but away from the coastal tourist zone, a more rural lifestyle is found in the towns and villages. Here, locals have managed to shrug off the effects of regular visitors and continue their

A splash of spiky green at Silves.

A bridge leads to the town of Silves in Algarve.

One of the domes of Loulé's market halls.

The Cathedral in Silves was formerly a mosque.

traditional ways. One of the most interesting places is **Silves** ③①, between Albufeira and Portimão. Silves was already populated by the 4th century BC and reached its greatest splendour under the Moors, who made it the capital of Algarve.

In its glory days Silves was the home of some of the greatest Arab poets. They recorded its ruin when the city fell to Portugal's King Sancho I in 1189: "Silves, my Silves, once you were a paradise. But tyrants turned you into the blaze of hell. They were wrong not to fear God's punishment. But Allah leaves no deed unheeded," wrote one. Two years later the Moors occupied Silves again, before it was finally reconquered by the Portuguese.

Yemenite Arabs built the walled city, but the **castle** (daily May–Sept 9am–7pm, Oct–Apr 9am–5.30pm) – atop a Roman citadel, itself built on Neolithic foundations – and the defensive towers were rebuilt in the later Almohad period (12th–13th centuries) and

heavily restored in modern times. The Moorish castle and the Christian cathedral dominate the city, the dark-red sandstone contrasting with the soft pinks and faded blues of the older surrounding houses. A sense of history still permeates Silves and the castle.

The Moorish cistern to the north once supplied the city's water, and is architecturally similar to 13th-century cisterns found in Palestine and in Cáceres, Spain. Built by both the Romans and the Moors, the advanced irrigation system transformed Algarve into the garden of Portugal.

The **Sé** (Cathedral; Mon–Sat 9am–1pm, Mon–Fri 2–6pm) is 13th-century Gothic, restored in the 14th century and almost destroyed by the earthquake of 1755. Its apse is decorated with square arches, pyramidal battlements and fanciful gargoyles. The inner chapel of João de Rego dates from the 1400s. Various tombs here are said to be those of crusaders who helped capture Silves from the Moors in 1244. Here, too, for four years lay the remains of João II, who died in nearby Alvor in 1495, aged 40 – from dropsy, according to some doctors, from poisoning according to others.

From Alte to Estói

Northeast of Albufeira on the N124 is **Alte** ③②, a graceful village lying at the foot of hills and huddled around its parish church. Nossa Senhora da Assunção dates from the 16th century and has magnificent 18th-century tile panels. The tiles in the chapel of Nossa Senhora de Lurdes, among the best in Algarve, are of 16th-century Sevillian origin. Alte is a typical village of the province with its simple houses, delicate white laced chimneys, and timeless serenity.

A nearby stream has transformed the area into an oasis amid the region's arid landscape. It's a lush garden of oleanders, fig and loquat trees and rose bushes. The blue-and-white tile panels at Fonte Santa (Holy Fountain) are inscribed with verses by a

local poet, Cândido Guerreiro. This area is perfect for picnics, or a walk up the Pena hill where you can visit the **Buraco dos Mouros** (Moors' Cave). Further up the mountain is the **Rocha dos Soidos**, a cave filled with stalactite and stalagmite formations.

Heading back towards Faro you reach **Loulé 33**, a small town whose old quarter – Almedina – is a maze of narrow streets, reminiscent of a North African casbah. The interior of the chapel of Nossa Senhora da Conceição (near the tourist office) is tiled with attractive 17th-century *azulejos*, and the Igreja da Misericordia has a fine Manueline doorway.

One of Loulé's greatest attractions is the Saturday **market**, held in the onion-domed market halls, selling food of every kind, from home-grown fruit to live chickens. It draws visitors in from all over the Algarve. Loulé also has an extremely lively carnival in February, one of the best in the country.

Take a very slight detour east before you reach Faro and you will come to **Estói 34**, a pleasant village with a fine parish church, but best known for its 18th-century **Palácio dos Condes de Carvalha**, which has been turned into a luxurious *pousada*. The highly ornamental gardens of this "Queluz of the south", with their statues and rococo fountains, and a splendid tiled staircase, are well worth seeing.

The town has a huge market – more of a country fair, held on the second Sunday of the month. It is a lively affair where you can buy a horse, sell a few sheep, stock up with fruit and vegetables or just buy sugared cakes to eat as you mingle with the crowds.

Vila Romana de Milreu

Close by is the Roman **Vila Romana de Milreu 35** (Tue–Sun Apr–Sept 9.30am–12.30pm, 2–6pm, Oct–Mar 9.30am–12.30pm, 2–5pm), a site discovered in the late 1800s. There are some lovely mosaics here, the remains of thermal baths, and a well-preserved villa dating from the 2nd century. The largest structure, a temple, was consecrated as a Visigothic basilica in the 3rd century.

A bronze statue of King Don Sancho in Silves.

The interiors of Palácio dos Condes de Carvalha.

ALGARVE ON A PLATE

Heaps of crustaceans, and other seafood, fresh-from-the-sea fish, eel and octopus are major elements of Algarve's culinary specialities, but it is also a region that is rich in fresh fruit and vegetables, ripened in the baking sunshine of the south. A much-loved dish is *amêijoas na Cataplana*, clams cooked in a copper pan of Arab origin, but other delights include slow-grilled sardines, sea bream or red mullet, razor clams or octopus, squid cooked in its ink, and bean stew with whelks. The rolling wooded hills of the interior mean that game and pork dishes are on the menu too. You can also discern the Arabic influence on cuisine here, particularly through the local sweets, usually created using nuts and dried fruits from Algarve's orchards.

The countryside of the Alentejo.

ÉVORA AND ALENTEJO

The Romans left more than a few footprints here, and there are historic towns and castles around almost every corner. Alentejo is one of the country's grandest landscapes.

Alentejo, literally "beyond the Tejo" (the River Tagus), has a distinctive character and beauty unlike that of any other Portuguese province. Its vast plains, coloured burnt ochre in summer, are freckled with cork oaks and olive trees, which provide the only shade for the small flocks of sheep and herds of black pigs. Nicknamed *terra do pão* (land of bread) because it is covered with field upon field of wheat and oats, Alentejo supports acres of grape vines, tomatoes, sunflowers and other crops.

The largest and flattest of the Portuguese provinces, about the size of Belgium, Alentejo occupies one-third of Portugal's total area yet has only six percent of its population. It stretches from the west coast east to the Spanish border and separates Ribatejo and Beira Baixa in the central regions from Algarve in the south. The open countryside is punctuated by picturesque whitewashed towns and villages, many built on the low hills that dot the horizon.

Alentejo is rich in handicrafts. Rustic pottery with naive, colourful designs can be found everywhere. In addition, certain towns specialise in particular crafts or products: hand-stitched rugs come from Arraiolos, loom-woven carpets from Reguengos, cheese from Serpa, tapestries from Portalegre, and sugar plums from Elvas.

Painted chairs for sale in Alentejo.

Getting familiar

Geographically the province is split into two regions, Upper *(Alto)* and Lower *(Baixo)* Alentejo. Évora is the capital of the former and Beja of the latter. To the east are two low mountain ranges, the *serras* of São Mamede and Ossa. Some of the towns in these ranges, particularly Marvão, have breathtaking, even precipitous, settings. Portugal's third-longest river, the Guadiana, flows through the province and in places forms the border between Portugal and Spain. This is

Main Attractions

Templo Romano, Évora
Sé, Évora
Évoramonte
Paço Ducal, Vila Viçosa
Monsaraz
Marvão
Vila Nova de Milfontes
Mértola

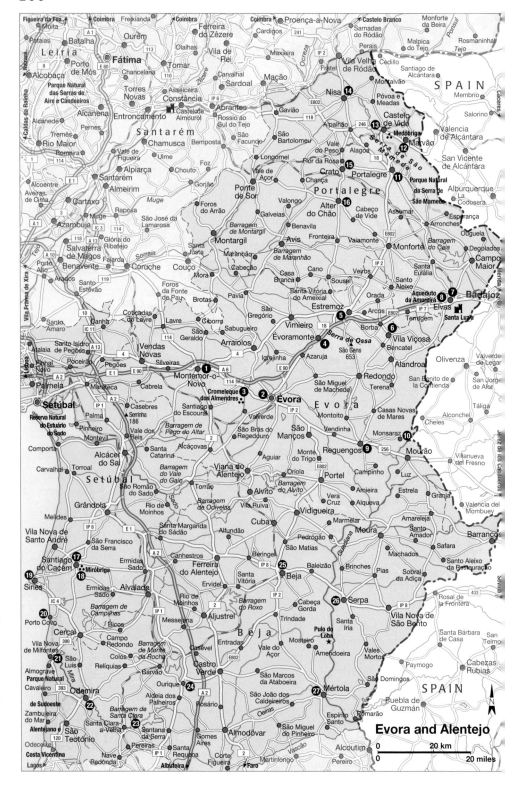

Evora and Alentejo

| 0 | 20 km |
| 0 | 20 miles |

by no means the only waterway, however. The region is criss crossed by a network of small rivers and dams.

Roads that connect the towns are excellent. Most of the traffic is local and slow moving. You will need to equip yourself with a reliable road map; signposting is limited, and without a map you could drive many kilometres before discovering you have taken a wrong turn.

The Portuguese in general are not renowned for their tidiness but the Alentejanos are the exception. The towns are litter-free and there is always a *dona de casa* in view whitewashing her already pristine home. Cool and simple is the theme for Alentejo architecture: low, single-storey buildings are painted white to deflect the sun's glare, and given a traditional blue or yellow skirting. Large domed chimneys indicate chilly winters. This practical style is followed from the humblest cottage to the large hacienda-style homes of the wealthy landowners; ornate and impressive architecture is reserved for cathedrals and churches.

Inland, Alentejo's temperature in the summer can reach inferno level: what little wind there is blows hot and dry from the continental landmass – no cooling sea breezes here. Temperatures can drop dramatically in winter, resulting in bitterly cold nights.

Alentejo's history

Alentejo is steeped in history, which goes back to the days of Roman colonisation. Later, it was the seat of the great landed estates *(latifundia)* of the Portuguese nobility and home to former kings. Even as late as 1828, Évora – the capital of the Alto Alentejo – was considered the second major Portuguese city, an honour that was first bestowed on it by King João I (1385–1433).

Estremoz, whose ancient castle has been converted into a comfortable *pousada*, was a nerve centre of medieval Portugal. Vila Viçosa was the seat

of the dukes of Bragança, whose royal dynasty began in 1640 with the coronation of João IV and ended in 1910 with the fall of the monarchy.

Politics, pastimes and popular song

Modern Alentejo is a far cry from the days of aristocratic domination, although farming techniques in the smallholdings have changed little. The greatest change is political: after the restoration of democracy in 1974 Alentejo became the heartland of Portuguese Communism. Many of the great estates – so vast that they included villages, schools and even small hospitals – were taken over by the farm workers during the revolution. Some of the landowning families were forcibly ejected, but the majority were absentee landlords anyway, living in properties nearer Lisbon or Porto. There is now a new landowning generation with a modern approach to agriculture and skilled at effective farm management.

Farming is the pulse of Alentejo, and the lives of its people revolve

FACT

To find out about the Rota dos Vinhos do Alentejo (www. vinhosdoalentejo.pt; Mon 2–7pm, Tue–Fri 11am–7pm, Sat 10am–1pm), visit the Alentejo Wine Route Support Office, at 20–1 Praça Joaquim António de Aguiar in Évora. There is a tasting room here as well so you can acquaint yourself with the region's different grape varieties.

Heading home from market.

TIP

Visit Arraiolos, 20km (12 miles) north of Évora, to see women at work on the town's famous hand-stitched carpets, based on Persian ones introduced in the 13th century. You can buy your own sample, large or small, to take home, and there's a fine pousada nearby if you want to stay over.

Lights decorate the Évora streetscape for Festa de São João.

around the seasons. Aside from Évora the towns are small and the population is scattered in hamlets linked to farms. Secondary schools are restricted to the larger towns; in the more remote areas the general practice among young people is to leave school early to work in the fields, or, as in so many rural regions, to head to the cities.

One of the main pastimes for menfolk is hunting birds, small prey or wild boar (today heavily controlled). During the season (roughly October to February) you will often see men out with their shotguns, pouches and a pack of dogs.

Singing and dancing are popular across the length and breadth of Portugal, and Alentejo does its share. Here, the folk songs are the domain of the men. These songs are slow, rather melancholic, but of a completely different style from the haunting fado that is heard elsewhere. A slow tempo is set by the stamping of the men's feet as they sing in chorus, swaying to the rhythm by the time they reach the end of the song. A performance is well

worth listening to; ask at an Alentejo tourist office about where to hear these songs, known as *ceifeiros*.

Évora, the capital of the Alto Alentejo, is the largest and the most important of all Alentejana towns. It is a superb city, full of fascinating sights, all of which are in a good state of preservation. Fortunately, they are likely to remain so, as the entire city has been proclaimed a World Heritage Site by Unesco.

It takes about two and a half hours to drive from Lisbon to Évora, and a tour could comfortably be managed as a day trip. But that would be a pity as it would not leave time to see the lovely towns and villages along the way. To base yourself in Évora is easy; there are plenty of small guesthouses and hotels.

The route from Lisbon

To reach Évora from Lisbon, cross the Tagus via the Ponte 25 de Abril and head south and east, bypassing Setúbal on the A6 (IP7). You will not need a welcome billboard to tell you when you reach the Alentejo; suddenly you will find yourself at the edge of the rolling plains. Look for the jumbled twigs on top of high chimneys and buildings – homes to the storks that flourish in the province. As you drive further inland you will also notice the waning breeze and the gradual increase in temperature.

Short detours off the main road lead to small Alentejo towns. **Pegões**, rather dry and dusty, is typical. Further along, **Vendas Novas** is shady and neat with an air of affluence.

Montemor-o-Novo ❶ can be seen from quite a long way off, its ruined medieval castle crowning its low *monte* (hill). The castle ramparts are thought to date from Roman times. The town is divided into the upper old town and lower new town. As you might expect, the old town is more interesting. It was here that St John of God (São João de Deus) was born in 1495. He was baptised in the parish church,

of which only the granite Manueline portal is still intact. In the square outside the church is a statue commemorating the saint, a Franciscan monk of great charity and humility. Although it does not have the population to support them, the town has five churches, three convents and two monasteries.

Évora: Alentejo's city

As you enter **Évora ②** on the main Lisbon road, there is a small tourist office just before the Roman walls, where you can pick up a street map marked with suggested walks that take in the most important sights. The best place to park is outside the walls, then walk to **Praça do Giraldo Ⓐ** at the centre of the city where the main tourist office is located (www.cm-evora. pt; daily May–Sept 9am–7pm, Oct–Apr 9am–6pm). This large square is arcaded on two sides and has a 16th-century church and fountain at the top. From here you can explore the inner city with ease.

The city's history can be traced back to the earliest civilisations on the Iberian peninsula. Évora derives its name from *Ebora Cerealis*, which dates from the Luso-Celtic colonisation. The Romans later fortified the city, renamed it *Liberalitas Julia*, and elevated it to the status of *municipium*, which gave it the right to mint its own currency. Its prosperity declined under the Visigoths, but was rekindled under Moorish rule (711–1165). Much of the architecture, with arched, twisting alleyways and tiled patios, reflects the Moorish presence. Évora was liberated from the Moors by a Christian knight, Geraldo Sem-Pavor (the Fearless), in 1165, in the name of Afonso Henriques I, Portugal's first king.

For the next 400 years Évora enjoyed great importance and wealth. It was the preferred residence of the kings of the Burgundy and Avis dynasties, and the courts attracted famous artists, dramatists, humanists and academics. Great churches, monasteries, houses and convents were also built. The splendour peaked in 1559, when Henrique, the last of the Avis kings (and also Archbishop of Évora), founded a Jesuit university. In 1580, following the annexation of Portugal by Spain,

Évora's Água de Prata Aqueduct was built in 1531–1537 by King João III and designed by the architect Francisco de Arruda, who previously built the Belém Tower.

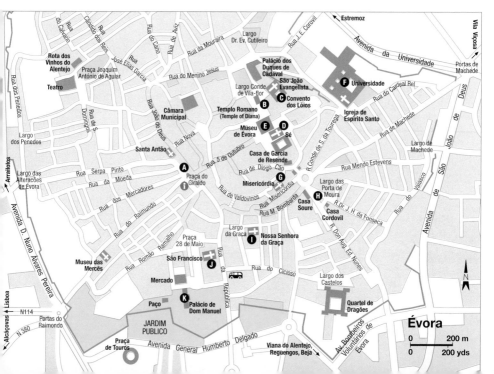

Inside the pousada in the old Convento dos Lóios.

Évora's glory waned. The Castilians paid little attention to it, except as an agricultural and trading centre, and even after Portuguese independence was restored in 1640, it did not regain its former brilliance.

Roman remains

The oldest sight in Évora is the **Templo Romano** ❸ (Temple of Diana), at the top of the lanes opposite the tourist office in Praça do Giraldo. It dates from the 2nd or 3rd century AD and is presumed to have been built as a place of imperial worship. The Corinthian columns are granite, their bases and capitals hewn from local marble. The facade and mosaic floor have disappeared completely, but the six rear columns and the four at either side are still intact. The temple was converted into a fortress during the Middle Ages, then used as a slaughterhouse until 1870, an inelegant role but one that nevertheless saved the temple from being torn down.

The ruins of a Roman temple – the temple of Diana – at Évora.

From a good viewpoint in the shady garden just across from the rear of the temple, you can look down over the lower town and across the plains: the tiny village of Evoramonte is just visible to the northeast. To the right of the temple is the **Convento dos Lóios** ❻ and the adjacent church of **São João Evangelista.** The convent buildings have been converted into an elegant *pousada* but the church is open to the public. Founded in 1485, its style is Romano-Gothic, although all but the doorway in the facade was remodelled after the 1755 earthquake. The nave has an ornate vaulted ceiling and walls lined with beautiful tiles depicting the life of St Laurence Justinian, archbishop of Venice, dated 1771 and signed by António de Oliveira Bernardes. The sacristy and wax room behind the altar contain paintings and part of the Roman wall, and beneath the nave you can see an ossuary and Moorish cistern. The church is privately owned, as is the neighbouring palace of the dukes of Cadaval, a wonderful building sometimes open for exhibitions.

The cathedral

The nearby **Sé** **D** (Cathedral; daily 9am–12.20pm, 2–4.50pm) is a rather austere building. Its granite, Romano-Gothic-style facade was built in the 12th century, while its main portal and the two grand conical towers – unusual in that they are asymmetric, with one tower adorned with glittering blue tiles – were added in the 16th century. Before going inside, take a close look at the main entrance, which is decorated with magnificent 14th-century sculptures of the Apostles. With three naves stretching for 70 metres (230ft), the cathedral has the most capacious interior in Portugal, and the vast broken barrel-vaulted ceiling is quite stunning.

Once you have seen the cathedral, it is worth paying the nominal sum to see the cloisters, choir stalls and **Museu de Arte Sacra** (Tue–Sun 9–11.30am, 2–4pm). The latter, in the treasury within one of the towers, contains a beautiful collection of ecclesiastical gold, silver and bejewelled plates, ornaments, chalices and crosses. The Renaissance-style choir stalls, tucked high in the gallery, are fashioned with a delightful series of wooden carvings with motifs both sacred and secular. From the choir stalls you get a good bird's-eye view of the cathedral. The marble cloisters are 14th-century Gothic, large and imposing, more likely to inspire awe than meditative contemplation.

Next door to the cathedral is the **Museu de Évora** **E** (Tue–Sun 10am–6pm), which has works by Josefa de Óbidos (1630–84), one of a small number of women painters of the time.

More Évora landmarks

At the old **Jesuit University** **F**, some elegant and graceful cloisters are visible. You have to follow a short road down to the east of the city to reach it. The marble of the broad cloisters seems to have aged not at all since the 16th century, and there is still the peaceful atmosphere of the serious academic.

The classroom entrances at the far end of the cloister gallery are decorated with *azulejos* representing each of the subjects taught. If you take a

TIP

If you're visiting Évora during the summer and want to cool off, go to one of the open-air municipal swimming pools (www2.cm-evora.pt/piscinasmunicipais) on the edge of town. Although well patronised because they are inexpensive, they are spotlessly clean, with plenty of lawn on which to stretch out and dry off.

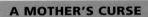

Carvings on the Cathedral in Évora.

A MOTHER'S CURSE

The church of São Francisco (see page 212) dating from the late 15th or early 16th century, has a remarkable chapel, the *Capela dos Ossos*. This bizarre and macabre room is entirely lined and decorated with the bones of some 5,000 people. It was created in the 16th century by Franciscan monks, when a large number of monastic cemeteries in the town were occupying valuable land. The skulls and bones have not merely been stored here in a random fashion; a lot of creative thought has gone into their placement. At the entrance you will see the inviting inscription: "*Nós ossos qui estamos, pelos vossos esperamos*" – "We bones lie here waiting for yours."

Most gruesome of all are the corpses of a man and a small child hanging at the far end of the chapel. These centuries-old bodies are said to be the victims of the curse of a dying wife and mother. Father and son were supposed to have made her life a misery and their ill-treatment eventually killed her. On her death bed she cursed them, swearing that their flesh would never fall from their bones. The corpses are far from fleshy, but there is plenty of leathery substance attached to their bones.

Braids of human hair dating from the 19th century are hung at the entrance of the chapel – votive offerings placed there by young brides.

Colourful, tranquil street, Évora.

The macabre Capela dos Ossos.

slow walk back up the hill and head for the Igreja São Francisco, you will pass by another church, the **Misericórdia G**, noted for its 18th-century tiled panels and Baroque relief work. Behind it is the Casa Soure, a 15th-century Manueline house that was formerly part of the Palace of the Infante Dom Luís.

As you walk along, have a good look at the houses. Nearly all of them have attractive narrow wrought-iron balconies at the base of tall rectangular windows. An odd tradition in Évora, as elsewhere in Portugal, is that visiting dignitaries are welcomed by a display of brightly coloured bedspreads hung from the balconies.

When you reach the Misericórdia church, take a brief detour to **Largo das Portas de Moura H**. The gates mark the fortified northern entrance to the city, which was the limit of construction and safety in medieval times. This picturesque square is dominated by a Renaissance fountain, which dates from 1556.

Heading west along the Rua Miguel Bombarda, keep an eye out for the church of **Nossa Senhora da Graça** ❶ (Our Lady of Grace), just off the Rua Miguel Bombarda. Built in granite, it is a far cry from the austerity of the cathedral. A later church (16th-century), its influence is strongly Italian Renaissance. Note the four huge figures supporting globes which represent the children of grace.

The most interesting thing about the **Igreja de São Francisco** ❶ is the **Capela dos Ossos** (daily 9am–12.45pm, 2.30–5.45pm; free; see page 211), but the chapterhouse is worth seeing too. It is lined with *azulejos* depicting scenes from the Passion and contains an *altar dos promessas* (altar of promises) on which are laid ex votos, wax effigies of various parts of the body given in thanks for cures. The church also has an interesting Manueline porch.

Évora's public gardens – the **Jardim Público** – near the church provide a very pleasant walk; if you're lucky you may catch the band playing on the park's old-fashioned wrought-iron bandstand. The delightful **Paláçio de Dom Manuel K** (1495–1521), or what

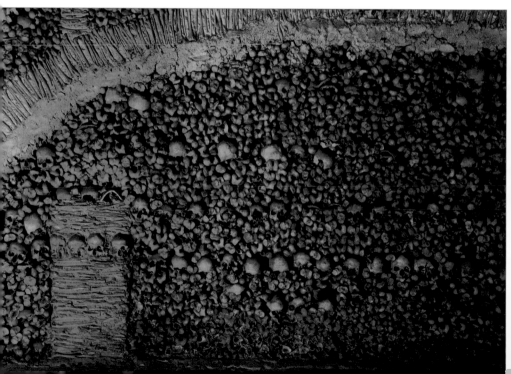

remains of it, stands in the park. It has paired windows in horseshoe arches, typical of the style that gained its name from Dom Manuel. Exhibitions are held in the long Ladies' Gallery.

If you're not intent on going inside Évora's monuments, a night stroll reveals its exterior architecture admirably. Nearly all the monuments are floodlit until midnight, and the winding narrow streets are extremely inviting on a balmy evening.

During the last week of June, Évora is filled with visitors who come to enjoy the annual **Feira de São João** (24–30 June). This huge fair fills the grounds opposite the public gardens. There's a local handicraft market, an agricultural hall, a display of local light industry, and the general hotchpotch of open-air stalls, as well as folk singing and dancing, and the restaurants serve typical local food.

Évoramonte and Estremoz

Alentejo has a number of megalithic monuments scattered across its plains, and some of the most important are just outside Évora (the tourist office will give you a map). The best preserved and most significant stone circle, or cromlech, on the Iberian peninsula is 12km (7 miles) west of the city. Close to the hill of Herdade dos Almendres, the **Cromeleque do Almendres ❸** has 95 standing stones.

Near to the agricultural department of the University of Évora in Valverde, just southwest of Évora, is the largest dolmen on the peninsula. The **Zambujeiro Dolmen** stands some 5 metres (17ft) high with a 3-metre (10ft) diameter and dates from about 3000 BC.

On the road from Évora to Estremoz lies **Évoramonte ❹**, a village at the foot of a 16th-century castle. It was here that the convention ending Portugal's civil war was signed on 26 May 1834. A commemorative plaque is placed over the house where the historic event took place. **Évoramonte Castle** perches high on a hill and offers remarkable views, well worth the clamber up to the top. Built in Italian Renaissance style with added Manueline knots, it grew out of a Roman fort.

Évoramonte Castle boasts fantastic views.

associated with King Dinis, whose residence it was in the 14th century. His wife, the saintly Queen Isabel of Aragon, is honoured by a statue in the main square, and a chapel dedicated to her can be seen in one of the castle towers (ask at the *pousada*).

The chapel is at the top of a narrow staircase; small, and highly decorated, it is where Isabel is said to have died, although some say that she died in the nearby King's Audience Chamber. The chapel walls are adorned with 18th-century *azulejos* and paintings depicting scenes from the queen's life. Behind the altar is a tiny plain room bearing a smaller altar, on which the Estremoz faithful have placed their *ex votos*, or offerings.

The most impressive part of the castle is the wonderful 13th-century keep, which is entered via the *pousada*. To get to the top you need to be fairly fit – or make a slow and steady ascent. The second floor has an octagonal room with trefoil windows. From the top platform there is a breathtaking view. The red rooftops contrast beautifully with the

Estremoz is famous for its pottery, which is on sale in shops all over town, and also at the Saturday market in Rossio, the main square of the lower town.

The castle in Estremoz.

Estremoz: steeped in history

About 22km (14 miles) northeast, in the centre of the marble-quarrying region, lies the lovely town of **Estremoz** ❺. Although much smaller than Évora, it has some fascinating monuments, and a pinky glow, courtesy of the local marble from which many buildings are constructed. The old part of town, crowned by a castle now converted into a *pousada*, was founded by King Afonso III in 1258, but is most often

whitewashed houses and the green plains beyond, much of which are planted with rows of olive trees.

Across the square from the *pousada* is King Dinis's palace. It must once have been a beautiful place, but all that remains standing after a gunpowder explosion in the palace arsenal in 1698 is the Gothic colonnade and star-vaulted **Audience Chamber**. It is used nowadays for exhibitions of work by local artists.

Having survived the narrow roads and hairpin bends on the drive up to the castle, the descent seems easy. The upper town is connected to the lower by 14th-century ramparts and modern buildings; the wrought-iron balconies are decorated with coloured tiles.

Estremoz is known for the small clay figures known as bonecas, which can be seen in the little municipal museum in Largo Dom Dinis.

If you like Portuguese wines then you may be familiar with the name Borba, where a cooperative produces a good red wine. The ancient village of **Borba** (about 11km/6 miles from Estremoz), which is said to date back to the Gauls and Celts, does not have much to show except for a splendid fountain, the Fonte das Bicas, built in 1781 from local white marble.

Vila Viçosa: the Braganças' base

Down the road from Borba is **Vila Viçosa ⑥**, the seat of the dukes of Bragança, an entire town built of shimmering white marble. Because the surrounding area is pocked by marble quarries, the usually expensive stone is in abundance. It is a place completely different in style from the Moorish-influenced towns perched on the hilltops. It is cool and shady, its large main square (Praça da República) is filled with orange trees, and elsewhere there are lemon trees and lots of flowers everywhere. Viçosa means lush, and its luxuriant boulevards are a pleasure to walk along.

A lovely, if rather overgrown, medieval **castle** overlooks the town square. It is very peaceful there, the only sound being the cooing of the white fantail doves that nest in the ramparts. The drawbridge is lowered

Old-fashioned street light in Estremoz.

The overgrown castle ruins at Vila Viçosa.

Alentejo is full of unexpected buildings such as this chapel transformed from what was once a mosque.

across the (dry) moat and the first floor has become a modest archaeological **museum** (Oct–Mar daily 9.30am–1pm, 2–5pm, Apr–Sept Tue–Fri 9.30am–1pm, 2.30–5.30pm, Sat–Sun to 6pm).

Vila Viçosa is best known for the **Paço Ducal** (the Ducal Palace of the Braganças; daily 10am–6pm), a three-storey building with a long facade, which is open to the public for guided tours. Its furniture, paintings and tapestries are very fine, and well worth seeing. The palace also contains an excellent collection of 17th- to 19th-century coaches.

The palace overlooks a square in which stands a bronze statue of João IV, the first king of the Bragança dynasty. To the north of the square is a striking gateway, the Manueline **Porta do Nó** (Knot Gate), a stone archway that appears to be roped together, and is part of the 16th-century town walls.

The medieval arches of Monsaraz.

From Elvas to Monsaraz

Heading east for about 28km (17 miles) from Estremoz, along the main road to the Spanish border, you will come to the strongly fortified town of **Elvas ❼**. Founded by the Romans, it was long occupied by the Moors and finally liberated from them in 1230 – about 100 years later than Lisbon. The town was of great strategic importance during the wars of independence in the mid-1600s. The fortress of **Santa Luzia,** south of town, was built by a German, Count Lippe, for the purpose of repelling the Spanish. The older castle above the town was originally a Roman fortress, rebuilt by the Moors and enlarged in the 15th century.

If you walk around the ramparts that once encircled the town you can't fail to be impressed by the effective engineering. The town itself is very attractive, from the triangular "square" of Santa Clara, with its 16th-century marble pillory, to the main Praça da República, with geometric mosaic paving.

The **Aqueduto da Amoreira ❽**, just outside the town, was designed

ALQUEVA DAM

The Alqueva dam on the Guadiana River, close to the Spanish border, is Europe's largest artificial lake, with a surface area of 250 sq km (96 sq miles). The idea was first mooted in 1957 under Salazar, but the controversial project stalled and was only completed in 2006. A Roman fort was encased in concrete before being submerged, and the village of Aldeia da Luz, which lay in the flood zone, was moved stone by stone and rebuilt. The commendable purpose of the dam project was to irrigate farmland, produce hydroelectric power, and provide a huge reservoir, but dams are rarely constructed without some destruction, and here the disadvantage was that waters submerged 160 rocks covered with Stone Age drawings and flooded the habitats of rare flora and fauna.

by a great 15th-century architect, Francisco de Arruda. Its 8km (5-mile) length and 843 arches took nearly 200 years to complete. The cost was borne by the people of Elvas under a special tax named the *Real de Agua*.

Handwoven rugs used to be manufactured throughout Alentejo, but nowadays the small town of **Reguengos 9** is the only place where they are still made, in a factory that has been using the same looms for the past 150 years. To reach it, return to Borba then travel south for about 60km (38 miles). Reguengos is a nucleus of megalithic stones and dolmens, found at several sites near the town, and is known for its wine.

About 16km (10 miles) northeast of Reguengos is the delightful walled town of **Monsaraz 10**, so small it can easily be explored on foot – leave your car at the gate. It was fortified by the Knights Templar when the Moors were the enemy. In time, Reguengos became more influential and Monsaraz less so, which helped it become the relaxed and peaceful village it is today. Its main street, Rua Direita, is all 16th- and 17th-century architecture, yet the town maintains a medieval atmosphere. In one Gothic house is a famous 15th-century fresco, an allegory on justice, *O Bom e o Mau Juiz* (The Good and the Bad Judge). From the ramparts there are great views over to the Alqueva dam.

Portalegre

The lush countryside that surrounds **Portalegre 11** is rather different from that in the low-lying lands. This area is in the foothills of the **Serra de São Mamede**, and the cooler and slightly more humid climate makes the landscape much greener. To get there, return to Estremoz and take the N18/E802 north – half of the route is now the IP2, a good road.

Quite a large town by Alentejo standards, Portalegre is unusual in that it is not built on top of a hill, but on the site of an ancient ruined settlement called Amaya. In the mid-13th century, King Afonso III issued instructions that a new city was to be built. He called it Portus Alacer: Portus for the customs gate which was

The Portalegre Avenue.

Marvão Castle offers spectacular views towards the Serra de São Mamede.

The white houses of Marvão.

to process Spanish trade and Alacer (*álacre* means merry) because of its pleasing setting. King Dinis ensured that the town was fortified in 1290 (although only a few of the ruined fortifications can be seen today) and João III gave it the status of a city in 1550.

The lofty 16th-century interior of the **Sé** (Cathedral; Tue 8.15am–noon, Wed–Sat 8.15am–noon, 2.30–6pm) is late-Renaissance in style. The side altars have fine wooden *retábulos* and 16th- and 17th-century paintings in the Italian style. The sacristy contains lovely blue-and-white *azulejo* panels from the 18th century, depicting the life of the Virgin Mary and the Flight to Egypt. The cathedral's facade is also 18th century, and is dominated by marble columns, granite pilasters and wrought-iron balconies.

Portalegre's affluence began in the 16th century, when its tapestries were in great demand. Continued prosperity followed in the next century with the establishment of silk mills. One tapestry workshop remains, the **Fábrica Real de Tapeçarias**, in the former Jesuit Monastery in Rua Fernandes, where looms are still worked by hand. Examples of the town's handiwork can be seen in the **Museu da Tapeçaria de Portalegre Guy Fino** (Tue–Sun 9.30am–1pm, 2.30–6pm), housed in an 18th-century mansion in Rua da Figueira.

Portalegre was home to one of Portugal's major writers: poet, dramatist and novelist José Régio (1901–69). His house has been opened as a museum. Of particular interest is his collection of regional folk art and religious works. Also of note is the 17th-century

Yellow Palace, where the 19th-century radical reformer Mouzinho da Silveira lived. The ornate ironwork here is quite remarkable.

Spectacular Marvão

Marvão ⑫ is one of the most spectacular sights of Alentejo. About 25km (15 miles) north of Portalegre, it is a medieval fortified town perched on one of the São Mamede peaks. Its altitude (862 metres/2,830ft) affords it an uninterrupted view across the Spanish frontier. The precipitous drop on one side made it inaccessible to invaders and an ideal defensive barrier.

At this height the land is barren and craggy. The seemingly impenetrable castle was built in the 13th century from the local grey granite. Clinging to the foot of the castle is the tiny village, just a few twisting alleyways flanked by red-roofed whitewashed houses. Close to the church of Espírito Santo, on the street of the same name, is a Baroque granite fountain. On the same street is the sober-looking Governor's House, its only decoration two magnificent 17th-century wrought-iron balconies.

On the road to Castelo de Vide are the ruins of the Roman settlement of **Medóbriga**. Many artefacts from here are now in Lisbon.

Castelo de Vide: fort and spa

Completing the triangle of noteworthy upper Alentejo towns is **Castelo de Vide ⑬**, a delightful town built in the shadow of an elongated medieval castle situated on the summit of a foothill on the northern *serra*. The town was originally a Roman settlement. Alongside it ran the major Roman road that traversed the Iberian peninsula. The settlement was sacked by the Vandals at the beginning of the 4th century, occupied by the Moors during their domination of the southern part of the peninsula, and eventually fortified by the victorious Portuguese in 1180.

Castelo de Vide is a spa town. You can drink its curative waters from plastic bottles, which are sold in the supermarkets, or sip from one of the numerous fountains located in and around the town. Perhaps its

Carrying greenery in the Jewish Quarter of Castelo de Vide.

The Fonte Da Vila, a 16th-century fountain in the historic town of Castelo de Vide.

prettiest outlet is the quadrangled, covered fountain (Fonte da Vila), set in the small square below the Jewish Quarter. The Baroque fountain has a pyramid roof supported by six marble columns. The central urn is carved with figures of boys, and the water spills from four spouts.

As in nearly all fortified Alentejo towns, Castelo de Vide has two very distinct faces. The first is the older one, situated next to the castle, and the most interesting and picturesque part of it is the medieval **Judiaria** (Jewish Quarter). This host of back alleys, cobbled streets and whitewashed houses is liberally splashed with green, as potted plants sprout their tendrils from every available niche, windowsill and step.

Notice the doors: this section of Castelo de Vide has the best-preserved stone Gothic doorways in Portugal. It also has the oldest synagogue, dating from the 13th century, although little remains of it now. The majority of the inhabitants of the neighbourhood appear to be elderly people who sit in the doorways of their homes calmly watching the world go by.

The picturesque Jewish Quarter in Castelo de Vide.

Further down the hill is the newer part of town: essentially 17th- and 18th-century buildings with wider, less steep streets, more space, more order and more elegance. On the main square, **Praça Dom Pedro V**, stand the grandiose 18th-century parish church and the old town hall, **Paços de Concelho**, remarkable for its huge 18th-century wrought-iron gate securing the main entrance.

Near the town you will find still more megalithic stones, including the 7-metre (22ft) Menhir da Meada. These *pedras talhas* seem to be everywhere, standing in fields, in open scrubland or in villages, inscrutable and ageless.

Portalegre's neighbours

Nisa ⑭ is a small, rather rambling town northwest of Castelo de Vide. It has the mandatory medieval castle, walls and an unusual squat, round-towered chapel. Home-made cheese is Nisa's speciality.

Some 24km (15 miles) south of Nisa on the road back to Estremoz is **Flor da Rosa**, where you may be able to buy local pots. But the most interesting place to see is the Convento de Flor da Rosa, dating from 1356 and founded by the Order of Knights Hospitallers of St John. An eclectic building, with a solid Gothic cloister, it was in use as a monastery right up until the end of the 19th century, and is now a pousada.

Two royal marriages took place in **Crato** ⑮, a couple of kilometres down the road. The first was that of Manuel I, who married Leonor of Spain in 1518 (his third marriage); the second was seven years later when King João III married Catarina of Spain. The main square is dominated by a splendid 15th-century stone veranda, the **Varanda do Grão-Prior**, which is all that survives of the priors' residence.

Some 13km (8 miles) further south, in countryside filled with olive groves, is **Alter do Chão** ⑯, a medieval town with equine traditions. It is from here that the Alter Real horse, closely related to the Lusitano breed, takes its name. The state-owned **Alter Stud Farm** (Coudelariade de Alter; tours mid-Sept–mid-May Tue–Sun 11.30am, 3pm, mid-May–mid-Sept 11.30am, 3.30pm) was founded in 1748 by José I (as he became two years later). Based on Andalusian stock, the animals thrived until the Napoleonic Wars when the best of them were stolen and the royal stables abolished. Happily, the breed, which excels in dressage, has been revived to a highly respected standard.

Unspoiled beaches

If you like unspoiled cliffs and beaches, quiet roads and villages, then you will delight in the Alentejo coast, although more and more tourists are discovering it. It borders on the open Atlantic and the ocean is therefore much rougher than on the south coast. There are plenty of sheltered bays for swimming, although the water is chilly.

Alentejo's coast is not renowned for its nightlife. Bars, discos and fancy restaurants hardly exist; nor do large hotels, except at Vila Nova de Milfontes. There are campsites, however, and all the villages have at least one *pensão*. You'd better bring along your phrase book. Where tourists are relatively few, so are local people who speak English.

Most people approach the coast from Lisbon, from where access is easy thanks to the extended motorway network. Heading south, the IP8 branches southwest just before Grândola to **Santiago do Cacém** ⓱, crowned by a castle built by the Knights Templar, which gives good views over the town and coast.

Anyone interested in things Roman should consider making a trip to nearby **Miróbriga** ⓲ (Tue–Sat 9am–12.30pm, 2.30–5.30pm, Sun 9am–noon, 2.30–5.30pm). This Iron Age

and Roman site is quite extensive and has been well excavated. There is also an interesting little Museu Regional nearby, concentrating mainly on the local cork industry.

Now it's just a short hop to Alentejo's largest coastal town, **Sines** ⓳, which is famous for being the birthplace of Vasco da Gama in 1460. It's not what you would call a beauty spot. The old part and the harbour are still picturesque, but the nearby oil refinery and power station are hard to ignore.

Leaving Sines to the south, you can clear your lungs at the village of **Porto Covo** ⓴. Though development has begun at the back of the village, it remains an intimate place, with cobbled streets swept scrupulously clean. The main square, grandly named Largo Marquês de Pombal, is very small, bordered by houses and the tiny parish church. A few small trees and plentiful benches surround the square. Down by the sea you can find shops, cafés and restaurants. Nearby secluded coves are easy to walk to.

Alentejo produces some fine wines. Its reds are full-bodied and mature well in the bottle.

The hotel Flor da Rosa, Crato.

Just off the coast of Porto Corvo is the fortified **Ilha do Pessegeiro** (Peach Tree Island), which in bygone days provided protection from raids by Dutch and Algerian pirates.

Returning to the main road, some 15km (9 miles) south of Porto Corvo is the small town of Cercal, beyond which you reach **Vila Nova de Milfontes ㉑**, the loveliest and most popular of Alentejo's resorts. The only time it gets really busy is in high summer when many Alentejanos and Lisboetas come for their annual holiday at the large campsite. There are a few bars, some seafood restaurants and a range of accommodation that includes the lovely up-market **Castelo de Milfontes** (tel: 283 998 231), converted from an ivy-clad fortress – drawbridge and all – which overlooks the estuary of the River Mira.

The river estuary provides long golden beaches and a calm sea. Park out at the headland overlooking the ocean, and you can turn back to see the town to your left, the winding river and the hills beyond – all very idyllic. If you are planning a day or two on this coast, then this is the place to stay. In early August it hosts the four-day Festival do Sudoeste, which could be described as Portugal's Glastonbury, and attracts top names.

Almograve and Zambujeira do Mar offer more stunning, often deserted beaches and some fine clifftop viewpoints across the basalt cliffs to the sea. Of the two very small villages, Almograve is by far the nicer. Between these two beaches is another, Cabo do Girão, but it is naval property and access is prohibited.

Southern Alentejo

You may well choose to start an exploration of the Lower Alentejo from a base in Lisbon, but you could start from here by going inland to the pretty town of **Odemira ㉒**, set on the banks of the Rio Mira, after which it is named. It is full of flowers and trees, so green that you are apt to forget that it is in Alentejo at all. Nearby is **Barragem de Santa Clara ㉓**, a huge dam on the Mira, where water sports are popular.

Ourique ㉔ is an agricultural town north of the dam. In its surrounding fields (Campo do Ourique), fruit, olives and cork trees grow. These fields, however, have seen far more than mere farming in their time. In the nearby hamlet of **Atalaia**, archaeologists have excavated an extraordinary Bronze Age burial mound. And it was on the site of a battle called Ourique in 1139 (which may or may not have been here) that a fateful encounter was fought between the Portuguese and the Moors. Afonso Henriques had just become the first king of Portugal, and the victory on this battlefield strengthened his determination to expel the Moors from all Portuguese soil, and gave a tremendous boost to the flagging morale of his battle-weary forces.

Beja: a hot place

The capital of Lower Alentejo, **Beja ㉕**, is the hottest town in Portugal

Milfontes, a village along the Mira river.

during the height of summer. It is a three-hour drive from Lisbon and an hour or so from Évora, or, if you are following the route from Ourique, it is about 60km (38 miles) on the IP2 (the old N123) or the N391.

A town existed on the present-day site as early as 48 BC, and when Julius Caesar made peace with the Lusitanians the settlement was named after this event, Pax Julia. During the 400-year Moorish occupation the name was adulterated to Baju, then Baja, until it finally became Beja.

It is now a fairly prosperous town, its income derived from the production of olive oil and wheat. A long-term German Air Force base here, dating from the 1960s, was turned over to the Portuguese in 1990. Beja is not a beautiful town, but it does have some interesting sights.

One of them is the 15th-century **Convento da Conceição**, a fine example of the the transition between Gothic and Manueline architecture. The Baroque chapel is lined with carved, gilded woodwork. The chapterhouse, which leads to

the cloisters, is tiled with superb Hispano-Arabic *azulejos* dating back to the 1500s. Their quality is rivalled only by those to be found in the Royal Palace at Sintra.

Legend has it that in the 17th century a nun at the convent fell in love with a French soldier, and when he returned to France she wrote him a number of love letters that were later published in Paris, and became something of a literary sensation.

Dissolved in 1834, the convent building also houses a notable **Museu Regional** (Tue–Sun 9.30am–12.30pm, 2–5.15pm; charge).

The small and modest Santo Amaro is the oldest church in Beja. It is thought to date back to the 7th century and is a rare example of Visigothic architecture. The Misericórdia church in the Praça da República is also worth a look. Beja's 13th-century castle (Tue–Sun May–Sept 10am–1pm, 2–6pm, Oct–Apr

Storks on a stalk, in Serpa.

Odemira, set on the banks of the Mira.

Pousada de São Francisco, Beja.

A church in Beja.

9am–noon, 1–4pm; free) still stands, and its castellated walls run around the town perimeter. The tall keep contains a military museum, and a narrow balcony on each side from which you can enjoy a remarkable view across the plains.

Driving in to **Serpa** (about 30km/18 miles east of Beja) is – as with so many small Alentejo towns – like driving into a time warp. The castle and fortified walls were built at the command of King Dinis. A significant difference here from other 13th-century walls is that these have an aqueduct built into them.

A well-preserved gateway is the **Portas de Beja**; the gates, along with the rest of the walls, were almost sold by the town council in the latter half of the 19th century. Cooler heads prevailed and the walls were saved, although a great part of them had been destroyed in 1707 when the Duke of Ossuna and his army occupied the town during the War of the Spanish Succession.

There are several churches worth seeing (notably the 13th-century Santa Maria), as well as the delightfully cool and elegant palace belonging to the counts of Ficalho, the **Paço dos Condes de Ficalho**. It was built in the 16th century and has a majestic staircase and lovely tiles. The present lady of the house, Dona Maria das Dores, Condessa de Ficalho, incidentally, is the granddaughter of José Maria Eça de Queiroz (1845–1900), one of Portugal's great 19th-century novelists (see margin).

The Rio Guadiana is considered the most peaceful of Portugal's three big rivers (the others being the Tagus and Douro), but an exception is at **Pulo do Lobo** (Wolf's Leap) between Serpa and Mértola. This is a stretch of high and wild rapids, which can be reached by road and is worth a visit if you are in the area – you will probably find you are the only tourist there.

Mértola

Mértola , an ancient fortified town set in the confluence between the Guadiana and the Oeiras rivers, is one of Alentejo's hidden gems. To get here from Serpa you can either take a secondary road to the south, or return to Beja, then take the main road south and turn off to the left. Whichever way you approach, the sight of the town's strongly built walls crowned by a sturdy **castle** (daily 9.30am–5.30pm; free) is as impressive as it is unexpected.

Mértola has a long history, reaching back to Roman times. For five centuries under the Romans it was an important port on the then navigable Guadiana for exporting mineral ores from the nearby Minas de São Domingos, near the Spanish border. Its importance continued under the Visigoths, whose handiwork can be seen in the castle tower, and later the Moors. Twice in the 11th and 12th centuries it was capital of a kingdom which included Beja. With the growth of agricultural produce in the region Mértola was active in exporting grain to North Africa. When the river eventually silted up, the town slipped quietly into oblivion.

Leave plenty of time to explore the astonishing remains of the Roman port, the parish church, the castle and several museums (a single ticket covers all the sites), as well as the **Igreja Matriz**. Outwardly a Christian church, this pristine white building was originally a mosque, one of the few in Portugal to have survived virtually intact.

The exhibition of Islamic pottery in the **Museu Islâmico** (Tue–Sun 9am–12.30pm, 2–5.30pm) is not enormous, but it is the finest in Portugal; and the **Museu Romano** (daily 9am–12.30pm, 2–5.30pm) is very sophisticated. The town hall here burned down some years ago, and during the clearing-up operation the remains of a Roman villa were discovered. After finishing an excavation, the town hall was rebuilt and the Roman villa turned into an elegant basement museum.

Sunset on the Senhora da Guadalupe chapel, Serpa.

Pork stew with clams.

FOOD AND DRINK

Alentejo's culinary specialities should not be missed. Try *sopa Alentejana* – a filling soup of bread, with lots of fresh coriander (a herb used a great deal in Alentejo cooking), garlic and poached eggs. One of the classic meat dishes is carne de *porco à Alentejana* – chunks of pork seasoned in wine, coriander and onions and served with clams. Two much heavier but delicious stewed dishes are *ensopada de cabrito* – kid boiled with potatoes and bread until the meat is just about falling off the bone, and *favada de caça*, a game stew of hare, rabbit, and partridge or pigeon, with broad beans. The best Alentejo cheese comes from Serpa. Made from sheep's and goat's milk, it has a creamy texture and a strong, slightly piquant flavour. Évora has its own goat's cheese, which is hard, salty and slightly acid. It is preserved in jars filled with olive oil.

Alentejo is a *região demarcada* – a demarcated wine region. Most towns have their own cooperative winery from which you can buy stocks at rock-bottom prices, and most restaurants have a low-priced cooperative house wine. In Lisbon, Alentejo reds are often drunk with *bacalhau*, instead of the more usual white. Try the reds from the Reguengos cooperative or those from Borba (see page 215), and white wines from the Vidigueira cooperative (www.adega vidigueira.com.pt).

PRESERVING ARTS AND CRAFTS

Local customs form a thread of continuity in rural Portugal, and none is stronger than the craft skills which are found throughout the country.

Portugal is a land rich in tradition, and in rural areas the skills and artistry of local craftspeople have been passed from generation to generation. Most skills are specific to one locality: pottery is perhaps the only national craft – although with important variations in design and decoration. Craft work is a significant cottage industry, but there is a danger of skills dying out, especially in regions with few visitors. To prevent this, EU funding has been channelled towards promoting the work of artisans to save skills, create employment and retain life in dying villages.

There are plenty of craft shops in the large towns, but the real joy is to stop in tiny villages and discover the spinning and weaving cooperatives formed by women, as in Mértola. See bobbin lacework, watch ceramics in the making, buy jute dolls, and marvel at the basket creations made from leaves of the dwarf fan palm.

The products of some regions have gained national importance. Arraiolos in Alentejo has a centuries-old tradition of rug- and carpet-making which has grown into a major industry; and the hand-embroidered bedspreads of Castelo Branco, which have been made since the 17th century, are also popular throughout Portugal and now in demand by tourists. You will see distinctive hand-painted furniture throughout the Alentejo. Estremoz sells little figurines in its weekend market; Caldas da Rainha is known for its ceramics; while Peniche, also in Estremadura, is famous for lace.

Clay-thrown, handpainted olive dishes, often embellished w the name of the locality, come with a separate nook for discarded olive pits.

Brightly coloured traditional costume.

Painted clogs in Viana do Castelo.

The ubiquitous Galo de Barcelos.

THE GALO DE BARCELOS

There is no escape from the Barcelos cockerel. Its fame arises from a legend (as colourful as the little figure itself), which has been embroidered and enlarged with every telling. The central theme relates the story of a murder committed in the northern town of Barcelos many centuries ago. A certain Galician pilgrim came under suspicion as the perpetrator, and no matter how strongly he protested, his pleas of innocence fell on deaf ears, and he was sentenced to death.

Before his execution he was granted a last wish: to make a final plea before the judge, who, in the midst of entertaining guests to dinner, agreed to see him. In desperation, the condemned man pointed to the roast fowl on the dinner table and cried, "As surely as I stand innocent, so will that cock crow." Miraculously, the rooster obliged. The judge forfeited his dinner, and the pilgrim gained his life.

Ceramic figures of the Barcelos cock are on sale everywhere. The symbol now also adorns everything from T-shirts to tea towels, and finds a place in most visitors' luggage.

a Real pottery is distinctively black and is made by covering with soil and ash to exclude oxygen and burning shwood over them.

dmade dolls in Marafona.

A skilfull resident of Obidos makes lace to sell at a local market.

ESTREMADURA AND RIBATEJO

Although ribboned with silver sand, the coast is not the major attraction in this region. It is inland that you will find some of the country's finest and best-loved monuments.

The region north of Lisbon reaching up towards Coimbra has not managed to establish itself as a major travel destination in spite of its many attractions. Bordered by an endless ribbon of silvery sand, the Costa de Prata – the Silver Coast – Nazaré apart, still only has small resorts. Most of the region's attractions, the monasteries at Alcobaça, Batalha and Tomar, the religious sanctuary at Fátima and the spectacular deep caves in the limestone *serras* are inland.

With its points of interest fairly widespread, it is an area tailor-made for a rambling tour. Allow around three days to take in most of the major sites and longer if you want to savour everything the region offers. The circular route described here goes anticlockwise from Lisbon up to Batalha and back.

North from Lisbon

The quickest ways to escape Lisbon are either by the A1 or the A8 heading north. Alternatively, for a slower but more interesting journey, cross the Rio Tejo on the Ponte Vasco da Gama and take the road on the eastern side of the river. The A1 will take you to the modest town of **Vila Franca de Xira,** the centre of Portuguese bullfighting. Every July and October the town comes alive with the bullfighting festival, known as

the Festas do Colete Encarnado (Festival of the Red Waistcoat) after the costumes of the *campinos*, traditional herdsmen.

Santarém ❶ is the central town of Ribatejo. It was named after Santa Iria, a young nun who was accused of being unchaste, and martyred in 653 near Tomar. Her body, thrown into the river, washed ashore here. A river-bank shrine has a statue whose feet act as a sacred gauge to the water level – if they are touched by floods, even Lisbon is in danger.

Main Attractions

Castelo de Almourol
Convento do Cristo, Tomar
Fátima
Mosteiro de Santa Maria da Vitória, Batalha
Cistercian Abbey, Alcobaça
Óbidos
Ilha Berlenga

Óbidos lacemaker at work.

Foreign visitors often prefer Portuguese bullfights (touradas) to those in Spain, since Portuguese bullfighters do not kill their bulls – at least not in public.

Among several fine churches, the Romanesque-Gothic church of **São João de Alporão** contains a good archaeological museum (Tue–Sun 9.30am–12.30pm, 2–6pm), as well as the beautifully carved tomb of Duarte, a son of Pedro I who died in battle in 1458. It contains just one of Duarte's teeth, the sole relic that was delivered to his wife.

In northeastern Santarém is the church of **Santa Clara** (Tue 2–6pm, Wed–Sun 9.30am–12.30pm, 2–6pm; free), originally part of a 13th-century convent, containing the elaborate tomb of Dona Leonor, daughter of Afonso III. The church of **Nossa Senhora da Graça** (Wed–Sun 9am–12.30pm, 2–5.30pm; free), a Gothic structure with a beautiful nave, holds several tombs, among them that of Pedro Alvares Cabral, discoverer of Brazil.

In **Alpiarça,** across the river, look for the 19th-century architectural gem of the **Casa dos Patudos** (Tue–Sun 10am–12.30pm, 2–5.30pm, summer to 6.30pm), today a wonderfully eclectic museum containing paintings by Portuguese artists including acclaimed naturalist painter Silva Porto, ceramics and more.

A diversion to **Abrantes** ❷ is worthwhile, if only to see the nearby Castelo de Almourol, romantically located on an island in the middle of the Tejo. The road on the east side of the river offers the most interesting route. Abrantes itself has little to offer visitors except perhaps for the castle of **Santa Maria do Castelo.**

Turn back along the north bank just before Tancos and look for the sign to **Castelo de Almourol** ❸ (daily Nov–Mar 10am–5pm, Apr–Oct 10am–7pm; free). It crowns a rocky island in the river and the ferryman (Sr João; tel: 914 506 562), who normally operates between 9am and 5pm, will row visitors across for €1.50. A trip around the island will cost more.

The Romans recognised the importance of the site on this key communication route and built a castle, although there may have been an earlier settlement. Later, the castle was occupied by the Visigoths, the Moors and finally the Christians.

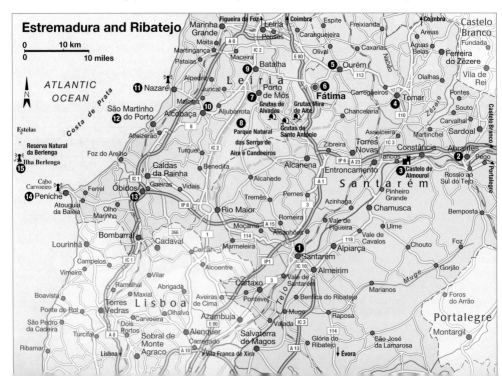

Afonso Henriques entrusted it to the Knights Templar in 1147 for help in fighting the Moors. The Grand Master Gualdim Pais rebuilt the castle leaving an inscription over the door, and it remained garrisoned for a time. When the Moors were expelled from Portugal the strategic importance of the castle declined and it eventually fell into disuse. It takes only a few minutes to wander around the walls of the fortress.

Tomar

From the castle it is a fairly short run north to **Tomar** ❹, a delightful town with a host of good points: a setting on the banks of the Rio Nabão; the splendid Convento do Cristo, which is a Unesco World Heritage Site; and medieval streets paved with stone and fancifully patterned with exuberant flowers. With its pleasing ambience and rich culture, its ancient legends and appealing daily life, Tomar is a town in which to linger and explore for a couple of days.

Tomar was the headquarters of the Knights Templar in Portugal, an order that was formed in 1119, during the crusades. The order spread quickly throughout Europe, gaining extraordinary wealth. It also made powerful enemies, and in the early 1300s, amid accusations of heresy and foul practices, and finally the suppression of the order altogether, the Knights took refuge in Tomar, where Grand Master Gualdim Pais had built a castle back in 1162. They re-emerged in 1320, reincarnated as the Order of Christ, whose proud symbol, the Cross of Christ, became the banner of the Age of Discoveries.

In Tomar they left behind the marvellous ruins of the old castle and, within its walls, the still-intact church and cloisters. The **castle** (Tue–Sun June–Sept 9am–6.30pm, Oct–May 9am–5.30pm; free) is set on a hill above the city, a 10-minute walk away, and commands a view over the rooftops of the old town.

Monastery and synagogue

The **Convento do Cristo** (www.conventocristo.pt; daily Apr–Sept 9am–6.30pm, Oct–Mar 9am–5.30pm) is a maze of staircases and passages, nooks and crannies. The seven cloisters (just four are open to the public) have been added at irregular angles and over several centuries, and even the beautiful main entrance is oddly tucked into a corner. The original Templar church is on the right, just inside the entrance. Begun in 1162, the octagonal temple was modelled on Jerusalem's Church of the Holy Sepulchre. Here, the knights would hear services while seated on their horses, and pray for victory in battle.

The chapterhouse and Coro Alto, added much later, provide a sharp contrast to the original temple, as does the adjoining 16th-century cloister with 17th-century tiles where some of the tombs of the knights are found. From here there is access to the upper level and then into the other cloisters. From the terrace of the small Claustro de Santa Bárbara,

The Convento do Cristo was built by the Knights Templar in around 1160.

The Convento do Cristo was built as part of a defensive system against the Moorish invaders.

Fátima, a place for pilgrims.

there is a view of the amazing, ornate Manueline window, structured around two deep relief carvings of ships' masts, knots, cork, coral and seaweed. The whole is topped by a shield, crown and cross, symbol of the union of church and king.

From the opposite side of the building you can see the castle yard where the knights trained their horses and spent their off-duty hours. Also on this side lies an unfinished chapel: bad luck during construction persuaded the superstitious knights to abandon it.

Tomar's synagogue in Rua Joaquim Jacinto is now **the Museu Luso-Hebraico de Abraão Zacuto** (daily July–Sept 10am–1pm, 2–7pm, Oct–June 10am–1pm, 2–6pm; free). Although a high percentage of Portuguese people have Jewish ancestry, and Tomar was once the home of a thriving Jewish community, there are very few Jews left. When King Manuel I married Isabella of Castile in 1497, a condition of the marriage contract was the expulsion of the Jews. They were allowed to remain if they converted, although laws governing fair treatment were not closely monitored. Later, the Inquisition legitimised brutal discrimination against them. The synagogue/museum is simple and moving, decorated with gifts from all over the world.

Other Tomar sights

The church of **São João Baptista** has a dark wood ceiling and a sombre atmosphere. Sixteenth-century wood-panel paintings on the walls depict scenes such as the Last Supper and Salome with the head of John the Baptist. On the left is a delicately carved pulpit.

Standing alone on the edge of town, **Santa Maria dos Olivais** is a simple church dating from the 12th century and containing many Templar tombs. The town's tourist office is on Avenida Dr Cândido Madureira, near the road to the castle, and there is a regional tourist office at 1 Rua Serpa Pinto.

En route from Tomar to Fátima, it is well worth a stop at **Ourém ⑤**, or more particularly at Ourém Velha, the fortified site on top of an easily defended hill. The history of the castle is known only from the time it was recovered from the Moors in 1148 by King Afonso Henriques. Little was attempted in the way of restoration until King Dinis (1279–1325) arrived on the scene. He rebuilt this as he did many other castles in Portugal.

The Lourdes of Portugal

Fátima ⑥, some 12km (8 miles) from Ourém, is not a place for non-believers, and there is even a notice to advise you of this. It is a place for pilgrims – of which there are up to 2 million a year. On 13 May 1917, three shepherd children had a vision of the Virgin here. Thereafter, she appeared before the children and, on one occasion, as a shining light to the townspeople who gathered with them on the 13th of the subsequent months (see page 74). The

two younger children died shortly after the apparitions, but one, Lucia de Jesus Santos, lived well into her eighties in a convent near Coimbra (she died in 2005). The processions that take place on the anniversaries of the visions – 13 May and 13 October – draw thousands of people from around the world.

Surrounded by acres of car parks is the vast white **basilica** (May–Oct Mon–Sat 9am–6.30pm, Sun 9am–6pm, Nov–Apr Mon–Sat 9am–6pm, Sun 9am–5.30pm), consecrated in 1953. In front of it is a huge esplanade large enough to hold 100,000 worshippers, and the **Chapel of Apparitions,** which Our Lady of the Rosaries ordered to be built in her sixth and final appearance on this spot. Inside the basilica lie the tombs of the two visionary children who died, Jacinta and Francisco Marto. Close by is a new church, congress and study centre dedicated to Pope John Paul II (hours as basilica).

Castles and caves

West of Fátima, along scenic well-paved roads, lies the pleasant town of **Porto de Mós** ❼, worth a brief stop even if only to look at the **castle** (Tue–Sun Oct–Apr 10am–12.30pm, 2–5.30pm, May–Sept 10am–12.30pm, 2–6pm), capped with green cones and standing on a hill. The castle has a fairly long pedigree and still contains some original Roman stonework. As with Ourém castle, King Afonso Henriques recovered it from the Moors in 1148. After several restorations, it remained in military use at least until the Battle of Aljubarrota in 1385, when João I is said to have rested his troops here before the fight. Afterwards the king rewarded his captain, Nuno Alvares Pereira, with the gift of this fortress for leading his troops so bravely. It was his grandson, Afonso, a cultured and much-travelled man, who endeavoured to convert the castle into a palace and disguise the strong military lines.

As a change from monuments, a diversion into the **Parque Natural das Serras de Aire e Candeeiros** ❽ offers fine limestone scenery and a chance to visit Portugal's largest caves. Take the N243 towards Torres Novas to find **Grutas Mira de Aire** (www.grutasmiradaire.com; daily Apr–May 9.30am–6pm, June, Sept 9.30am–7pm, July–Aug 9.30am–7.30pm, Oct–Mar 9.30am–5.30pm), **Grutas de Santo António** (www.grutassantoantonio.com) and **Grutas de Alvados** (www.grutasalvados.com). The latter two lie on a spur off the main road. All three are different enough to be worth visiting. If you only have time for one, then perhaps Grutas Mira de Aire is the best choice. The caves are reached down more than 600 steps through well-illuminated caverns with imaginative and descriptive names, to the underground river. Fortunately, there is a lift for the return to the surface.

Batalha: an essential stop

Batalha ❾ is one of Portugal's most beautiful monuments, and another

The Basilica of Our Lady of the Rosary was built to commemorate the events of 1917, when three peasant children claimed to have seen the "Virgin of the Rosary".

Fátima statuary.

A characteristically graceful vaulted dome inside the monastery at Batalha.

Portugal's largest cave in Parque Natural de Serras de Aire e Candeeiros.

Unesco World Heritage Site. The origins of **Mosteiro de Santa Maria da Vitória** (www.mosteirobatalha.pt; daily Apr–Sept 9am–6.30pm, Oct–Mar 9am–5.30pm), to use its full name, lie in Portugal's struggle for independence from Castile. One of the decisive battles for independence was fought at Aljubarrota, not far from Batalha. The Castilian king, Juan, who based his claim to the throne on his marriage to a Portuguese princess, invaded Portugal in 1385. The 20-year-old Dom João, Master of the Order of Avis and illegitimate son of Pedro I, promised to raise a monastery to the Virgin Mary if the Portuguese won. With his young general, Nuno Alvares Pereira, João defeated the Castilians, and became João I. The monastery was constructed between 1388 and 1533.

On the other side of the building you may enter the **Claustro Real** (Royal Cloister). Arches filled with Manueline ornamentation surround a pretty courtyard and are patterned with intricate designs. The chapterhouse is the first room off the cloister. It has an unusual and beautiful ceiling and its window is filled with a stained-glass Christ on the Cross, remarkably rich in colour. This chamber holds the tombs of two unknown soldiers, whose remains were returned to Portugal from France and Africa after World War I, a war that claimed 8,145 Portuguese soldiers' lives. The sculpture of "Christ of the Trenches" was given by the French Government, and a photograph of its extraordinary discovery on the battlefields of Flanders can be seen in the refectory opposite, where there is a small World War I museum.

To reach the **Capelas Imperfeitas** (Unfinished Chapels), go outside the monastery. This octagonal structure is attached to the outside wall and its rooflessness is a shock. Ordered by King Duarte I to house the tombs of himself and his family, the chapel was begun in the 1430s but construction was never finished – no one is quite certain why. The shell contains simple chapels in each of seven walls.

The chapel opposite the door holds the tomb of the king and Leonor, his wife. The eighth wall is a massive door of limestone, with endless layers of beautifully detailed ornamentation in carved Manueline style.

Alcobaça

Twelve km (8 miles) south of Batalha is the town of **Alcobaça** ❿, named after two rivers, the Alcoa and the Baça. At its heart is the magnificent **Cistercian Abbey** (www.mosteiroalcobaca.pt; daily Apr–Sept 9am–7pm; Oct–Mar 9am–5pm), yet another Unesco World Heritage Site. The first king of Portugal, Afonso Henriques, founded it to commemorate the capture of Santarém from the Moors. He laid the foundation stone himself in 1148.

The abbey's Cistercian monks were energetically productive. Numbering, it is said, 999 ("one less than a thousand" according to records), they diligently tilled the land around the abbey, planting vegetables and fruit. In Sebastião I's reign, the exceedingly wealthy and powerful Santa Maria Abbey, as it is also known, was declared by the Pope the seat of the entire Cistercian order. The monks here were particularly known for their lively spirits and lavish hospitality. They ran a school, perhaps the first public school in Portugal, and a sanctuary and hospice as well. In 1810, however, the abbey was sacked by French troops. In the liberal revolution of 1834, when all religious orders were expelled from Portugal, the abbey was again pillaged.

The long Baroque facade, added in the 18th century, has twin towers in the centre, below which are a Gothic doorway and rose window surviving from the original facade. Directly inside the serene and austere church, the largest in Portugal, three tall aisles and plain walls emphasise the clean lines. In the transepts are the two well-known and richly carved tombs of Pedro I and Inês de Castro (see box, page 36). Off the south transept

are several other royal tombs, including those of Afonso II and Afonso III, and a sadly mutilated 17th-century terracotta of the Death of St Bernard. To the east of the ambulatory there are two fine Manueline doorways that were designed by João de Castilho.

An entrance in the north wall of the church leads to the 14th-century **Claustro de Silencio** (Cloister of Silence). Several rooms branch off the cloister, including the chapterhouse and a dormitory. There is a kitchen, with an enormous central chimney and a remarkable basin through which a rivulet runs: it supposedly provided the monks with a constant supply of fresh fish. Next door is the refectory, with steps built into one wall leading to a pulpit. To the left of the entrance is the **Sala dos Reis**, with statues of many of the kings of Portugal, probably carved by monks themselves. The panel in the same room, which tells

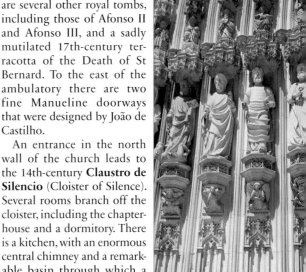

The exterior of Batalha Abbey.

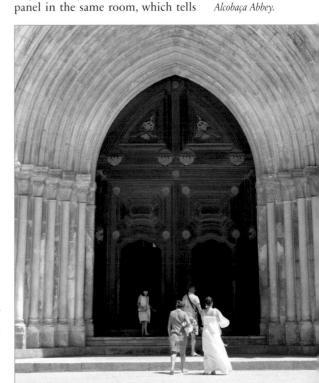

The main entrance to Alcobaça Abbey.

The arches of Alcobaça Abbey.

Powerful waves rock the shore at Costa de Prata.

the history of Alcobaça Abbey, is a rare example of a manuscript *azulejo* panel.

Alcobaça today is the centre of a porcelain and pottery industry. There are numerous shops around the central square, and some factories welcome visitors.

The Silver Coast

From Alcobaça, it is a relatively short drive out to the coast to reach the fishing port **Nazaré** , which nestles along a sweeping bay. In summer, thousands of holiday-makers pack the beach in rows of peaked, brightly striped canvas tents that create a striking image.

Nazaré, named after a statue of the Virgin that a 4th-century monk brought to the town from Nazareth, lives literally on two levels. In the lower part of town, small, white-walled fishermen's cottages line the narrow alleyways. High above on the cliff that towers 109 metres (360ft) over the old town is the quarter

known as **Sítio.** Reached by a funicular that climbs the tallest cliffside in Portugal, Sítio is dominated by a large square, and on its edge a tiny chapel built to commemorate a miracle in 1182, when the Virgin saved the local lord by stopping his horse plunging off the cliff as he pursued a deer.

The 17th-century **Nossa Senhora da Nazaré** on the other side of the square is the focus of festivities during the second week of September that include processions and bullfights in the Sítio bullring. The steep, narrow pathway and steps from the lighthouse west of the church afford stirring views of Atlantic breakers.

The abundance of tourists vitiates some of Nazaré's charm, but it also assures that all the visitor's desires will be catered to. Pleasant seafood restaurants and small hotels line the sandy bay; esplanade cafés, bars and souvenir shops abound. But the life of the hardy fishermen goes on.

Because they had no natural harbour, the fishermen used to launch their boats from the beach. They managed this by pushing their craft down

log rollers into the sea then clambering aboard and rowing furiously till they overrode the incoming breakers. When they arrived home again, the boats were winched ashore by oxen and later by tractors. The building of a modern anchorage to the south of the beach has relieved the Nazaré fishermen of this arduous task.

The Nazaré fisherfolk's traditional dress is today seen more in souvenir shops than on the street. Some women still wear coloured petticoats under a wide black or coloured skirt and cover their heads with a black scarf; the men still favour woollen shirts in traditional plaids, but few wear the distinctive black stocking bonnets.

Calm waters and a walled town

The road south out of Nazaré leads first past the new fishing harbour and then down the coast to **São Martinho do Porto ⑫**. Here a huge encircling sandbank creates a virtual lagoon, although there is a small opening to the sea. These calm, shallow waters are readily warmed by the sun but, with only a limited exchange of water, the risk of pollution in the bay is high. Moving south again, the road sweeps grandly by the university town of **Caldas de Rainha** (Queen's Spa) – where there is a regular morning fruit market and the charming Museu de Cerâmica (Tue–Sun 10am–12.30pm, 2–5pm; free), which contains local and international ceramics dating from the 17th century. The road then continues on to Óbidos.

A picture-postcard view of town walls crowned by a castle announces **Óbidos ⑬**. The old walled town, its streets tumbling with bougainvillea, presents a well-groomed appearance to the steady influx of day-trippers. The pretty town retains some authenticity, as no new building has been permitted, and only the existing structures within the walls can be used as tea shops, residences and gift shops. Everything in the narrow jumbled streets is painted white, with blue or yellow trimmings, and there are some colourful window boxes.

The town has a long history: it was occupied by the Moors before falling

Mending nets, a task that stays unchanged.

The medieval market of Óbidos.

into Christian hands. King Dinis, the indefatigable castle-builder, tidied it up and restored the **castelo** early in the 14th century. Damaged in the great earthquake of 1755, the castle was subsequently restored and has been converted into a delightful *pousada*. It is the place where everyone wants to stay, and gets booked up well in advance (tel: 262 955 080).

Apart from wandering around unprotected town walls and enjoying the ambience of the town, there is little to see in the way of monuments. The 17th-century **Igreja de Santa Maria** (1634–84) dominating the market square attracts the most attention, chiefly for the religious paintings by Josefa de Óbidos, the female artist born in the town in the 17th century.

Back to the coast

Like many of Portugal's coastal towns, **Peniche** ⓮ has no natural harbour, only a bay sheltered by the rocky promontory of **Cabo Carvoeiro**, the second most westerly point in Europe. A sea wall has been built to protect the bay. Peniche is a town of around 27,000

people. Here, the spare white houses cling to the slopes for shelter from the sweeping northwesterly winds. Too stark and exposed for tourism to have taken hold, the town typifies life in Portuguese fishing communities.

The **Fortaleza** physically dominates the town. The veteran leader of Portugal's Communist Party, Alvaro Cunhal, escaped from this notorious prison in 1960 by climbing down the cliffs to a waiting boat that reportedly took him to a Soviet-bloc submarine. Today, the building serves as a local museum (Tue–Fri 9am–12.30pm, 2–5.30pm, Sat–Sun 10am–12.30pm, 2–5.30pm).

You can get a powerful sense of the Atlantic swell that is the fisherman's constant companion by taking the ferry from Peniche out to **Ilha Berlenga** ⓯, 7km (4 miles) offshore. The ferry runs from June to September and the journey takes an hour (for more on the island, see the box on page 240).

The return to Lisbon is best made via the new highway from Óbidos, entering Lisbon via the IC2.

A gilded statue in Óbidos church.

ILHA BERLENGA

It's an adventure to discover Portugal's beautiful Ilha Berlenga, a rocky chunk of island that looks as if part of the Hebrides drifted out into the Atlantic. Visiting the island, once out of the shelter of the peninsula, powerful currents rock the boat with unexpected force, but the destination is worth the discomfort. A 17th-century fortress, now converted to an inn, a lighthouse and a few fishermen's cottages are the only buildings.

The entire island has been designated a national bird sanctuary, and seagulls and eider ducks are everywhere. Officials patrol the makeshift paths to ensure that visitors do not disturb the birds. The greatest excitement lies in taking a trip around the reefs, caves and smaller islands, past a breathtaking sea tunnel called the Furado Grande.

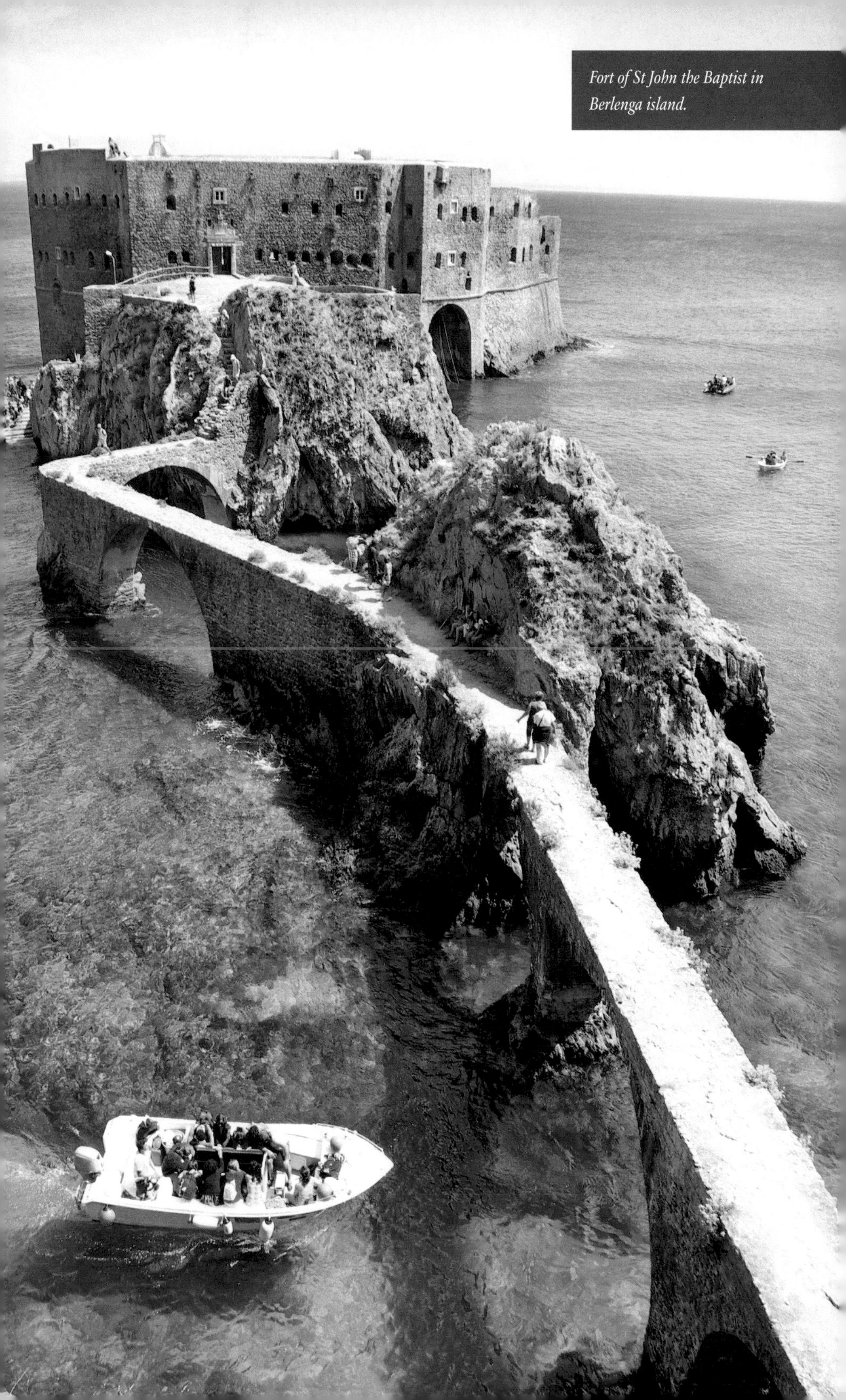

Fort of St John the Baptist in Berlenga island.

A mural map of Portuguese exploration.

COIMBRA

Coimbra grows old but never grows up. University freshers arrive each year to revitalise traditions and pour their souls into *fado*. For visitors it is a great mix of history and youthful exuberance.

Perched on a hill overlooking the Rio Mondego, **Coimbra** ❶ is surrounded by breathtakingly beautiful countryside. The city itself is an exciting mixture of ancient and new, rural and urban. The tourist office is located in the centre of the lower town, in Largo da Portagem; it will provide you with a good map of the city.

The university is the most stalwart guardian of Coimbra's colourful past. Students clad in black capes, the traditional academic dress, resemble oversized bats as they flit around town. The hems of the capes are often ripped, a declaration – at times – of romantic conquest. But these capes have only come back into style relatively recently, as for a time they were associated with Salazar's New State, and therefore not worn in the years after the 1974 revolution.

In May each year, the university celebrates the *Queima das Fitas*, the "burning of the ribbons", when graduating students burn the ribbons they have been wearing, the colour of which signifies their faculty – yellow for medicine, and so on. The celebrations last a week, and their grand finale is a long drunken parade.

Another Coimbra tradition is fado, a more serious cousin of the Lisbon variety. The sombre Coimbra fado

theoretically requires you to clear your throat in approval after a rendition, and not applaud. It is performed only by men, often cloak-wrapped graduates of the university.

The country's third-largest city, Coimbra lies at the centre of an agricultural region and has a large market. The students are not the only ones in black: it is the traditional dress of many of the rural women who come into town as well. Coimbra also has a considerable manufacturing industry.

Main Attractions
Biblioteca Joanina
Museu da Ciência
Museu Machado de Castro
Sé Velha
Mosteiro de Santa Cruz
Jardim da Manga

Scientific decorations at the University of Coimbra.

A decorative doorway in Coimbra.

The city's history

Coimbra traces its roots to the Roman municipality of *Aeminium*. It gained in importance when the nearby city of Conímbriga (see page 255) proved vulnerable to invasion. Convulsions in the empire and various invasions brought an end to Roman rule in the city. The Moors took over in 711, ushering in 300 years of Islamic rule, with a few interruptions. One such occurred in 878 when Afonso III of Asturias and León captured the city. Coimbra was not permanently retaken by Christian forces until 1064. It then became a base for the reconquest, and the city was walled. From 1139 to 1385 Coimbra was the capital of Portugal.

The 12th century was an age of considerable progress for Coimbra – including the construction, which began in 1131, of the city's most important monastery, Santa Cruz, still standing today. A lively commercial centre, the city included both Jewish and Moorish quarters. Division was not only by religion, but also by class. Nobles and clergy lived inside the walls in the upper town, while merchants and craft workers lived outside in what is today known as the Baixa, the lower area, down by the river, and heart of the modern town.

The university, founded in 1290 in Lisbon, moved to Coimbra in 1308 only to return to Lisbon nearly 70 years later. It was not until 1537 that the university settled permanently in Coimbra. A few years later, it moved to its present site at the top of the hill.

Most areas of interest are easily reached on foot. There is also a handy elevator which rises from Avenida Sá da Bandeira to Rua Padre António Vieira. Don't try to drive within the city. The old city and the university crown Coimbra's central hill, and the Baixa, which is the main shopping and eating district, lies at the foot of the hill along the Rio Mondego. Santa Clara lies across the river, while the tourist office, *Turismo*, is conveniently located at the northern end of the road bridge. Linking the two banks of the river, too, is a hi-tech footbridge with bright zigzag railings, and there are plenty of picturesque riverside restaurants.

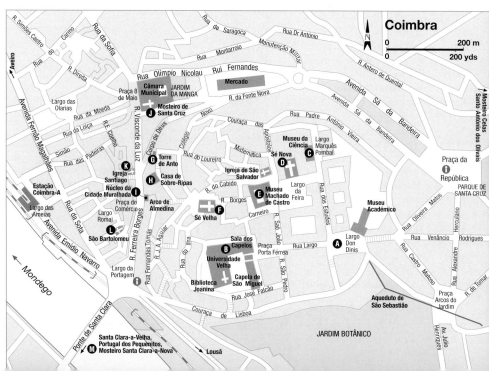

The old city and university

Once enclosed within walls, the old city is a tangle of narrow streets and alleys, lined by ancient buildings and filled with squares and patios. The university buildings are a compelling mix of styles, from the odd Baroque **Torre**, a clocktower, to bleakly Salazarist faculty blocks. The modern centre of the university is the statue of King Dinis, its founder, on the site of an earlier castle in **Largo Don Dinis ⓐ**, also home to the **Museu Académico** (Academic Museum; Mon–Fri 10am– 12.30pm, 2–5pm), where the displays include historic university capes and posters. Nearby stand the buildings that house the faculties of science and technology, medicine and letters and the New Library.

Of more historical interest than these stolidly functional buildings is the Pátio das Escolas (Patio of the Schools), within the **Universidade Velha ⓑ**, the Old University. To enter the patio, pass through the 17th-century Porta Férrea, a large portal decorated in the Mannerist style, to a large, dusty courtyard that is used for parking. Here are some of the oldest and stateliest buildings of the university. The figure of João III, who installed the university in Coimbra, still reigns from the centre of the patio. Behind him, there is a magnificent view of the river.

The building in the furthest corner from the Porta Férrea is the **Biblioteca Joanina** (daily Mar–Oct 9am–7.30pm, Nov–Feb 9.30am–1pm, 2–5.30pm), among the world's most resplendent Baroque libraries. The three sumptuous 18th-century rooms were built during the reign of João V, whose portrait hangs at the far end. Bookcases, decorated in gilded wood and oriental motifs, reach gracefully to an upper galleried level; even the ladders are intricately decorated. Note the fine frescoes on the ceilings. More than 300,000 books fill the cases and are still consulted by scholars.

Next door is the **Capela de São Miguel** (St Michael's Chapel), begun in 1517, and remodelled in the 17th and 18th centuries. The chapel is notable for its carpet-style tiles, the painted ceilings, the altar and the Baroque

FACT

Trains from Lisbon (Oriente) take 1.5–2 hours and stop at Coimbra B station 3km (2 miles) north of the centre, where passengers take a linking train to Coimbra A, the delightful little station in the middle of town. You don't need a separate ticket.

A mosaic welcomes you to the university at Coimbra.

MUSEU DA CIÊNCIA

Several small university museums were merged to form the impressive **Museu da Ciência ⓒ** (Science Museum; www.museudaciencia.pt; Tue– Sun 10am–6pm), located in Largo Marquês de Pombal. One of Europe's most important science collection, this award-winning museum has some 250,000 objects on display. Categories include botany, mineralogy, geology, palaeontology, astronomy and medicine, with information provided in both English and Portuguese.

This museum is a great choice for families as there are plenty of child-friendly interactive displays, including the key "Secrets of Light and Matter", and some fascinating visual exhibits, such as a bed of flowers seen from the perspective of a bug-eyed insect.

organ. Beside the chapel is a small museum of sacred art.

The arcaded building to the right of the Porta Férrea on the Via Latina houses the **Sala Grande dos Actos** (Mon–Fri 9am–1pm, 2–5.30pm, Sat–Sun 10.30am–4.30pm), where degrees are conferred and academic ceremonies take place. Portraits of Portugal's kings hang from its walls. Other rooms that you may enter are the rectory and, right by the bell tower, the **Sala do Exame Privado**, the Private Exam Room.

Old and New cathedrals

A short walk down from the university takes you to the **Sé Nova** **D** (New Cathedral; Mon–Sat 9am–6.30, Sun 10am-12.30pm; free), whose sand-coloured facade presides over a rather uninteresting square. Built for the Jesuits in 1554, it became a cathedral in 1772. Inside, the altar and much else is of lavishly gilded wood. Many of the paintings around the altar are copies of works by Italian masters.

The **Museu Machado de Castro** **E** (daily Apr–Sept 10am–6pm, Oct–Mar 10am–12.30pm, 2–6pm) is housed in the old Episcopal palace and the neighbouring 12th-century church of São João de Almedina. Constructed over the city's Roman forum and *cryptoporticus* (underground galleries), the palace was the residence of Coimbra's early bishops. The museum is named after Portugal's greatest sculptor Joaquim Machado de Castro (1732–1822), who was born in Coimbra. It holds an extensive and varied collection of medieval sculpture, as well as superb later pieces.

The **Sé Velha** **F** (Old Cathedral; Sun–Thu 10am–6pm, Fri 10am–4pm; free except for the cloisters), renovated in the 20th century, was built between 1162 and 1184. It served as a cathedral until 1772, when the episcopal see was moved to the Sé Nova. The fortress-like exterior is relieved by an arched door with an arched window directly above. The intricate Gothic altar within is of gilded wood, created by two Flemish masters in the 15th and 16th centuries. Sancho I was crowned king here in 1185, and João I in 1385. There are several tombs in the cathedral, including those of the 13th-century Bishop Dom Egas Fafe (to the left of the altar) and Dona Vetaça, a Byzantine princess who was a governess in the Coimbra court in the 14th century. Construction of the early Gothic cloister began in 1218.

Work on the **Colégio de Santo Agostinho**, on Rua Colégio Novo, was started in 1593. The ecclesiastical scholars and monks who first occupied it would probably be astonished by its present-day purpose, for this pleasant building, lined with pretty *azulejos*, is now home to the university's Psychology Department.

Nearby, on Rua Sobre-Ripas, the medieval **Torre de Anto** **G** (Anthony's Tower) was once part of the 12th-century city walls. Much later it was the home of the poet António Nobre (1867–1900) during his days as an undergraduate student.

The **Casa de Sobre-Ripas** **H**, on the same street, is an aristocratic 16th-century mansion. Note the archetypal Manueline door and window, but

The Old Cathedral of Coimbra, built in the 12th century.

don't bother knocking: it is the Faculty of Archaeology, and not open to the public. Here, it is believed, Maria Teles was murdered by her husband João (eldest son of the tragic Inês de Castro) who had been convinced by the jealous Queen Leonor Teles that his wife – the queen's sister – was unfaithful to him.

The **Arco de Almedina**, an entrance to the old city just off Rua Ferreira Borges, was also part of the medieval walls that encircle the old town hill. Housed in the tower here is the **Núcleo da Cidade Muralhada** ❶ (Tue–Sat 10am–1pm, 2–6pm), a model display of the town with its original town plan and defensive towers, plus details of its history. Head upstairs for superb views and to spy down through the holes carved into the stone floor. In times of war or invasion, boiling oil was poured through these holes to thwart potential aggressors.

Baixa Coimbra

The Baixa is the busy shopping district, and Rua Ferreira Borges, with many fashionable shops, is the busy, principal street. Although this district lay outside the walls of the old city, it dates back to almost the same time.

The **Mosteiro de Santa Cruz** ❷ (Tue–Fri 9am–5pm, Sat 9am–noon, 2–5pm, Sun 4–5.30pm; free) in Praça 8 de Maio (a continuation of Rua Ferreira Borges) was founded in 1131 by the St Augustine fathers. In the 14th century a grim scene was enacted when Dom Pedro had the body of his murdered lover exhumed, crowned and propped on a throne here, forcing his courtiers to pay homage to her corpse and kiss her decomposing hand. The facade and portal of the church date from the 16th century. Inside, the small church is light and spacious. Eighteenth-century *azulejos* adorn the walls: the right side depicts the life of St Augustine of Hippo; on the left, scenes relate to the Holy Cross.

Another striking work by a major 16th-century artist is the exquisite

pulpit on the left-hand wall, by sculptor Nicolau Chanterène. The **sacristy** (charge) contains several interesting paintings including *The Pentecost* by the 16th-century Grão Vasco, a silverwork collection, and some clerical vestments. You can see the tombs of the first two kings of Portugal, Afonso Henriques and Sancho I, ensconced in regal monuments. The chapterhouse and the lovely Cloister of Silence may also be visited.

Behind the church of Santa Cruz lies the **Jardim da Manga** (Garden of the Sleeve), so named because Dom João III reputedly drew this oddity of a garden on his sleeve – although the design has also been attributed to João de Ruão, a French sculptor working in Portugal in the 16th century. Curiously modernistic, this monumental garden was completed in 1535, and intended as a representation of the fountain of life. Beside the church is an atmospheric café in an ecclesiastic setting that was clearly part of the church.

If you wander down Rua da Sofia, which turns off 16th-century Praça 8 de Maio, you may be struck by the

Museu Machado de Castro.

TIP

To find the boisterous student nightlife, head for the restaurants around Rua la Sota, one street back from the river in Baixa Coimbra. And try the *chanfana* – goat stewed in wine – a dish from the Beira Litoral, to the north.

fact that it is extraordinarily wide for a street of that period. It was the original base for several colleges of the university before they were moved to new homes.

Praça do Comércio, off Rua Ferreira Borges, is an oddly shaped square lined with 17th- and 18th-century buildings. At the north end stands the sturdy **Igreja Santiago** , a church dating from the end of the 12th century. The capitals are decorated with animal and bird motifs. At the square's south end is the **Igreja de São Bartolomeu** , built in the 18th century.

Santa Clara

The Santa Clara section of town lies across the river. **Mosteiro Santa Clara-a-Nova** (New Santa Clara Monastery; Tue–Sun winter 9am–5pm, summer 9am–6.30pm) is worth a visit if only for the view over Coimbra. Inside is the tomb of Queen Isabel, who was canonised in 1625 and became the city's patron saint. Closer to the river, too close for its own comfort in fact, is **Santa Clara-a-Velha**, the old Santa Clara Monastery. This 12th-century edifice is simpler and more lovely than its replacement, for which it was abandoned in 1677. Waterlogged for centuries, it has been successfully restored.

Nearby **Quinta da Lágrimas** is where Inês de Castro is believed to have been murdered (see page 36). The family home is now a luxurious hotel and the grounds contain the **Fonte das Lágrimas**, the spring which is said to have risen on the spot where the luckless Inês cried for the last time and met her violent end.

To the east of the city, the **Mosteiro Celas** is notable for its cloister, and the pretty church of **Santo António dos Olivais** was once an old Franciscan convent.

Shops, parks and boats

The lanes of the Baixa have some delightfully old-fashioned shops. The covered market on **Rua Olimpio Nicolau** is open daily.

Coimbra has numerous parks: the **Jardim Botânico** (Botanical Garden, Apr–Sept Tue–Fri 9am–5.30pm, Sat–Sun 2–8pm; Oct–Mar Tue–Fri 9am–5.30pm, Sat–Sun 11am–5.30pm; free except for greenhouses), on Alameda Dr Júlio Henriques, next to the 16th-century Aqueduto de São Sebastião, is a lovely garden, laid out in the 18th century.

The **Portugal dos Pequeninos** (www.portugaldospequenitos.pt) is an outdoor theme park displaying small-scale reproductions of traditional Portuguese houses and monuments, which children love to clamber over and explore.

Other parks are **Santa Cruz**, off Praça da República, and **Choupal**, west of the city – a larger green space that is good for walks and bicycle rides. Tiny **Penedo da Saudade** has a nice view.

If you want some physical exercise, and a complete change from historical monuments, there are canoes and pedaloes for hire on the river. Basófias (Tue–Sun) offer river cruises lasting an hour.

Exploring Portugal dos Pequeninos.

A stroll in the Jardim Botânico.

A SALINEIRA

SIDE TRIPS FROM COIMBRA

Within easy reach of Coimbra you will find gleaming
lagoons, colourful fishing villages, exotic forests,
and the most extensive Roman ruins in the country.

Coimbra ❶ might be the main
focus of interest in this vicinity,
but there are plenty of opportunities for short excursions to other
noteworthy places. The countryside
towards the coast is especially bucolic
with an old-fashioned rural way of
life. The coast also offers plenty to see,
especially Aveiro with its canals and
lagoons. Castles and palaces feature
too, as well as Roman ruins.

Conímbriga

Portugal's largest excavated Roman
ruins are at **Conímbriga** ❷ (daily
9am–7pm; charge), 15km (9 miles)
south of Coimbra, near the town of
Condeixa; the drive is easy, and there
is a bus service. The site is complemented by the **Museu Monográfico
de Conímbriga** (daily same hours),
one of the country's finest museums.

As you enter the site, you are walking down the road that gave Conímbriga its original importance: the
highway from Olisipo to Bracara
Augusta. In front of you is an enormous wall. Passing through the main
entrance and continuing along the
path to the right, you will come to the
arch of the aqueduct (rebuilt), parts of
the aqueduct itself, and the remains of
several buildings that were possibly
small shops.

The building known as Cantaber's
House stretches to the south. The

house is full of ornamental fountains
and pools, but more interesting are
the baths, which lie at the extreme
south end. They are easily recognisable by their hexagonal and round
shapes, and by the piped heating system (that great Roman innovation),
visible through the stone grid covering the floors. Around the other side
of the wall you can see more baths:
public ones. For Romans, bathing
was an important daily ritual, and the
bathroom was also a place to discuss
politics. Beyond the baths is an area of

Main Attractions
Conímbriga
Serra do Buçaco
Aveiro
Vista Alegre
Praia de Mira
Figueira da Foz

A Roman mosaic, Conímbriga.

marvellously patterned mosaics; some are covered to protect them from the elements. The museum is small but carefully designed. A long case displays ceramics, jewellery, and artefacts relating to weaving, agriculture, lighting, writing and hygiene. There are also statues and a model of the forum and temple.

Serra do Buçaco

Northeast of Coimbra lies the **Serra do Buçaco** ❸ (Buçaco Forest), a darkly haunting area which for centuries has been protected, enabling 700 varieties of native and exotic trees to flourish. Benedictine monks established a hermitage here in the 6th century. The Carmelites, who built a monastery in 1628, began cultivation

of the forest, planting species brought back from sea voyages, including Himalayan pines, monkey puzzles, Japanese camphor trees, huge Lebanese cedars, and ginkgoes. In 1643 the pope threatened to excommunicate anyone harming the trees.

A royal hunting lodge was built in neo-Manueline style at the end of the 19th century, next to what remained of the convent. The Italian architect Luigi Manini, somehow managed to inject his own interpretation of Romantic Revivalism into the construction and the intended modest hunting lodge turned into a sumptuous palace. After the fall of the monarchy in 1910, it became the spectacular and luxurious **Palace Hotel do Buçaco** (where you may still, at

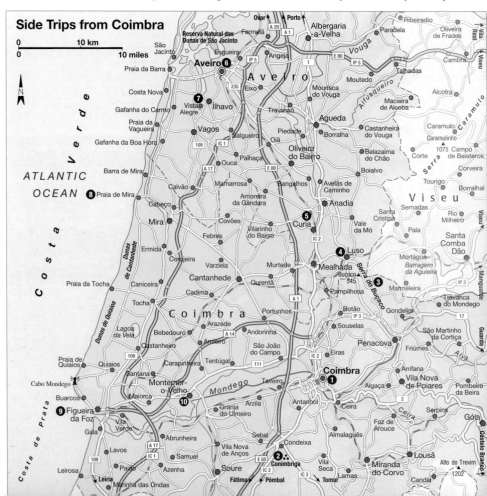

Side Trips from Coimbra

a price, lodge in the suite of the last king, Manuel II). A small church, the cloister, and several monks' cells remain from the monastery. In one of these cells the Duke of Wellington spent the night before the Battle of Buçaco on 27 September 1810. His victory in this battle was the first serious setback suffered by Napoleon's army, as the French attempted for the third time to conquer Portugal. The victory is still celebrated annually on the anniversary, with a re-enactment of the battle, in full period costume. A military museum is among a host of sights.

A high-quality wine is produced on the estate and is available in the restaurant. If you are keen to try it, book yourself in for lunch at the hotel and enjoy a real treat (www.palacehoteldo bussaco.com).

Downhill from Buçaco is the village of **Luso ❹**, renowned as a spa for the water that flows freely from fountains and which is available bottled throughout Portugal. A common sight here is of local people overburdened with an assortment of plastic water bottles jostling to fill them at Fonte de São João (St John's Fountain).

The N1/IP2 north towards Aveiro leads through the heart of the Barraida wine country. A slight diversion into **Curia ❺** allows the opportunity of picking up a special map of the region from the *Turismo*. Armed with this, you can find your way to the local winery at Sangalhos, Caves Aliança (www.alianca.pt), where you can taste wine or visit the fabulous museum in its cellars, which displays beautiful artefacts collected by José Berardo, one of Portugal's richest men. The collection includes 1,500-year-old phallic symbols from Niger and a fine collection of fossils and ethnographical items. .

To the coast and Aveiro

Aveiro ❻ has been described as the Venice of Portugal. The comparison, although exaggerated, stems from the canals that traverse the city and the boats that ply them. The canal system is modest, however: there is only one main canal, with two smaller ones along the edges of town. But they are

Flowers seem to drip from every wall in Buçaco.

Details from Hotel Buçaco Palace.

CONIMBRIGA'S PAST

Conímbriga was probably settled as early as the Iron Age (800–500 BC), and it was not until the latter part of the 2nd century BC that the Romans arrived. Conímbriga profited from its location by the Roman road between Olisipo (Lisbon) and Bracara Augusta (now Braga), and around AD 70 was designated a municipium.

Conímbriga's prosperity was not to last. Crises in the empire and Barbarian incursions prompted the construction of the defensive wall, still prominent today, but despite this, in 464 the Suevi successfully attacked the city. Conímbriga continued to be inhabited, but lost to neighbouring Aeminium (Coimbra) its status as an important centre.

Only part of the estimated 13-hectare (32-acre) site has been excavated.

Visitors will find it hard to forget that Luso is a spa town.

Colourful moliceiros take to the water in Aveiro.

linked with the *ria*, the lagoon that extends 47km (29 miles) just inland of the Atlantic and is fringed by dunes and long sandy beaches. Known to the Romans as Talabriga, Aveiro once lay directly on the ocean, but over the centuries a strip of sediment has built up, creating the *ria* but blocking ships and trade.

The lagoon plays a significant part in Aveiro's economic importance as an expanding port for fishing fleets and industrial cargoes. Other important local industries include wood, cork, and ceramics from nearby Vista Alegre. Next to the canals are large saltpans, another local resource. Once the lagoon was famous for brightly painted *moliceiros*, the boats with large graceful prows that were widely used to gather *moliço* (seaweed) for fertiliser, and which today are used for transporting tourists.

Aveiro was a small settlement during the Middle Ages. It was designated a town in the 1200s, and in 1418 was encircled by fortified walls, at the suggestion of Infante Prince Pedro after whom the city park is named. Shortly after this, Aveiro was granted the concession of a town fair; the March Fair continues to this day with local produce on display.

The 16th century was a time of growth and expansion for the town. With dredged access to the sea and to the interior, Aveiro became a trade centre from which products of the entire Beira region were exported. In 1575, a violent storm shifted the sandbanks in the lagoon, blocking the canal from the sea. The inevitable decline in Aveiro's importance encouraged emigration, which caused a dramatic decrease in population (to about one-third). In 1808, another storm reopened the sea passage, but it was not until the last half of the 19th century that Aveiro's fortunes picked up.

Exploring Aveiro

Aveiro makes a good base for a trip on the *ria* or to nearby beaches, but the city is worth exploring as well. The best way to get around Aveiro is to

pick up a free bicycle from a BUGA park, under a local scheme to encourage cycling in the town. Aveiro is divided in two by the principal canal. The southern part is where the aristocracy once lived; the northern half is the old fishermen's section.

The southern half centres around the **Praça da República**. In the simple square, the nicest building is the solid and rather prim town hall. On the east side of the square, the 16th- and 17th-century **Misericórdia** church has a lovely Renaissance portal and 19th-century tiles on its facade. In a square further south the 17th-century **Carmelite Convent** once housed the barefoot Carmelite order, who embraced a simpler way of life, focusing on solitude. Note the paintings on the ceiling, which depict the life of St Teresa of Avila.

The town's **Museu de Aveiro** (Tue–Sun 10am–5.30pm) is housed in the 15th-century **Convento de Jesus**. The convent has some fine 17th-century paintings and its church is effusively gilded. Arching over the choir are lovely hand-painted ceilings, and off the choir is a chapel with beautiful tiles. Just outside is the tomb of Santa Joana Princesa, daughter of Afonso V and patron of the city, who lived in the convent for 14 years until her death in 1489. Intricately carved in coloured marble and delicate inlays, with statues supporting and crowning it, the tomb took 12 years to construct.

The **São Domingos Cathedral** is near the museum. Its Baroque facade has twisted columns and sculpted figures of Faith, Hope and Charity. Inside, an enormous skylight over the altar lends the church an airiness that many Baroque churches lack. The huge blue altar rises strikingly in the all-white interior. The tomb of Catarina de Ataíde is here, a woman honoured, under the name Natércia, by the poet Luís Camões in his sonnets. The church was founded in 1423 and remodelled during the 16th and 17th centuries.

Several blocks away is the refreshing **Parque Dom Infante Pedro**, in the grounds of the old Franciscan Monastery. Colourful flowers, lush trees, fountains, and a small lake where you can hire paddle boats make this a nice spot for a break.

The old quarter

North of the canal lies the fishermen's section, where narrow houses support facades that sometimes rise beyond roof levels. The arches and curves on these false fronts are reminiscent of the fishing boats and their curved prows. The fish market, where the catch is sold each morning, is in this area. There is also the white, oddly shaped chapel of **São Gonçalinho** and the church of **São Gonçalo**. Inside this 17th- and 18th-century building gleam a gilt altar and newly placed tiles.

The beautiful *ria* is a prime reason for coming to Aveiro. You can tour its length by boat, car or bus, although boat is by far the most rewarding. The lagoon and its subsidiary canals extend as far south as Mira and as far

Public art in Aveiro.

The striped houses of the Costa Nova.

north as Ovar. There is a fair range of hotels in the area and many campsites. You will see traditional colourful *moliceiros* (the annual regatta is in July), shorelines dotted with saltpans, forests and villages, glorious sea birds plummeting into the water, and the sandbar that blocks the city's access to the sea. A road bridge takes you over the mouth of the estuary to **Costa Nova**, where there are brightly coloured traditional houses and excellent fish restaurants. Just 3km (2 miles) north of here, **Praia da Barra** is home to the Iberian peninsula's tallest lighthouse and (together with Costa Nova) is famed for its great surfing conditions. For information on the town, head to the tourist office, in an Art Nouveau building at Rua João Mendonça 8.

Continuing north, São Jacinto is a bustling port and part of the **Reserva Natural das Dunas de São Jacinto** (www.icnf.pt), an inviting little nature reserve with ponds and trails, which is famed for its birdlife. Visitor numbers are limited, so it is advisable to reserve online in advance.

Castles and candy stripes

From Aveiro a good road leads south to Figueira da Foz and back to Coimbra along the riverside. Fairly soon after leaving Aveiro, past Ilhavo, divert right to **Vista Alegre** for its porcelain factory (www.vistaalegreatlantis.com; Mon–Fri 9am–noon, 2–5pm). Famous throughout Portugal, it started production in 1842 and is still run by the same family. There is a shop and small museum (Tue–Fri 9am–6pm, May–Sept Sat–Sun 9am–12.30pm, 2–5pm, Oct–Apr Sat–Sun from 10am).

Mira lies close to the road a little further south. Keep going through the town and head for **Praia de Mira** ❽ on the coast. This is the most southerly point of the lagoon and canal system that surrounds Aveiro. Candy-striped beach huts add a jaunty air to the resort, but the main attraction is the inland lagoon, where there is safe boating and where picnickers enjoy shade from the surrounding pine trees.

Heading south, dip into the attractive quieter beach at **Praia de Quiaios**, situated just 10km (6 miles) north of the major holiday resort of **Figueira da Foz** ❾; the latter is favoured by both Portuguese and Spanish visitors. Turn a blind eye to the high-rise blocks and look at the broad expanse of beach and the gaily coloured beach huts, again in delightful candy stripes.

There is a fast road along the north side of the river to **Montemor-o-Velho** ❿, dominated by a 14th-century castle (daily May–Sept 10am–8pm, Oct–Apr 10am–5pm; free) on a prominent mound. Like many in Portugal, it was held by the Moors before being taken by the Christians. Within the walls are gardens, the ruins of a 16th-century Manueline palace and the restored **Igreja de Santa Maria da Alcáçova**, built around the time the castle was restored. To enjoy a rural atmosphere on the return to Coimbra, take the road from here along the south side of the river.

The striped houses of the Costa Nova.

A shrine high in the mountains.

BEIRA ALTA AND BEIRA BAIXA

This is a region of extreme contrasts, incorporating the Serra da Estréla (the highest mountain range in Portugal), areas of sheep and cattle, and sturdy castles.

The provinces of Beira Alta and Beira Baixa, the Upper and Lower Beiras, constitute a large rural section of eastern Portugal – a modest and hardy geographical region in a country that is among the poorest in western Europe. But it is rich historically, marked over centuries by the invasion routes of both Spaniards and Moors, in defensive castles and remnants of fortresses. The area has its natural attractions as well: the dramatic mountains of the Serra da Estréla and the stark plains and plateaux of the Baixa are some of the most beautiful natural landmarks in Portugal. The region is bounded by the Spanish frontier to the east, the Rio Douro to the north, and the Tejo (Tagus) to the south. The western boundary is a ragged line 60km (38 miles) east of Oporto.

Beira Alta

Guarda ❶ is the principal city and administrative capital of the Beira Alta's eastern district. The charter of Guarda was granted by Sancho I, Portugal's second king, in 1199, although the city had been established by 80 BC when it had a role in the attempted secession from Rome. Roman ruins can be found just outside town, near the Romanesque chapel of Póvoa de Mileu, notable itself for a small rose window and nicely carved capitals. Three town gates from the 12th- and

13th-century castle and town walls still stand: the Torre de Ferreiros (Blacksmiths' Tower), the Porta da Estréla (Star Gate), and the Porta do Rei (King's Gate), along with the castle keep. From the top there is a magnificent view of the mountains, and the broad plains to the north.

The **Sé** (Cathedral) was built of granite cut from the surrounding area. Work started in 1390 and was not completed until 1540, so that there were many Renaissance and Baroque elements added to the original Gothic.

Main Attractions

Viseu
Termas de São Pedro do Sul
Santar
Castelo Branco
Palácio Episcopal
Monsanto

Beira Alta farmer on his way home.

Portugal has about 15 varieties of cheese, most made with goat's or sheep's milk.

Diogo Boytac (1494–1520) worked on the cathedral, which bears some resemblance to Batalha. The exterior has flying buttresses and fanciful gargoyles. Inside, the 16th-century stone *retábulo*, later highlighted with gilt, represents scenes from the life of Christ; the stone carving is the work of João de Ruão, also known as Jean de Rouen (1530–70). A beautiful Renaissance doorway, off the north aisle, leads to the Capela dos Pinas, which contains the late Gothic tomb of a bishop.

The town museum in a 17th-century seminary has archaeological finds and a range of paintings, while a large park by the station includes an excellent, modern children's playground.

Guarda has been dubbed the city of four Fs – *fria, farta, forte e feia*, which means: cold, plentiful, strong and ugly. The predominance of heavy grey granite may be ugly to some, but the old parts of the city are pleasant. "Strong" in this context alludes to Guarda's history as a defence point against the Moors and Castile. "Plentiful" refers, no doubt, to the rich land surrounding the town, noted particularly for its sheep farming. Cold it certainly is, in winter: situated some 1,066 metres (3,500ft) above sea level, Guarda is Portugal's highest city – high enough for frost and snow in winter.

Around Guarda

Northwest of Guarda is the quintessential fortress village of **Trancoso**, a delightful tangle of cobbled lanes surrounded by 13th-century walls. Don't

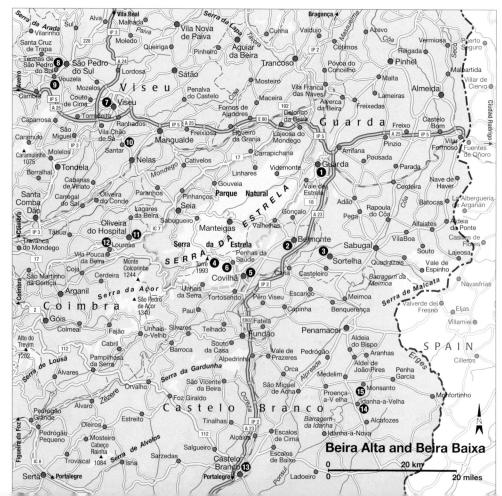

Beira Alta and Beira Baixa

miss the castle with its unusual Moorish tower and the medieval *juderia* (Jewish district). South of Guarda lie two handsome castle towns: on the main road to Castelo Branco is **Belmonte ❷**, birthplace of Alvares Cabral, who discovered Brazil, and home to the **Museu Judaico de Belmonte** (Tue–Sun 9.30am–12.30pm, 2–6pm; free), portraying the fascinating history of Judaism in the town, and how it continued in secret some 500 years after the Inquisition. Just south of here is **Sortelha ❸**, a tiny village with a castle surrounded by rocky crags, within a "magic ring" of stone. Ancient civilisations may have shaped some of the rocks, and they certainly mined in the area – there are entrances to mines that have been closed for centuries.

Stretching southwest is the **Serra da Estréla**, the highest mountains in the country and the source of Portugal's most highly rated *serra* cheese, whose production is centred on Covilhã (see below). The highest point of all is the over-commercialised **Torre ❹**, at nearly 2,000 metres (6,500ft). Nearby is a pilgrimage site, a statue of the Virgin carved into the rock, to which the faithful journey on the second Sunday of August.

The Serra offers skiing in winter and pleasant walking (or driving) with grand views in all directions. The prime winter resort is **Covilhã ❺**, southeast of Torre. It is too low to receive much snow itself, but it is a short drive to the ski area at **Penhas da Saúde ❻**.

Viseu: hub of Beira Alta

The western district of Beira Alta is governed by the city of **Viseu ❼**, about halfway between Guarda and Aveiro. In the 2nd century BC the Romans built a fortified settlement here, and some of their road system can still be seen, along with a number of Latin-inscribed stones.

A thorn in the side of the colonisers was a rebel Lusitanian named Viriathus, who harassed Roman legions

until he was finally betrayed and killed. A monument to him lies at the edge of a park – the Cova do Viriato – on the site of a Lusitanian and Roman military encampment. Here, you can still see the old earthworks once used by the Romans. Viseu was made a bishopric during the 6th century AD, the time of the Suevian-Visigothic kingdom, and a record still exists: a signature of the Bishop of Viseu, dated AD 569.

The city suffered alternating invasions of Moors and Christians from the 8th to the 11th centuries. Fernando the Great of Castile and León captured it for the Christians in 1057. Teresa, mother of the first king of Portugal, granted the city its first charter in 1123. From the 14th to the 16th centuries, building in Viseu seems to have been concentrated in the upper part of town. About this time an active Jewish colony evolved here. In 1411 the Infante Dom Henrique (Prince Henry the Navigator) became Duke of Viseu, and towards the end of that century the town walls were completed. But the surrounding area was becoming a centre of vigorous agricultural

FACT

The information offices for the Parque Natural da Estréla in Guarda, Seia, Gouveia, and Manteigas have details of hiking routes with places to stay.

The exquisite vaulting in Viseu's cathedral.

activity, and by the 16th century the walled area was becoming depleted.

Perhaps this was fortunate, because over the next two centuries much of this space was filled with a lavish assortment of Baroque churches, chapels, mansions and fountains. Today the architectural richness lends a dignified air to the enclosed city.

Pure Baroque

A city highlight is the 13th-century **Sé** (Cathedral; daily 8am–noon, 2–7pm; free). The ribbed vaulting is beautifully carved to look like knotted cables, and the ceiling of the sacristy is extravagantly painted with animals and plants. The twin-towered **Igreja da Misericórdia** across the square is whitewashed granite and pure Baroque. You should also save some time for the **Museu Grão Vasco** (Wed–Sun 10am–12.30pm, 2–5.30pm, Tue 2–5.30pm), in the old Bishop's Palace in the same square. Many of the works represent the fine school of Portuguese primitive painting that flourished here in the 16th century, and of which Grão Vasco

Fernandes (see page 112) was the acknowledged master.

The **Feira de São Mateus**, held annually from mid-August to mid-September, is a major event in Viseu, with music, food and fireworks. A Tuesday market is held year-round. Viseu is well known for its lace, carpets and black pottery.

Around Viseu

Northwest of Viseu is the small town of São Pedro do Sul and, some 4km (2.5 miles) southwest, the **Termas de São Pedro do Sul ❽**, which are probably the oldest as well as the best known and most frequented hot springs in the country. Sinus problems, rheumatism, hangovers or a foul temper – the springs are said to be a cure for all ailments. There are other delightful villages in the area, too. Just south of São Pedro do Sul is **Vouzela ❾**, with a lovely 13th-century church, and close by is the village of **Cambra**, clustered around the remnants of its castle.

South of Viseu, just off the secondary road to Nelas, **Santar ❿** is a little gem of a place, once known as

A cloudless day in Santar.

the Court of the Beiras. Due south is **Oliveira do Hospital** ⓫, a small town that once belonged to the Hospitallers. As a mark of this, tombs of the Ferreiros in the parish church (the Igreja Matriz) are crowned by a carving of an equestrian knight on the wall above.

Southwest (continue down the main road in the direction of Coimbra), in the village of **Lourosa** ⓬, is the ancient church of São Pedro. Spain's King Ordoño II ordered its construction in 911; it has a central nave, horseshoe arches, Moorish windows and Visigothic decoration.

Beira Baixa

Travelling south now towards the Beira Baixa, you come to the Rio Zêzere, which roughly divides Beira Alta from Beira Baixa. The river flows most swiftly from early April to late June. A good place for water sports is the **Barragem de Castelo do Bode**, a dam that blocks the flow of the River Zêzere to form a long, many-armed lake that runs south into the province of Ribatejo. (The most direct route is to take the IC3/N110, then turn left

about 8km/5 miles south of Tomar.) Both the river and the lake have fine fishing, with canoeing, waterskiing and windsurfing available in places.

The Rio Tejo marks the southern limit of Beira Baixa. Upstream the Tejo crosses into Spain. On both sides of the border is desolate scrub country. The gorge formed by the river is steep-sided and virtually inaccessible for vehicles other than four-wheel-drives. Along much of the Portuguese side of the river runs an ancient Roman road, which was originally the route from Vila Velha de Rodão to the Spanish town of Santiago de Alcántara. Water now conceals large chunks of the work, but where the road rises above the surface, you will see that instead of building the road with flat stones, the entire way is paved with local slate stood on edge, its upper surfaces rutted by centuries of cart traffic.

Castelo Branco

The capital of Beira Baixa is **Castelo Branco** ⓭, which stands at the junction of the IP2/E802 and the N112. It is an ancient city whose origins, like

Castelo Branco became a city in 1771.

Looking out over Castelo Branco from the old battlements.

A Roman settlement was recorded at Idanha-a-Velha in the first century.

those of so many communities in Portugal, are lost in time. Its "modern" history dates back to 1182, when it and the surrounding area were given as a gift to the Knights Templar by Dom Fernão Sanches. It received a charter in 1213 and became a city in 1771, in the reign of José I. The battlements of the "white castle" that gave the city its name provide a fine view, though the castle itself is in ruins. The old town is delightful, with narrow winding streets. Points of interest include two churches, São Miguel and Misericórdia Velha, the latter a 16th-century structure with a notable doorway; and **Praça Velha**, also called Praça de Camões – a fine medieval square near the ancient municipal library.

The most important thing to see in Castelo Branco is the splendid **Palácio Episcopal**, built on the orders of the Bishop of Guarda, in 1596. It served as the winter residence of the bishops of the diocese. It now houses the **Museu Francisco Tavares Proença Júnior** (Tue–Sun Oct–Apr 10am–5.30pm, Apr–Oct 10am–7pm), which displays archaeological and regional items, but

is most interesting for its large collection of *colchas*, the beautiful hand-embroidered bedspreads for which the town is famous.

In 1725, Bishop João de Mendonça commissioned a **garden** to be laid out beside Castelo Branco's Palácio Episcopal. Although relatively small, it is considered one of Portugal's finest formal gardens, and is an extraordinary sight, with a multitude of statues fountains and pools. The statues have been placed in homage to just about everybody and everything the bishops thought important: the kings of Portugal, of course; the saints, Apostles and evangelists, along with the virtues; and the seasons of the year, the signs of the zodiac and the elements of the firmament. There were even more statues, but the invading French armies of 1807 carted off the best. The plinths have been left standing in their places, in many cases with the name of the missing item clearly engraved.

Monsanto

From Castelo Branco it is easy to get to the small village of **Idanha-a-Velha** ⑭, northeast of the city. This was an episcopal see until 1199, when the see was moved to Guarda. There remains a strange, ancient basilica with dozens of Roman inscriptions inside. It is said that Wamba, the king of the Visigoths, was born here. A Roman bridge in the village is still in use, and various coins, pottery and bones have been found.

Nearby is the granite village of **Monsanto** ⑮, once declared "the most typical Portuguese village", with many of its houses tucked between giant boulders. Built around and atop a steep rocky mass in a broad valley some 50km (30 miles) northeast of Castelo Branco, Monsanto sits in the middle of a major invasion route. Its intriguing castle commands a superlative view in every direction. It is thought that this *monte* has been fortified since Neolithic times, and the castle is so well integrated into the natural rock it looks as if it grew here.

Some say it was during the Roman invasion in the 2nd century BC, others claim it was some 1,400 years later during a Moorish invasion, that the people of Monsanto, under a long siege and nearly out of food, fooled their attackers by killing a calf, filling its belly with rice, and hurling it off the ramparts. The attackers were so impressed with the evidence of ample supplies that they packed up and left. One of the biggest feast days is on 3 May, when young villagers toss down pitchers filled with flowers from the battlements, symbolically re-enacting the event.

Much of the castle was destroyed at the beginning of the 19th century. One Christmas Eve there was a tremendous thunderstorm, and a bolt of lightning hit the gunpowder magazine. The gunpowder exploded, and the irons flew from the hearth and struck dead the governor, an unpopular figure who that year had forbidden the traditional burning of a tree trunk in front of the parish church. Divine retribution, the people of the village believed.

The folk music of the Monsanto area is charming if strange. Half chanted, half sung, there is nothing quite like it elsewhere in the country. Its rhythm is beaten out with the assistance of a square tambourine known as an *adufe*.

The great Idanha plain stretches south from here, beyond Castelo Branco, where there are large areas of pine and eucalyptus. It is a vast area of cattle-raising country: bitterly cold in winter, scorching hot in the summer months, it is not a region that is much visited by tourists.

Idanha-a-Velha is one of the oldest towns in Portugal, but has a very small population.

Giant boulder at Monsanto.

COLCHAS

If you have been impressed by the beautiful linen bedspreads you saw in the museum, or those being made in the attached embroidery school, you might be inspired to buy a modern version to take home with you. Since the 17th century it has been the custom for brides-to-be to hand-embroider their wedding bedspreads. From this practice and skill, a cottage industry was born. Traditionally the spreads were white, but in recent years, they have become available in interwoven colours. Earlier patterns were geometric, echoing Persian carpets, but other decorative themes have become popular as well, including those showing flowers and birds. The intricate work involved means that a single item can take up to a year to complete, and prices are accordingly high.

Porto, as viewed from the Douro river.

PORTO

An evocative city on the Rio Douro, Porto's charms lie in its time-worn sun-baked buildings, vibrant riverfront cafés and ancient cobbled back-streets. The flipside is a vibrant commercial centre and a lucrative port-wine trade.

Porto ❶ is the commercial centre of northern Portugal, a fascinating city with a long and colourful history that is reflected in the culture, lifestyle and architecture. Its historic centre is a Unesco World Heritage Site. In many ways, Porto is a northern European city, with granite church towers, stolid dark buildings, and hidden Baroque treasures. But there is a real southern European feel here, as well, particularly around the Ribeira *bairro* where the narrow backstreets, hung with washing, and dusty old-fashioned shops have a hint of Naples about them.

Posed majestically on the rocky cliffs overlooking the Rio Douro, Porto is linked by six bridges to Vila Nova de Gaia, where most of the port-wine lodges are located, fronted by their moored *barcos rabelos* (see page 281). These days, large ships dock at the seaport of Leixões, but coal barges, fishing trawlers and other small vessels still sail up the river, and a river trip is a great way to see the city. The climate in town is temperate, and the Portuenses, as the inhabitants are called, are traditionally industrious – as reflected in the well-known Portuguese saying: "Coimbra studies, Braga prays, Lisbon shows off and Porto works."

In Roman times, the twin cities at the mouth of the Douro were known as Portus on the right bank and Cale on the left. During the Moorish occupation, the entire region between the Minho and Douro rivers was called Portucale. When Afonso Henriques founded the new kingdom in 1143, he took the name of his home province and called it Portucalia.

Porto prospered from the seafaring exploits of the golden epoch of discoveries. Its shipyards, adapting Douro river *caravelas*, produced caravels that sailed around the world. Prince Henry,

Main Attractions

Casa do Infante
Centro Português de Fotografia
Rua Santa Catarina
Port Wine Museum
Casa da Música
Port-wine lodges

Driving over Dom Luís Bridge.

Flower sellers add colour to the streets of Porto.

who initiated and inspired exploration, was born here.

The wine trade

In the 17th and 18th centuries, the wines of the Upper Douro were robust table reds. Then, in 1820, a "climatic accident" occurred, with warm weather producing unusually sweet grapes, with a resulting sweet tipple, particularly appreciated by the British. In the following years, the wine companies added *aguardente*, or brandy, to stop the fermentation and fix the sugar content. This was the beginning of the sweet fortified wine so famed today. England's long connection with the city they called Oporto had been developing with the wine trade (see Wines of Portugal, page 93). The Methuen Treaty of 1703 opened English markets to Portuguese wines, and the English shippers of Porto became increasingly rich and powerful. In 1727 they established a Shippers' Association, which regulated the trade and controlled prices paid to Portuguese growers. Thirty years later, to combat the English monopoly, the Marquês de

Pombal founded the Alto Douro Wine Company. Today the business is organised and controlled by the city-based Port Wine Institute.

Porto is an energetic and lively commercial city with an individual taste in food and drink. Regional specialities include roast pork, fresh salmon, lamprey, trout and tripe. The most popular bars and restaurants (justifiably so) are by the river around Cais de Ribeira and in Vila Nova de Gaia opposite. You may hear fado in a few restaurants, such as Mal Cozinhado at Rua Outerinho 13, while those seeking a more vigorous nightlife head for Foz de Duoro 4km (2 miles) downstream by the sea.

The old city

The heart of the city is the **Praça da Liberdade Ⓐ**, with its central equestrian statue of Pedro IV. On the north side of the square is the broad Avenida dos Aliados, its bright flowerbeds covering part of the city's new Metro. The avenue leads uphill to the **Câmara Municipal Ⓑ** (Town Hall) and the modern statue of Almeida Garrett

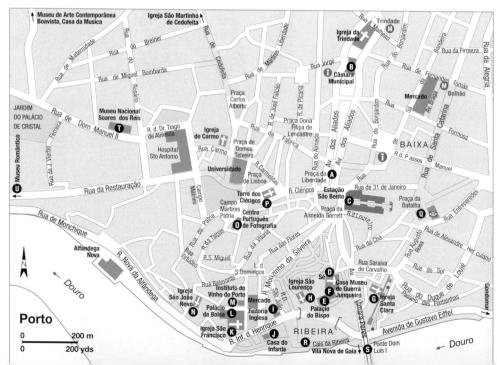

Porto

0   200 m
0   200 yds

(1799–1854), liberal poet and novelist, and native son of Porto.

To the southeast of Praça da Liberdade lies the Praça da Almeida Garrett, where the railway station, the **Estação São Bento** Ⓒ, has a fine entrance hall decorated with traditional *azulejos* depicting historical scenes. From here you can catch a train for a journey along the Rio Douro to Pocinho.

Heading south, you arrive at the 12th-century **Sé** Ⓓ (Cathedral; www. diocese-porto.pt; Mon–Sat Apr–Sept 9am–12.30pm, 2.30–7pm, Nov–Mar to 6pm; free). It was here that King João I married Philippa of Lancaster in 1387, the year after the Treaty of Windsor was signed with England. The Gothic cloister is decorated with fine tiles. Just below, in the Medieval Tower, is a tourist office offering tours of the city and river (tel: 351 222 000 073; www. portotours.com). There is a good choice, to suit various time frames and budgets, particularly the river trips, which vary from a 50-minute cruise of the bridges for €10 to a two-day cruise, including sightseeing and meals, starting from €135.

Nearby, on Pena Ventosa, the site of an ancient citadel, is the impressive 18th-century **Palácio do Bispo** Ⓔ (Bishop's Palace). Just beyond is the **Casa Museu de Guerra Junqueiro** Ⓕ (Tue–Sat 10am–12.30pm, 2–5.30pm, Sun 2–5.30pm), in the house of the highly regarded poet of that name, who died in 1923. His memorabilia and furnishings are on display.

Across the avenue stands the 15th-century **Igreja Santa Clara** Ⓖ (Mon–Fri 9–noon, 3.30–6pm, Sat 3–6pm, Sun 10am–11am; free), next to one of the best-preserved sections of the old city wall. Santa Clara has been rebuilt several times but is noted for its splendid gilded wood choir stalls and altars. Sacheverell Sitwell wrote: "After it, every other building in Porto, even São Francisco, is drab and dull."

To the west, the **Igreja São Lourenço** Ⓗ (Tue–Sat 10am–1.30pm, 2.30–5pm; free), better known as Igreja dos Grilos (after the crickets that lodge there), was built in 1570 and is one of the earliest examples of Portuguese Baroque.

The name of Praça da Liberdade, or Liberty Square, was adopted in 1910.

Praça da Liberdade is considered the centre of Porto.

The western side

The well-known Sandeman silhouette is hard to avoid in Porto.

At the end of Rua Infante Dom Henrique stands the bastion of English life, the **Feitoria Inglesa** (English Factory House). Here, the old British port-wine shippers do their business, play billiards or cards, read English newspapers and enjoy English food, as they have for the past 200 years.

Around the corner, on Rua da Alfândega, stands the much-restored **Casa do Infante** (Tue–Sat 10am–1pm, Sun 2–5.30pm; free Sun), where Prince Henry the Navigator was born in 1394. For a time it served as the customs house; it is now a museum with three floors of exhibits relating the history of Porto's trade and industry. Also on display are the Roman foundations and mosaics discovered during excavation.

Going by the Praça do Infante Dom Henrique, you reach the **Igreja São Francisco** (daily July–Aug 9am–8pm, June, Sept–Oct 9am–7pm, Nov–May 9am–5.30pm), founded by King Sancho II in 1233 and rebuilt in the 14th century. The interior glitters in Baroque splendour with gilded

Colourful laundry on the line.

columns, arches and statues. On the site of a convent, which burnt down in 1832, is the **Palácio da Bolsa** (Stock Exchange; www.palaciodabolsa.pt; guided tours Apr–Oct 9am–6.30pm, Nov–Mar 9am–12.30pm, 2–5.30pm), noted for its opulent reception hall. Up the hill is the **Instituto do Vinho do Porto** (Port Wine Institute), the government agency established in 1932 to control the quality of port.

Following the Rua Belmonte past old homes with balconies and tiled walls, you arrive at the church of **São João Novo**, built in 1592.

The road leads to the **Centro Português de Fotografia** (www.cpf.pt; Mon–Fri 10am–12.30pm, 2–6pm, Sat–Sun 3–7pm; free), housed in a former prison and mainly showcasing the work of Scottish-born photographer Frederick William Flower (1815–89), who lived in Porto for most of his life.

Just beyond here is the singular 18th-century **Torre dos Clérigos** (torredosclerigos.pt; daily 9am–7pm), the tallest granite tower in Portugal. This was designed, along with its church, by Nicolau Nasoni, who was also architect of the fine Baroque Solar de Mateus near Vila Real. Unless you really have no head for heights it is worth climbing the 225 or so steps for the view over the city. Just north of the tower lies the main **university** building, a handsome granite structure built in 1807 as the Polytechnical Academy.

East of São Bento railway station lies the busy **Praça da Batalha**, with a statue of Pedro V in the middle, and the imposing 18th-century church of São Idelfonso with a facade of bright blue-and-white tiles. The main shopping street is **Rua Santa Catarina**, where bargains may be found in a variety of goods, from shoes to pottery. Rua das Flores has the best gold and silver shops.

Cais da Ribeira

Take the steep roads down to the river, and you will find yourself drawn to

the **Cais da Ribeira** ®, one of the liveliest parts of the city and a Unesco World Heritage Site. Many small shops and restaurants are built right into what remains of the old city wall, some showing watermarks around 2 metres (6ft) from the floor where the river has burst its banks. During the day you can take a river trip from here, and in the evening its restaurants brim with customers.

Ten minutes' walk downriver brings you to the *electrico* stop, a tram that goes out to Castelo de Queijo on the coast. Just beyond is an excellent **Port Wine Museum** (Tue–Sat 10am–5.30pm, Sun 10am–12.30pm, 2–5.30pm).

The splendid steel arch further upriver is a railway bridge, **Ponte de Dona Maria Pia**, built in 1876 to plans by Alexandre Gustave Eiffel and only recently put out of use by the new Ponte São João. In the centre of Porto is the handsome **Ponte Dom Luís I** ®, built in 1886, which provides splendid views. This two-storey iron bridge has two decks, the upper of which will carry the new Metro

line, and leads directly to port cellars in Vila Nova de Gaia (see page 280).

Outside the old town

On the western side of the city, in the old royal Palácio dos Carrancas, is the **Museu Nacional Soares dos Reis** ® (www.museusoaresdosreis.com; Wed–Sun 10am–6pm, Tue 2–6pm), named after a 19th-century sculptor. It has a fine collection of archaeological artefacts, religious art, regional costumes, ceramics and contemporary paintings, as well as sculpture. Paintings by Grão Vasco are on display, among them pictures of St Catherine and St Lucy.

On the western side of the Jardim do Palácio de Cristal (entered from Rua Entre Quintas) is the intriguing **Museu Romântico** ® (Mon–Sat 10am–5.30pm, Sun 10am–12.30pm, 2–5.30pm), which recreates and evokes the life of the Portuguese 19th-century bourgeoisie. It's located in the Quinta da Macieirinha, where King Carlo

Porto is often called the invincible city, because of its resistance against Napoleon during the Peninsular War.

Casa da Música is the major concert space in Portugal.

FACT

On the Festa de São João (23–24 June), festivities take place near the Ponte Dom Luís I. There is a regatta of the port-wine boats, and people sing, dance around bonfires and feast on roast kid and grilled sardines – and hit each other over the head with plastic hammers.

Alberto died in 1849, after abdicating the throne of Sardinia. The mansion is set in a rose garden and contains most of its original furnishings.

North of here, via Rua de Don Pedro V, is the splendid **Casa da Música** (www.casadamusica.com; tours daily 11am and 4pm in Portuguese, 4pm in English). Designed by top Dutch architect Rem Koolhaas, this ultra-modern geometric building has an extraordinary interior space. Regular concerts are staged here, ranging from fado to classical music, and the building may also be visited and appreciated for its innovative architecture and interior design.

To the northwest, in Boavista, is the Art Deco **Museu Serralves** (www.serralves.pt; Tue–Fri 10am–5pm, Fri–Sat 10am–8pm), set in an attractive 18-hectare (44-acre) estate. The mansion holds temporary exhibitions of modern art. In the grounds is the stunning **Museu de Arte Contemporânea** (hours as above), designed by Porto architect Alvaro Siza Vieira, which has both permanent and temporary exhibitions. As well as a large,

The azulejos-rich exterior of Igreja do Carmo, a Carmelite church.

light exhibition space, the building comprises an auditorium, a restaurant and a library.

Port-wine lodges

Porto is best known for being the home of port which, in the last few years, has made something of a comeback, shedding its previous stuffy image as being primarily a gentleman's after-dinner drink to be enjoyed, typically, with a fat cigar.

Vila Nova de Gaia, across the Ponte Dom Luís I, is an industrial zone with ceramic, glass, soap and other factories. But above all, Gaia is the true seat of the port-wine industry, where most warehouses or lodges are to be found. There are about 80 port-wine lodges here: many of the larger ones welcome weekday visitors to tour the installations and, better still, taste their wines (which most visitors will then purchase). Most prominent is Sandeman (www.sandeman.eu; Mon–Fri Mar-Oct 10am–12.30pm 2–6pm, Nov–Feb 9.30am–12.30pm, 2–5.30pm), whose distinctive silhouette, designed in 1928, rises on the skyline. Another good choice is British-owned Taylor's (Mon–Fri 10am–6pm, Sat–Sun 10am–5pm; free). The port-wine lodges line the waterfront and fly their flags from *barcos rabelos* moored alongside.

In spring, the new wine is brought down from the Upper Douro by truck, and is then left to mature in 530-litre (140-gallon) oak casks, or pipes. Here the blending takes place, with wines from different vineyards and different years blended to produce a distinctive aroma, taste and colour before the wine is bottled and again left to mature.

In the evening, many people cross the bridge to eat and enjoy a great view of the city opposite. Apart from traditional restaurants, at the far end of the quay there is a wide choice of places to eat and drink in the modern riverside Cais de Gaia complex, with terraces and river views.

Barcos Rabelos

The *barcos rabelos* have become a symbol of port wine, the product with whose destiny they have been entwined for hundreds of years

On his return to Lisbon after discovering the sea route to India in 1498, Vasco da Gama proclaimed *"Somos a gente do mar"* (We are the people of the sea). Using small, light, high-prowed caravel sailing ships based on an ancient Mediterranean design, 15th- and 16th-century Portuguese explorers voyaged the world and Portugal became the greatest maritime nation on earth.

A generation later Portugal lost its superior position, but numerous seafaring traditions were still in place. And as Portugal retreated into centuries of introspection, the boat-building techniques and traditions left by ancient mariners were retained.

Best known are the flat-bottomed, square-rigged *barcos rabelos*, which are a familiar sight in Porto.

Viking similarities

In traditional *barco rabelo* building the hull's shell is laid first, then the ribs are placed. This is the Nordic "clinker building" method which may be a direct Viking legacy. A comparison between the bare hull of a *rabelo* and that of a reconstructed longboat in Oslo's Viking Museum shows striking similarities. Other features of the *rabelo's* design evolved in the 17th century, the nascent period of the trade in port wine. Ever since then the grapes for port have been grown in the upper reaches of the Douro valley, from where the wine is transported to Vila Nova de Gaia for shipment abroad. The adapted indigenous boats of the Douro were constructed in large numbers and put to this use on the treacherous river, stacked with casks of wine. Flat bottoms were needed to shoot the rapids, negotiate the shallows, and achieve high loading ratios. A tall platform at the stern gave the helmsman a clear view over the rows of casks, and a huge steering oar, or *espadela* – effectively a rudder – was needed to change course rapidly. This also had to be capable of being levered out of the water to avoid smashing in the rapids and rocky shallows. Intrepid boatmen slept and ate on board, suspending cauldrons from a beam and boiling their traditional dishes of *bacalhau* (dried cod).

The damming of the Douro for hydroelectric power brought an end to the *rabelo's* interdependence with the port trade. But although port now makes the journey from the Upper Douro by road, the *rabelo* has proved an irrepressible symbol of the product. Boats are still constructed, at great expense, to compete in the annual race of *rabelos* owned by the port-shipping firms. The regatta, enthusiastically contested, is held on 24 June, the festival of São João (Porto's patron saint), when the city erupts in revelry. Boats set off from the mouth of the Douro, with the race climaxing at the Dom Luís I bridge.

The set of rules ensuring that the *rabelos* are constructed precisely according to the specifications evolved during their heyday is taken very seriously. The craft have to be built in yards along the Douro, with the hull constructed from maritime pine, and laid down by the "clinker building" technique. The largest *rabelos* are around 24 metres (80ft) long by 5.5 metres (18ft) wide with 80 sq metres (860 sq ft) of sail billowing in the wind, and need at least a dozen crew members. Payloads are up to 65 casks, each holding 522 litres (138 gallons) of port.

The regatta proves that the boats are more than advertisements for their owners' wares.

Boats along the Douro River.

Rio Tâmega.

Amarante on the hillside.

THE DOURO VALLEY

Renowned worldwide for the wine it produces, the Douro valley is graced by its centuries-old vineyards growing on steeply terraced hillsides.

Map on page 286

The romantic history of port wine has endowed the Douro region with unrivalled respect. Douro means "of gold" and the river, gleaming at sunset, does resemble a twisting golden chain as it winds through the narrow valley between the steep hills and terraced vineyards. The countryside is exceptionally beautiful, particularly in spring and autumn, and is enhanced by the neat rows of vines which grace the hillsides.

Although the Douro stretches from Spain to the Atlantic at Porto, only the inland part of the valley, the Alto Douro, is recognised for growing the grapes used for port wine. The demarcated region starts some 100km (60 miles) upstream from Porto at Barqueiros, just before Régua, and follows the river all the way to Spain. Some of the tributaries of the Douro – the Corgo, Torto, Pinhão and Tua – are included in the area. It was Portugal's authoritarian Marquês de Pombal who staked out the Douro in 1756, making it the first officially designated wine-producing region in the world. Subsequent legislation designated the Upper Douro as the port-wine region.

Characteristically, the schistose soils are stony and impoverished and the climate extreme. Summers are very hot and dry, and made hotter by the direct rays of the sun reflected on the crystalline rock; winters are cold and

wet. The large lumps of surface schist act as storage heaters, absorbing the sun's heat in the day and releasing it throughout the night. The slopes nearest to the river grow the finest grapes and this land is highly prized.

Choosing a base

Peso da Régua (see page 288) is the capital of the Douro valley, with an office of the Port Wine Institute; it is also the headquarters of the portgrowers' association, which grades and certifies the wine travelling to Porto.

Main Attractions

Amarante
Quinta da Aveleda
Lamego
Parque Arqueológico do Vale Côa
Mateus
Vila Real

Amarante's historic bridge.

Balconies overhang the Rio Tâmega in Amarante.

The smaller town of Pinhão 25km (15 miles) further upstream is regarded as the centre of the wine industry, and this is where all the famous names have their farms. It is a handy place to stay although it is hardly bristling with hotels. Taylors have restored and extended a *quinta* on the banks of the Douro, now the Vintage House Hotel, providing quality accommodation. The area has a number of restored houses and farms that are part of the manor house system (see page 117), some of them in very fine locations.

Casa de Casal de Loivos, above Pinhão, has a fine overview of the Douro or, if you prefer to bury yourself in the country, Casa da Lavada, a restored 14th-century fortified manor house, provides modern comforts. It is high in the mountains of the Serra do Marão in a village where visitors are still a curiosity. Traditional hotels are found in the surrounding towns of Amarante,

Vila Real or Lamego. **Porto ❶** is a good base for organised trips into the surrounding area. Coach trips are well advertised but it is easy enough to catch a train from São Bento station on the Douro line. The end of the line is Pocinho, not too far from the Spanish border. There are branch lines to Amarante, Vila Real and Mirandela. The river is now navigable for much of its length and boat trips up the river are a regular feature and a pleasant way to see the countryside. One option is to go by boat as far as Pinhão and return by train.

Upriver from Porto

There is little to detain the motorist between Porto and Amarante so the fast A4 is the best way to travel. It speeds up what would otherwise be a very slow journey through *vinho verde*-growing countryside. The main area for *vinho verde* lies to the north in Costa Verde and Minho.

Amarante ❷, on the banks of the Rio Tâmega, is delightful, at least in the old part of town. Geese paddle contentedly among punts and trailing

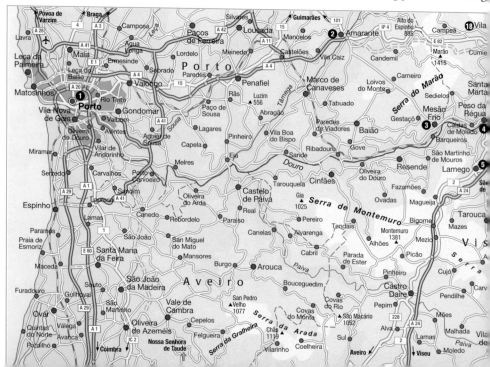

illow trees on the river, while afternoon tea-takers look on from over-
hanging wooden balconies. Dominant
in the town is the three-arched **Ponte
de São Gonçalo**, built in 1790. It
became a battleground in the Peninsular War in 1809 when General
Silveira, supported by Marshal Beresford's troops, successfully fought off
the French.

The bridge leads to the **Convento
de São Gonçalo** (Mon–Sat 8am–7pm,
Sun 8am–8.15pm; free), named after
the local patron saint, and protector of
marriages.

Amarante's association with fertility rites reaches back into the mists
of time, and some claim the town's
name is derived from *amar*, meaning
to love". These ancient beliefs have
empowered São Gonçalo, beatified in
1561, to assist believers in everything
pertaining to love and marriage. He
is honoured every June by a festival
which, as you may imagine, is a particularly raucous occasion, with the
local men out in the streets offering
distinctly phallic-shaped cakes to any
women prepared to accept them.

The convent, however, is much
more sombre. It was begun in 1540
but not completed until 1620. Inside
is the tomb of São Gonçalo, who died
about 1260, and some lush gilded
carved woodwork. Anyone aspiring to
love and marriage need only touch the
effigy of the saint to be blessed within
the year. Sadly, the limestone effigy is
now quite worn in places.

Above the rear cloister is the
Museu Amadeo de Souza-Cardosa
(Tue–Sun June–Sept 10am–12.30pm,
2–6pm, Oct–May 9.30am–12.30pm,
2–5.30pm), which has some superb
contemporary and Modernist Portuguese paintings – Souza-Cardosa
was a Cubist artist who came from
Amarante.

Nearby is the **Quinta da Aveleda**
(tel: 255 718 200; www.aveleda.pt;
daily visits at 10.30am, noon, 3pm
and 4.45pm), seat of one of Portugal's main wine empires and a leading exporter of the country's famous
vinho verde. A visit to the *quinta*
includes a tour of the beautiful gardens, as well as the bottling plant.
At the wine lodge you can taste two

FACT

Boat trips on the river
are privately run and
therefore not promoted
through tourist offices.
Trips last from a few
hours to a few days,
and most hotels and
quintas will tell you
what's on offer.

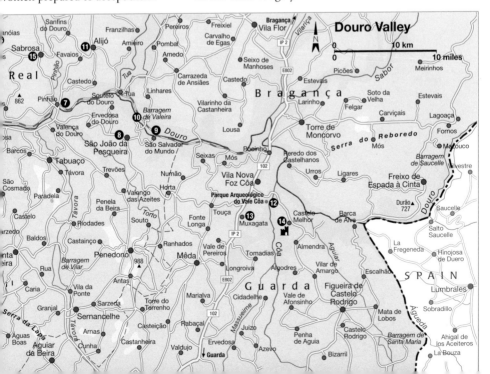

Ready to pour one of the Douro valley's excellent wines.

Nossa Senhora dos Remédios church.

different types of vinho verde, accompanied by local cheese, and buy a bottle or a case from the old distillery, which has now been converted to a store. If you want to have lunch here or would like a more personalised tour, including a visit to the production facility, you must book in advance.

Beyond Amarante the road turns abruptly south to twist and climb through the Serra do Marão. *Vinho verde* vines climb the trees here and huge granite tors stand in the summit region. Beyond is a descent to the small village of **Mesão Frio** ❸, and a sweeping view of the Upper Douro winding peacefully through the gorges of the port-wine country.

The road follows the river's north bank, passing through the small spa town of **Caldas de Moledo** before reaching **Régua** ❹ (its full name is Peso da Régua), a busy river port

and the headquarters of the **Casa do Douro**, an organisation that has a great deal of power in the regulation of port-wine production. In this area lie some of the oldest British and Portuguese estates, and information about them can be had from both the Casa do Douro and the tourist office near the market. Here the road crosses the Douro and runs along the picturesque southern bank.

South of the river

Before following along the south bank towards Pinhão, there is a worthwhile diversion to **Lamego** ❺, which is a city of historical importance. The Lusitanians arose in revolt against the occupying Romans, refusing to pay the heavy taxation, so the Romans burned the town to the ground. Fernando de León and Castile took the city, aided by the legendary El Cid, and allowed the Muslim *wali* to continue to govern Lamego, as long as he converted and paid tribute to the king. But the city's most significant moment in Portugal's history was in 1143, when the *cortes* met

PILGRIMAGE CHURCH

Atop Lamego's other hill is the visually striking church of **Nossa Senhora dos Remédios,** crowning a vast stairway reminiscent of Braga's Bom Jesus. The first chapel was founded by the Bishop of Lamego in 1361, and dedicated to St Stephen. In 1564, it was pulled down, and a new one built. From that time, there has been a steady stream of the faithful seeking cures. The first week in September is the time of the major pilgrimage, and there is a jolly accompanying festival which seems to have little to do with healing or piety. The present sanctuary was started in 1750, and was consecrated 11 years later – but the magnificent Baroque-style staircase leading up to it, begun in the 19th century, was completed only in the 1960s. Fountains, statues and pavilions decorate each level.

for the very first time. At this meeting, the nobles declared Afonso Henriques to be Afonso I, the first king of Portugal.

Lamego's 12th-century castle, on one of the city's two hills, preserves a fine 13th-century keep, with windows that were added later and a very old and unusual vaulted cistern. The cistern is possibly Moorish, with monograms of master masons.

The **Sé** (Cathedral; daily 8am–1pm, 3–7pm), a Gothic structure, was built by Afonso Henriques in 1129. Only the Romanesque tower is left from the original building. The city museum, housed in the 18th-century Bishop's Palace, has a collection that includes Flemish tapestries dating from the 16th century and works by Grão Vasco.

Just outside Lamego (start on the Tarouca road), in the valley of the Rio Balsemão, is the tiny **São Pedro de Balsemão ⑥**, a Visigothic church believed to be the oldest in Portugal, with parts of the structure dating back as far as the 6th century.

Following the south bank of the Douro towards Pinhão is a rewarding drive; you can enjoy the flowing lines of vineyards patterning the hillsides and broken only by signs displaying such well-known names as Sandeman, Barros and Quinta Dona Matilde.

Pinhão ⑦, on the north side of the river, seems an unlikely town to lie at the heart of the port-wine region. There is little to visit but it is worth a stop at the railway station to see the *azulejo* panels depicting scenes of the Rio Douro or to taste some wine in the barrel-shaped café by the river. The tourist office (Rua António Manuel Saraiva; tel: 254 731 932) has information about the wine estates in the region.

A scenic circular tour

A tasty sampler of typical Douro scenery and traditional villages can be enjoyed on a short circular tour from Pinhão, taking around half a day. It starts on the south side of the river, along the road climbing the hillside to **São João da Pasqueira ⑧**. This village has some fine 18th-century houses mixed with surprisingly modern properties. Follow left-turns signposted Barragem de Valeira to drive through dilapidated, overgrown vineyards ravaged by the Phylloxera scourge in the 19th century and never replanted. Watch out on the descent towards the *barragem* (reservoir) for the pointed hill, **São Salvador do Mundo ⑨**, which is littered with churches and chapels.

Around where the **Barragem de Valeira ⑩** now stands is where Baron Forrester, the 19th-century English pioneer, lost his life in 1861: in those days the river here tumbled over dangerous rapids. Born in Hull in 1809, Joseph James Forrester came out to Portugal as a young man to work for his uncle in Porto. He was fascinated by the wine industry and spent many years boating up and down the river making a detailed map. His widely acclaimed work

TIP

The best time to visit the Douro valley is during the *vindima*, in September, when the grapes are being collected. Some vineyards give tourists the chance to participate in the grape harvest, joining in with the picking and then trampling the fruit barefoot in the pressing basins to release the juice.

The pilgrims' stairway at Nossa Senhora dos Remédios.

Azulejo is a tin-glazed, ceramic tilework that has become a hallmark of Portugal.

Historical re-enactors dress up for a medieval festival in Lamego.

won him his title in 1855, the first foreigner to earn such an honour. It was the river that eventually claimed his life at the age of 51. He was out boating with António Adelaide Ferreira and others when they ran into trouble at the Cachão de Valeira rapids. The boat capsized and Baron Forrester drowned, dragged down, it is said, by the weight of his money belt. António Adelaide Ferreira survived, helped by the buoyancy of her crinoline dress.

Cross the *barragem* to regain the north shore and zigzag up the hillside towards Linhares. Vineyards make the patterns and create the scenery for much of the way towards Tua and Alijó. **Alijó ⓫** is one of the bigger towns in the area and is the location of a *pousada* named after Baron Forrester. The route back heads through Favaios to Pinhão.

Rock art

Winding eastwards from Pinhão through **São João da Pasqueira** and along the hill contours, past quaint churches and villages, you will come to Vila Nova de Foz Côa and the valley of the Rio Côa. Work in the 1990s to build a dam in this remote region uncovered a remarkable collection of rock paintings.

In 1996 the Portuguese Government declared the Côa valley protected as the **Parque Arqueológico do Vale Côa ⓬** (www.ipa.min-cultura.pt/coa; tel: 279 768 260; Tue–Sun 9am–12.30pm, 2–5.30pm; visits must be reserved in advance). In 1998, the park, which has the largest area of palaeolithic engravings in Europe, was declared a Unesco World Heritage Site.

At present, only three rock-art sites in the valley can be visited, not by individuals, but on a guided tour with a vehicle. These are at Penascosa, Ribeira de Piscos, Canada do Inferno and Fariseu (seasonal). The tours all last around 90 minutes. Tours to Canada do Inferno start from the Museu do Côa; tours to Ribeira de Piscos

start from the visitor centre at **Muxa-gata** ⓭, while tours to Penascosa leave from the reception centre in **Castelo Melhor** ⓮.

The stunning Museu do Côa (Tue–Sun 10am–1.30pm, 2–5.30pm) stands in the middle of nowhere like an installation in the landscape. The museum houses cutting-edge displays on the rock paintings, as well as temporary exhibitions, and has a restaurant with wonderful views over the park.

North to Vila Real

Going from Pinhão to the north leads to **Sabrosa** ⓯, the birthplace of Fernão de Magalhães, known in English as Ferdinand Magellan, the man who led the first circumnavigation of the world between 1519 and 1522 under the Spanish flag. Just before Constantim, look out on the right for a diversion to the sanctuary of **Panóias** ⓰ where there is a field with a series of enormous carved stones, believed to have been used as altars for human sacrifice. Inscriptions in Latin invoke the ancient god Serapis, known to both Greek and Egyptian mythology.

Beyond Constantim but before Vila Real is the village and fantastical palace of **Mateus** ⓱ (www.casademateus. com; May–Sept 9am–7.30pm, Nov–Apr 9am–6pm) with its celebrated gardens. It was built by Nicolau Nasoni in 1739–43 for António José Botelho Mourão. Today, an illustration of the palace graces the distinctive label of the popular rosé wine from this area, even though there is no formal connection. Mateus Rosé is still Portugal's best selling wine export, with distribution in more than 150 countries. The exquisite building, with its striking Baroque facade, double stairway and huge coat of arms, frequently hosts musical events.

Vila Real

An ancient settlement in the Terra de Panóias, **Vila Real** ⓲ was founded and renamed by King Dinis in 1289. Its name, "royal town", is appropriate, as Vila Real once had more noble families than any city other than the capital. Walking through ancient streets, you will see many residences marked, often above the main entrance, with

FACT

Pressure to stop the flooding of the Côa Valley included a rap song recorded by high-school students from Vila Nova de Foz Côa, with the line "Petroglyphs can't swim". Although the dam project was abandoned in 1995, many carvings had already been submerged by the construction of the Pocinho dam in 1982.

Vineyards in the Douro River.

An architectural detail in Vila Real.

A bridge over the Douro Valley.

a lively bustling industrial centre. Vila Real is one of the largest towns in the region.

The **Sé** (Cathedral) was originally the church of a Dominican convent. Although much of the present building dates from the 14th century, Romanesque columns still remain from an earlier structure. The oldest church is the ancient **Capela de São Nicolau**, on a promontory of high land behind the municipal hall, overlooking the valley of the Rio Corgo. Another church of note is **São Pedro**, whose Baroque touches were completed by Nicolau Nasoni (1691–1773), the Tuscan-born architect who designed the manor house in Mateus. Among fine houses dating from the 15th–18th centuries is the **Casa de Diogo Cão**, an Italian Renaissance-style building that was the birthplace of Cão, the navigator who discovered the mouth of the River Congo in 1482.

the original owners' coats of arms. As likely as not, descendants of the family will still be living there.

The 19th-century writer Camilo Castelo Branco lived in Vila Real and wrote many of his most enduring works using the town as a backdrop.

Vila Real became a city proper only in 1925, but the importance of the region dates from 1768, when the vineyards were developed commercially: the area has good red and white wines, but it is the rosé that is best known – especially Mateus. Now

As far as local crafts are concerned, the Vila Real region is noted for the black pottery of Bisalhães and the woollen goods of Caldas do Alvão and Marão.

Selling baked goods at the market in Amarante.

PORT WINE, THE DOURO'S TREASURE

The story of port wine is one of triumph over adversity. From bare, inhospitable terrain came an extraordinary wine that is famed the world over.

Upstream from Porto lies the country's most inhospitable region. Dry and stony, with barely a covering of dusty soil and with excessively high summer temperatures, combined with months of drought, the Upper Douro seems an unlikely area to have emerged as a global producer of world-famous port wine.

Covering a vast area of some 243,000 hectares (600,000 acres) with around 15 percent under vines, the history of port production has its roots in a modest cottage industry where the discerning locals were producing exceptionally high-quality wine for their own use. Exploiting the region to produce wine in commercial quantities was beset by huge problems, but it seemed that every disadvantage, every deterrent, contributed to its success. The soil, or rather the lack of it, was just one. Vines planted into the schist (rock) sent their roots searching deep down through the cracks and crevices to find water. The vast root system that developed allowed the plants to survive burning summers without irrigation, so yielding grapes high in sugar.

The pre-dammed Rio Douro, steep banked and virtually unnavigable, was another apparent drawback that proved essential to the region's success, for without it there would have been no means of exporting the wine. Grapes harvested at the steep higher levels were transported to the split-level factories below, and the resulting wine was then lowered to the river for transport on the distinctive flat-bottomed *barcos rabelos*.

More than 80 varieties of grape have been used in port wine but modern plantings are limited to about six varieties.

Teams, mainly of women, spread along the rows and sweep systematically across the vineyard; strong young men carry away the baskets. The close-packed vineyards create geometric green patterns on the hillsides transforming the rolling landscapes of this region.

In the Douro region of Portugal there are still Port producers who crush their grapes by the traditional method: by foot.

Enjoying a glass.

BRINGING IN THE HARVEST

The Upper Douro is a pleasure to visit at any point during the summer, but harvest time is the most rewarding. The harvest *(vindima)* usually starts towards the end of September – the exact date being dictated by the conditions of any particular year – and by this time temperatures have cooled to a pleasant heat.

In spite of recent mechanisation, grape picking is still largely done by hand. Extended families of itinerant workers from surrounding villages often return year after year to the same farms to bring in the harvest. Traditionally, men and women adopt different roles in the field, but they all come together at meal times. Lunch is almost party time: the estate owners provide an abundant meal and the pickers relax and enjoy it.

When the mood is right, and with a contented team of workers, the sound of singing can be heard emanating from the vine terraces. It is a time of great celebration, of relief that the crop has survived the vagaries of the weather and of thanksgiving for a harvest, even in years when it is not at its most bountiful.

The flat-bottomed rabelos, designed to suit the shallow waters of the Douro, carry the port barrels downriver.

Grapes from an Alentejo vineyard.

Port casks.

Along the waterfront near Peneda-Gerês National Park.

Grapevines growing in Minho.

COSTA VERDE AND THE MINHO

Verdant and lush, this is a land of vineyards, tranquil
riverside towns, busy markets, and a great European
wilderness: the Peneda-Gerês National Park.

Main Attractions
Braga
Barcelos
Viana do Castelo
Vila do Conde
Peneda-Gerês National Park
Ponte de Lima

The Minho region north of Porto is often described as Costa Verde, or the Green Coast, a reference to the vineyards and lush green of its well-watered landscape. In reality it is a much larger area than just the coast. It extends northwards to the Rio Minho, the boundary with Spain, eastwards to include the Parque Nacional da Peneda-Gerês and south to encompass Braga and Guimarães. It is a region of great natural beauty, especially the verdant Lima Valley and the wild and mountainous Peneda-Gerês, where farming techniques and lifestyles pass from generation to generation with relatively little change.

Grapes are grown everywhere. They hang from trees, pergolas and porches, and climb along slopes and terraces. They grow in poor rocky soil where little else flourishes. To get the most out of the land, the Minhotos train their vines to grow upwards, on trees, houses and hedges, leaving ground space for cabbages, onions and potatoes. This freewheeling system made it difficult to modernise grape production, but for many years the larger vineyards have been using a system of wire-supporting crosses called *cruzetas*.

The *vindima*, or grape harvest, is still done by hand and is a wonderful sight to behold. Harvesting takes place in September and October and lasts until early November. It can be

a hazardous task, requiring towering 30-rung ladders to get at the elusive treetop grapes, although most vines now are trained at tractor height. In the hilly country, men still carry huge baskets of grapes weighing as much as 50kg (110lb) on their backs. On some back roads, squeaky ox-carts transport the grapes to wine-presses. In these modern times, however, the fruit is generally transported in trucks.

While harvest is still a festive occasion, it no longer involves quite the unbridled merrymaking of yore. In

Decorations for the Braga folklore festival.

TIP

The Comissão de Viticultura da Região dos Vinhos Verdes in Porto can provide information on *vinho verde* wine routes and estates to visit (tel: 226 077 300; http://rota.vinhoverde.pt).

the old days, workers used to perform a kind of bacchanalian dance, their arms linked, stamping on the grapes with their bare feet. It was said that this was the only way to crush the fruit without smashing the pips and spoiling the flavour of the wine. This was often accompanied by music and clapping, glasses of spirits and a good deal of sweat. Nowadays, mechanical extractors often remove the pips, and presses are generally used to crush the grapes, although treading still takes place in a few vineyards.

There is a second style of agriculture here which is even more distinctive and unique to this region of Portugal. It is known as dune agriculture, and involves digging small depressions in the actual sand dunes, which then capture the moisture from the sea mist and protect the crops from the sometimes strong winds. These sandy allotments are traditionally fertilised by dried seaweed, which many people believe contributes to the consistently high quality of the produce that is grown here. The seaweed is harvested in early autumn, collected by enormous nets and then spread out to dry in the sunshine.

Braga

Some people still refer to **Braga** ❶ somewhat wistfully, as "the Portuguese Rome". In Roman times, as Bracara Augusta, it was the centre of communications in north Lusitania. In the 6th century two synods were held here. Under Moorish occupation,

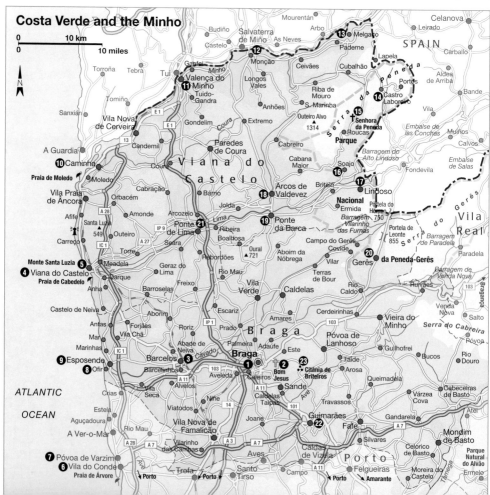

Costa Verde and the Minho

Braga was sacked and the cathedral badly damaged, but in the 11th century the city was largely restored to its former eminence by Bishop Dom Pedro and Archbishop São Geraldo. The archbishop claimed authority over all the churches of the Iberian peninsula, and his successors retained the title of Primate of the Spains for six centuries.

Like a Renaissance prince, one of his successors, Archbishop Dom Diogo de Sousa, encouraged the construction of many handsome Italian-style churches, fountains and palaces in the 16th century. Zealous prelates restored many of these works in the subsequent two centuries, but often with unfortunate results. Braga lost its title as ecclesiastical capital in 1716, when the patriarchate went to Lisbon. But it is still an important religious centre, and the site of Portugal's most elaborate Holy Week procession.

A visit to Braga usually begins at the **Sé** (Cathedral; daily Apr–Oct 8.30am–6.30pm, Nov–Mar 8.30am–5.30pm), which was built in the 11th century on the site of an earlier structure destroyed by the Moors. Of the original Romanesque building there remains only the southern portal and the sculpted cornice of the transept. Although it has been greatly modified by various restorations, the cathedral is still imposing. The interior contains some fine tombs, including those of the founders, Count Henri and his wife Teresa, a granite sculpture of the Virgin, an 18th-century choir loft and organ case, and richly decorated chapels and cloister.

Of particular interest is the **Tesouro da Catedral** (Cathedral Treasury; Tue–Sun Apr–Oct 9am–12.30pm, 2–6.30pm, Nov–Mar 9am–12.30pm, 2–5.30pm), with a fine collection of 15th-century vestments and silver chalices and crucifixes dating from the 10th and 12th centuries.

Nearby, with plain west walls set off by an 18th-century fountain, is the **Palácio de Arzobispo** (Archbishop's Palace), built in the 14th century and

reconstructed several times. The palace now houses the Public Library, with city archives dating back to the 9th century, 300,000 volumes and 10,000 manuscripts. On the western side of Praça Agrolongo stands one of Braga's Rome-inspired churches, **Nossa Senhora do Pópulo**, built in the 17th century and remodelled at the end of the 18th. It is decorated with *azulejos* depicting scenes from the life of St Augustine.

The **Palácio dos Biscainhos** (Tue–Sun 10am–12.15pm, 2–5.30pm) just across the way is a 17th-century mansion with lovely gardens and fountains. It houses the municipal museum with an impressive collection that includes 18th-century tiles, ceramics, jewellery and furniture.

The city has been digging into its past in recent years and uncovered such riches as Roman baths, a sanctuary called Fonte do Idolo and the remains of a house: Domus de Santiago. An archaeological museum, the **Museu Dom Diogo de Sousa** (http://mdds.imc-ip.pt;Tue–Sun 10am–5.30pm) displays the finds, with fascinating

Splendid wooden doorway of Braga Cathedral.

The grand stairway of Bom Jesus.

exhibits, including mosaic flooring dating from the 1st century AD. The museum is a short walk from the ruins of the above-mentioned **Termas Romanas** (Tue–Fri 9am–12.30pm, 2–5.30pm, Sat–Sun 11am–5pm), dating from the 2nd century AD.

On the northern side of the city, the church of **São João de Souto** was completely rebuilt in the late 18th century. But here you will find the superb **Capela do Conceição**, built in 1525, with crenellated walls, lovely windows and splendid statues of St Anthony and St Paul.

Bom Jesus

There are many other churches and chapels of interest in the centre, but the best known is **Santuário Bom Jesus** ❷ (daily 8am–8pm; free) which is conspicuously set on the wooded Monte Espinho, about 5km (3 miles) outside Braga. This popular pilgrimage centre is remarkable for its grandiose Baroque stairway and the view from its terrace of the Rio Cávado valley with the mountains in the distance. The double flight of stairs is flanked by chapels, fountains and often startlingly bizarre figures at each level, representing the Stations of the Cross.

If you don't wish to climb the steps, there is a funicular (daily 8am–8pm) and a winding road to the top. There, among oak trees, eucalyptus, camellias and mimosa, stands the 15th-century church, rebuilt in the 18th century. In its **Capela dos Milagres** (Chapel of Miracles) are votive offerings and pictures left by past pilgrims. Several hotels, souvenir shops and restaurants are also located in the vicinity of the sanctuary.

Barcelos: cock and bull

Just northwest of Braga is the charming market town of **Barcelos** ❸, on the north bank of the Rio Cávado. Barcelos has 15th-century fortifications, a 13th-century church and a 16th-century palace, but more than that, it has one of the best markets in the country. Every Thursday, traders and artisans display their crafts, textiles and other goods in the centre of town. There are also plenty of food stalls to ensure you won't go hungry.

It was here that the late Rosa Ramalho, the most famous folk-art sculptress in Portugal, created her world of fanciful ceramic animals and people – a style that has been continued by her granddaughter..Head to the Centro de Artesanato de Barcelos (Rua Dom Diogo Pinheiro 25) to browse local crafts. It displays copperware, handmade rugs, wooden toys, bright cotton tableware, and, of course, the *galo de Barcelos* – the ubiquitous Barcelos cockerel.

A monument, the so-called Senhor do Galo cross, is the most apt reminder of the extraordinary legend that lies behind the rooster's elevation to Portugal's unofficial national emblem (see page 227). There is an excellent pottery museum, the **Museu de Olaria** (www.museuolaria.org; Tue–Sun 9.30am–noon, 2–5pm), featuring traditional ceramics and pottery from all over the country, including the Azores.

Feeding the hens.

An old gate in Braga.

Viana do Castelo

A lively fishing and shipbuilding port at the mouth of the Rio Lima, **Viana do Castelo ❹** was called Diana by the Romans. This was the centre of Portugal's wine trade until the port declined in the 18th century and Porto became pre-eminent. There is a good deal to see in the centre of Viana, as well as beyond: the town is home to several of the region's most enticing sweeps of sand. In the central Praça da República there is a beautiful 16th-century fountain and the remarkable Misericórdia hospital, with a three-tiered facade supported by caryatids. There is also a museum here, the **Museu do Traje** (Costume Museum; Tue–Sun June–Sept 10am–1pm, 3–7pm, Oct–May 10am–1pm, 2–6pm), with two floors of colourful traditional costumes. Nearby stands the handsome 15th-century parish church with a Gothic portal and Romanesque towers.

The town is dominated by **Monte Santa Luzia ❺**, with a large and inappropriate modern basilica. To get here, hop on the funicular railway (daily 8am–dusk). Alternatively, energetic souls can climb the stairs just past the hospital. To the west of the town, the Baroque Nossa Senhora da Agonia church is the site of a popular pilgrimage each August. Dancers, musicians and other celebrants, wearing vivid embroidered traditional costumes, come from all over the Minho to take part in the three-day *festa*, which is among Portugal's most spectacular.

Moving to the waterfront you come to the **Gil Eannes** (www.fundacaogile-annes.pt; Apr–Sept 9am–7pm, Oct–May 9am–5.30pm), a former naval hospital ship, now a floating museum dedicated to the ship's former function, which was mainly servicing the cod fishermen in Greenland and New-foundland. Part of the ship is now also used as an unusual youth hostel.

Across the river is the enticing **Praia de Cabedelo** beach, accessible via a five-minute ferry ride from the harbour (hourly May–Sept). There are more good beaches nearby, including at the small resort of Carreço, just 5km (3 miles) to the north.

There is no escaping the Barcelos cockerel.

Traditional dancing in Viana do Castelo.

Walk or cycle along the Ecopista, heading east from Valença to Cortes (13km/8 miles). This former railway track has been converted to a signposted paved pathway and is flanked by beautiful countryside, including bubbling streams, vineyards and mountains.

Capela das Malheiras chapel, Viana do Castelo.

Coastal route from Porto

An alternative route into the Minho is by driving up the coast from Porto and returning by the inland route. The Atlantic beaches are generally broad, with fine sand, but the sea is cold and rough. A fishing town and resort, **Vila do Conde ⑥**, is the site of the vast Convento de Santa Clara, which was founded in 1318, the 16th-century parish church of São João Baptista and a lovely 17th-century fortress. Travellers are welcome to watch how fishing boats are made and to visit the lace-making school and museum, the Museu das Rendas de Bilros (Tue–Sun 10am–noon, 2–6pm; free). Nearby, **Póvoa de Varzim ⑦** is another popular fishing port-resort, with an 18th-century fort and a parish church. There is also a casino and a modern luxury hotel, the Axis Vermar, with heated swimming pools and tennis courts. Further north, **Ofir ⑧** is a delightful seaside resort set amid pine forests. Just across the Rio Cávado lies the town of **Esposende ⑨** with the remains of an 18th-century fortress. There are many new, often garishly

painted, houses in towns and villages along the way, which have often been built by emigrants returned from France, Germany and elsewhere.

Along the Rio Minho

Continuing northwards, beyond Viana do Castelo, the road leads to **Caminha ⑩** on the banks of the Rio Minho, an attractive town with echoes of its past as a busy trading port. The church, dating from the 15th century, has a beautiful ceiling of carved wood. There are several lovely 15th- and 16th-century buildings near the main square.

At the estuary of the Minho, the road turns inland and follows the river, which forms the border with Spain. **Valença do Minho ⑪** is a bustling border town with shops and markets. Spaniards come here regularly to purchase items that include table linen and crystal chandeliers. The Portuguese, on the other hand, cross the border to Tui or Vigo to buy canned goods such as asparagus and artichokes, as well as clothing. The old town of Valença is still fairly intact, with cobbled streets and stone houses with iron balconies, surrounded by 17th-century granite ramparts. The ancient convent, with a splendid view of the Minho and of Spain, is now a *pousada*.

From **Monção ⑫**, a fortified town known for its spring water and classy *vinho verde*, you can either take the road south through the heart of the Minho, or continue along the riverside and cross over the mountains of Serra da Peneda and sense the isolation. Either way, the routes meet at Ponte da Barca.

The mountain route

Follow the river as far as **Melgaço ⑬**, another fortified town, and turn inland for **Castro Laboreiro ⑭**, an ancient settlement with an 11th-century castle, which is most renowned for a large breed of working dog that was introduced to protect the villagers from marauding wolves.

Take the road from here to **Senhora da Peneda ⑮** to find an amazing

Bom Jesus-style church, in the middle of nowhere. A long flight of steps ascending to the church is adorned with 14 chapels, each containing a tableau depicting a major event in the story of Christ.

Dramatic mountain scenery opens up as you pass through a number of villages, including Rouças and Adrão, to meet the road outside the village of **Soajo** ⑯, where there is a colourful market on the first Sunday of the month. Of particular interest here are the communal *espigueiros*, granite grain stores built on mushroom-shaped legs, and grouped around a threshing floor.

The road onward leads southeast to **Lindoso** ⑰ (the name comes from *lindo* meaning beautiful) and a finely situated border castle keeping watch for invaders from Spain. Below the castle ramparts lies another cluster of *espigueiros*. Return from Lindoso on the road to Ponte da Barca. You will see lush countryside, crisscrossed by rivers with medieval stone bridges; simple white churches with elaborate granite doorways and windows;

and, of course, unending vineyards. Due to the high population density, the land has been divided and subdivided for generations, so the average property now consists of just a hectare or two.

The road now passes **Arcos de Valdevez** ⑱, an attractive hillside town built on the banks of the Rio Vez, with a magnificent view of the valley. Just to the south, **Ponte da Barca** ⑲, on the south bank of the Rio Lima, has a lovely 15th-century parish church and an old town square, but the principal attraction is the fine arched bridge, after which the town is named, built in 1543 and often restored.

This is a possible starting point for a visit to the stunning **Peneda-Gerês National Park** (see page 306 for a suggested route). Covering a vast 703 sq km (272 sq miles), the park encompasses wild plains with grazing cattle, pine-clad mountain ranges and lush forests. It is the wettest region of Portugal, and there are streams and rivers and a flourishing plant life with some 17 species found nowhere else, as well as extensive forests of oak and

Grapes grow everywhere, even on telegraph wires.

The unusual grain stores of Soajo.

FACT

Guimarães' Festival of St Walter, the Festas Gualterianas, dates from the middle of the 15th century. This three-day celebration, on the first weekend in August, includes a torchlight procession, a fair with traditional dances, and a medieval parade.

pine. Wild ponies, deer, wolf, golden eagles, wild boars and badgers also live within the boundaries.

The park encompasses fascinating ancient villages with stone houses, cobbled streets and a predominance of elderly women dressed in black. You may fish, go horse riding, hike and mountain climb amid the breathtaking scenery. There are also dolmens, perhaps 5,000 years old, and milestones that once marked the old Roman road to Braga.

The bustling, central little spa town of **Vila do Gerês** ⑳ (also called Caldas do Gerês) has plenty of places to stay and a popular spa centre (May–Oct). There are also some good hiking trails surrounding the town; detailed maps are available at the tourist office. Nearby, tiny **Rio Caldo** is the park's centre for water sports, including kayaking, waterskiing and rowing.

The Lima valley and the south

Here you might turn westwards, along the beautiful valley of the Lima River, which the Romans believed to be the *Lethe*, the mythical River of Forgetfulness. The area has numerous great estates or *solares*, which stand as a tangible reminder of the glories of the old empire. Some are now guesthouses, and arrangements to visit or stay in these manors should be made beforehand, if possible (see page 117).

Ponte de Lima ㉑ is one of the loveliest towns in Portugal, mainly because of its location on the south bank of the Lima and its picturesque historic centre. There is a popular market, held every other Monday, resembling a splendidly colourful "tent city" on the river bank. It sells everything from local cheese to cotton underwear.

The town faces a magnificent Roman bridge with low arches, and remains of the old city wall still stand. A 15th-century palace with crenellated facade now serves as the town hall. Across the river, the 15th-century **Convento de Santo António** has beautiful woodwork, including two Baroque shrines.

Enjoying watersports in the national park.

PARQUE NACIONAL DA PENEDA-GERÊS

It is easy to make a round trip of the Peneda-Gerês National Park by car, taking in some of the most spectacular scenery on both sides of the border. From Ponte da Barca take the road east towards Lindoso, past the hydro scheme to the border at Madaleina. Cross into Spain – there are no formalities – and continue alongside the reservoir until you come to a right turn signposted Lobios and Portela do Homen. Take this turn and you eventually cross back into Portugal.

On the Portuguese side you have a choice: continue straight down the "main" road to the old spa town of Caldas do Gerês then towards Braga, or, shortly after crossing back into Portugal, take the right turn down the road which follows the Vilarinho reservoir to Campo do Gerês, which has an excellent visitor centre portraying traditional life in Vilarinho das Furnas, the village submerged by the reservoir. Then drive towards Covide, passing a well-stocked craft shop, then west to Vila Verde. Of the two options, the latter is the more interesting. Roads can get very busy at weekends in summer, and at peak times the park authority may impose traffic restrictions.

If you plan on camping in the national park, be sure to use a designated site, or you could be faced with a hefty fine. Tourist offices have lists of official sites which are, generally, of a very high standard.

Continuing towards Viana do Castelo, you pass more manor houses, such as the Solar de Cortegaça, with its great 15th-century stone tower. This is a working manor, with wine cellars, a flour mill and stable. Guests are welcome to take part in the farm life (tel: 258 971 639).

Guimarães: birthplace of a nation

A busy manufacturing town noted mainly for textiles, shoes and cutlery, **Guimarães ㉒** still possesses many reminders of its past glory as birthplace of the Portuguese nation. Around the year 1128, an 18-year-old boy named Afonso Henriques proclaimed independence for the region of Portucale from the kingdom of León and Castile. In the field of São Mamede, near Guimarães, the young Afonso Henriques defeated his mother's army, which was battling on behalf of Alfonso VII, king of León and Castile.

Guimarães has long been the centre of the Portuguese linen industry. It still produces high-quality, coarse linen from home-grown flax naturally bleached by the sun. The region is also known for its hand embroidery.

A good place to begin a tour is at the 10th-century **castelo** (daily 10am–6pm), on the northern side of town. It is believed that Afonso Henriques was born here in 1110, the son of Henri of Burgundy, Count of Portucale, and his wife Teresa. The castle is a large mass of walls and towers on a rocky hill with a magnificent view of the mountains. The dungeon and fortifications were restored many times. Early in the 19th century, the castle was used as a debtors' prison; it was restored again in 1940. At the entrance stands the small Romanesque chapel of **São Miguel do Castelo** with the font where Afonso Henriques was baptised in 1111.

Heading into town, you pass the 15th-century Gothic **Paço dos Duques de Bragança** (daily 10am–6pm), now occasionally used as an official residence by the president of the Republic. This massive granite construction consists of four buildings set around a courtyard and has

The Roman bridge at Ponte de Lima.

Traditional honeypots for sale. Bee keeping is a practice well established in most regions, producing a variety of honeys from wild lavender to orange blossom.

Guimarães is famous for its medieval historic monuments.

been completely restored. Outside stands a fine statue of Afonso Henriques by Soares dos Reis. Visitors may also view the splendid chestnut ceiling of the Banquet Hall, the Persian carpets, French tapestries, ancient portraits and documents.

The Rua de Santa Maria, with its cobblestones and 14th- and 15th-century houses, leads to the centre of town. On the left lies the **Convento de Santa Clara**, built in the 1600s and now used as the town hall.

The church of **Nossa Senhora de Oliveira**, dating from the 10th century, was rebuilt by Count Henri in the 12th century and has undergone several restorations. Still visible are the 16th-century watchtower and 14th-century western portal and window. The church takes its name from a 7th-century legend of an old Visigoth warrior named Wamba who was tilling his field nearby when a delegation came to tell him he had been elected king. Refusing the office, he drove his staff into the ground, declaring that not until it bore leaves would he become king. It turned into

an olive tree and the church was later built on the spot.

Adjacent to the church of Oliveira, the convent now holds the **Museu de Alberto Sampaio** (http://masampaio.imc-ip.pt; Tue–Sun July–Aug 10am–midnight, Sept–June 10am–6pm) displaying the church's rich treasury of 12th-century silver chalices and Gothic and Renaissance silver crucifixes, as well as 15th- and 16th-century statues, paintings and ceramics.

The busiest square in Guimarães is the Largo do Toural. Just beyond, the **Igreja São Domingos** was built in the 14th century and still has the original transept, rose window and lovely Gothic cloister. The latter houses the **Museu Arqueologico Martins Sarmento** (Tue–Sat 9.30am–noon, 2–5pm, Sun 10am–noon, 2–5pm), named after the man who was responsible for the excavation of the Citânia de Briteiros (see page 309) and displaying objects from that site and other *citânias* (ancient Iberian fortified villages) of northern Portugal, as well as collections of Roman inscriptions, ceramics and coins.

Continuing along the broad garden called the Alameda da Resistência ao Fascismo, you reach the **Igreja São Francisco**, founded in the 13th century. There is little left of the original Gothic structure, but the sacristy has impressive 17th-century gilt woodwork and ceiling, as well as some striking *azulejos*.

High on the outskirts of the city stands **Santa Marinha da Costa**, founded as a monastery in the 12th century and rebuilt in the 18th century. The church functions regularly and may be visited. The cells of the monastery, which were badly damaged by fire in 1951, have been restored and turned into a luxury *pousada* (one of two *pousadas* in the town; for details, check www.pousadas.pt). A 10th-century Mozarabic arch and vestiges of a 7th-century Visigothic structure are visible in the cloisters, and the veranda is decorated with magnificent 18th-century tile scenes and a fountain.

Citânia de Briteiros

After the Briteiros exhibit at the Martins Sarmento museum, you could visit the original site, 11 km (7 miles) north of Guimarães. At first, the **Citânia de Briteiros** ㉓ (daily 9.30am–6.30pm) appears to be nothing more than piles of stones on a hillside, but it is in fact one of Portugal's most important archaeological sites. Here are the remains of a prehistoric fortified village said to have been inhabited by Celts. It was discovered in 1874 by archaeologist Francisco Martins Sarmento.

Near the summit, two round houses have been reconstructed. Also visible are the remains of defensive walls, ancient flagstones and the foundation walls of more than 150 houses. The houses were circular with stone benches running around the walls. A large rock in the centre supported a pole which would in turn have held up a thatched roof. Several of the houses are larger, with two or more rectangular rooms, presumably the homes of prominent members of society. The town evidently had an efficient water system: spring water flowed downhill through gutters carved in the paving stones to a cistern and a public fountain.

Statue of Afonso Henriques at Guimarães.

Restored houses of the ancient settlement Citânia de Briteiros.

Bragança countryside.

TRÁS-OS-MONTES

Isolated by distance and mountains, Trás-os-Montes
has developed an individuality that distinguishes it
from the rest of Portugal.

To most Portuguese, the remote
northeastern province of Trás-os-
Montes (Behind the Mountains)
could be on the other side of the
moon. Lisboetas are inclined to look
at it as from a vast distance – albeit
with fierce affection. The word *"trás"*
– "back" or "behind" – fits the region
like a glove. Before Portugal joined
the EU, this region was backward in
almost every aspect: cut off from the
rest of the country by mountains,
poor road and rail systems, and grinding poverty that drove the workforce
of almost every village to migrate to
urban areas, or emigrate to the more
advanced economies of northern
Europe, or overseas. Now, improved
roads, better communications and
farming subsidies have led to rapid
improvements in living standards,
although pockets of poverty still exist.

Regional differences

There has been higher emigration
from the north of Portugal than from
the south, and one of the principal
reasons is the division of land. The
south is an area of *latifúndios* – large
landholdings – while the north has
minifúndios – smallholdings. A farmer's land in the north is often insuf-
ficient to provide him and his family
with a living; the terrain, with its steep-
sided valleys and high mountains, also
makes farming here a challenge.

A more subtle factor affecting
Portugal's conservative north is the
Church. While all Portugal is Roman
Catholic, the sheer remoteness of
the northeast corner has meant
that national government has little
impact, while tradition and religion
predominate. This has affected education, particularly; not so long ago the
only educated man in a village was
the priest, whose wisdom and opin-
ion would be sought on every matter
ranging from the spiritual to aspects
of crop harvesting.

Main Attractions
Parque Natural do Alvão
Atei
Montalegre
Chaves
Parque Natural de Montesinho
Bragança
Rio de Onor
Miranda do Douro

Goats in Portugal are used mainly for their milk.

Who will buy?

Geographically, Trás-os-Montes covers the extreme northeast corner of the country, from Bragança in the north to the Rio Douro in the south and west to Chaves and Montalegre. Climatically, the region is different, too. Cut off from the influence of the Atlantic, it is hotter and drier in summer and colder in winter, especially in the far northeastern Terra Fria, the cold lands. Trás-os-Montes remains one of the most interesting areas of the country, for its towns, its countryside and its historical connections.

Entering the region

You can enter the region, which includes the Alto Douro, from a number of directions. Northern border crossings from Spain are at Vila Verde da Raia, on the road leading south to Chaves (this is a historical invasion route – employed by the armies of Napoleon in the early 1800s); at Portelo, in the Parque Natural de Montesinho; from the east at Quintanilha, east of Bragança; and at Miranda do Douro and Bemposta, where the Douro forms the frontier. From inside

Portugal, the main routes into the region are from Porto or Lamego via Vila Real; or from Guarda via either Torre de Moncorvo or Freixo de Espada à Cinta.

This itinerary enters the region at Vila Real and follows a meandering route to absorb the sights and atmosphere of the area without ignoring the major points of interest.

Serra de Alvão

Two scenic routes lead north out of Vila Real, one on each side of the high Serra da Padrela – to Chaves in the north, and Bragança in the northeast. But the adventurous traveller may strike northwest into the rugged Serra de Alvão, and be treated to one of the most lavish vistas the country has to offer. The road leads through the **Parque Natural do Alvâo**, an exceptionally beautiful and pristine natural park with mountains, a river and a wide range of flora and fauna. Continue across the Rio Olo to **Mondim de Basto** ❶ on the banks of the Rio Tâmega. There it forms the border between Trás-os-Montes and the Minho.

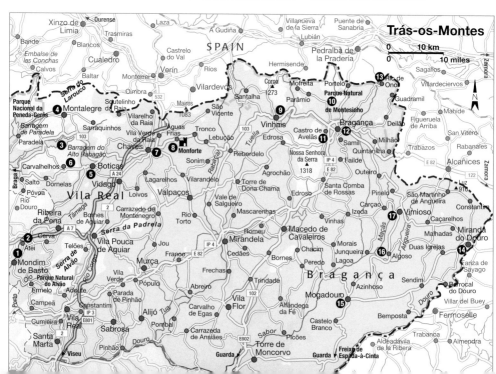

Granite gives way to slate – many of the houses are roofed by it – and in the high passes you can hear the rushing of mountain waters and the tinkle of goat bells. In the winter there is snow here, but at other times of the year you are likely to encounter a profusion of wild flowers and pine forests. Pine resin, which is used in the manufacture of paints and turpentine, is a major product of this area.

A side trip of some 12km (8 miles) from Mondim de Basto will take you to **Atei ❷**, a delightful little village containing numerous archaeological remnants of Roman occupation. From here a curious subterranean passage of either Roman or Arab construction (opinions vary) leads down to Furaco on the banks of the Tâmega.

Leaving Mondim de Basto, the road winds northwards to Cabeceiras de Basto, in Minho province, at the head of a small "peninsula" that juts up into Trás-os-Montes. Stop at the imposing Baroque Mosteiro Refóis before heading into the high Serra de Cabreira and back into Trás-os-Montes at Póvoa.

Barroso district

You soon join the main Braga–Chaves road that runs beside the gigantic expanse of lake formed by **Barragem do Alto Rabagão ❸**, a huge dam, but here again another side trip could take you north – to Montalegre, the towering Serra do Larouco, and the primitive villages of the Barroso district.

As the largest town in the area, **Montalegre ❹** might be considered the capital of Barroso. Given a charter in 1273 by King Afonso III, and restored and expanded in turn by King Dinis and King Manuel I, Montalegre is thought to have enjoyed its status from a much earlier time, for the pillory in the centre of town carries the coat of arms of King Sancho I, who reigned from 1185 to 1211.

The town commands a view over an extensive area, so understandably

it has been a military centre for centuries. Montalegre is rich in archaeological finds. Lusitanians, Romans, Suevi and Visigoths were all here, and the magnificent four-towered castle was much used during the many wars that Portugal fought against Spain.

North of the region rises the Serra do Larouco, the second-highest range of mountains in the country (after the Serra da Estrela), with a number of passes leading into Spanish Galicia.

The district of Barroso stretches from the foothills of the Serra do Larouco southeast towards the city of Chaves. There is no absolute boundary, but it would include such villages as Meixido, Padornelos and Tourém. If you can close your eyes to the "emigrant architecture" – uncontrolled modern housing that is built with money saved by the Portuguese who work abroad – you will find in these settlements a sense of history utterly remote in time.

Trás-os-Montes e Alto Douro means "beyond the mountains and the Douro".

A farmer in Portugal works with his hay.

The ancient houses are built of enormous granite or slate blocks. Doors, windows and balconies are of weathered antique wood. Until recently, many houses were thatched. Once common, dirt streets are rapidly becoming paved, and electricity has only recently been installed. Almost every church is Romanesque, with the typical facade rising to a twin-columned peak to house the church bell.

For centuries the people of Barroso lived out their lives cut off from the outside world. They developed their own customs, songs, festivals and habits. In many corners of the world under similar circumstances, local people may treat outsiders with suspicion or alarm, but this is certainly not the case in Barroso. It is hard to imagine a more warm-hearted, hospitable people, willing to share the peculiarities of their daily lives with those who come to visit them.

Communal bulls

One of the region's most colourful festivals is the annual **Chega dos Toiros**, an inter-village competition. The name means "The Arrival of the Bulls". Each village takes enormous pride in its own bull, a communally owned animal bred especially for the purpose of inseminating the various cows owned by the individual farmers. This bull, by both tradition and breeding, is the biggest and fiercest animal imaginable, intended as much to gain the honours at the annual competition as it is for stock purposes.

Held in June, July and August, the Chega is essentially a bullfight, where the bull of one village is pitted against another in a fierce battle. Each animal is decorated and fêted by his villagers, and paraded to the accompaniment of noisy bands and crowds. The fight itself is in deadly earnest, with the champions of each bull goading their animal into combat. The fight continues until one animal is injured, or turns and runs. The victor is then led away by his villagers with much celebration.

At the end of the season there will be a regional champion, and this is the lucky animal who will be put out to pasture with the region's cows.

A rustic doorway in the Barroso district.

Wine of the dead

Boticas ❺ is the place to drink *vinhos mortos*, "wine of the dead". In order to protect their wine stocks from the French during the Peninsular War in the early 1800s, the villagers buried it in the ground. When it was later retrieved, the wine was found to be much improved. The practice is still followed, with good results. To sample another regional drink, make a short diversion west to the spa village of Carvalhelhos ❻. The spring water here is particularly sweet and is sold all over the country. Most refreshing is *com gas*, the sparkling version.

Chaves

Chaves ❼, just a few kilometres down the road from Barroso, seems a world away. An ancient city, the fortified Lusitanian village of the present site was captured by the Romans in AD 78. The Emperor Flavius founded the city of Aqua Flaviae there, inaugurating the still-popular hot springs and baths. Chaves is now a bustling town with a population of about 41,000. An agricultural and textile centre, it is famous for its *presunto*, or smoked ham (see margin tip page 318); you can taste it, with a glass of wine, at Faustino's, a former winery that claims to be the largest taverna, or *tasca*, in Portugal. More wine tasting is available at the **Adega Cooperativa de Chaves** (Mon–Fri 9am–6pm), located about a kilometre north of town and open for tours and tasting of the local red, white and sparkling wines.

The town is also well known for its natural spa, which was first discovered and developed by the Romans. The town's Parque Termal (Largo das Caldas) offers a wide range of treatments said to cure everything from arthritis to obesity. You can also join the queue waiting for a mug full of the steamy water.

Situated on the Rio Tâmega, Chaves commands a strategic position in a wide valley that extends from the Spanish frontier into the heart of Trás-os-Montes. Just about every invader who set his heart on Portugal, or chunks of it, routed his armies through this channel. Here

Dom Afonso, standing proud in the centre of Chaves.

The modern town of Chaves was once known to the Romans as Aquæ Flaviæ.

On the road to Bragança.

the Romans built one of the largest of their bridges in the Iberian peninsula. Completed in AD 104, it has 20 arches, is 140 metres/yds in length, and is still very much in daily use. In the middle of the bridge are two inscribed Roman milestones. Chaves means "keys" in Portuguese, but the ancient Aqua Flaviae was later shortened to Flavias, and local mispronunciation may have produced the current name.

Sights include the parish church, rebuilt in the 16th century; and the former Bragança ducal palace, now the **Museu Região Flaviense** (museusdechaves.com; June–Sept Mon–Fri 9am–12.30pm, 2–5.30pm, Sat–Sun 2–5.30pm, Oct–May daily 9am–12.30pm, 2–5.30pm), in the Praça de Camões. Prior to the formation of Portugal, the fortified city was a part of the original county of Portucale. Various of Portugal's early kings added significantly to its castle, one of the most important in the land.

A second castle, also once an integral part of the defences of this strategic valley, still stands at **Monforte ❽**, about 12km (8 miles) to the northeast.

East from Chaves

Heading east towards Bragança you will pass the old town of **Vinhais ❾**. Its castle is barely more than a ruin, although there was a significant population here. The town is set high in the Serra de Montesinho, on the south flank of the **Parque Natural de Montesinho ❿**, a wildly rugged park of heath-like scenery, the habitat of rare wolves, boars and foxes, as well as many varieties of flora and fauna. The area survives on agriculture, particularly vines, woodwork, weaving and basket-making.

To explore the region, first stop at the tourist office in Bragança (Avenida Cidade de Zamora; tel: 273 381 273) and ask for a book about the park, which contains a detailed map of the area. Be aware that not all of the roads are paved. Whichever direction you take, you will have a journey through spectacular country.

A mountain, Cidadela, rises behind Vinhais. Over it passed the Roman road that led from Braga to Astorga; today this ancient route is rich in archaeological discoveries. In the 11th

and 12th centuries there was a general movement by the population of this area towards the more fertile farmlands of the south. To prevent this, various monasteries were founded and encouraged by the early rulers of the region to develop their own agriculture and cottage industries. One of the most important of these was the **Mosteiro de Castro de Avelãs** ⑪, a few kilometres west of Bragança. Parts of the church of the Benedictine abbey have been incorporated into the present-day parish church.

Bragança: a fascinating city

With a population of some 30,000, **Bragança** ⑫ is the administrative capital, a university town, and also an agricultural trade centre (for livestock, vineyards, olives and grains). It has a thriving textile industry, and has been famous for its ceramics since prehistoric times (in a nearby cave at Dine, archaeologists have found pottery dating from the Palaeolithic period).

Known as Brigantine to the Celts and Juliobriga to the Romans, Bragança received its first foral (royal charter) from King Sancho I in 1187 – when the family from which the dukes of Bragança are descended started building their feudal castle there. The Braganças – still pretenders to the throne of Portugal – provided the land's kings and queens consistently from 1640 until the formation of the republic in 1910, and the emperors of Brazil from 1822 to 1889. In 1662, Catherine of Bragança, daughter of the first Bragança king João IV, became queen to Charles II of England, thus renewing the long alliance between the two nations. Since the fall of the monarchy, a foundation, the Fundação da Casa de Bragança, has managed all royal properties, including the family's 16th-century ducal palace in Vila Viçosa.

Bragança's ancient castle still stands – with a Princess' Tower full of ghosts. The keep of the castle houses a **military museum** (Tue–Sun 9am–noon, 2–5pm; free). You can also see an

A statue and fountain in Bragança. The city was originally a celtic settlement known as Brigantion.

Bragança Castle is an excellent example of civic Romanesque architecture.

MONTESINHO PARK

The stunning Parque Natural de Montesinho still has a tangible feeling of being stuck in a time warp. The dramatic countryside is stippled with ancient villages that preserve their age-old customs, and many still bear their ancient Roman or Visigothic names. The protected area covers 751 sq km (290 sq miles), but you don't have to have your own vehicle to explore it, as this is great hiking country as well. There are at least a dozen well-marked hiking trails running throughout the park, which vary in duration and difficulty. Coroa (1,273 metres/4,175ft) and Montesinho (1,486 metres/4,874ft) are the highest points. Pick up a route map at one of the park information offices and follow the waymarks. Don't forget to carry drinking water with you.

unusual medieval *pelourinho* (pillory), its shaft piercing a granite boar. Also within the castle walls, you will find the 12th-century five-sided Domus Municipalis, the oldest municipal hall in Portugal. The town walls, with their 18 watchtowers, are still largely intact, and the city has a fine cathedral and fascinating museum of archaeology, furniture and ethnography, the **Museu do Abade de Baçal** (Tue–Fri 10am– 5pm, Sat–Sun 10am–6pm), in what used to be the Bishop's Palace.

Another fascinating museum is the **Museu Ibérico da Máscara e do Traje** (Tue–Sun 10am–12.30pm, 2–6pm), with a display of colourful ribboned costumes and masks worn during the annual Carnival and similar festivities. The **Centro Ciência Viva** (Tue–Fri 10am–6pm, Sat–Sun 11am–7pm) celebrates the city's economic reliance on silk from the 15th to the 19th centuries, while the **Centro de Arte Contemporânea Graça Morais** (Tue–Sun 10am–12.30pm, 2–6.30pm), has a permanent exhibition of paintings by local artist Graça Morais, as well as regular temporary exhibitions featuring Portuguese and Spanish contemporary artists and sculptors. The Museu Dr Belarmino Afonso (Mon–Fri 9am–12.30pm 2–5.30pm) has an interesting ethnographical collection.

Excursions north

Basing yourself in this historic city it is relatively easy to make short day trips out into the surrounding region. First, to the north, in the furthest corner of Portugal, there is **Rio de Onor** , a tiny village that straddles the border with Spain. It took a rare presidential visit for the village to acquire its first bus service. The people of Rio de Onor developed their own dialect and intricate communal social system. In their music and folk dances a common instrument is the *gaita-de-foles* – a bagpipe, with Celtic associations similar to those of Scotland and Ireland.

A good time to visit the villages that extend in an arc from Vinhais, across Bragança, and down as far as Miranda do Douro and Freixo de Espada-à-Cinta, is between Christmas Day and

A farmer in the Rio do Onor region of Portugal.

Epiphany (6 January), when the local population celebrates a number of feasts connected with the Christian calendar – but incorporating ferocious masks and bizarre costumes. These celebrations date back to the dawn of time, when the agrarian people of these pastoral regions practised fertility rites and paid more than passing attention to magic.

Carnival, in February, is another good time to visit. Forty days before Easter the masks and costumes come out again, and you cannot be sure if it is the Christian spirit or the bogeyman that dominates the season. As in so many places, the Catholic Church incorporated pagan elements in order to appease the local people, and the rites became entangled.

Excursions south

South of Bragança you may head towards the Spanish frontier at **Miranda do Douro** ⓮. This fortified town sits above a craggy gorge overlooking the Douro. Like many of the country's border towns, it has suffered a turbulent history in its attempts to keep out the Spanish. These days invaders from across the river are welcomed with open arms – provided they bring a supply of euros.

Fifteenth-century houses with granite doorways, a 16th-century cathedral with a sequence of gilded wood altarpieces, an excellent folk museum, the **Museu da Terra de Miranda** (May–Sept Wed–Sun 9.30am–12.30pm, 2–6pm, Tue 2.30–6pm, Oct–Apr Wed–Sun 9am–12.30pm, 2–5.30pm, Tue 2–5.30pm), and the medieval Rua da Costanilha make it a worthwhile stop.

It is possible to make a circular tour by following the road on to the quiet town of **Mogadouro** ⓯, which nestles in the shadow of a 12th-century castle built by King Dinis on earlier Roman foundations.

If you like castles, don't miss the impressive ruins at **Algoso** ⓰, on the way back to **Vimioso** ⓱. Since the 12th century, this fortress has guarded the area surrounding its lofty perch – a hill called Cabeça da Penenciada – while 500 metres (1,650ft) below, the Rio Angueira flows westwards to the Rio Maçãs.

The church at Miranda do Douro.

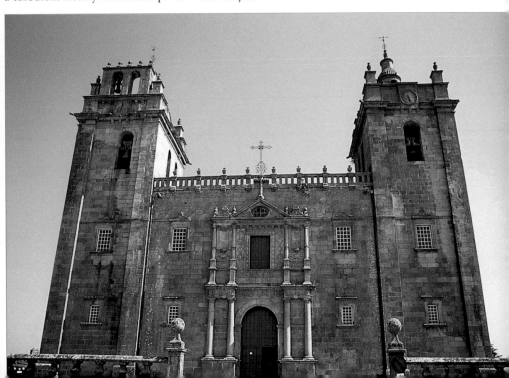

Mountain scenery at Pico do Arieiro.

MADEIRA

The archipelago has an individuality that distinguishes it from the rest of Portugal. Its beauty is varied, from the flowery elegance of Funchal to the remote inland craters.

The discovery of the Madeiran archipelago, 608km (378 miles) west of Morocco, was an early triumph for the ambitious seafarers inspired by Prince Henry the Navigator. In 1418, while sailing south to explore the West African coast, the caravels of João Gonçalves Zarco and Tristão Vaz Teixeira found shelter on a low-lying island they called, in gratitude, Porto Santo (Holy Port). Two years later they returned, to discover a large mountainous island 37km (23 miles) to the southwest, which they named Ilha da Madeira – the Island of Wood. Madeira Island and Porto Santo remain the only two inhabited islands in the archipelago.

Modern explorers will find that Madeira is still a wild and idyllic place to visit. Its great forests have gone – burnt down by the first settlers with fires that got out of control and are said to have raged for years – but man has contributed his own wonders to an Atlantic island whose natural splendour has earned it such titles as "God's Botanical Gardens" and "The Floating Flowerpot".

The city of Funchal

A statue of Gonçalves Zarco now stands as a central landmark in **Funchal ❶**, the capital of Madeira and home to a third of the 270,000 islanders. The city squats in the centre of

a wide bay on the sunnier south side of the island, its name inspired by the wild fennel (*funcho*) that the discoverers found growing on the surrounding plain. Behind it rises a natural amphitheatre of terraced hills and mountains that provide shelter from the northeasterly winds that frequently blow over the island – rain, storms and consolatory rainbows are the price you pay for Madeira's splendid verdant landscape.

Cruise-ship passengers and tourists with limited time usually settle

Main Attractions
Funchal
Old Blandy's Wine Lodge
Pico do Arieiro
Santana
Curral das Freiras
Porto Santo

Dancers at the Funchal Spring Flower Festival.

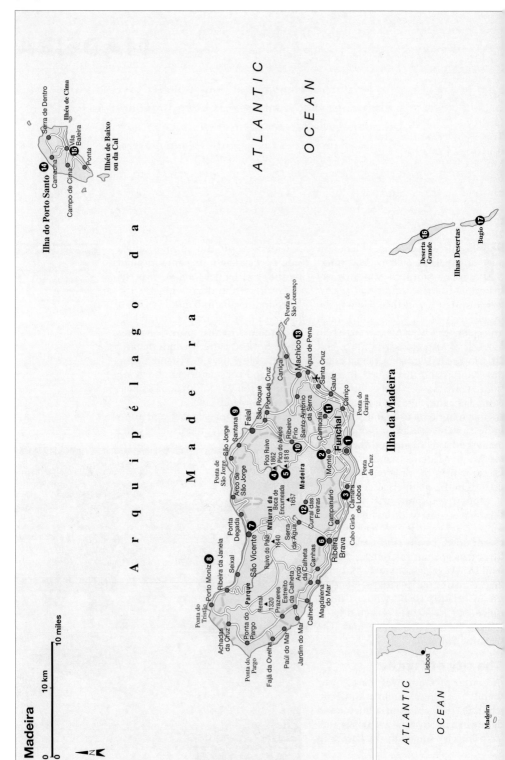

Madeira

0
10 km
10 miles
N

Arquipélago da Madeira

ATLANTIC OCEAN

Ilha do Porto Santo ⓰

Serra de Dentro
Ilhéu de Cima
Campacha
Vila
Campo de Cima ⓯ Baleira
Ponta
Ilhéu de Baixo
ou da Cal

Ilha da Madeira

Ponta de São Lourenço
Machico ⓭
Santa Cruz
Água de Pena
Caniçal
Canical
Gaula
Porto da Cruz
Caniço
São Roque
Santo António
da Serra
Camacha
Ponta do
Garajau
Ribeiro
Frio
Santana ⓮
São Jorge
Faial
Pico Ruivo
▲1862
Pico do Arieiro
▲1818
⓾
Funchal ❶
Monte
❷
Ponta de
São Jorge
Ponta da Cruz
São Jorge
Arco de
São Jorge
Madeira
Camacha ⓫
Parque
Natural da
Boca de
Encumeada
▲1657
Curral das
Freiras
⓬
Campanário
Câmara
de Lobos
❸
Ponta
Degada
Serra
de Água
Seixal
São Vicente ❼
Ribeiro do Paúl
▲1640
Cabo Girão
Ribeira
Brava
❻
Ribeira da Janela
Porto Moniz ❽
Achadas
da Cruz
Canhas
Arco
da Calheta
Prazeres
Estreito
da Calheta
Calheta
Magdalena
do Mar
Ponta do
Tristão
Ponta do
Pargo
Fajã da Ovelha
Paúl do Mar
Jardim do Mar

ATLANTIC OCEAN

Lisboa
Madeira

for the two essential Madeiran experiences, the Monte toboggan ride and tea at Reid's Palace Hotel. The first of these involves taking the cable car or driving up to **Monte ❷**, a cool and leafy hilltop resort with *quintas*, sanatoriums and the **Monte Palace Tropical Gardens**. The nearby twin-towered church of Nossa Senhora de Monte contains the tomb of Emperor Charles I of Austria. From here you can descend to Funchal by *carro de cesto*, a kind of wicker sofa attached to wooden runners that is guided 2km (1.2 miles) down the steep lanes by a pair of drivers wearing boaters and white flannels. This unique form of transport was invented by an English resident looking for a speedy way to get down to his office from his *quinta*.

Tea at **Reid's Palace Hotel** is far less strenuous, and simply involves climbing into a wicker armchair, and ordering a pot of Earl Grey tea and some crustless cucumber sandwiches. A world-famous five-star hotel with a prestigious site overlooking Funchal harbour, Reid's was opened in 1891 to cater for the growing number of well-to-do visitors to the island – particularly the British, who liked to stop over en route to and from their colonies.

The British presence on the island has proved influential in many ways – besides endorsing Madeira's reputation as a refined holiday destination acclaimed for its civility and hospitality, their fondness for cane furniture, acquired in the Orient, stimulated the island's wicker industry centred on the eastern town of Camacha (see page 331). Another important cottage industry, the production of an intricate and understandably expensive kind of embroidery (*bordados*), is indebted to an Englishwoman, Elizabeth Phelps, who introduced it to supplement local incomes after disease devastated the island's vines, with disastrous effects on the islanders' living standards, in the 1850s. Rua dos Murcas is the best place to buy.

More recently, there has been another presence on the island that has hit the headlines: Cristiano Ronaldo. Recognised as one of the world's top footballers, Ronaldo is now Madeira's most famous native son, and just about everywhere you go in the capital you will see his face staring out from mugs, T-shirts and dishcloths. It's an image that also reminds visitors that Madeira has moved on from its bygone image of starched British gentility.

Lomquats and scabbard fish

Funchal's true pleasures are woven into the everyday life of the city. A visit to the **Mercado dos Lavradores** (Workers' Market), a cornucopia of good things, costs nothing – unless, of course, you are tempted to buy some lomquats, tomarillos, pittangas or any of the many other exotic fruits and vegetables grown on the island.

Venture into the *mercado's* inner halls and you can gaze in safety upon the gloriously ugly *espada* (scabbard fish) that frequently features on

São Lourenco Fortress in Funchal.

Funchal's Mercado dos Lavradores.

You will find flowers for sale in many corners of Funchal.

Madeiran menus (not to be confused with the equally common traditional dish called *espetada* – beef cooked on a skewer over a wood fire scented with laurel twigs). Despite its vicious teeth and eel-like appearance, *espada* tastes good and is something of a rarity as it is only caught here and off the coast of Japan. The most important catch in the archipelago, the fish lives at a depth of up to 760 metres (2,500ft) and is hunted year-round by fishermen from **Câmara de Lobos** ❸, just west of Funchal. They use lines with baited hooks and flies spaced at regular intervals that can be more than 1.6km (1 mile) in length.

For a rewarding insight into Madeira's past, there are several places worth visiting: the oldest wine lodge, **Old Blandy's Wine Lodge** (www.theold blandywinelodge.com; Mon–Fri 10am– 6.30pm, Sat 10am–1pm; charge for tours) on Avenida Arriaga, dates in part from the 16th century, and you can wander around at will or join a tour where the process behind the famed Madeiran wine production is explained. Tasting is also available.

Pretty square, Funchal.

For a photographic glimpse into the past, check out the **Museu de Fotografia Vicentes** (www.photo graphiamuseuvicentes.com.pt; Mon–Fri 10am–12.30pm, 2–5pm) in Rua da Carreira, which houses a collection of old photographs of life on the island as recorded since 1865 by the Vicente family. Continue your history lesson at the Museu **Quinta das Cruzes** (Calada do Pico 1; Tue–Sun 10am–12.30pm, 2–5.30pm), the former residence of João Gonçalves Zarco, who discovered Madeira and became its first governor. The *quinta* is now packed with art treasures and the attractive gardens stay open throughout the lunch break. They are one of several exotic oases around the city, which include the **Boa Vista Orchids** and, the largest, **Jardim Botânico** (Botanical Gardens), on Caminho do Meio.

Housed in a beautiful 17th-century palace at Rua Mouraria 31, the Museu **Municipal do Funchal** (**História Natural**) (Tue–Fri 10am–6pm, Sat– Sun noon–6pm) documents the fauna and flora of the island.

Most of Madeira's hotels are located on the west side of the capital – only a short bus or taxi ride from Funchal's main square, **Praça do Município.** Decorously paved with black and white stones, this is bordered by imposing buildings with whitewashed facades and dark basalt outlines that remind visitors how Church and State have lorded it over this Portuguese outpost. A Jesuit church and college, founded in 1569, fills its north side, while the 18th-century **Câmara Municipal** (Town Hall) to the east was once the palace of the Conde de Carvalhal. The count's country residence was at **Quinta do Palheiro Ferreiro**, 8km (5 miles) east of Funchal, which is now a 320-hectare (800-acre) estate owned by the Blandy family, with magnificent gardens open to the public (www.palheirogardens.com; daily 9am–4.30pm).

On the south side of Praça do Município, the former Bishop's Palace houses Madeira's principal art museum, the **Museu de Arte Sacra** (Museum of Sacred Art; www.museuartesacrafunchal. org; Tue–Sat 10am–12.30pm, 2.30–6pm, Sun 10am–1pm). Among its exhibits is a fine collection of 15th- and 16th-century Flemish paintings acquired during the island's profitable trade in sugar with Flanders. "White gold" was the spur that provoked Madeira's rapid colonisation – by the 1450s merchants from Lisbon had established lucrative plantations on the island, worked by slaves brought over from Africa and the nearby Canary Islands, 416km (258 miles) to the south. By the 17th century, most of Madeira's terraces had been given over to producing its eponymous fortified wine, originally derived from Cretan vines introduced to the island by Henry the Navigator. Among these was the sweet *malvoisie* grape, which gave rise to the malvasia or malmsey wines that so besotted Europe in the 16th century. In Shakespeare's *Henry IV*, Falstaff is accused of selling his soul for "a cup of Madeira and a cold capon's leg".

For exquisite tiles, check out the delightful little **Casa-Museu Frederico de Freitas** (Tue–Sat 10am–5.30pm) on Calçada de Santa Clara, which has an exhibition of tiles from around the world, including Turkey, Syria and Holland, as well as other beautiful decorative arts dating from the 16th century.

Wine routes

Madeira wine travels and keeps well and few visitors leave without a bottle or two. Funchal has many invitingly fusty wine lodges and tasting bars where you can indulge in some serious research. **D'Oliveiras** on Rua dos Ferreiros, is worth seeking out, while **Barbeito Wine Lodge** on Estrada da Ribeira Garcia is a smaller traditional producer with a small tasting room and shop. The most comprehensive initiation into the history and production of Madeira wine is provided by Old Blandy's Wine Lodge (see page 328).

Take any road out of Funchal, and the arduous work required to produce the island's wines, fruit and other

TIP

Madeira's network of buses provides an excellent way of travelling around the island, if you don't feel like driving. Buses serve virtually every corner of the island, originating from Funchal's various privately run bus terminals. Tickets can be bought on board and timetables are available at Funchal's main tourist office.

Toboggan men waiting at the top of the run.

crops soon becomes apparent. The true heroes of Madeiran history are its farm labourers and their enslaved predecessors, who over the centuries toiled to win cultivable land from the island's steep and irregular terrain. Workers resolutely sculpted the island with staircases of tiny stone-walled fields – sometimes built by suspending men on ropes from above, with baskets of soil carried up from the river beds far below. These *poios*, or terraces, are fed by a phenomenal network of irrigation channels, known as *levadas*, that today run for thousands of kilometres (see margin), including 40km (25 miles) through tunnels.

Peaks, cliffs and villages

Even without the terracing that has transformed the island's landscape into a precipitous work of art, Madeira would be staggeringly attractive. A range of volcanic mountains runs east–west across the island, rising to a central conference of peaks, of which the highest is **Pico Ruivo ❹** at 1,862 metres (6,109ft). The nearby summit of **Pico do Arieiro ❺**, which

can be comfortably reached by car, provides a physical and spiritual high point. From here, providing you have prayed away the clouds, you can follow an exhilarating on-top-of-the-world path across the peaks to **Achada do Teixeira**.

From all sides of these central mountains, deep ravines run seawards to boulder-strewn beaches where small villages have grown up – most spectacularly at **Ribeira Brava ❻** and **São Vicente ❼**, directly opposite each other on the south and north coasts respectively. The ridges above them invariably culminate in sheer cliffs that are among the highest in the world. If you have the head for it, a viewing platform at **Cabo Girão** enables visitors to contemplate a vertical drop of 580 metres (1,900ft).

Along Madeira's wild north coast, narrow roads have been stitched into the cliffsides, threading through tunnels, round hairpin bends and under waterfalls that provide a free and unexpected car wash. **Porto Moniz ❽**, a weatherbeaten town on the island's northwestern tip, with several small

Picturesque São Vicente.

hotels, fish restaurants and volcanic rock pools, provides a welcome goal for adventurous motorists searching for the raw side of Madeira.

Other popular ports of call are the village of **Santana** ❾, on the northern coast, where the islanders' traditional A-shaped thatched cottages have been colourfully restored, with a couple open for visitors; the forest resort of **Ribeiro Frio** ❿ on a winding road that traverses the island between Funchal and Santana; and, closer to the capital, the wicker-making centre, **Camacha** ⓫, towards the east of the island.

For all this natural drama, Madeira is a fundamentally benign and relaxing island. Blessed with fertile soil, abundant water and an equable subtropical climate, the countryside is graced with a profusion of native plants and flowers that have been supplemented by exotic imports. Orchid enthusiasts can check out the **Jardim Orquídea** (Pregetter's Orchid Garden; www.madeira-orchid.com; daily 9am–6pm) on Rua Pita da Silva in the capital, which has thousands of varieties on view. The island is a heaven for walkers and the botanically inclined, with the mountain pass at **Boca da Encumeada** and the **Parque das Queimadas** popular starting points for hikers.

Two-thirds of the island is a protected area, and the **Laurisilva forest**, which occupies one-fifth of the land between 330 metres (1,000ft) and 1,300 metres (4,250ft), is a Unesco World Heritage Site.

Off the beaten track

Like all good islands, Madeira has plenty of secrets. An easy and worthwhile trip from Funchal is up to **Curral das Freiras** ⓬ (Corral of the Nuns), a secluded crater-like valley that until the late 1950s could only be reached by the narrow mountain paths that still snake down its sides. It gets its name from the nuns of Funchal's Santa Clara Convent, who fled here in 1566 when French pirates

sacked the capital. Another pleasant surprise lies to the west of Ribeira Brava – a plateau of austere and often misty moorland known as the **Paúl da Serra**, where a tiny white statue, Nossa Senhora da Serra, supervises the grazing sheep and cows.

The east side of Madeira is less mountainous and is consequently the most developed part of the island. Here you can find the airport, two golf courses, stretches of intensive farmland and **Machico** ⓭, which can claim to be Madeira's second city even though it only has 13,000 inhabitants, one high-rise hotel and a seafront commandeered by a sandy football pitch.

In the northeastern corner of the island the mood changes again as the land narrows to a low-lying, sandy peninsula called **Ponta de São Lourenço**, reached through a tunnel to the north of Machico. Here Caniçal was, until 1981, the island's principal whaling station.

Continue to the end of the headland, which offers good views and blustery walks, and you will often

Basket-making is a traditional industry in Camacha.

A classic A-shaped cottage in Santana.

meet old men selling souvenirs carved from redundant stocks of whalebone.

Porto Santo and other islands

The arid landscape of Ponta de São Lourenço provides a foretaste of that found on Madeira's neighbouring island, **Porto Santo** . The sleepy world of Porto Santo is a relatively accessible one, connected daily by ferry (two hours) and aeroplane. The island is a complete contrast to Madeira: while the former has a surplus of mountains, water and vegetation but no beaches to speak of, Porto Santo has just a few parched volcanic hills and a south coast that is one long, 7km (4-mile) stretch of unspoilt sand. It is as if God were planning to add beaches to Madeira but, like a builder who leaves a pile of sand outside your front door then disappears, he somehow forgot.

This divine oversight is a blessing both for beach-lovers and for connoisseurs of small-island life, as well as wind- and kite-surfers who hold competitions here. Plagued by rabbits and erosion, and vulnerable to attack by pirates, Porto Santo has always been ignored in favour of its lush and fertile neighbour, but it is nevertheless well worth a visit.

The capital, **Vila Baleira** ⑮, makes a virtue out of such inertia, and has only recently made efforts to cash in on its most famous resident, Christopher Columbus. The explorer was among the many sugar buyers who came to the islands in the 1470s, and later married the daughter of Porto Santo's first governor, Bartolomeu Perestrello. It is a leafy and attractive town with a palm-shaded main square and a tempting beach.

During the summer, holidaymakers from Funchal and mainland Portugal flock to Porto Santo, giving it the semblance of a seaside resort. But even at the height of the season there is space enough to wander along its magnificent beach. And, if that is your thing, to enjoy the island's 27-hole golf course.

Porto Santo is linked underwater to another separate group of islands, the barren **Ilhas Desertas**. Only 16km (10 miles) southeast of Madeira, they rise as high as 480 metres (1,570ft) and can easily be seen from the main island's southern shores. Despite repeated attempts over the centuries, settlement of the two islands – **Deserta Grande** ⑯ and **Bugio** ⑰ – has proved impossible. They are now a nature reserve where sea birds, wild goats, venomous black spiders and a colony of monk seals live in curious harmony. The Ilhas Desertas can sometimes be visited by boat trips from Funchal, and if you are interested in wildlife and wilderness regions it is worth enquiring at the tourist office.

Another set of islands also belongs to the Madeiran archipelago and is even more inhospitable than the Ilhas Desertas. Known as the **Ilhas Selvagens**, these lie 215km (135 miles) south of Madeira. Despite being closer to the Spanish Canaries, they remain under Portuguese jurisdiction.

Splashes of vivid bougainvillea.

Volcanic crater at the Reserva
Natural da Caldeira do Faial.

Holy pilgrimage at Convento de Nossa Senhora da Esperanza.

THE AZORES

Time seems to have stood still in the beautiful Azores islands. Way out in the Atlantic Ocean, they have a character of their own, yet are redolent of Portugal's maritime history.

The nine islands of the Azores floating in the Atlantic Ocean are gratifyingly rich in romantic history, cryptic legend and stunning natural beauty. You cannot ignore their volcanic origins – deep craters or calderas are their most outstanding feature. But greenery and trim, patchwork fields impose order and a surprising gentleness. With their tall cliffs and farm-quilted countryside, their tiny homesteads sprinkling the lush landscape, the islands are a magical presence in a volatile ocean.

To Portuguese explorers, who first mapped them in the 15th century, the Azores (Açores in Portuguese) became vital stepping stones in an expanding empire. Christopher Columbus, returning from his momentous 1492 voyage to the New World, took on water at the eastern island of Santa Maria. For centuries the Azores have offered a safe haven and restful stopover for other mariners.

This remote island group has an extra dimension if you share the view that the 650km (400-mile) -long archipelago's two tiny, westernmost islands, Flores and Corvo, more than a third of the way across the Atlantic, mark the true outermost limit of Europe. The Azores' capital, Ponta Delgada, is on São Miguel, the largest island in the group. The islands are meteorologically important to weather forecasters

– an Azores High (high-pressure area) extending to the east means fine weather for western Europe.

Origins

The name Açores was bestowed on the archipelago by Gonçalo Velho Cabral who, with Diogo de Silves, landed at Santa Maria in 1427. These daring seafarers mistook the many buzzards there for hawks, which are called *açores* in Portuguese. But from myth, fable and fanciful charts, another legend persists. Here, some believe, is the

Main Attractions

Ponta Delgada
Caldeira das Sete Cidades
Furnas
Santa Maria
Angra do Heroismo
São Jorge
Horta
Graciosa

Hot ferrous waterfall in São Miguel.

Hot springs bubble away, sending steam into the air.

lost Atlantis, from Plato's account of a sunken empire lying beyond the Pillars of Hercules. Yet chroniclers wrote that all the islands were uninhabited when the Portuguese arrived.

In 1439, settlement officially began on the seven then-known islands (Flores and Corvo were not discovered until 1452), through the efforts of Prince Henry the Navigator. His colonisation policy was so zealous that he offered land to Flemish farmers (the connection was through his sister, Isabel, who was married to the Duke of Burgundy, ruler of Flanders). Prince Henry not only foresaw the role of the islands in his larger purpose of African discovery but, in his businesslike way, realised they could be productive and profitable, and organised the planting of wheat and sugar cane.

Throughout Portuguese history, the islanders have held themselves apart from Lisbon, and have often chosen an opposing path. During the 19th-century War of the Two Brothers – the Miguelist Wars between two sons of King João VI – islanders supported the liberal Dom Pedro IV against his absolutist brother, Dom Miguel, wh had the support of most of Portugal.

Hardy islanders today still live b farming and fishing. There's a signif cant dairy industry. You will see cow milked on steep hillsides, their mil occasionally still carried in churn by farmers on horseback. But ther are more cerebral pursuits, too, an from the Azores have emerged man of the finest poets, novelists and ph losophers in Portuguese culture. On of several daily newspapers, O *Açor ano* is the third oldest in Europe. Th islands' identity was established lon; ago; autonomous government cam< in 1976, two years after the coup tha toppled Salazar's dictatorship (se< page 65).

Island attractions

The Azores are gradually attracting more tourists, but still remain off the radar. Great for walking holidays, they are full of pleasant surprises, and invite the visitor to explore. In other words a dream world for anyone seeking unspoilt nature, tranquillity and the chance to "get back to basics". What

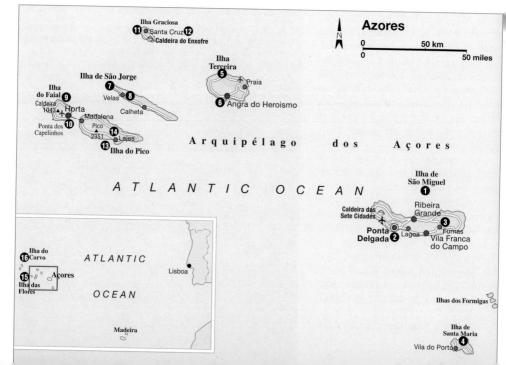

they are not, though, are bland resorts for sophisticates or sun worshippers. There are relatively few sandy beaches, and these are mostly volcanic black. The weather is mild (the winter averages 14°C/57°F, summer 23°C/74°F) but except for June to September, it is often wet and windy.

Island pleasures are unpretentious and relaxed. You will discover awe-inspiring scenery of stunning beauty, luxurious vegetation with exotic plants (50 of 850 species are endemic), enchanting lakes amid extinct craters, tranquil hill country with rolling fields and lush meadows, magnificent coasts lined by picturesque villages and historical towns, and spectacular hydrangea hedges crisscrossing the landscape. There is also much to see in the daily working life, which still has a rather traditional aspect. Entertainment is generally limited to discos and bars. Custom and religion are served by frequent *festas*, and the striking Baroque churches carved from basalt.

You can see the relics of a long tradition of whaling, and will encounter the sons and grandsons of whaling men – and, in summer, numerous emigrant families on annual trips home. The Azores are worth a visit even if you only have time to see São Miguel. The Government Tourist Office (*Turismo*) is very friendly and helpful, and the Portuguese Tourist Board will provide plenty of information (see page 375).

The islands are ideal for walking. The more ambitious can climb Pico (Peak) on Pico island: at over 2,300 metres (7,550ft), this is Portugal's highest mountain, but there are numerous less demanding hikes. Additionally, an expanding number of sports facilities range from deep-sea fishing, whale-watching and diving to golf and tennis.

The islands divide naturally into three groups: São Miguel and Santa Maria in the east; Terceira, São Jorge, Graciosa, Faial and Pico in the centre; and Flores and Corvo to the west.

São Miguel

São Miguel ❶ is perhaps the most varied of the islands. It is also the largest, measuring 65km by 16km (40 miles by 10 miles), and the most

TIP

The main tourist office in the Azores is on Avenida Infante Dom Henrique, in Ponta Delgada, São Miguel island, tel: 296 288 082; www.visitazores.com.

A flower vendor in Ponta Delgada.

ESPÍRITO SANTO CULT

On the island of Terceira, gaudy chapels *(impérios)* reflect the islanders' ardour for the Espírito Santo cult, which originated in medieval Germany and was promulgated in Portugal through the teachings of the 17th-century Jesuit priest, António Vieira, and brought to the Azores by early Portuguese settlers. On Whit Sunday, the day of the Holy Spirit, there are processions in towns and villages throughout the island, and many villages have regular Sunday celebrations. A child is usually crowned as an 'emperor', and bears a sceptre, overseeing the ensuing festivities. Local people believe that worship of the Holy Spirit – whose insignia, a crown, sceptre and a white dove, are kept in the *impérios* – will protect their communities from volcanic eruptions, earthquakes, and damage from storms.

A banana tree on the Azores island of San Miguel.

Milk cows grazing on a pasture overlooking the Atlantic.

populated, with nearly half the archipelago's population of 250,000.

On the south coast, the capital of **Ponta Delgada ❷** sprawls behind the waterfront – the Avenida Infante Dom Henrique – with its arcades and 18th-century city gates. The town is dramatically set off against numerous small volcanic cones rising on the distant hills. City sights include several fine Baroque churches, among them the 16th-century parish church, Igreja Matriz de São Sebastião. Also of architectural interest are the Palácio da Conceição, which houses the government; and the curious Baroque Casa de Carlos Bicudo with its mermaid facade.

For a view that overlooks the city, head for the **Reduto da Mãe de Deus**, where in 1944 an ill-informed anti-aircraft battery shot at an aircraft carrying General Eisenhower on his way home. There's a good museum, the **Museu Carlos Machado** (museucarlosmachado.azores.gov.pt; Tue–Fri 10am–12.30pm, 2–5.30pm, Sat–Sun 2–5.30pm), in the 16th-century Convento de Santo André, with exhibits on the island's natural history and ethnography, as well as folk art, paintings and sculpture.

In the west of the island are the enchanting twin lakes within the **Caldeira das Sete Cidades** (Cauldron of the Seven Cities). This is best viewed from Vista do Rei (The King's View), but you will be able to spot only one sleepy village in the crater. In sunlight, one lake is blue, the other green – stemming, legend has it, from the tears of a princess forced to part from her shepherd lover. A half-day circuit of the island might lead past pineapple plantations (visitors welcome) just north of the capital, on to Sete Cidades and the promontory of **Ponta dos Mosteiros**, eastwards to Capelas and its tobacco fields, and finally to the historical town of **Ribeira Grande**. Further east are the Caldeiras da Ribeira Grande, a small spa in picturesque surroundings, and the tea plantations of Gorreana (www.gorreanatea.com; open to the public).

Eastwards from Ponta Delgada, past sandy beaches, are the potteries of **Lagoa** and the diving centre at Caloura, and, beyond, the attractive town of **Vila Franca do Campo** with three ornate Baroque churches. The municipal museum has a good collection of musical instruments and pottery. Above Vila Franca, the pilgrimage chapel of **Senhora da Paz** affords a splendid view over the south coast. Just offshore, accessible from the pretty harbour, is the tiny crater island of **Ilheu**, with a natural seawater swimming pool.

Northeast and inland, past the crater lake of Lagoa das Furnas, is the village of **Furnas ❸**, with hot springs and boiling mud cauldrons that give off the rich stink of sulphur. But here, too, is a famous botanical park, a volcanically heated lake you can swim in, and a pleasant hotel and restaurant, the **Terra Nostra Garden Hotel**. The dish of the house is *cozido à Furnas* – meats and vegetables steamed in underground ovens. For a picnic, you can boil your own eggs in the hot springs beside the crater lake.

Santa Maria and Terceira

The island of **Santa Maria ❹**, only 17km by 9km (10 miles by 5 miles), has peaceful fields and red-roofed whitewashed houses in a southern Portuguese style (initially settlers came from Algarve and Alentejo). Today there are some 6,000 inhabitants. Apart from the underlying volcanic massif, there is also sedimentary rock, and the beaches therefore are a shining gold, in bright contrast to the more usual volcanic black. Santa Maria is the driest, sunniest island, often called the "Algarve of the Azores". Just north of the airport in Anjos is the reconstructed church, where Christopher Columbus once knelt in prayer. The main town is **Vila do Porto**.

In the central group, **Terceira ❺** (29km by 17km/18 miles by 10 miles) derives its name from the fact that it was the third island in the archipelago

to be discovered. All the settlements on Terceira stretch along the coastline, while the unpopulated interior of the island – a wild and rugged landscape partly covered with native brushwood of tree heather, juniper and mosses – is often enveloped in clouds.

Terceira is distinguished by its capital, **Angra do Heroismo ❻**, which is, deservedly, on Unesco's World Heritage list as it is undoubtedly the most beautiful town in the archipelago. Once the capital of the Azores, it was granted its heroic title by Queen Maria II, the daughter of Dom Pedro IV, whose regency the island stoutly supported. Severely damaged by an earthquake in 1980, Angra has largely recovered. Its cathedral, several churches, castles and palaces are of considerable interest. A circuit of the island encompasses stunning views of green patchwork fields subdivided by stone walls. Terceira's most boisterous *festas* are around 24 June, the day of São João (St John the

Looking down on the red roads of São Jorge.

Hot springs, or furnas, on San Miguel.

WHERE

Between April and October, daily whale-watching trips are organised by Espaço Talassa in Lajes, on Ilha do Pico (tel: 292 672 010; www.espacotalassa. com). Trips last around three hours and are preceded by a multimedia presentation (on dry land) all about the creatures you are hoping to see.

The harbour at Terceira island.

Baptist), and include *touradas à corda*, the running of rope-restrained bulls.

From São Jorge to Corvo

Beautiful **São Jorge** ❼, 56km (35 miles) long by only 8km (5 miles) wide, rises abruptly from the sea and culminates in a mountain ridge that is often shrouded in mist. Besides its glorious natural setting, São Jorge affords magnificent views of all the central islands. Almost all the villages are set on small coastal plains (*fajãs*) at the foot of tall cliffs; some hamlets can only be reached via narrow footpaths. This island is another excellent choice for walkers. **Velas** ❽, with stunning views across to Pico, is the main town and a good base to explore the island and to buy the excellent local cheese.

Faial ❾ rises almost symmetrically on all sides to the central **Caldeira**, an eerie crater with a depth of some 300 metres (1,000ft). Faial's epithet, "Blue Island", was inspired by its hydrangea hedgerows running like blue ribbons over the countryside in June and July – a stunning sight for people used to

seeing these bushes only in neat parks and gardens.

The lively capital of **Horta** ❿ is extremely pleasant, with some interesting museums and churches. Its harbour is a port of call for transatlantic sailors, with each crew commemorating their journey by painting a picture on the *mole* (breakwater). **Ponta dos Capelinhos** is a dramatic contrast to the lively town and flowery countryside: here, in 1957–8, an undersea volcanic eruption rumbled and grumbled and left a legacy of vast, grim dunes of dark cinder.

Graciosa ⓫ is as gracious as its name suggests, with soft sloping hills and peaceful villages scattered over the island. Yet it also has a volcanic heritage: in Caldeira do Enxofre you may descend 182 stone steps to a huge cavern (*furna*) with a sulphurous subterranean lake. In the small, tidy capital of **Santa Cruz** ⓬ it becomes obvious why Graciosa was known as the "White Island": all its houses are traditionally whitewashed.

The towering peak which gives the island its name is the main reason to

visit **Ilha do Pico** ⑬, but a look round the island reveals fertile countryside in the east and bizarre rocky regions (called *mistérios*) in the west, which have been flooded by lava comparatively recently. In the sheltered enclosures between dry-stone walls, grapes are grown to produce the local wines.

In **Lajes** ⑭, a small whaling museum, the **Museu dos Baleeiros** (Tue–Fri Apr–Sept 9.15am–12.30pm, 2–5.30pm, Sat–Sun 2–5.30pm) recalls the all-too-recent past, when men went out hunting the giant creatures: Herman Melville's *Moby Dick* is set in these waters. Rising to over 2,350 metres (7,700ft), majestic Pico is the highest mountain not only in the Azores but in the whole of Portugal. To climb the main peak (this is best done in summer), you will need proper gear and a reliable route-finder.

Ilha das Flores ⑮ (17km by 12km/ 10 miles by 7 miles) does not abound in flowers, as its name suggests. But it is the most humid island of the Azores, its wet climate accounting for the lush evergreen vegetation. Flores offers some wild landscapes

that are quite different from those of the other islands: basalt predominates, in the form of high-lying, boggy plateaux where waterfalls plummet down over steep rock faces. In the capital, Santa Cruz, there is the charming ethnographic Museu das Flores (Mon–Fri 9am–12.30pm and 2–5.30pm), in a converted convent, with displays about life on the island and interesting, quirky artefacts.

From Flores, a boat runs daily, weather permitting, to **Ilha do Corvo** ⑯ (corvo means crow in Portuguese), which measures only 6km by 3km (4 miles by 2 miles). It is the smallest and quietest island in the archipelago, with the 468 inhabitants all living in **Vila Nova**, which is the only village. Corvo's prime sight is a tranquil lake embedded in an isolated crater, whose swampy islets reputedly resemble a map of the Azores. The voracious birds after which the island was named can still be seen around the shores.

Typical whitewashed houses on Santa Maria.

View of Horta harbour with Pico Mountain at dusk.

Ponte de Lima azulejo.

INSIGHT GUIDES TRAVEL TIPS
PORTUGAL

TRANSPORT

GETTING THERE AND GETTING AROUND

GETTING THERE

By Air

Scheduled Flights

tap Air Portugal (www.tap.pt) is Portugal's national airline and it has wide international links. Flights, particularly from Paris, can get very heavily booked in the summer (July/August) and around Christmas and Easter.

Many major airlines make non-stop direct flights to Lisbon from capital cities in Europe and other continents. There are several flights a week from New York, Los Angeles and Boston.

You may also, from some countries, fly directly to Porto in the north, Faro in the south and to Madeira and the Azores. Links with London are particularly good.. Budget airlines also operate between the UK and Lisbon, including Easyjet (www.easyjet.co.uk), Ryanair (wwwryanair.com) and Monarch (www.monarch.co.uk).

Visitors from the USA and South America can travel on Sata Airways (www.sata.pt) which has seasonal flights from São Salvador da Bahia (Brazil) to Lisbon; between Porto and Lisbon; between Oakland, California and Terceira, Azores; and between Boston and Lisbon, Porto, and Ponte Delgada, Azores; as well as various routes between Portugal and the rest of Europe.

Between regular airlines and charter companies the choice is considerable – and ticket prices vary a great deal.

Charter Flights

Because Portugal is a popular tourist destination, charter flights from Britain and continental Europe to Lisbon and Faro are frequent in summer, less so in winter. There are similar flights from the United States. Although primarily intended for holiday-makers buying a complete package, including accommodation, spare capacity is sold off as seat only, and often at a discounted rate.

Airports

In Lisbon and Porto the international airports are on the outskirts of the city. Taxis will take you to the city centre. All have meters and lists of charges for out-of-town journeys. The website for Portugal's airports is www.ana.pt. In Lisbon, taxis cost around €10 and drivers are entitled to charge an excess for luggage over 30kg (66lb). The easiest way to reach the town centre, if you don't have much luggage, is the Metro extension, which was completed in 2012. The red line runs from Aeroporto, and you can change at S. Sebastião for the blue line to Restauradores or Baixa-Chiado, which will take around 35 minutes; trains run from 6.30am to 1am. The Aerobus runs from the yellow bus stop outside the airport every 20 minutes and takes about 20 minutes to the centre of town, and can be quicker than a taxi when traffic is heavy. Tickets allow you a free day's travel on the city's transport system. Porto and Faro also have bus services to their city centres and good air links with each other.

Aeroporto de Lisboa
Tel: 218 413 500
Aeroporto Dr Francisco Sá Carneiro (Porto)
Tel: 229 432 400

Aeroporto de Faro
Tel: 289 800 800
Aeroporto da Santa María (Azores)
Tel: 296 820 020
Aeroporto des Horta (Madeira)
Tel: 292 943 511

By Train

Nowhere in Portugal is yet linked to the superfast tgv system, but there's a busy international (and national) train service run by the national railway company, **CP (Caminhos de Ferro Portugueses;** www.cp.pt). A daily train, the Sud-Express, runs as a night train between Lisbon and Irun, from where you can take the TGV to Paris; likewise there are night trains on the Paris–Porto route, changing at Irun. The Madrid to Lisbon/Porto service (usually twice a day) is a sleeper and takes around 10 hours.

There are also routes from northern Spain (Galicia) or southern Spain (Seville) into Portugal. These latter services tend to be slow and time-consuming. Once in Portugal, you have a good, fast north–south route (Porto–Lisbon–Faro) as well as slow, scenic rides, if you care for them, especially in the north.

Special Tickets

Various discounts are available, including for groups, seniors, students, youths and children. Eurail offer train passes for periods of three, four, five or six days

By Road

By Car

Good roads link Portugal with its Spanish neighbour at numerous border points. Main east–west

Oriente Station was designed by Santiago Calatrava.

routes to Lisbon are from Seville via Beja; from Badajoz via Elvas; from Salamanca via Viseu (via the IP5 highway).

If driving from England, using the channel ferries, or the Channel Tunnel, allow three days; or, via Plymouth–Santander or Portsmouth–Bilbao, two.

By Bus

Eurolines (www.eurolines.com) operates buses between Paris and Lisbon. Although cheap, it may not be as cheap as a no-frills carrier. Tickets tend to be open, so make sure you book a seat for the return journey. Busabout (www.busabout.com) offer seven-day day 'adventure' bus tours around Spain and Portugal aimed at young travellers.

GETTING AROUND

By Car

Thanks to EU funding, many of Portugal's roads have improved considerably over the past decade or so. However, many rural routes continue to be poorly maintained and narrow. In the cities, traffic can be heavy, especially in rush hour, and towns can be difficult to negotiate. The best plan is to find a car park and walk. Remember to drive on the right, giving priority to traffic on your left.

You will need a blue zone parking permit to park in most major cities. You can acquire these free of charge from the local police. Do not park within 18 metres (60ft) of a road

junction, 15 metres (50ft) of a bus or tram stop. Park facing the same direction as the moving traffic on your side of the road. Car parks are increasing in number and are obviously the most secure option.

Seat belts are compulsory in both front and rear seats, and children under 12 must travel in the back. Talking on a mobile phone while driving is also illegal. Offending against these and other regulations is subject to heavy on-the-spot cash fines. Watch out for compulsory dipped-headlight signs on motorways in the north. By law you should also have a red warning triangle and a fluorescent yellow jacket in the car (provided in rental cars). If you break down, 24-hour assistance is available via the Automóvel Clube de Portugal (www.acp.pt).

The alcohol limit is 0.5g/litre and a blood/alcohol reading of more than 0.12 percent will result in steep fines. There are four categories of highway: **AE** are motorways on which tolls are levied (120kph/75mph speed limit) **IP** are *itinerários principais* (main trunk roads, 100kph/62mph) **IC** are *itinerários complementares* (complementary trunk roads, 100kph/62mph) **AN** are *estradas nacionais* (main roads, 90kph/53mph) The speed limit in urban areas is 50kph (30mph).

Car Hire

To get the best car hire deals, book in advance with internet-based brokers, like Holiday Autos (www.holidayautos. com). Alternatively, the major international car hire companies have offices at the airport, including Hertz,

Avis, Alamo and Europcar – along with several local, generally less expensive, companies. Reliable local choices include Auto Jardim (www. auto-jardim.com) and Guerin (www. guerin.pt); the latter has offices at Faro and Lisbon airports, as well as in the cities of Porto and Lisbon.

To rent a car in Portugal, most agencies require you to be at least 21 years old and to have had a valid driving licence for a minimum of one year. An international licence is not necessary.

By Air

tap Air Portugal is the national airline. There is daily service between Lisbon, Porto, Faro, Madeira and the Azores.

The airline Portugália also operates a solid domestic and international service, and has a good reputation. The offices are located at Rua C - Edifício 70, 1749-078 Lisbon, tel: 218 425 500.

By Train

Trains in Portugal range from the comfortable and speedy alfa *rápidos* to the painfully slow *regionais*. Generally, the most efficient routes are the Lisbon–Coimbra–Porto and the Lisbon–Algarve lines. Algarve trains depart from Gare do Oriente. Santa Apolónia is where to catch trains to northern and central Portugal. *Rápidos* (alfa)are fast and punctual and cost more. Some *rápidos* have first-class carriages only; others have a very comfortable second class as well. Next in line are the *directos intercidades*, which make more stops and travel more slowly.

These have both first- and second-class compartments; second-class here is likely to be less comfortable than in the *rápidos*.

Finally, the *semi-directos*, and especially the *regionais*, seem to stop every few metres and take longer than you could have believed possible. On *directos*, *semi-directos* and *regionais*, second-class seats are not assigned, and the train company, **Caminhos de Ferro Portugueses (CP)**, has no qualms about issuing more tickets than seats if the need arises. If you want to be certain of a seat, board early. On rural routes, trains are almost always punctual.

Furthermore, to reach more remote – or even not-so-remote – destinations, it may be necessary to change trains, and timetables are seldom coordinated. Unless you are catching *rápidos* (and *intercidades*), which are punctual, leave yourself plenty of time between transfers. Note also that only the international trains like the Sud-Expresso and the Faro–Porto Comboio Azul have restaurant cars.

Stations in Lisbon

There are four railway stations in Lisbon. Cais do Sodré and Rossio are commuter stations. International and long-distance trains to the north and east leave from Santa Apolónia, just to the east of Praça do Comercio. Trains south to Alentejo and the Algarve leave from Gare Oriente.

Stations in Porto and Coimbra

Porto and Coimbra each have two railway stations. Porto's São Bento and Coimbra A are located in the respective town centres. Most long-distance trains, however, arrive and leave from Porto's Campanhã station and Coimbra B station, outside the cities, and there are shuttle services between the central and outlying stations.

By Bus

Bus networks are privately run. The major carriers are Rede Expressos (www.rede-expressos.pt) and **Eva Transportes** (http://www.eva-bus.com).

Except for routes between major cities, the bus is often faster than the train, and the system is certainly more extensive. This is particularly true in the north and between the smaller towns in Algarve and Alentejo.

There are quite a few private bus lines which specialise in particular areas of the country. Often they have more direct routes to smaller towns.

Many travel agencies can book tickets on a private line, or may even run their own.

Boat Trips

Boat trips are offered in a variety of vessels, traditional and modern, on the country's three main rivers, the Tejo, Douro and Minho. Many are privately run, so tourist offices do not necessarily have all the information. Hotels, particularly in the Douro region, should be able to tell you all the options.

Rio Tejo Lisboa Vista do Tejo is a state-run lunch and dinner cruise from Alcântara docks (tel: 213 913 030; www.lvt.pt).

Rio Douro Boats depart from the Cais de Ribeira in Porto. Trips range in length from an hour to several days, visiting quintas and stopping en route. The largest operating company is **Douro Azul** in Porto (tel: 223 402 500; www.douroazul.pt). The French shipping company **Croise Europe** (www.croisieurope.travel) has three boats. **Portowellcome** in Vila Nova de Guia also organises trips (tel: 223 747 320; www.portowellcome.com). The government-backed PortoTours, in the Torre Medieval just below Porto's cathedral, organises boat and other tours (tel: 222 000 045; www.portotours.com).

Transport in Lisbon

Trains

Commuter trains to Cascais (stopping in Carcavelos, Estoril and other towns along the western coast) depart from Cais do Sodré station, west of the Praça do Comércio. Trains depart roughly every 15 to 20 minutes; the journey to Cascais (the end of the line) takes 35–40 minutes.

Trains to the northwestern suburbs, including Sintra, leave from the Rossio station at 15-minute intervals. The trip to Sintra takes about 45 minutes and operates from Campolide.

Buses and Trams

The city bus company, Carris, runs an extensive system of buses, trams *(eléctricos)* and funiculars. Bus stops are clearly marked by signposts or shelters. All stops display a diagrammatical map of the bus route; many have a map of the entire city system.

Pre-World War I trams ply the smaller, steeper streets where buses

are unable to navigate. Some of them are quite beautiful, inside and out; they are slower and cheaper than the buses and are a good way to see the city. The tram is also supplemented with some larger, more modern vehicles operating along the riverside.

Carris also runs two funiculars and an elevator. The Santa Justa Elevador is near the Rossio. One funicular climbs the steep Calçada da Glória from Praça dos Restauradores, the other is in São Paulo. You pay on board, or they are covered by Carris tickets and passes.

Tickets and Passes

It is worth considering buying a Viva Viagem or 7Colinas card. These cost €0.50, and you can then charge up the card. You thus pay less per journey than you do if you buy regular tickets. They can be charged so that they're useable only on the Carris network, or so that they can be used on the Carris and the Metro networks. Buying tickets for each journey works out more expensive. Don't board the bus without paying, as ticket inspectors appear from time to time and the fine is steep.

The Carris information kiosks scattered all over the city provide information and sell tickets and passes. Two of the most convenient kiosks are in Praça da Figueira, near the Rossio, and near Eduardo VII Park.

Metro

The metro is useful for travel in the central zone of the city and travelling to/from the airport. The system is easy to use and cheap. You can buy single tickets and validate them at the machines next to the ticket booths. Carris kiosks and Metro stations also sell a one-/five-day Bilhete Carris/Metro ticket valid for buses, trams, funiculars and the metro. Alternatively the Viva Viagem or 7Colinas cards may be charged so that they are valid on the Metro.

Taxis

In all Portugal's cities, taxis are plentiful and cheap. The great majority of them are cream, while older ones are black with green roofs. In the city, they charge a standard metered fare, with no additions for extra passengers. (They carry up to four people.) Outside city limits, the driver may use the meter or charge a flat rate per kilometre, and is entitled to charge for the return fare (even if you don't take it). You should tip taxi drivers between 5 and 10 percent.

ACCOMMODATION

HOTELS, YOUTH HOSTELS, BED & BREAKFAST

CHOOSING A HOTEL

Accommodation ranges from 5-star luxury hotels with fantastic facilities to basic private rooms for rent, or from boutique, charming converted mansions, to glamping-style yurts in the middle of the North Portugal countryside. The middle range of reasonably priced accommodation has been considerably expanded thanks to an increase in the number of both Portuguese- and foreign-owned hotels, and there is also now a far greater supply of designer boutique options and luxury hotels across the country, particulary in and around Lisbon, Porto and Algarve. Hotels in Portugal offer great value when compared with places elsewhere in Europe. This is particularly the case at the luxury end of the market. Here, you can stay in gorgeous properties in glorious settings at prices far lower than equivalent places in some other European countries.

Pousadas & Manor Houses

It's well worth trying to stay in some pousadas while you are in Portugal, as these are a speciality of the country, the like of which you won't find elsewhere. Pousadas are national inns in architecturally special buildings, which provide stylish and comfortable accommodation, usually in great settings. They are to be found in most parts of the country, some in historic castles, some in converted convents or grand country houses, and the majority serve excellent regional food. For reservations,

contact the *pousadas* directly or call the central number (tel: 218 442 001; www.pousadas.pt or check www.pousadasofportugal.com). If you're able to book some time ahead, there are some excellent deals on offer. For more information on these and on the Turihab scheme, which offers places to stay in other Portuguese architectural gems, see *Pousadas and Manor Houses*, page 116).

For self-catering countryside villas, also under the Turihab scheme, try Casas no Campo, www.casasnocampo.net.

Guesthouses

Portugal has some very charming, modest guesthouses. These often have a lot of local character, and are well located, but are well kept and appealing. Bed and breakfasts in private homes are designated by an official TER symbol on a metal plaque and the logo of the State Tourist Office (Direcção-Geral do Turismo); there are three categories:

TH *Turismo de Habitação*: in houses of architectural merit.
TR *Turismo Rural*: characteristic rural houses.
AT *Agroturismo*: houses forming part of a farm estate.

Apartment & Villa Rental

There are apartments, villas and *quintas* for rent all over the country, which can be the most convenient and comfortable choice when travelling as a family. To seek out the perfect place to stay, try websites such as www.ownersdirect.co.uk, www.chooseportugal.com, www.villasandcottages.com and www.homeaway.co.uk.

Hotels

Hotels in Portugal come in several guises. They offer amenities such as restaurants and room service. All rooms have bathrooms. Hotels are rated from 1 to 5 stars:
5 stars: a luxury hotel.
4 stars: not luxury but close.
3 stars: good value but sometimes run-down.
1 and 2 stars: basic places to stay.
Albergarias are essentially hotels offering 4-star comfort and meals.
Estalagems are very similar but may be 4- or 5-star.
Residencials have star gradings and are like small hotels but generally do bed and breakfast only. They usually have an "R" on a sign outside.
Pensãos are more basic, and again do bed and breakfast only. You can find 4-star *pensãos*, but the majority offer fewer comforts than that.

HOTEL LISTINGS

The list below includes a small sample of the wide variety of hotels in Portugal. Remember that you will probably have difficulty finding a decent room in July and August if you haven't made an advance reservation, and you'll also get better deals if you book ahead.

The following hotels are listed by area, following the order of the regions in the Places section of this book, beginning with Lisbon; Estoril, Cascais, Sintra and Setúbal have been grouped together under Around Lisbon. In each place, places to stay are listed in order of comfort, beginning with the most luxurious.

Note that *pousadas* and manor houses are included with hotel listings.

TRANSPORT

ACCOMMODATION

EATING OUT

ACTIVITIES

A – Z

LANGUAGE

LISBON

Residencial Alegria
Praça da Alegria, 12
Tel: 213 220 670
www.alegrianet.com
A small family-run hotel with plenty of charm, where the simple rooms are brightened with painted wooden furniture. It's conveniently situated just off Avenida do Liberdade. €€

Hotel Avenida Palace
Rua 1º de Dezembro
Tel: 213 218 100
www.hotelavenidapalace.pt
A grand 19th-century building, smack in the old town centre, between the Rossio and Praça dos Restauradores, this has sumptuously decorated rooms, with lots of oil paintings and polished antique furnishings. €€€€

Bairro Alto Hotel
Praça Luís de Camões, 2,
Tel: 213 408 288
www.bairroaltohotel.com
Chic boutique hotel in the heart of Lisbon, with gorgeous, soberly decorated rooms, snow-white linen, city views, free-standing bathtubs, and all comforts.Rooms are air- and sound-conditioned. €€€€

Hotel Botânico
Rue da Mãe d'Agua, 16–20
Tel: 213 420 392
www.hotelbotanico.net
Handily located between the Bairro Alto and the Avenida da Liberdade and close to Avenida Metro station, Hotel Botânico is comfortable, with plain, unfussy rooms. €€€

Hotel Britânia
Rua Rodrigues Sapaio, 17
Tel: 213 218 200
Small, comfortable Art Deco hotel

The Lapa Palace's "Royal Terrace".

that dates from the 1940s and exudes modernist style, set on a quiet street parallel to the Avenida da Liberdade. €€€

Hotel Diplomático
Rua Castilho, 74
Tel: 213 839 020
www.viphotels.com
Centrally located, Hotel Diplomático is a smart 4-star, business-oriented hotel that has appealing, brightly decorated rooms, and is comfortable and efficient. €€

Residencial Dom João
Rua José Estêvão, 43
Tel: 213 144 171
www.residencialdjoao.com
A modern residence with spacious rooms, this is located in a quiet residential neighbourhood, slightly off the beaten track, but only a 15-minute walk to the Praça Marquês de Pombal. €€

VIP Executive Suites Éden
Praça dos Restauradores, 24
Tel: 213 216 600
www.viphotels.com
The Art Deco Eden Theatre has been converted into a beautiful hotel that contains well-appointed one-bedroom and studio apartments. The icing on the cake is the wonderful rooftop pool with city views. €€€

Hotel Eduardo VII
Avenida Fontes Pereira de Melo, 5
Tel: 213 688 822
www.hoteleduardovii.pt
This Best Western option is near the park with a beautiful view from the restaurant; rooms are old-fashioned but comfortable, and it has a small and intimate feel, rather like a private club. €

Fluorescente Residencial
Rua das Portas de Santo Antão, 99
Tel: 213 426 609
www.residencialflorescente.com
With traditionally tiled hallways and bright, clean rooms, some with full-length baths, this guesthouse is centrally located in a street of restaurants, near Praça dos Restauradores. €€

The Independente
Rua de Sao Pedro de Alcantara, 81
Tel: 213 461 381
www.theindependente.pt
In a great central location close to Principe Real, Bairro Alto and Chiado, the Art Deco Independente Hostel & Suites is a gorgeous budget option, with 90 beds in 11 dorms, plus four spacious suites. €–€€

As Janelas Verdes
Rua de las Janales Verdes, 37

Casa da Calcada.

Tel: 213 218 200
www.heritage.pt
Next to the Museum of Ancient Art, this noble mansion belonged to an 18th-century writer. Beautifully furnished, with a lovely library and terrace for guests, and some rooms with river views. €€€

Lapa Palace
Rua do Pau de Bandeira, 4
Tel: 213 949 494
www.lapapalacelisbon.com/
This glamorously restored 19th-century mansion in the best residential quarter has a discreetly opulent feel, with gorgeous rooms, balconies overhung with greenery, and marble bathrooms. €€€€

Hotel Miraparque
Avenida Sidónio Pais, 12
Tel: 213 524 286
www.miraparque.com
The Miraparque proffers decent rooms with unfussy décor. This is excellent value in a good location on a quiet street with lush views overlooking the park and the city. €

Pálacio Belmonte
Páteo Dom Fradique
Tel: 218 816 600
www.palaciobelmonte.com
A place for a special treat: beautiful bedrooms and enormous suites, with eclectic, out-of-this-world decoration, have been created in this 15th-century palace beneath the castle. The black marble pool is divine. €€€€

Pestana Palace Hotel
Rua do Jau, 54
Tel: 213 615 600
www.pestana.com

Classy, superbly restored 19th-century palace a short taxi ride from the centre. Five-star luxury with pool, gardens, oriental pavilion and luxurious rooms in the new wing. Wonderful food. **€€€€**

Hotel Regency Chiado
Rua Nova Do Almada, 114
Tel: 291 724 276
www.hoteldochiado.com
A modern yet classic hotel that rose from the ashes of the 1996 Chiado fire. Beautiful designed rooms with balconies have fabulous city views, as does the bar terrace. **€€€**

Roma Residencial
Travessa da Glória, 22-A
Tel: 213 460 557/8/9
www.residencialroma-lisbon.com
This simple, unfussy hotel has all the requisite amenities including private bath and TV in every room, plus small wrought-iron balconies, and is situated in a handy location in the heart of Baixa. **€**

Sana Rex Hotel
Rua Castilho, 169
Tel: 213 882 161
www.sanarexhotel.com
The Rex is a nice, centrally located, 3-star hotel, with small, comfortable rooms with wood-panelled furniture. **€€€**

Pensão São Jão de Praça
Rua de São Jão de Praça, 97
Tel: 218 862 591
In the atmospheric Alfama district,

right below the cathedral, this is a charming pension with sunny rooms. Some rooms have river views, some are without showers. Clean and friendly. **€**

Albergaria Senhora do Monte
Calçada do Monte, 39
Tel: 218 866 002
http://www.albergariasenhoradomonte.com/
This fantastically located small hotel has smart, comfortable rooms and beautiful views overlooking São Jorge Castle, Alfama and down to the Tejo. **€€€**

Solar do Castelo
Rua das Cozinhas, 2, Castelo
Tel: 213 218 200
www.heritage.pt
In an 18th-century mansion in a unique location inside the castle walls, this has had a stylishly contemporary makeover; and is a fantastically romantic place to stay. **€€€**

Solar dos Mouros
Rua do Milagre de Santo António, 4
Tel: 218 854 940
www.solardosmouros.com
Dramatic interiors that combine African artworks and contemporary paintings against brilliant, bright-walled rooms by the artist-owner Luís Lemos, high up in the picturesque Alfama district with river and castle views. **€€**

Tiara Park Atlantic Hotel
Rua Castilho, 149

Tel: 213 818 700
www.tiara-hotels.com
This modern, large hotel has 331 spacious rooms overlooking the park; executive rooms are worth the extra cost as they have sweeping views over Lisbon and the river. **€€€€**

Hotel Tivoli Jardim
Rua Julio C. Machado, 9
Tel: 213 591 000
www.tivolihotels.com
Run by the same company as the friendly Tivoli Lisboa, this has lovely, spacious rooms with big plate-glass windows, snow-white linen and contemporary style. **€€€–€€€€**

Hotel Tivoli Lisboa
Avenida da Liberdade, 185
Tel: 213 198 900
www.tivolihotels.com
Big, handsome and handy for all parts of town, this welcoming hotel has superb views from its Terraço and Sky bars and a lush Elements Spa by Banyan Tree. **€€€€**

York House Hotel
Rua Janelas Verdes, 32
Tel: 213 962 435
http://www.yorkhouselisboa.com/
In a class by itself: comfort and charm combined. The great favourite of Graham Greene, among others. An interesting neighbourhood, about 15 minutes by bus from the Rossio. Reserve well in advance. The annexe is down the street at number 47. **€€€€**

AROUND LISBON

Cascais

Farol Design Hotel
Avenida Rei Humberto II de Itália, 7
Tel: 214 823 490
www.farol.com.pt
Next to the lighthouse above the sea, this wonderfully bright and sunny, stylish boutique hotel has stunning, contemporary rooms that are mostly white with flashes of colour, plus a salt-water swimming pool. **€€€€**

Fortaleza do Guincho
Estrada do Guincho
Tel: 214 870 491
www.relaischateaux.com/guincho
A superlative hotel within a handsomely renovated fortress, complete with canons and flags, and right by the beach. Rooms overlook the ocean, and there's a Michelin-starred restaurant. **€€€€**

Oitavos Hotel
Rua de Oitavos, Quinta da Marinha
Tel: 214 860 020
www.theoitavos.com
Designer looks complement the

The Farol Design Hotel in Cascais.

landscape along the Cascais coast at this 5-star hotel, with rooms decorated in slate-greys and overlooking the sea. **€€€€**

Onyria Marinha Edition Cascais
Quinta da Marinha, Rua do Clube
Tel: 214 860 150
http://www.onyriamarinha.com
This sumptuous designer boutique

PRICE CATEGORIES

Price categories are based on the cost of a double room for one night in high season.
€ = up to €70
€€ = €70–140
€€€ = €140–200
€€€€ = above €200

hotel opened in 2011. Choose between rooms and modernist villas, with glorious infinity pools and close to lush gardens, woodlands, and a golf course. €€€€

Estoril

Palácio Estoril Hotel & Golf
Rua Particular
Tel: 214 648 000
www.palacioestorilhotel.com
To feel like an off-duty James Bond, stay at this monumental palace, with plenty of glamour, 5-star luxury, tradition, all the comforts and a famous casino. €€€€

Hotel Smart
Rua Maestro Laçerda, 6
Tel: 214 682 164
www.hotel-smart.net
Immaculate little guesthouse, this is a good-value option close to the casino, with smart rooms, a terrace, pleasant garden and a swimming pool. €€

Setúbal

Pousada de Palmela
Palmela
Tel: 212 351 226

www.pousadas.pt
Near Setúbal, this pousada is spectacularly set on a hill top. It's inside the ancient castle walls and the conversion makes use of the ruined convent within to create a unique place to stay. €€€€

Pousada São Filipe
Setúbal
Tel: 265 555 070
www.pousadas.pt
In a 17th-century fortress, this pousada is a superb place to stay, with lovely views overlooking the harbour, the River Sado and the Natural Park of Arrábida. €€€€

Pousada Vale do Gaio
Barragem Tito Morais, Torrão
Tel: 265 669 610
www.valedogaio.com
Southeast of Setúbal, this is set in the countryside of the Alentejo, and is a small, gorgeous, chic pousada beside a lake, with sunny terraces and a great restaurant. €€€

Sintra

Convento de Sao Saturnino
2705-001 Azóia-Sintra

Tel: 219 283 192
www.saosat.com
In a beautifully tranquil setting, this converted convent has whitewashed rooms, a labyrinth interior, and six gorgeously decorated rooms and three suites under wood beamed ceilings and with paintings covering the walls. €€€€

Lawrence's Hotel
Rua Consiglieri Perdosa, 38–40
Tel: 219 105 500
www.lawrenceshotel.com
Lord Byron stayed in this 5-star hotel, the oldest in Portugal, in the heart of Sintra, founded in 1764. Just 11 rooms and an excellent restaurant. Delicious breakfasts. €€€€

Hotel Sintra Jardim
Quinta Visconde de Trojal, Travessa dos Avelares, 12
Tel: 219 230 738
http://pensaoresidencialsintra.pai.pt/
On the road to Cascais, this grand family guesthouse has nice, old-fashioned rooms with lots of character, and an attractive gardens and pool surrounded by lush greenery. €–€€

ALGARVE

Albufeira

Residencial Limas
Rua de la Liberdade, 25–7
Tel: 289 514 025
www.limasresidencial.com
Cheerful small hotel, with brightly decorated blue and yellow rooms, in the thumping heart of Albufeira's always lively resort and close to lots of

Hotel Eva is centrally located in Faro.

bars and restaurants. €

Rocamar Beach Hotel
Largo Jacinto D'Ayet, 7
Tel: 289 540 280
www.rocamarbeachhotel.com
Set high up on a rocky outcrop, overlooking the beach and ocean, this is one of Albufeira's mid-range choices, with sea-view rooms in

1950s style with picture windows and balconies. €€

Cabanas

Forte de São João da Barra
http://www.fortesaojoaodabarra.com/
A converted 17th-century fortress, perched on the coast a short distance from the pretty seasidetown of Cabanas. The 10 rooms are stylish and contemporary. €€€

Faro

Hotel Dom Bernardo
Rua General Teófilo da Trindade, 20
Tel: 289 889 800
www.bestwesterndombernardo.com/
This Best Western hotel is conveniently located near the centre of Faro, and has presentable, neat rooms with terracotta floors in a smart, modern building. €€€

Estalagem Aeromar
Avenida Nascente, 1, Praia de Faro
Tel: 289 817 189
www.aeromar.net
On the beach in the direction of the airport, this modern hotel has views over the River Formosa and the beach, and comfortable rooms. €€

Hotel Eva
Avenida da República, 1
Tel: 289 001 002
www.tdhotels.pt

A link of the TD chain, this is a good choice, a central, comfortable hotel that has all mod cons and a rooftop pool. Make sure your room overlooks the harbour. €€€

Residencial Samé
Rua do Bocage, 66
Tel: 289 824 375
One of a dozen *pensãos* in town, this homely choice is centrally located and has small, basic, simple, but clean rooms, and is good value for those on a small budget. €

Lagos

Hotel Belavista da Luz
Praia da Luz
Tel: 282 788 655
www.hotelbelavistadaluz.com
An excellent family-oriented choice, this modern hotel with good sports and entertainment facilities has rooms with balconies, centred around two large swimming pools. €€

Albergaria Marina Rio
Avenida dos Descobrimentos
Tel: 282 780 830
www.marinario.com
A smart white-washed hotel with a great marina-side location, this has balconies making the most of the view overlooking the bobbing boats and glittering water. €€

Quinta das Achadas
Estrada da Barragem Odiáxere
Tel: 282 798 425
http://algarveholiday.net/Quinta_das_Achadas
Surrounded by luxuriant gardens, this has loads of charm and rooms in converted stables, with wrought-iron beds and bathrooms tiled in traditional azulejos. €€€

Hotel Tivoli Lagos
Rua António Crisógono Santos
Tel: 282 790 079
www.tivolihotels.com
This fine 4-star has nautical blue and white rooms and plenty of facilities, including a large pool, plus a central location in Lagos. €€

Loulé

Hotel Loulé Jardim
Praça Manuel Arriaga
Tel: 289 413 095
www.loulejardimhotel.com
A handsome early 20th-century building near the centre of the historic town of Loulé, this is set near gardens, and has a cosy, comfortable atmosphere, but no restaurant. €€

Portimão

D. João II Pestana Hotel
Praia do Alvor
Tel: 282 400 700
www.pestana.com
A modern place, with good sports and recreational facilities, the D. João II Pestana has cool contemporary rooms and is set up above several white-sand miles of beach. €€€

Pensão Alcaide
Praia do Vau, Portimão
Tel: 282 401 462
www.hotelalcaide.com/
A comfortable 18-room hotel, this basic and homely choice has small, simple rooms with tiled floors and balconies. €

Pestana Delfim Hotel
Praia dos Três Irmãos, Alvor
Tel: 282 400 800
www.pestana.com
Set high above the sea, a 5-minute walk from the beach; modern, with good sports facilities, this comfortable option is an all-inclusive hotel, which means all meals are included in the price. €€€

Praia da Rocha

Hotel Algarve – Casino
Avenida Tomás Cabreira
Tel: 282 402 000
www.solverde.pt
This is a grand, late 20th-century, rather ugly hotel, but with great views and comfortable rooms, plus casino and cabaret, set on a gorgeous beach. €€€

Hotel Bela Vista
Avenida Tomás Cabreira
Tel: 282 450 480
www.hotelbelavista.net
This is Praia da Rocha's most characterful hotel, a beautiful boutique place in a renovated historical property. It's exquisitely decorated with brilliant tiling and linens, and with a gorgeous pool surrounded by day beds. €€€€

Sagres

Hotel de Baleeira
Baleeira, Sagres
Vila do Bispo
Tel: 282 624 212
www.memmobaleeira.com
With ocean views, the Baleeira has designer boutique rooms that are decorated with minimalist styling and relaxing hues of white, and has a seawater pool and tennis court. €€

Navigator
Rua Infante Don Henrique
Tel: 282 624 354
http://navigator.sitex.us/
This apartment hotel has a pool and other facilities, and is well-appointed with appealing rooms with balconies. It's next to the *pousada* with equally wonderful ocean views. €€

Pousada do Infante
Tel: 282 620 240
www.pousadas.pt
Near Cape St Vincent in the village of Sagres, this historic pousada is a memorable place to stay: it has a fantastic clifftop postion and incredible sea views. €€€

São Brás de Alportel

Vila Monte
Sítio dos Caliços
Tel: 289 790 790
www.vilamonte.com
Ten minutes from the sea, this handsome hotel with Moorish influences is in an old manor house, with a pool, tennis courts, terraces and gardens. €€€

Tavira

Convento da Graça
Rua Dom Paio Peres Correia
Tel: 281 329 040
www.pousadas.pt
A lovely old converted Franciscan convent with tons of character and atmosphere, close to the centre of Tavira and within easy access of some beautiful beaches. €€€€

Mare's Residencial
Rua José Pires Padinha, 24
Tel: 281 325 815
www.residencialmares.com
Small family-run hotel set in a beautiful location on the river bank; rooms are simple but comfortable and the best have balconies overlooking the water. €

Vila Galé Albacora
Rua 4 de Outubro
Tel: 281 329 900
www.vilagale.co.uk
On the banks of the river, this is a large 4-star hotel with 268 rooms, centred around a large swimming pool, and located close to Tavira's centre as well as within easy reach of Parque Natural da Ria Formosa.

Vilamoura

Hotel Dom Pedro Marina
Av. Tivoli
Tel: 289 381 000
www.dompedro.com
A modern establishment benefitting from a great location near the waterfront and marina, this has lovely views and 100 smart rooms, plus four suites with Jacuzzis on each balcony. €€€

PRICE CATEGORIES

Price categories are based on the cost of a double room for one night in high season.
€ = up to €70
€€ = €70–140
€€€ = €140–200
€€€€ = above €200

UPPER ALENTEJO

Alendroal

Casa de Terena
Rua Direita, 45
Tel: 268 459 132
www.casadeterena.com
Restored 200-year-old house in centre of the very pretty village of Terena, 10km (6 miles) from Alendroal and perfectly set for exploring the beautiful Alentejo countryside. €€

Herdade Dom Pedro
Tel: 268 459 137
http://montedompedro.no.sapo.pt/
Period Alentejo farmhouse set amid 100 hectares (250 acres) of olive groves in a peaceful country location, with a swimming pool and opportunities to go horse riding. €€

Estremoz

Pousada da Rainha Santa Isabel
Largo Dom Dinis
Tel: 268 332 075
www.pousadas.pt
In a dramatic setting in a former castle, this pousada has amazing views over the surrounding plains, and is furnished by beautiful antiques. €€€€

Évora

Hotel D. Fernando
Avenida Dr Barahona, 2
Tel: 266 741 717
www.hoteldomfernandoevora.com
Well-appointed 3-star hotel with bright, cheerful rooms that's centred around a swimming pool surrounded by lawns, and located centrally. €

Évoramonte
Quinta do Serafim
Tel: 268 959 360
www.quintadoserafim.pt

This gorgeous rural option, centred around an ancient olive mill, is close to the picturesque small village of Évoramonte and has three self-contained antique-furnished villas. €€

Hotel M'ar de Ar Muralhas
Travessa da Palmeira, 4
Tel: 266 739 300
www.mardearhotels.com
Luxury hotel inside the city walls, this has a lovely garden with manicured lawns that's bordered by the castellated city wall and rooms decorated in powdery colours, with lovely terracotta floors. €€

Pensão Giraldo
Rua dos Mercadores, 27
Tel: 266 705 833
A friendly, inexpensive pensão in the main square, this is a good-value choice and picturesquely located, but don't expect any frills. €

Pensão Policarpo
Rua da Freira de Baixo, 16
Tel: 266 702 424
www.pensaopolicarpo.com
The most atmospheric place to stay in Évora: this charming guesthouse is set in an old nobleman's house with a courtyard for breakfast. €

Pensão Riviera
Rua 5 de Outubro, 47–9
Tel: 266 703 304
www.riviera-evora.com
This is a small, old-fashioned place near the centre, a cosy choice that proffers white rooms with dark wooden furniture. €€

Pousada dos Lóios
Largo Conde de Vila Flor
Tel: 266 730 070
www.pousadas.pt
Former monastery, centrally located opposite the Roman temple, with

rooms set in the ancient chambers of the Canons Regular. Very popular – book early. €€€€

Best Western Plus Hotel Santa Clara
Travessa da Milheira, 19
Tel: 266 704 141
www.hotelsantaclara.pt
Good value andvery central – only a few paces from Praça do Giraldo – this Best Western lives up to the chain's usual standards, with smart, comfortable rooms. €€

Solar de Monfalim
Largo da Misericordia
Tel: 266 750 000
www.monfalimtur.pt
A lovely converted palace in Evora town centre, this is great value and an atmospheric choice, with simple rooms furnished with wrought-iron furniture. €€

Marvão

Pousada de Santa Maria
Rua 24 de Janeiro, 7
Tel: 245 993 201
www.pousadas.pt
Near Portalegre, within a walled hilltop town, this gorgeous pousada has lots of character and is set in two converted traditional houses, with breathtaking countryside views. €€–€€€

Redondo

Hotel Convento de São Paulo
Serra de Ossa, Aldeia da Serra
Tel: 266 989 160
www.hotelconventospaulo.com
With beautiful antique furnishings and fine gardens, this hotel is set in a glorious converted convent that's surrounded by a lush national forest. €€–€€€

LOWER ALENTEJO

Serpa

Casa da Muralha
Rua Portas de Beja,43
Tel: 284 543 150
www.casadamuralha.com
Extremely attractive lodging in a whitewashed house tucked beside a historic aqueduct in the centre; rooms are very appealing, whitewashed, with traditional handpainted Alentejan furniture. €€

Vila Nova de Milfontes

Casa Amarela
Rua Dom Luis Castro e Almeida

Tel: 283 996 632
www.casaamarelamilfontes.com
Casa Amarela is a cheery place with a cheery owner; it has small rooms with bright paintings and bright bedspreads, a comfy lounge and shared kitchen. €

Casa da Eira
Rua Casa da Pedra
Tel: 283 99 70 01
www.casadaeira.com
Set in three converted houses, Casa da Eira has bright, sunny rooms full of jazzy colour and a lovely pool,

and the management can organise adventure holidays. €€

Vila Viçosa

Pousada de Dom João IV
Tel: 268 980 742
www.pousadas.pt
Located in a converted 15th-century convent, this grand and lavishly decorated pousada has lovely rooms and is in the heart of the town, close to the Ducal palace. €€€

ESTREMADURA

Batalha

Hotel Residencial Casa do Outeiro
Largo Carvalho do Outeiro, 4
Tel: 244 765 806
www.casadoouteiro.com
At this modern-style residencial with
a pool, all the rooms have balconies
where you can sit out, and are bright
and sunny. Ask for one with a view
towards the monastery. €€

Óbidos

Albergaria Josefa d'Óbidos
Rua Dom João d'Ornelas
Tel: 262 959 228
www.josefadobidos.com
Near the old town, this guesthouse
has comfortable, clean rooms, some
of which are old-fashioned and
traditional, while others are more
contemporary. €€

Mansão da Torre
Tel: 262 959 247
www.hotelmansaodatorre.com
A modern hotel, 2km (1 mile) out of
town towards Caldas da Rainha, this
has serene rooms with contemporary
style, decorated in earthy and
subdued colours €€

Pousada do Castelo
Paço Real
Tel: 262 955 080
www.pousadas.pt
In the castle, within the walled town,
this is one of Portugal's finest and
most dramatically sited pousadas,
with great countryside views.
€€€€

Porto de Mós

Quinta do Rio Alcaide
Tel: 244 402 124
www.rioalcaide.com/
Here you have a choice of a small
group of houses set in an active
quinta in the Parque Natural das
Serras de Aire e Candeeiros. €€

Santarém

Casa da Alcáçova
Portas do Sol
Tel: 243 304 030
www.alcacova.com
This is a fine 17th-century manor
house, where all the rooms have
splendid 19th-century decor, some
with four-posters, all with antiques
and lots of polished wood. €€

Tomar

Estalagem de Santa Iria
Parque de Mouchão
Tel: 249 313 326
www.estalagemsantairia.com
This is the sole building on a
small island in the middle of the
river, accessible via bridge. The
charming building has an acclaimed
restaurant, as well as lovely
traditional rooms with leafy outlooks.
€€

Hotel dos Templários
Largo Cândido dos Reis, 1
Tel: 249 321 730
www.hoteldostemplarios.pt
This modern hotel is surrounded
by lush grounds, with balconies
overlooking the River Nabao, and is
located a short walk from the Unesco
World Heritage Site, the Convento de
Cristo. €€€

Residencial União
Rua Serpa Printa, 94
Tel: 249 323 161
Central and popular, set around
a courtyard, this residence is a
charming place to stay with lots of
character and simple rooms. €

COIMBRA

Hotel Astória
Avenida Emídio Navarro, 21
Tel: 239 853 020
www.almeidahotels.com
A classic, Belle Epoque hotel on the
river front, with elegant, antique-
filled rooms – this has lots of charm
and character. Good restaurant with
Buçaco wines. €€

Dona Inês
Rua Abel Dias Urbano, 12
Tel: 239 855 800
www.hotel-dona-ines.pt
This modern hotel, with clean, smart
rooms, is just a few minutes walk
from the centre yet is in a quiet,
tranquil location. €

Hotel D. Luís
Santa Clara Coimbra
Tel: 239 802 120
www.hoteldluis.pt
A modern place, pleasingly set on the
southern bank of the Rio Mondego
with grand view of Coimbra, this Best
Western offers good value. €–€€

Pensão Santa Cruz
Praça 8 de Maio, 21
Tel: 239 826 197
www.pensaosantacruz.com
Centrally located in a square, this
pensão is a good-value choice with
plenty of character: it has large,
traditional rooms, with whitewashed
walls and carved antique furniture. €

Hotel Quinta das Lágrimas
Santa Clara
Tel: 239 802 380
www.hotelquintadaslagrimas.com
This is full of history: an 18th-century
palace converted to a small hotel, in
the park where Inês de Castro is said
to have met her violent end. €€€

Hotel Tivoli Coimbra
Rua João Machado
Tel: 239 858 300
www.tivolihotels.com
On the western outskirts; this lovely,
comfortable 4-star is up to Tivoli's
usual good standards, and has
neutrally decorated, serene rooms.
€€€

BEIRA LITORAL

Águeda

Estalagem da Pateira
Rua da Pateira, 84
Tel: 243 721 205
www.pateira.com
A few kilometres from the A1, this is a
57-room modern hotel on a peaceful
lake shore, with boats and a heated
pool. €€

Aveiro

Hotel Afonso V
Rua Dr Manuel das Neves, 65
Tel: 234 425 191
www.hoteisafonsov.pt
Near the city centre, this old-
fashioned, traditional hotel offers
inexpensive, spacious rooms that are
good value for money. €€

PRICE CATEGORIES

Price categories are based on the
cost of a double room for one night
in high season.
€ = up to €70
€€ = €70–140
€€€ = €140–200
€€€€ = above €200

TRANSPORT

ACCOMMODATION

EATING OUT

ACTIVITIES

A – Z

LANGUAGE

Pensão Avenida
Avenida Dr Lourenço Peixinho, 256
Tel: 234 423 366.
http://pensaoavenida.planetaclix.pt/
A simple, Art Nouveau pension with bright, simple rooms, this is a great-value choice, close to the train station and a short walk from the city centre. €

Hotel Imperial
Rua Dr Nascimento Leitão
Tel: 234 380 150
www.hotelimperial.pt/
Modern and central, this has very traditionally styled rooms with wrought-iron balconies, decorated in rich colours with polished wood accents. €

Hotel Moliceiro
Rua Barbosa de Magalhães, 15
Tel: 234 377 400
www.hotelmoliceiro.pt
Comfortable hotel overlooking the canal in the historic centre, this is decorated in Art Deco-style, with particularly lavishly decorated superior rooms. €€

Buçaco

Bussaco Palace Hotel
Tel: 231 937 970

www.almeidahotels.com
This is a superb old place, a luxury hotel in a sumptuous old hunting lodge set in a forest. Nearby is the Military Museum with exhibits from the Peninsular War. €€€€

Guarda

Residencial Santos
Tel: 271 205 400
www.hotelsantos.pt
Guarda is the highest town in Portugal, and this charming guesthouse is built into the city walls; there's a roof terrace that offers fantastic views. €

Leiria

Hotel Eurosol
Rua Dom José Alves Correia da Silva Leiria
Tel: 244 849 849
www.eurosol.pt/leiria
Modern, with views over the old town and castle, the Hotel Eurosol is a reliable and comfortable choice, with rooms decorated in neutral colours. €€

Murtosa

Pousada da Torreira
Torreira

Tel: 234 860 180
www.pousadas.pt
On an isthmus between the ocean and the lagoon, this modern building is well integrated within the dramatic surrounding landscape and has a peaceful setting overlooking the estuary. €€€

Oliveira do Hospital

Hotel São Paulo
Rua Prof. Antunes Varela, 3
Tel: 238 609 000
www.ftphotels.com
This 3-star, 44-room modern block, mainly aimed at business travellers, is nothing flashy, but friendly, and with plain rooms with dark wood furniture and balconies. €–€€

Viseu

Pousada de Viseu
Tel: 210 407 610
www.pousadas.pt
Once a hospital, this is now a sumptuous place to stay. The neoclassical building with beautiful minimalist rooms is centred on a glorious courtyard, and there's a gorgeous pool. €€€

PORTO

Hotel Boa Vista
Esplanada do Castelo, 58 Foz do Douro
Tel: 225 320 020
www.hotelboavista.com
Set where the Rio Douro meets the Atlantic, this hotel occupies a

The sleek lobby of the Sheraton Hotel & Spa.

150-year-old building, with spacious, light rooms and amazing views. €€

Hotel da Bolsa
Rua Ferreira Borges, 101
Tel: 223 398 500
www.hotelbolsaporto.com

This elegant hotel near the old Stock Exchange has pleasant, warm-hued rooms. River views cost a few euros extra, which are well worth paying. €€

Grande Hotel do Porto
Rua Santa Catarina, 197
Tel: 222 076 690
www.grandehotelporto.com
Close to the main square, this wonderfully lavish hotel dates from 1880. The lobby may be all marble columns, but the rooms are coolly styled in neutral colours. €€

Infante de Sagres
Praça D. Filipa de Lencastre, 62
Tel: 223 398 500
www.hotelinfantesagres.pt
The most splendid old hotel in town, just off the main avenue; full of character and with a sense of former glories, with rooms decorated in sumptuous dark colours. €€€€

Hotel Inca
Praça Coronel Pacheco, 52
Tel: 222 084 151
www.bestwesternhotelinca.ca
Central andwell placed for shops and sightseeing, this Best Western is a pleasant place, if in need of some updating. €€

Hotel Internacional
Rua do Almada, 131

Tel: 222 005 032
www.hi-porto.com
One block west of the main Avenida dos Aliados, this handsome building dates from the early 1900s and was completely remodelled in 2010. Single, double and triple rooms. €€
Hotel Ipanema Park
Rua de Serralves, 124
Tel: 225 322 100
www.hoteisfenix.com
A modern hotel, with excellent service and beautiful views over the River Douro. A rooftop pool makes this a superlative choice, perfect for hot summer days. €€
Mercure Porto Central Hotel
Praça da Batalha, 116
Tel: 222 000 571
www.mercure.com
Near the centre, this is a 4-star hotel and a reliable choice, with smart rooms decorated in inoffensive, neutral shades of brown and white. €€
Residencial Pensão Pão de Açucar
Rua do Almada, 262
Tel: 222 002 425
www.residencialpaodeacucar.com
In a quiet location just west of the main avenue, this family-run pension is in an elegant building and has

pleasant, old-fashioned rooms. €
Hotel Peninsular
Rua Sá de Bandeira, 21
Tel: 222 003 012
With a tiled entrance and Art Deco upper floors, this friendly hotel is near the São Bento station. Many rooms are furnished by carved antique wooden furniture. €
Pestano Porto Hotel
Praça do Ribeira, 1
Tel: 223 402 300
www.pestana.com
Wonderfully situated hotel, right on the quayside, with all amenities, and wonderful views of Douro river, Torre dos Clérigos and Sé do Porto. €€€
Quality Inn
Praça da Batalha, 127
Tel: 223 392 300
www.continentalhotels.eu
In the centre of town, this friendly, welcoming hotel has a very convenient location and comfortable, if simple rooms. Ask for a room with a balcony. €
Hotel Rex Porto
Praça da República, 117
Tel: 222 074 590
www.rexhotel-porto.com/
A grand, central pensão, this is set in a stately old building, with

parking available. Rooms have high ceilings, and some are furnished with antiques. €
Sheraton Porto Hotel & Spa
Rua Tenente Valadim, 146
Tel: 220 404 000
www.sheratonporto.com/en/
Glass and steel give this tall, light and airy building an ultra-modern allure. Cool interior design has plasma TVs in the rooms and a posh spa. By contrast, the restaurant serves delicious traditional convent puddings. €€€€
Hotel Tuela Porto
Rua Arq. Marques da Silva, 200
Tel: 226 004 747
www.hoteisfenix.com
In central Porto, this 154 room hotel has been renovated in a crisp contemporary style with all modern comforts and lots of designer chic. €€
Residencial Vera Cruz
Rua Ramalha Ortigão, 14
Tel: 223 323 396
www.residencialveracruz.com
An inviting family-run hotel off Avenida dos Aliados, this residence is pleasant with airy, smart rooms. The rooftop breakfast room is a nice touch. €

DOURO

Alijó
Pousada de Barão Forrester
Rua José Rufino
Tel: 259 959 467
www.pousadas.pt
This famous town house, a *pousada* since 1983, is near Vila Real and close to the Douro river, and surrounded by rolling, vine-covered hills and lush forests. €€€

Amarante
Casa da Calçada
Largo do Paço, 6
Tel: 255 410 830
www.casadacalcada.com
Elegant and beautifully furnished hotel in parkland in the heart of town. It not only has stylish, extremely comfortable, contemporary rooms, but a fine restaurant and a pool. €€€€
Casa da Levada
Travança do Monte Amarante
Tel: 255 433 833
www.casalevada.com
Surrounded by chestnut woods and beautiful countryside, there are superb rural views from this 16th-century house, with a castellated tower and atmospheric

rooms decorated in antique carved wooden furniture. €€
Pousada de São Gonçalo
Serra do Marão
Tel: 255 460 030
www.pousadas.pt
In the Marão mountains, between Amarante (24km/15 miles) and Vila Real (20km/12 miles), this pousada stands at an altitude of 880 metres (2,890ft) and has a lovely setting and amazing views. €€€€

Lamego
Quinta de Vista Alegre
Tel: 255 880 150
www.quintavistalegre.com
This grand country house has good views – as its name suggests. The gardens are lush and green, and the rural setting makes it a wonderfully relaxing choice. €€
Vila Hostilina
Tel: 254 612 394
www.villahostilina.com
Difficult to find, but worth seeking out, this small *quinta* on the Lamego–Porto road is extremely tranquil. The house is furnished by antiques and surrounded by fruit trees, and there's a large swimming pool. €€

Pinhão
Quinta de la Rosa
Tel: 254 732 254
www.quintadelarosa.com
This spectacular country house has an incredible setting above the River Douro, with views across the river and vineyards. The estate produces ports, wines and olive oil. €€
Vintage House Hotel
Tel: 291 724 240
http://hotelvintagehouse-douro.com/
Beside the Douro in the heart of port-wine country; bougainvillea-clad terrace, riverside gardens, tennis court and pool. A wine academy for tasting and first-class restaurant. €€-€€€€

PRICE CATEGORIES

Price categories are based on the cost of a double room for one night in high season.
€ = up to €70
€€ = €70–140
€€€ = €140–200
€€€€ = above €200

MINHO

Amares

Pousada de Santa Maria do Bouro
Tel: 253 371 970
A splendid conversion of a12th-century monastery by architect Eduardo Souto de Moura. It's surrounded by gorgeous gardens and convenient for the Peneda-Gerês National Park. €€€

Arcos de Valdevez

Casa do Adro
Lugar de Eiró Soajo
Tel: 258 576 327
www.casadoadroturismorural.com
Fine old granite house in the centre of this mountain village, 15km (9 miles) from Arcos. €€
Casa do Rio Vez
Estrada de Seleiros, Bouça Couto
Tel: 258 526 078
Mobile: 93406 4577
www.casadoriovez.com
Five spacious rooms (including a self-contained loft) in a former olive-oil mill on the banks of the Rio Vez. Contemporary styling and a lovely pool. €€
Residencial Dona Isabel
Rua Mário Júlio Almeida Costa
Tel: 258 520 380
Close to the bridge, this neat little guesthouse is a bargain. Rooms are smart and well kept, and bathrooms sparkling clean; some river views. €

Braga

Albergaria Bracara Augusta
Tel: 253 206 260
www.bracaraaugusta.com
A grand town house with smart rooms with traditional styling, this has a colonnaded restaurant and a leafy garden. €€
Hotel do Elevador
Bom Jesus do Monte
Tel: 253 603 400
www.hoteisbomjesus.pt
Just 4km (2 miles) from Braga, this grand renovated mansion has a fantastic setting and lavishly decorated rooms and lounges. There's a recommended panoramic restaurant, which specialises in local regional cuisine. €€€
Pousada Sao Vicente Braga
Largo das Infias
Tel: 253 209 500
www.pousadas.pt
A relatively recent addition to the pousada collection, this is a beautifully converted 19th-century mansion. Rooms have antique carved wooden beds, there are spacious bathrooms, and a pool surrounded by

sunshaded tables. €€
Albergaria da Sé
Rua Gonçalo Pereira, 39–51
Tel: 253 214 502
www.albergaria-da-se.com.pt/
This central, modern hotel has traditional-style architecture, and is a charming, small place, well-furnished and in a pretty setting not far from the cathedral,with appealing, plain rooms. Good value. €
Albergaria Senhora Branca
Largo Senhora a Branca, 58
Tel: 253 269 938
www.albergariasrabranca.pt
Comfortable modern hotel that's conveniently and peacefully located on a large piazza in the centre of town; the comfortable rooms have a charming, old-fashioned feel, and some have balconies overlooking the garden €€

Caniçada

Pousada do Gerês - Caniçada, São Bento
Vieira do Minho
Tel: 253 407 650
www.pousadas.pt
This *pousada* is a restored hunting lodge on the edge of Peneda-Gerês National Park. Panoramas include views over the Caniçada dam in the Cavado River and over to Spain.€€€€

Guimarães

Casa de Sezim
Rua de Sezim, Santo Amaro
Tel: 253 523 000
www.sezim.pt
An estate near Guimarães with a splendid 18th-century facade and beautifully decorated boutique rooms, each with a lounge area and a private terrace. The estate is well known for the high quality of its white wine. €€€
Hotel Fundador D. Pedro (Residencial)
Avenida D. Afonso Henriques, 740
Tel: 253 422 640
www.hotelfundador.com
A modern, 3-star neighbour to the costlier Hotel de Guimarães, this is another good choice, for comfort rather than character, with simple modern rooms. €€
Hotel de Guimarães
Rua Eduardo de Almeida Guimarães
Tel: 253 424 800
www.hotel-guimaraes.com
The 4-star Hotel de Guimarães is a modern, contemporary choice, with sleek rooms, a spa and a health club, just 10 minutes' walk from the city centre. €€€

Ponte de Lima

Casa do Outeiro
Arcozelo
Tel: 258 941 206
www.solaresdeportugal.pt
This glorious 16th-century country house, 2km (1 mile) from town, has lovely antique-filled rooms, a gorgeous library lined with books from floor to ceiling, a great country kitchen, and a greenery-framed terrace. €€
Casa do Pinheiro
Rua General Norton de Matos, 50
Tel: 258 943 971
Charming antique-furnished guesthouse, with lots of polished wood and tall windows. Outside are lush gardens and a beautiful little pool, with lawns and yellow sunshades. €€
Paço de Calheiros
Calheiros
Tel: 258 947 164
www.pacodecalheiros.com
Located 7km (4 miles) outside Ponte de Lima, this is a splendid 17th-century manor house full of character and approached via a tree-lined drive. It's owned by the Count of Calheiros, who proudly shows guests around. €€

Viana do Castelo

Casa Dos Costa Barros
Rua de São Pedro, 28
Tel: 258 823 705
www.solaresdeportugal.com
An old town house right in the historic centre, in the Manueline style of the 16th century, which has been in the family since 1765. It's beautifully decorated with antiques. €€
Caso Melo Alvim
Avenida Conde Carreira, 28
Tel: 258 808 200
www.meloalvimhouse.com
Very comfortable *estalagem* in a restored period house in the historic centre, this has beautifully decorated, romantic rooms with lovely outlooks. Some have carved wood four-poster beds, and some have balconies. €€€€
Jardim (Residencial)
Largo 5 de Outubro, 68
Tel: 258 828 915
http://residencialjardim.com.sapo.pt
By the riverfront gardens, near the centre of town, this is a pleasant hotel with spacious rooms, decorated in strong colours. €
Viana Sol Hotel
Largo Vasco da Gama
Tel: 258 828 995

www.hotelvianasol.com
Near the old docks, 10 minutes' walk from town centre, this is a lovely grand building, and is comfortable, although feeling a little faded. €€

Vila Nova de Anha
Quinta do Paço d'Anha
Lugar dos Penedos
Tel: 258 322 459
http://pacoanha.com/html/
A grand 16th-century farming estate centred on an ancient manor house near Viana do Castelo, which produces its own *vinho verde*. There are fantastic views across the landscape and the sea. €€€

TRÁS-OS-MONTES, BEIRA ALTA AND BEIRA BAIXA

Bragança
Ibis Bragança
Rotunda do Lavrador Transmontano
Tel: 273 331 675
A comfortable, simple hotel with 70 rooms. It's a modern place that lacks character but has a great, central location. €
Pousada de São Bartolomeu
Estrada do Turismo

Tel: 273 331 493
This modern *pousada* is perched on a hilltop and has splendid views over the city of Bragança, and it lies close to the Parque Natural de Montesinho. €€

Manteigas
Pousada de São Lourenço
Tel: 275 980 050

www.pousadas.pt
High in the Serra da Estrela, with the freshest, cleanest air in summer and views of snowcapped mountains in winter, this granite-built place has a panoramic restaurant from which to enjoy the views over the river valley. €€€

MADEIRA

Funchal
Casa Velha do Palheiro
Rua de Estalagem, 22
Tel: 291 790 350
www.casa-velha.com
Once a hunting lodge, this has been converted into an extremely comfortable country house hotel, set between a golf course and lush gardens a few kilometres inland from Funchal. €€€€

Estalagem Quintinha Sao Joao
Rua da Levada de Sao Joao, 4
Tel: 291 740 920
www.quintinhasaojoao.com
Set a little way back from Funchal, overlooking the bay, this is a lovely spot, with a rooftop pool and lush gardens. Rooms are spacious, comfortable and bright and furnished with traditional wooden furniture €

Reid's Palace Hotel
Estrada Monumental, 139
Tel: 291 171 171
www.reidspalace.com
Reid's Palace is the most famous hotel on the island, still touched with Edwardian splendour. It's perched on the coast and surrounded by subtropical gardens, and rooms have a countrified look, decorated in pale colours. €€€

AZORES

São Miguel
Hotel Camões
Largo de Camões, 38
Tel: 296 209 580
www.hotelcamoes.com
A reasonably priced 4-star establishment right in the heart of Ponta Delgada, this is nicely furnished with polished wooden furniture and

View of Reid's Palace, Funchal.

has comfortable, inviting rooms. €€
Convento de São Francisco
Vila Franca do Campo
Tel: 296 583 532
http://conventodesaofrancisco.arteh-hotels.com/
There are 10 rooms, decorated in an elegant, pared-down baroque style, in this beautifully renovated 17th-century convent. The

surrounding countryside is perfect for country walks and activities. €€

Terceira
Pousada Forte de Angra do Heroísmo, São Sebastião
Angra do Heroísmo
Tel: 295 403 560
www.pousadas.pt
Atop a cliff, this is a strikingly designed boutique *pousada* in a 16th-century fortress. Sleek designer rooms are floored in warm polished wood, and there's a coolly contemporary restaurant serving creative cuisine. €€€

PRICE CATEGORIES

Price categories are based on the cost of a double room for one night in high season.
€ = up to €70
€€ = €70–140
€€€ = €140–200
€€€€ = above €200

TRANSPORT
ACCOMMODATION
EATING OUT
ACTIVITIES
A – Z
LANGUAGE

EATING OUT

RECOMMENDED RESTAURANTS, CAFÉS & BARS

WHAT TO EAT

Portuguese food is simple and fresh, abundant and filling, with few complicated sauces, but strong flavours and lots of garlic, olive oil and herbs. Portions are more than filling, and you will often have to work hard to clean your plate. Shellfish is popular and is usually served by the gram: about 300 grams (10oz) is enough for one. (For more details about Portuguese food, see page 85.)

One word of caution: when you sit down for a meal you are often presented with a plate of appetisers – cheese, meat pastes, shellfish. These are not gifts of the house, as they might appear, and you will be

Fortaleza do Guincho, Lisbon.

charged for anything you eat or pick at. Shellfish, in particular, can be expensive.

Meal times are relaxed: lunch is between 1 and 3pm; dinner usually between 8 and 9.30pm. The *menu* or *ementa turistica* is a set menu, which usually includes a *prato do dia* (dish of the day) and is inexpensive; this may only be served at lunchtime. Eating out is generally cheap by European standards.

CHOOSING A RESTAURANT

Restaurants in Portugal are rated on a scale of one to four stars, depending on expense, decor and service. The quality of food does not necessarily relate to the rating: there are plenty of 1- and 2-star neighbourhood places that serve great food but don't have any fancy trimmings.

Below are a few recommended restaurants, but there are, of course, many more. *Pousada* dining rooms are of consistently high standard (and are also usually expensive).

DRINKING NOTES

Port, the country's major gift to the wine world, is drunk as an aperitif as well as a *digestif*. The best places to try it are the clubby Port Wine Institutes in Lisbon, at Rua São Pedro de Alcântara in the Bairro Alto, and the Solar do Vinho do Porto in the Jardim do Palacio de Cristal in Porto.

Madeira can be an aperitif, generally when it is dry (Sercial) or medium (Verdelho). A sweet version,

Bual or Malmsey, is best for dessert.

Wine is red (*tinto* or *maduro*, mature), white (*branco*) or slightly sparkling *verde* (literally "green", but *vinho verde* can be either white or red). Always try to drink the local wines. *Vinho verde* should be sampled in the north of the country, Ribatejo wines in the centre and Alentejo and Algarve wines in the south. (See Wine feature, page 93.)

Adegas are wine cellars, the equivalent of Spanish *bodegas*. These can also be small restaurants.

Cervejarias are bars specialising in beers, but they are often indistinguishable from other bars. Beer (*cerveja*) is served by the bottle (*garrafa*), glass (*imperial*) or mug (*caneca*).

Ginginha or cherry brandy is a speciality of Lisbon and there are several tiny *ginginha* bars selling nothing else. A serving in a small paper cup, usually with a few black cherries, costs less than a euro.

Aguardente, the local eau de vie, is widely available, as is brandy. An *aguardente velha* for many Portuguese is a fine *digestif*.

Favourite Foods

Caldo verde, a cabbage and potato soup with *chouriço* (sausage). *Bacalhau* (salt cod) is a national obsession. There are, supposedly, 365 ways to prepare it. *Carne de porco á Alentejana* (clams and pork with fresh coriander) is a favourite meat dish. Sardines: fat, fresh and ubiquitous near the coast. *Doces de ovos*, or egg sweets, made with egg yolk, sugar and cinnamon and served as dessert.

LISBON

It is wise to reserve a table at the more expensive restaurants. Bairro Alto is the best place to head for intimate *tascas*, the typical restaurants of the city.

A Commenda
Praça do Império, Belém (inside Cultural Centre)
Tel: 213 648 561
International and Portuguese cooking is on offer at this smart, chic restaurant, which has a great terrace with views over the sparkling blue Tagus. €€

Adega Tia Matilde
Rua do Beneficência, 77
Tel: 217 972 172
This charming family-run restaurant has a friendly atmosphere and serves up traditional homestyle Portuguese cooking . €€

Hotel Altis Belêm
Doca do Bom Sucesso
Tel: 210 400 208
A Michelin-starred choice, where Chef José Cordeiro blends exotic flavours from former Portuguese colonies with local traditions to create innovative, exciting cuisine, and you dine in a gorgeous contemporary setting. €€€

Bica do Sapato
Cais da Pedra á Bica do Sapeto
Tel: 218 810 320
Close to Lux club (see page 367), set on the waterfront with views over the Tagus, this offers enduringly trendy creative cuisine that is beautifully presented; the restaurant, like Lux, is part-owned by John Malkovich. €€€

Bocca
Rua Rodrigo da Fonseca, 87D
Tel: 213 808 383
Contemporary, sophisticated, this hip, stylish restaurant serves creative Portuguese cuisine. You can view the kitchen through a window from the dining room, and there's a long and impressive wine list. €€€

Bonjardim
Travessa de Santo Antão, 12
Tel: 213 427 424
Some say it's the best roast chicken in town. This is where to head when you're in the mood for simple comfort food: piri-piri chicken, perfectly roasted, with heaps of chips. €

Bota Alta
Travessa da Queimada
Tel: 213 427 959
With lots of paintings and pictures on the walls, and cheery gingham tablecloths, this is a popular place in Bairro Alto, with hearty Portuguese dishes on the menu and a lively, convivial atmosphere. €

Buenos Aires
Calcada Escadinhas do Duque, 31B
Tel: 213 420 739
Melt-in-the-mouth Argentinian steak at this intimate yet lively restaurant set on a long flight of cobbled steps in Chiado; this is a romantic choice – for non-vegetarians, that is. €€

Casa do Leão
(in São Jorge castle)
Tel: 218 875 962
Not only does this place provide traditional Portuguese cuisine at its best, but it has an incredible setting on the castelo walls, and amazing views across the city. A tranquil, unparalleled spot. €€€

Cervejaria da Trindade
Rua Nova da Trindade, 20c
Tel: 213 423 506
www.cervejariatrindade.pt
Wall-to-wall tiled in ornate traditional, hand-painted tiles, which date from the 19th century – a roomy and very popular restaurant housed in the former refectory of the Trinos Friars. Go early at weekends. €

Doca Peixe
Doca de Santo Amaro, Armazém 13, Alcântara
Tel: 213 973 565
Down on the rejuvenated docks there is a wide choice of restaurants, and this is one of the best choices, serving superlative fresh fish and seafood, beautifully and simply cooked. €€

Eleven
Rua Marquês da Fronteira
Tel: 213 862 211
Set at the top of Eduaordo VII park, this is a minimalist, Michelin-starred choice, with lush city views through its huge plate-glass wall. €€€

Forno Velho
Rua do Salitre, 42
Tel: 213 533 706
A traditional setting and traditional food including goat roasted in the wood-fired stove and bacalhau con natas (cod cooked with cream); grilled fish and seafood soup are other specialities. €

Gambrinus
Rua das Portas de Santo Antão, 23
Tel: 213 421 466
In a pedestrianised street of restaurants, this is one of Lisbon's most venerable choices, an elegant, traditional restaurant, with excellent seafood. Service is very good and the wine list is impressive. €€€

El Gordo II
Travessa dos Fiéis de Deus, 28
Tel: 213 426 372
This intimate place in the heart of

Bairro Alto has a few tables out on the narrow street and serves delicious tapas. €€

Martinho da Arcada
Praça do Comércio
Tel: 218 879 259
Vintage restaurant serving Portuguese staples, such as bacalhau (cod) various different ways, under the arcades and yellow awnings at the corner of grand Praça do Comércio, close to the river. €€€

Pap' Açorda
Rua da Atalaia, 57 (Bairro Alto)
Tel: 213 464 811
This characterful restaurant in Bairro Alto sees diners seated under huge glass chandeliers. It's enduringly fashionable, with an excellent reputation, delicious traditional Portuguese cooking (açorda is a type of soup made with bread), and waiters with attitude. €€

Restô
Costa do Castelo, 7
Tel: 218 867 334
Set atop Alfama, this is the restaurant section of a performance arts cooperative. The food is nothing out of the ordinary, but there are fantastic views, as if you're floating above the city; or opt for barbecue in the leafy courtyard. €€

Sol Dourado
Rua Jardim do Regador, 19–25 (off Restauradores)
Tel: 213 472 570
Cheerful setting, with a vaguely 1980s-feeling, red and black interior, tasty food. There are plenty of fish specialities, but grilled meats are also on offer. €

Solar dos Presuntos
Portas de Santo Antão, 150
Tel: 213 424 253
www.solardospresuntos.com
Hearty Minho food, specialising in seafood, this is a cheerful, welcoming place, in the street-of-many-restaurants. It attracts local business people, who come in droves to dine on octopus, lobster and so on. €

Tavares Rico
Rua da Misericórdia, 35–7
Tel: 213 421 112
Chandeliers, gold-framed stucco,

PRICE CATEGORIES

The restaurants are divided into the following price categories based on a meal for two:
€ = under €25
€€ = €25–50
€€€ = above €50

gilded mirrors: this is Lisbon's oldest and most sumptuous restaurant, enduringly exclusive, with a 19th-century ballroom feel. Cooking is sophisticated, traditional Portuguese,

and service is helpful. €€€
Terreiro do Paço
Lisboa Welcome Centre, Praça do Comércio
Tel: 210 312 850

This has a fabulous location next to the Tagus river, with terraces overlooking the water. It also offers excellent Portuguese cuisine. Closed dinner Saturday and all Sunday. €€€

AROUND LISBON

Cascais

Fortaleza do Guincho
Estrada do Guincho
Tel: 214 870 491
A splendid setting in an 18th-century fortress beside the sea; imaginative, well-presented food that combines French and Portuguese flavours and has earned the restaurant a Michelin star. €€€
Villa Albatroz
Rua Fernando Tomas, 1

Tel: 214 847 380
All the elegance of Cascais, this is part of a swish local boutique hotel, with a sunny terrace and wonderful panoramic sea views. Good seafood and gourmet Mediterranean cuisine. €€€

Sintra

Café de Paris
Praça da República
Tel: 219 232 375

In central Sintra, this long-standing restaurant has been open since 1920. It serves delicious fresh fish and seafood dishes. Friendly and efficient service. Good *menu*. €€
Hotel Palácio de Seteais
Avenida Barbosa du Bocage, 8
Tel: 219 233 200
Great food is served in marvellous style, within beautifully frescoed walls in an elegant dining room swathed in long draped curtains. €€€–€€€€

ALGARVE

Specialities *Ameijoas na cataplana* (clams with ham, sausage, parsley and pepper); fried sardines; snails; seafood in general.

Albufeira

A Ruina
Cais Herculano
Tel: 289 512 094
Enjoy good food and good views overlooking the ocean. Open since 1971, A Ruina has a terrace for the summer months, and an ancient well room in the interior. €€
Vila Joya
Tel: 289 591 795
Praia de Gale
With two Michelin stars to its name, this is a fabulous restaurant under the stewardship of Austrian Chef Dieter Koschina, at a 5-star boutique resort, which also offers sea views. The wine cellar has over 12,000 bottles. €€€€

Almancil

Henrique Leis
Vale Formoso
Tel: 289 393 438
The eponymous Brazilian chef of this exciting Algarve restaurant mixes the flavours of his homeland with French cuisine, to create wonderful,innovative dishes. The setting is a wooden house,filled with huge paintings. €€€
São Gabriel
Estrada Vale do Lobo–Quinta do Lago
Tel: 289 394 521
At lush resort Quinta do Lago, Chef Torsten Schulz heads up this splendid

and creative Michelin-starred restaurant, with fantastic fusion cuisine served in a beautifully light, bright interior under wrought-iron chandeliers. €€€
Sr Frango
Estrada da Fonte Santa, Escanxinas
Tel: 289 393 756
With bright-coloured walls and brilliant-coloured paintings, this is a cheerful restaurant that's renowned for one thing: chicken, charcoal-grilled to perfection. €

Faro

Adega Nova
Rua Francisco Barretto, 24
Tel: 289 813 433
Popular rustic place, with wood-beamed ceilings, housed in a cellar that was once a storehouse for tiles and bricks; it serves excellent, good-value food. €€
O Farol Cervejaria
Largo Dr Francisco Sá Carneiro
Tel: 289 813 394
Set next to Faro's covered market, this offers tasty fresh fish, seafood and meat dishes it a simple setting with a large sun-shaded terrace. €€

Lagos

Adega Tipica A Forja
Rua dos Ferreiros, 17
Tel: 282 768 588
This always packed-out, buzzing, bustling place with excellent food, proffers excellent cuisine and service with tables crammed close together. €–€€

Don Sebastião Restaurante
Rua 25 de Abril, 20
Tel: 282 762 795
This white-arched restaurant serves top-quality fresh fish and seafood. On summer evenings it's perfect to sit out at the tables out on the cobbled street. €€€
No Pátio
Rua Lançarote de Freitas, 46
Tel: 282 763 777
Quality food served in a pleasant courtyard setting in old Lagos; this English-owned place has a rustic feel and delicious cooking. €€

Loulé

A Muralha
Rua Martin Moniz, 41
Tel: 289 412 629
This has lots of charm, with white-washed walls laden with bourgainvillas. Varied menu including *cataplana*, seafood and chicken piri-piri served in the secluded walled garden or indoors. €€
Monte da Eira
Clareanes, on road from Loulé to Querença
Tel: 289 438 129
A modest farmhouse turned into a delightful restaurant. The interior is white-washed with arching wood beams, and they serve up Portuguese food with flavour and imagination. €€€

Olhão

O Lagar
Pechão, Belmonte de Cima.
Tel: 289 715 437

TRANSPORT
ACCOMMODATION
EATING OUT
ACTIVITIES
A – Z
LANGUAGE

Porco à alentejana, Portugal's most famous pork dish.

Olhão is a splendid place to sample seafood, and this family-run place is a good choice for eating and relaxing in an agreeable atmosphere, with excellent steaks as well as fish. €€

Portimão

Dona Barca
Largo da Barca

Tel: 282 484 189
A great place to linger over a lazy lunch, this is a popular spot in the middle of town, full of locals, and serving up traditional Portuguese dishes, grilled fish, seafood soup, and so on. €€

Taberna da Maré
Largo da Barca

Tel: 282 414 614
The Taberna da Maré is another reliable fish restaurant, dating to 1946. It has wooden trestle tables and benches outside, and a characterful, rustic interior – a great setting for eating the freshest seafood. €€

Sagres

A Tasca
Tel: 282 624 177
A large, popular restaurant above the fishermen's bay, with a fantastic harbourside location and sea views to die for: its shellfish and fish are good and prices are reasonable considering the location. €€

Tavira

Quatro Aguas
Quatro Aguas
Tel: 281 325 329
A lovely, lively restaurant on the road south of Tavira, on the way to the Ilha de Tavira ferry, this has excellent fish and meat dishes and is a popular choice. €€€

Vilamoura

Willie's
Rua do Brazil, 2
Tel: 289 380 849
Chef Willie Wurger, originally from Germany, specialises in the cuisine of Central Europe, and his eponymous restaurant serves up Michelin-starred cooking in a softly coloured, romantic and intimate setting. €€€

ALENTEJO

Specialities *Açorda de alhos* (bread soaked in broth that is strongly spiced with garlic); *carne de porco á Alentejana* (clams and pork with fresh coriander). *Serpa* and *Beja* cheeses.

Évora

Botequim da Mouraria
Rua da Mouraria, 16A
Tel: 266 746 775
Tiny, tucked away place: this has not many seats and a small menu

of local specialities. The food and atmosphere are fantastic. €€
Dom Joaquim
Rua dos Penedos, 6
Tel: 266 731 105
Delicious dining in a chic contemporary setting, this is a contender for Évora's best restaurant, with fantastic seafood dishes. €€€
Fialho's
Travessa das Mascarenhas, 16
Tel: 266 703 079

You should book ahead for this place, a Portuguese favourite for classic regional food. Specialities include wild boar and slow-cooked lamb. €€€
Tasquinha do Oliveira
Rua Cândido dos Reis, 45-A
Tel: 266 744 841
This is a small restaurant (book ahead) offering typical, splendidly home-cooked Alentejan cuisine. There's a good wine list and a friendly atmosphere. €€

ESTREMADURA

Specialities Estremadura has excellent seafood, including *arroz de marisco* (seafood and rice). Ribatejo wines.

Tomar

Bela Vista
Traversa Fonte Choupo, 6

Tel: 249 312 870
This is an excellent, inexpensive restaurant with a fantastic setting by the river and a charming, rustic feel. Prices are very reasonable and food is superb. €€

PRICE CATEGORIES

The restaurants are divided into the following price categories based on a meal for two:
€ = under €25
€€ = €25–50
€€€ = above €50

COIMBRA AND BEIRA LITORAL

Specialities The area is particularly well known for *chanfana* (kid stew); *leitão* (roast suckling pig); *pastéis de Santa Clara* (pastries).

Aveiro

Mercado do Peixe
Largo da Praça do Peixe
Tel: 234 383 511
Locations don't get much more convenient for fresh seafood than this: overlooking fish market. This popular, stylish restaurant is full of locals dining on the freshest possible fish. €€

Coimbra

Dom Pedro
Avenida Emidio Navarro, 58

Tel: 239 829 108
This is Coimbra's top restaurant, located near the tourist office, with a wonderfully traditional, tiled interior. It serves hearty regional cooking, such as *chanfana* (kid stew). €€€

Molho de Brocolos
Avenida Sa da Bandeira, 33–5
Tel: 239 091 309
Vegans and vegetarians don't have it easy in Portugal, and thus a vegetarian restaurant is a welcome find: non-meat-eaters will be thrilled to enjoy some variation in their omelette-dominated diets. Varied and good food at reasonable prices. €€

Hotel Quinta das Lagrimas
Rua António Augusto Gonçalves

Tel: 239 802 380
A handsome 18th-century palace with lovely gardens – this hotel is the perfect setting for a splendid, special-occasion meal, with lavish Portuguese dishes on the menu and a great wine list making it a worthy holder of its Michelin star. €€€

Ze Manel dos Ossos
Beco do Forno, 12
Tel: 239 823 790
Charming little rustic place that is always packed, in tribute to great Portuguese food, with hearty dishes. Pork is the speciality, with dishes such as stewed pork with beans. €€

BEIRA ALTA

Covilhã

Solneve
Rua Visconde de Coriscada, 126
Tel: 257 323 001
www.solneve.pt
This cheerful, large-scale hotel restaurant serves up solid traditional cooking, specialising in meat dishes, such as roast kid and baked veal. €

Guarda

Hotel de Turismo
Tel: 271 223 366
At this well-maintained old hotel, you can expect good food and service in grand, old-school surroundings, with

white linen tablecloths and lots of dark wood. €€

Seia

Hotel Eurosol Seia-Camelo
Avenida 1 de Maio
Tel: 238 310 100
This pleasing hotel is a good choice for lunch or dinner. It contains the wood-panelled restaurant Camelo, which specialises in local regional cuisine, served in a pleasant atmosphere. €€

Restaurante Regional de Serra
Avenida dos Combatentes da Grande Guerra, 14
Tel: 238 312 717

A popular place for hearty local specialities, the centrally located Restaurante Regional de Serra offers home-style cooking in substantial portions. €€

Viseu

Muralha da Sé
Adro da Sé, 24
Tel: 232 437 777
Near the cathedral, serving regional cooking, this smart, atmospheric choice has lots of rustic charm, with exposed flagstone walls. Delicious specialities include various octopus dishes, including roasted with red wine. €€

PORTO

Specialities Port, of course, plus *tripas á moda do Porto* (tripe with butter beans) and *presunto* (ham) from Lamego.

O Escondidnho
Rua Passos Manuel, 144
Tel: 222 001 079
O Escondidnho offers high-quality food, with a Portuguese-French menu, served in traditional surroundings, with lavishly tiled walls, dark wooden furniture, and antique ceramics on the walls. €€

Mercearia
Cais da Ribeira, 32–3A
Tel: 222 004 389
One of Porto's best typical Portuguese places, the restaurant is named in tribute to the local fish

market, and specialises in beautifully cooked seafood. €€

O Paparico
Rua de Costa Cabral
Tel: 225 400 548
This traditional restaurant with lots of atmosphere and rough-stone walls serves good food: select from a small but interesting menu of Portuguese specialities. €€

Portucale
Rua da Alegria, 598
Tel: 225 370 717
On the 13th floor of an old tiled building, Portucale is a long-standing favourite, a fine restaurant with a fine view over Porto's rooftops. The service and the food are considered and superlative. €€€

Ze Bota
Travessa do Carmo, 16–20
Tel: 222 054 697
This tucked-away place is a lively, atmospheric choice. It serves good hearty Portuguese food and is deservedly popular with local people. €€

Vila Nova de Gaia

Yeatman
Rua do Choupelo
Tel: 220 133 100
A new restaurant that's already earned a Michelin star, thanks to Chef Ricardo Costa, formerly of Largo do Paço in Amarante. Cooking is traditional Portuguese given a creative makeover: try the tasting menu. €€€

MINHO

Specialities Minho is the source of the great *caldo verde* (cabbage soup). *Arroz de sarabulho com rojões* (rice and pork) and lamprey. To drink there are *vinho verde* wines.

Amarante

Casa da Calçada
Largo do Paço, 6
Tel: 255 410 830
A fine, Michelin-starred restaurant in a magnificent 5-star residence in a pretty river town, near port-wine country. Cuisine is creative yet traditional and beautifully presented, and service also receives plaudits. €€€

Braga

Hotel Elevador
Bom Jesus do Monte
Tel: 253 603 400

Excellent regional cuisine in a hotel at the sanctuary (see page 302), which is architecturally impressive and has wonderful views – the restaurant has sweeping panoramas across Braga city centre. €€–€€€

Inácio
Praca Conde S. Joaquim, 4
Tel: 253 613 235
Regional food, with enormous portions of dishes such as bacalhau (cod) and veal, served in a very pleasant setting, with spotless white tablecloths in a lovely wood-beamed old building. €€

Viana do Castelo

Estalagem da Boega
Quinta do Outeiral, Gondarém, near Vila Nova da Cerveira
Tel: 251 700 500
Set in glorious countryside, and in

a grand 17th-century mansion, this is the place for distinguished Minho cuisine. It is best to book in advance. €€€

Pousada de Monte Santa Luzia
Monte de Santa Luzia
Viana do Castelo
Tel: 258 828 889
This hilltop hotel with a grand view serves international and Portuguese food. The dining room is splendid, with a formal look, gilded chandeliers and fine views. €€–€€€

Os Três Potes
Beco dos Fornos, 9
Tel: 258 829 928
A charming, rustic restaurant housed in what was once a bakery, this offers a traditional setting in which to enjoy good regional food. Expect dishes such as caldo verde (a soup made from greens and vegetables) and bacalhau. €€

TRÁS-OS-MONTES

Specialities Hearty favourites in Trás-os-Montes include *chouriços de sangue* (blood sausage), *feijoada* (bean stew), goat, rabbit, trout, lamprey.

Bragança

O Geadas
Rua de Loreto, 4
Tel: 273 326 002/1
www.geadas.net
This exceptional restaurant specialises in regional cooking, with beautifully presented dishes, in a smart but casual setting, and attracts hordes of locals, who rate it highly. €€

Solar Bragançano
Praça da Sé, 34
Tel: 273 323 875
A cosy place with rustic decor that is popular among local people, this has starched white tablecloths and wood-panelled walls, and offers delicious seasonal Portuguese cooking. €€

Chaves

Carvalho
Alameda do Tabolado
Tel: 276 321 727
This modern-looking restaurant is much favoured by locals, and serves up huge portions of typical hearty Portuguese food, with great service and in an appealing setting. €€

O Celeiro
Alameda do Tabolado, 7
Tel: 276 321 971

A fabulous deli that's packed from floor to ceiling with Portuguese speciality foodstuffs, including tasty local smoked ham and sausages. €€

Macedo de Cavaleiros

Restaurante Montanhes
Rua Camilo Castelo Branco 19
Tel: 278 422 481
A traditional local restaurant that's a good choice for Portuguese traditional dishes, with sympathetic service and in relaxing surroundings – wooden furniture and exposed stone walls give the place a rustic feel. €€

Mogadouro

A Lareira
Avenida Nossa Senhora do Caminho
Tel: 279 342 363
A big restaurant for this town, owned by a French-trained chef. Regional and French food, with splendid steaks and great seafood. Excellent value. €€€

Pinhão

CS Vintage House Hotel
Lugar da Ponte
Tel: 254 730 230
www.hotelvintagehouse-douro.com
A fine choice of ports, as can be expected, but there are also appealing menus from which to select dishes in a comfortable house-hotel run by CS. €€€

A simple dish of king prawns.

PRICE CATEGORIES

The restaurants are divided into the following price categories based on a meal for two:
€ = under €25
€€ = €25–50
€€€ = above €50

ACTIVITIES

NIGHTLIFE, FESTIVALS AND HOLIDAYS, SPORTS, PARKS AND SHOPPING

NIGHTLIFE

Portugal's nightlife is liveliest in Lisbon, and Lisbon's nightlife – from fado to great bars and discos – throbs in three main areas: in the picturesque district of Bairro Alto, a tightly knit grid where tiny bars spill into the streets, providing a party atmosphere; in the Cais do Sodré area behind the Avenida 24 de Julho; and around the reclaimed dockside at Alcântara.

Look out, too, for events in the **Fundação Calouste Gulbenkian** and the **Centro Cultural de Belém**. The **Coliseu dos Recreios** in Rua das Portas de Santo Antão is the main venue for popular music performances. Major theatrical events are staged in the **Teatro Nacional Dona Maria II** in Rossio Square and in the Casino-Auditório in Estoril. The **Teatro Camões** in the Parque das Nações is the main home of La Companhia Nacional de Bailado, the national ballet compay.

The **Teatro Nacional São Carlos** in Chiado is the city's opera house, which has a winter season. The **São Luís Teatro Municipal** is the capital's principal classical music venue, but look out for concerts in romantic settings, such as the São Roque church, and at Sintra and the palace at Mafra.

Tickets for many events can be obtained from the fifth floor of the Fnac department store in Chiado.

The **Orquestra Nacional do Porto** is a major national orchestra, and Porto has a prime classical music venue in the striking **Casa da Música** as well as the **Auditório Nacional Carlos Alberta;** and popular music is staged at the Coliseu de Porto.

The Orquestra do Algarve holds concerts throughout the year and there are a number of festivals along the coast. **Loulé** has a renowned jazz festival.

There are a number of music festivals around the country throughout the summer, including the **Festival do Sudoeste** in the Alentejo and the **Rock in Rio** in Lisbon.

Any town or village is lively until late on the night of a festival but at other times of the year the tourist towns and resorts in **Algarve** are among the few places to keep late hours; here summer visitors like to stay up until the early hours. Lagos, especially, is a fun party town.

For a list of what's going on where, look for one of the many free listings magazines, such as *Agenda Cultural Lisboa*, a free monthly magazine which is available at the airport and tourist centres. Even if you can't read Portuguese, the listings are comprehensible.

Music

Although Portugal's nightlife usually comes to an end fairly early, music, in fado houses, concert halls and nightclubs alike, tends to start fairly late, around 10pm.

The Portuguese musical tradition is much broader than simply fado. Folk music, very different from fado, is surprisingly vibrant in Portugal, as is jazz. There are several Lisbon nightclubs devoted only to African music, which are the places to go to hear the latest in African-influenced sounds.

Lisbon

Many of Lisbon's fado houses are located in the Bairro Alto. There are

World Music

In Portugal you can hear local music played on unusual instruments and rooted in deep traditions, and you can hear world music, brought in from the former colonies in Africa and Latin America.

Festas have kept alive local folk groups, which show no signs of dying out, and modern musicians often turn to these roots for inspiration, from the Arabic-inspired songs of Alentejo to the bagpipe wails of Trás-os-Montes. There is a rich variety of instruments, notably the *guitarra portuguesa*, a 12-string instrument that has several versions, and the four-string *cavaquinho*, the ancestor of the ukelele. There is also a strong a capella tradition, and you may hear student groups break into song in the streets of Porto or Coimbra.

Brazilian music has come to the fore in recent years, and Portugal is a good place to hear it. You can also seek out venues with music from Africa, or from Cabo Verde, a small Atlantic island and former colony with a disproportionate number of talented singers, such as Cesaria Évora.

others in the older neighbourhoods – the Alfama, Alcântara and Lapa. They usually serve dinner (optional) and often charge a fairly steep entrance or minimum consumption charge. Singing starts around 10pm. It's best to book in advance.

Adega Machado
Rua do Norte, 91
Tel: 213 422 282.
www.adegamachado.pt

Easter is a high point in the festival calendar.

Arcadas do Faia
Rua da Barroca, 54–6
Tel: 213 426 742
www.ofaia.com
A Sévera
Rua das Gáveas, 51–7
Tel: 213 461 204
www.asevera.com (Closed Wednesday)
Clube de Fado
Rua São João da Praça, 92–4
Tel: 218 852 704
www.clube-de-fado.com
Senhor Vinho
Rua do Meio, 18 (in Lapa)
Tel: 213 972 681
www.srvinho.com

Coimbra
This is a university city, full of young
people, so there is lots in the way
of nightlife. But best of all is the
enthusiasm for their own brand of
fado. Among the best places are:
A Capella
Rua do Corpo de Deus
Tel: 239 833 985
www.acapella.com.pt/
Diligência Bar
Rua Nova
Tel: 239 827 667
The **Teatro Gil Vicente** (www.tagv.pt)
usually has a bright weekly programme
of concerts and other events.

Discos and Clubs

Bars with live music – and often
dancing – are called *boîtes*.
Discotecas, or discos, occasionally
have live music as well.

Lisbon

Most are in or near the Bairro Alto,
Rato and São Bento – areas west and
up from Avenida da Liberdade – or in
a cluster in the Cais do Sodré area off
Avenida de 24 de Julho.
Frágil
Rua da Atalaia, 126
Tel: 213 469 578
Among the trendiest discos in town.

Right in the Bairro Alto. Good music.
Closed Tuesday.
Hot Clube
Praça de Alegria, 39 (just above
Avenida da Liberdade)
Tel: 213 467 369
www.hotclubedeportugal.org
The best place in town for jazz.
Incognito
Rua Poiais de S. Bento, 37
www.incognitobar.com
Open Thursday to Saturday. You have to
ring a bell to get into this appropriately
named place. One of Lisbon's oldest
clubs, hosting alternative sounds.
Jamaica
Rua Nova do Carvalho, 6 (near Cais
do Sodré railway station)
Tel: 213 421 859
Fantastically random crowd in a
small and unfancy dive, good music,
ranging from 70s and 80s tunes to
reggae. In the city's red-light district,
but not sleazy.
Kremlin
Rua das Escadinhas da Praia, 5
Tel: 218 957 101
Also in the Alcântara area; lively.
Lux
Avenida Infante D. Henrique Armazem
A Santa Apolónia
Tel: 218 820 890
www.luxfragil.com
Very trendy and popular, this club in a
converted dockside warehouse near
Santa Apolónia station has an easy-
going atmosphere. You can eat here,
too. Closed Sunday and Monday.
Music Box Lisboa
Tel: 213 473 188
Rua Nova Do Carvalho, 24
www.musicboxlisboa.com
Managed by a record label, this is
a club and cultural space with a hip
music policy, hosting great live gigs
and DJs.

Porto

Aniki-Bobo
Rua Fonte Taurina (next door to the
Postigo do Carvão)

Tel: 223 324 619
No food but good music.
Indústria
Avenida do Brasil, 843
Tel: 226 176 806
One of the trendiest places to be for a
young crowd, filling up at around 2am.
Maus Habitos
Rua Passo Manuel, 178
Tel: 222 087 268
www.maushabitos.com
Arty venue with DJs.
Pitch Club
Rua Passos Manuel, 34–38
Tel: 222 012 349
http://pitch-club.com
A popular club, featuring music styles
including drum and bass and reggae,
spread across three floors.

Cinema

All films in Portugal are subtitled, not
dubbed, so they are accessible to
non-Portuguese speakers. There are
dozens of cinemas in Lisbon – 14 in
the El Corte Inglés department store
alone. In towns elsewhere there are
also plenty of cinemas.

FESTIVALS AND HOLIDAYS

January

1 January: New Year's Day (national
holiday).
20 January: Festa das Fogaceiras in
Santa Maria da Feira – young girls
in traditional dress carrying castle-
shaped *fogaças* cakes on their heads.

February

February/March (depending on date
of Easter): Carnaval celebrated all
over Portugal, but especially in Lisbon,
Loulé, Nazaré and Viana do Castelo.

March

Late March/early April (week
preceding Easter): **Semana Santa
(Holy Week).** Celebrated nationwide,
with local variations such as Senhor
Ecce Homo festival in Braga featuring
barefoot, torch-bearing, hooded
penitents.

April

25 April: Dia da Liberdade (Liberty
Day) celebrates the 1974 revolution.
Late April: Ovibeja Agricultural Fair.
Nine-day Beja fair, nightly concerts.

May

1 May: Labour Day
2–3 May: Feira das Cantarinhas. Fair of traditional handicrafts in Bragança.
Early May: Queima das Fitas, Coimbra. Local students go mad with parades, fado and the burning of gowns.
Early May: Festa das Cruzes. Festival of the Crosses in Barcelos, with concerts nightly.
13 May: Fátima Romaris. Celebrates the vision of the Virgin at Fátima. Rock in Rio, Lisbon. Huge rock festival.

June

10 June: Portugal Day.
13 June: Festa de Santo António. Celebrated all over the country, but especially in Lisbon.
Mid-June: Corpus Christi celebrations, Monção. A procession and a battle between the forces of good and evil.
23–4 June: Festa de São Joao (John the Baptist), celebrated especially in Porto, Aveiro and Braga. In Porto large parties are held where people are hit over the head with inflatable mallets.
29 June: Festa de Sao Pedro (St Peter). Music, dancing and processions.
Late June: Feira Nacional da Agricultura, Santarém. Features horse racing, bullfights and bull-running in the streets.
Late June: Festa de São Gonçalo, Amarante. A large procession with single people exchanging phallic-shaped cakes as love tokens.
Late June: Festas Populares. Huge Alentejo country fair in Évora.

July

First weekend of the month, every four years, 2015, 2019 etc: Festa do Colete Encanado, Vila Franca de Xira, has bull-running in the streets; and Festa dos Tabuleiros, Tomar, showcases a procession of girls dressed in white, balancing large trays of bread and wheat on their heads.
Mid-July: Festival Marés Vivas. Cool music festival in Porto.

August

Early August: Festival do Sudoeste, Zamujeira do Mar. Large music festival with hip international stars.
Mid-August: Festival do Marisco, Olão. Celebration of shellfish.
15 August: Feast of the Assumption.
20 August: Romaria da Nossa Senhora da Agonía (Our Lady of

Sorrows), Viana do Castelo. Parade of floats, music, fireworks and lots of drinking.
Mid-August to 21 September: Feira de São Mateus, Viseu. An agricultural fair featuring bullfights, fado and folk dancing.
Late August: Folkfaro, Faro, Algarve. Lots of live music.

September

8 September: Nossa Senhora da Nazaré, Estremadura. Folk dances, bullfights and processions.
Late September: Feiras Novas, Ponte de Lima, the Minho. Huge market and fair.

October

5 October: Republic Day.
13 October: Fátima Romaris, Fátima. Celebrates the vision of the Virgin; similar to the May festival.
Late October: Feira de Santa Iria, Faro, Algarve. Honouring St Irene with music and a fun fair.

November

1 November: All Saints' Day.

December

1 December: Independence Day.
8 December: Feast of the Immaculate Conception.
25 December: Christmas Day.

SPORTS

Participant Sports

Golf

The standard of golf courses in Portugal is very high. Those in the Estoril/Sintra area and in Algarve are particularly popular. The following is just a selection of the many clubs around the country. Among useful and comprehensive websites are www.portugalgolfe.com and www.algarve-golf.com.

Lisbon
Clube de Campo Aroeira 1
Herdade da Aroeira, south of the River Tagus.
Tel: 212 979 100
www.aroeira.com
Estoril Golf Club
Avenida da República, Estoril
Tel: 214 680 176
www.palacioestorilhotel.com

Estoril-Sol Golf Club
Quinta do Outeiro, near Sintra
Tel: 219 240 331
Lisbon Sports Club
Casal da Carregueira, Belas, near Queluz
Tel: 214 310 077
www.lisbonclub.com
Penha Longa Club (Atlântico)
One of two fine Penha Longa club courses near Sintra.
Tel: 219 249 011
www.penhalonga.com
Praia d'El Rey
Between Óbidos and Peniche, easily accessible via the A8 motorway
Tel: 262 905 010
www.praia-del-rey.com

Setúbal
Tróia Golf Club
Torralta, Tróia
Tel: 265 494 024
www.troiagolf.com

Algarve
This is a selection from a large number of excellent courses:
Le Méridien Penina Golf Club
Penina, near Portimao
Tel: 282 420 200
www.lemeridienpenina.com/en
Oceânico Golf
Tel: 289 310 333
www.oceanicogolf.com
Has no fewer than five courses on the Vilamoura estate near Loulé – of which the so-called Old Course is the most famous.
Onyria Palmares Golf Club
Meia Praia, near Lagos
Tel: 282 790 500
www.onyriapalmares.com
Quinta do Lago Golf Club
Almancil, near Loulé and Faro
Tel: 289 390 705
www.quintadolagogolf.com
Vale do Lobo Golf Club
Vale do Lobo, near Loulé
Tel: 289 353 465
www.valedolobo.com

Costa de Prata
Vimeiro Golf Club
Praia do Porto Novo, Vimeiro, about 65km (40 miles) north of Lisbon
Tel: 261 980 800
www.turismovimeiro.com

Porto
Miramar Golf Club
Praia de Miramar, Avenida Sacudira Cabral, Valadares, near Porto
Tel: 227 622 067
Oporto Golf Club
Lugar do Sisto, near Espinho
Tel: 227 342 008
www.oportogolfclub.com

Tennis

In Lisbon, the **Marinha Golf Club** and Lisbon Sports Club *(listed above, under Golf)* have tennis courts. Try also:
Club de Ténis do Estoril
Tel: 214 662 770
www.clubedetenisdoestoril.com
Lisboa Tennis Clube
Tel: 217 609 952
In Algarve, there are courts at the Jim Stewart Tennis Academy (www.playtennisalgarve.com) at the **Quinta do Lago**, and more courts at **Vale do Lobo** (tel: 289 357 850), **Vilamoura Ténis Centre** (tel: 289 324 123) and at many hotels. Several towns have their own municipal courts.

Water Sports

There are few facilities for hiring equipment outside Algarve. In the Lisbon area you will find surfboards and other equipment for hire at the beaches. For sailing, there's **the Cascais Naval Club** (www.cncascais.com) Windsurfers head for the long beaches and wild waves at Guincho, farther out. For deep-sea fishing, check with the local tourist office.
In Porto, the **Porto Golf Club** (tel: 227 342 008) has skin-diving facilities. You can also try the Leça da Palmeira Beach (to the north) for sailing.
In Algarve, all the larger tourist beaches and towns have some facilities. Near Lagos, there are windsurfing and waterskiing facilities at Luz, São Roque (Meia Praia) and Alvor beaches; the latter two also have sailing facilities. Praia da Rocha has sailing, windsurfing and waterskiing facilities; sailing and windsurfing are practised at Armação de Pera, near Albufeira. Vilamoura has extensive water sports facilities, as does Vale do Lobo. The wild coast near Sagres is particularly popular with surfers.

Walking & Hiking

The many national parks in central and northern Portugal are ideal for walking and hiking: the Serra da Estrela and Peneda-Gerês and Montesinho National Parks are three of the best. The beaches and cliffs

To Ski or to Scu?

The Serra da Estrela is the place for the little that Portugal has to offer in the way of winter sports. Visitors ski here, but mostly they *scu* – a combination of the words ski and *cu*, which means rear end in Portuguese. To *scu*, you grab a plastic bag, sit on it, and slide downhill.

along the Algarve coast are also excellent for walking, as are the hills around Mogadouro in Trás-os-Montes. Various local organisations offer hiking and climbing excursions.

Horse Riding

There are stables all around the country where horses can be hired. Algarve in particular has a number of riding centres. Most of the horses you will encounter are at least in part Lusitano, a famous and sure-footed Portuguese breed. Adventure centres in northern Portugal also offer horse riding trips, such as around Campo do Gerês in the Minho.

Spectator Sports

Football

Football dominates Portuguese sports life. From the 10-year-olds playing in the street to the hundreds of professional, semi-pro and amateur teams, to the massive coverage the sport is given on TV and in the papers, football in Portugal is inescapable.
The three most important teams in the country are FC Porto, from Porto, Benfica and Sporting, the latter two from Lisbon. Just about everyone in Portugal, no matter where they are from, is a loyal fan of one of the three.
The football season stretches from September or October to July. Tickets for the big three teams are difficult to get, as there are many season-ticket holders. In Lisbon, try the ticket kiosk located in Praça dos Restauradores; elsewhere, try the stadiums themselves. Games are usually held on Sunday afternoon.

Bullfighting

Portuguese bullfighting is different from the Spanish variety. It is considered less violent because the bull is not killed in the ring (however, it is killed later, out of public view). Nonetheless, it is bloody enough to upset the sensibilities of many people. The star Portuguese bullfighters are on horseback, the horses beautifully bedecked and highly trained. A striking aspect of the Portugese *corrida* is the team of *forcados* – eight unpaid local men, colourfully dressed in short coats, tight pants, waistbands and stockings – who face the bull bare-handed in an exhibition of pure machismo.
Bullfighting is popular primarily in Ribatejo (just outside Lisbon) and in Lisbon itself. The season runs from spring to autumn. In Lisbon, *corridas* are held in the Campo Pequeño

The Algarve is for watersports.

bullring. There is also a ring in Cascais. The most famous bullfights, however, are held in Santarém and Vila Franca da Xira, northeast of Lisbon (take the train from Santa Apolónia.)
Ribatejo festivals, which are frequent in the summer, almost always feature bullfighting and the freeing of bulls in the streets.

NATIONAL PARKS

Parque Nacional da Peneda-Gerês

The Peneda-Gerês (see page 305) park extends over some 700 sq km (270 sq miles) and is located in the far north of the country. The highest peak in the Peneda-Gerês is 1,544 metres (5,065ft), with a view of the Minho, Trás-os-Montes, and across the border into Galicia.
The lush plant life is fed by heavy rainfall. The park is home to 17 species of plants that are found nowhere else, as well as extensive forests of oak and pine. Wild ponies, deer, wolves, golden eagles, wild boars and badgers, as well as many other animals, live within the boundaries.
You may fish, go horse riding, hike and mountain climb amid the breathtaking scenery in the park. You can also visit picturesque ancient villages. There are dolmens, perhaps 5,000 years old, and milestones that once marked the old Roman road to Braga.
Entrance to the Peneda half of the park – the northern section – is from Melgaço, at the Galician border, and Ponte da Barca. The entrance to Gerês is off the Braga–Chaves road (take the turn-off to Caniçada). There is a *pousada* at the edge of the park, in Caniçada.

Tourist offices in the Minho, especially in Braga, can provide information about the park.

Parque Natural Montesinho

In the far northeastern corner of Portugal, Montesinho lies between Bragança, Vinhais, and the Spanish border (see page 318). As in Peneda-Gerês, many varieties of flora and fauna abound. There is not only wild, heath-like scenery but also ancient villages preserving their age-old customs. Access is from Bragança or Vinhais.

Parque Natural Serra da Estrela

Granite peaks, glacial valleys and streams, lakes and boulders lie within the natural park of the Serra da Estréla (see page 267). The highest peaks in Portugal are also quite accessible by car (although in winter roads may briefly be blocked). The prettiest season, with wild flowers everywhere, is spring.

There are places to stay in the larger towns in or near the Serra, which include Gouveia, Seia, Covilhã and Guarda. There is a *pousada* in Manteigas. The Serra is about two hours by car from Coimbra.

Serra da Arrábida

Just south of Lisbon, the Serra da Arrábida's natural beauty is accessible to anyone with a car (see page 181). The steep hills, with a wide variety of flowers and trees, and the blue ocean for contrast, are beautiful. The Serra da Arrábida provides wonderful views all along the highway, west from Setúbal.

A good map will show you where to find Portugal's several other protected areas. These include Algarve's southwestern coast, and a coastal wetland, the Parque Natural da Ria Formosa, which is important to migrating birds. Many other rural areas outside parks are also astonishingly beautiful and rich in birdlife.

SHOPPING

What to Buy

Portuguese handicrafts range from hand-carved toothpicks to wicker furniture to blankets and rugs. The most famous items are ceramic tiles (azulejos – see page 160) and pottery, Arraiolos rugs, embroidery and lace (see page 226). The beautiful Vista Alegre porcelain and Atlantis crystal bear comparison with the best in the world.

Pottery Different varieties of ceramic work are produced all over the country; in Alentejo, for example, you will find examples of *barro* pottery, a simple brown clay, sometimes decorated, sometimes glazed. Decorations on ceramics tend to be paintings of fruit or flowers, or sometimes scenes of rural life. Fine pottery from around Coimbra often carries animal motifs, and looks quite intricate in comparison with the simple Alentejano decorations. Further north, blue-and-white glazed pottery appears.

Rugs Arraiolos rugs, by contrast, come from only one place, the one from which they take their name: Arraiolos, in Alentejo. (They are, however, sold in other parts of the country, especially in Lisbon.) The art of designing and stitching these rugs probably goes back to the Middle Ages.

Where to Shop

Lisbon

Lisbon is particularly appealing for its small-scale, stuck-in-time shops and new bijou fashion boutiques. The best shopping areas are central Baixa, around Rua Garrett and in Avenida da Roma, while for boutiques you are best off heading to Bairro Alto.

Lisbon also has several large shopping centres: Colombo, Iberia's largest shopping mall, to the north of the city; Amoreiras – Lisbon's first; the sleek Vasco da Gama in the Parque das Nações; and El Corte Inglés, the city's largest department store. Near Cascais, Cascaishopping is just off the expressway and Cascais itself has a

Pottery crafted in the Alentejo.

shopping centre called Cascais Villa.

While many regional crafts are sold in Lisbon, there is usually a much wider and more authentic selection in the provinces. The following is a list of the traditional crafts produced in particular areas:

Alentejo

Cane and wicker-work, cork products (baskets, coasters, sculpture), wool blankets, Arraiolos rugs, ceramics *(barro)*, traditional hand-painted furniture, copper goods and lace.

Algarve

Palm and wicker-work, copper and brass articles, candles, earthenware pottery.

Coimbra and the Beiras

Ceramics (colourful animal motifs from near Coimbra; elegant Vista Alegre porcelain from the Aveiro region; black clay pottery from the Viseu region); woven rag quilts from the Serra da Estrela; as well as lace and embroidery.

Douro and Minho

Ceramics; wicker-work; straw baskets and hats; embroidery, crochet work, and regional costumes (especially from the Viana do Castelo area); religious art (from Braga). The Thursday market in Barcelos, north of Porto, has lots of handicrafts for sale. Porto is, of course, the ideal place to buy port, but it can be found throughout the country. Similarly, Amarante is the heart of the *vinho verde* production so it is good to buy the wine direct from local *quintas*.

Trás-os-Montes

Blankets; weaving and tapestries; crocheted bedspreads; black pottery from Bisalhóes (near Vila Real).

TRANSPORT

ACCOMMODATION

A – Z

A HANDY SUMMARY
OF PRACTICAL INFORMATION

A

Admission Charges

Portugal's museums and galleries are relatively inexpensive, ranging from around €3–6 for an adult ticket. Over-65s and students generally pay half price upon proof of identification. You can expect to pay in the region of €15 for entrance to theme parks and water parks.

Both Lisbon and Porto offer discount cards: the Lisboa Card and the Porto Card, which offer substantial discounts on multi-sights and also often include some transport options. For more information, check the respective tourist offices or online.

B

Budgeting for your trip

Portugal remains one of the cheapest countries in southern Europe for tourists.

To help you budget, here are some average costs:
A beer: €1
A glass of house wine: €1.50
Main course at a budget/moderate/expensive restaurant: €8/€10/€20
Double room in a cheap/moderate/deluxe hotel: €50/€70/€170
Taxi journey from Lisbon airport to the centre: €10
Single bus ticket or metro ticket: €1.40

C

Children

Like its neighbour, Spain, Portugal is a seriously child-friendly country. Children are made welcome just about everywhere, including hotels, restaurants and bars. There are plenty of kiddie-geared activities on offer, as well, particularly in Algarve, with water parks, boat trips and beaches. Watch the strength of the sun in summer, however, and always ensure your child is wearing a hat and plenty of sunblock. Most hotels can supply a cot if notified in advance, and babysitting is generally provided at 4- and 5-star hotels. Otherwise, tourist offices may be able to recommend babysitting services. Children's meals are not always available, but most restaurants are happy to provide a smaller portion. On public transport, children under five travel free while 5- to 11-year-olds pay half fare (on trains only; full fare on Metro and buses).

Climate

Spring and summer are the best times of year to visit Portugal. Southernmost Algarve enjoys mild winters with many fine sunny days.
Around Lisbon, winters are mild with an unpredictable mixture of sunny and showery days, while in the northern and central regions winters are rainy, and while not freezing, are surprisingly chilly. In the mountains it's even colder, and variable snow falls on the Serra da Estrela and mountains to the north

and east between November and February (sometimes enough for ski enthusiasts, although conditions are far from ideal). Winters are short, beginning in November or December and ending in February or March.

Generally, the weather starts getting warm in May and June throughout the country, and usually stays warm to very hot until September.

Along the western coast, the Atlantic tends to be cool (22°C/72°F) until July. The southern coast warms up earlier.

Some inland areas experience extremely high temperatures in summer – Alentejo in the south and the Upper Douro in the north often top 40°C (104°F) for long periods. Algarve in contrast tends to be moderately hot in summer (31°C/88°F), enjoying the benefit of cooling westerlies.

Customs Regulations

You can bring currency up to €10,000 into the country without declaration.

EATING OUT

ACTIVITIES

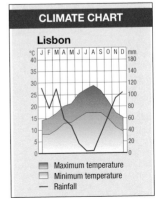

CLIMATE CHART

Lisbon

°C | J F M A M J J A S O N D | mm

- Maximum temperature
- Minimum temperature
- Rainfall

A – Z

LANGUAGE

The duty-free allowance for travellers over 17 years of age from non EU countries is 200 cigarettes and 1 litre of spirits or 4 litres of wine. EU residents can bring in 800 cigarettes, plus 10 litres of spirits, 20 litres of fortified wine, 60 litres of sparkling wine, 90 litres of still wine or 110 litres of beer.

D

Disabled Travellers

Portugal is gradually catering more to travellers with disabilities and there is a handful of organisations that may be able to advise you further. Accessible Portugal (Rua João Freitas Branco, 21D, Lisbon, tel: 926 910 989, www. accessibleportugal.com) offers a wide choice of itineraries, including city breaks, overnight trips, accommodation and tours. They speak English. Ourico do Mar (tel: 289 414 687; www.ouricodomar.com) offer wheelchair-accessible holiday accommodation, with wheelchair-accessible transport on the Algarve. Newer and larger hotels generally have disabled-accessible rooms and adapted toilets, and museums and major sights are gradually providing ramped access.

E

Electricity

Mains voltage is 220V, which is fine with equipment intended for 240V. Plugs are the European two round-pin variety. Adaptors are sold at airports, hardware stores and supermarkets.

Embassies

Embassies are listed in phone books (under *Consulado* or *Embaixada*). Most are in Lisbon, Porto or Faro.

Embassies in Lisbon:
Australia
Avenida da Liberdade, 200
Tel: 213 101 500
Canada
Avenida da Liberdade, 196, Edifico Victoria
Tel: 213 164 600.

Republic of Ireland
Rua da Imprensa à Estrela, 1, 4°
Tel: 213 308 200.
South Africa
Avenida Luís Bivar, 10/10 A
Tel: 213 192 200.
UK
Rua de São Bernardo, 33
Tel: 213 924 000
US
Avenida das Forças Armadas, 16
Tel: 217 273 300.

Emergencies

To contact the emergency service (police, ambulance or fire) dial **112** (toll-free). Most operators speak at least two foreign languages, usually including English.

Entry Requirements

Visas & Passports
European Union nationals may enter Portugal with only a national identity card. Citizens of Great Britain and Australia need only a valid passport for a three-month stay. The same applies to Americans and Canadians staying for 60 days or less.

All other non-EU visitors must show a valid passport when entering Portugal, and this will be stamped with a 60-day tourist visa. No one with a tourist visa is permitted to work.

Bureaucracy is a serious problem, so you should apply for an extension at least one week before your time runs out.

Visas or extended-stay visas can be obtained at any Portuguese consulate abroad, or contact the Serviço de Estrangeiros (Foreigners' Service) at Avenida António Augusto de Aguiar, 20, tel: 213 144 053, Mon–Fri 8.30am–4.30pm, www. sef.pt.

The British office that deals with extensions to visas is at the Portuguese Consulate, 62 Brompton Road, London SW3 1BY, tel: 020-7581 8722.

Etiquette

The Portuguese are usually courteous and hospitable. Taking a short while to learn the language basics, and liberal use of these thereafter, will serve you well. (Turn to the Language section on page 376 for some useful words and phrases.)

Here are a few helpful hints:
If you are invited to someone's house, it is polite to bring flowers for the hostess or a small toy or sweets if

there are young children.
There are always orderly queues at bus stops. Be certain to respect them. For some reason, stretching in public (on the street or at the table) is considered rude. Otherwise, use common sense and a smile and you shouldn't go far wrong.

G

Gay and Lesbian Travellers

In a country heavily influenced by the Catholic Church, attitudes towards gays are not as tolerant as elsewhere in Europe. Lisbon is the most important city in Portugal's gay scene and offers a number of bars and clubs catering to a gay crowd. In certain enclaves of the Algarve, such as "the Strip" in Albufeira, gay visitors will find accommodating bars and restaurants.

The website www.portugalgay. pt contains a travel guide with information in English and other languages.

H

Health and Medical Care

Portugal enjoys a healthy climate and no vaccinations are necessary. Bring enough prescription medication to last through your stay, if only to avoid confusion with brand names and/or language. Although the Portuguese health service has reciprocal emergency-treatment arrangements with other EU countries (take your ehic card, available on line at www.ehic.org. uk and from main post offices), it is advisable to have additional health insurance, as well as insurance against loss, theft, etc.

All narcotics and illegal drugs are banned and customs keep a close watch.

There are no special health precautions. Beware of sunburn, especially on misty days when the combination of a cool breeze and filtered sunshine can cause serious burning. Use sunscreen, and wear a hat if the sun is fierce.

Tap water is generally safe but sometimes not very palatable, so it is best to use bottled water (*água mineral*).

Insect bites (usually by mosquitoes) can be a problem in the summer, so bring repellents. In the countryside, snakes are not uncommon but they are rarely a problem: apart from one species of viper in the north, other venomous snakes have fangs at the back of their mouths, so even if they were to strike, it is unlikely to do you any major harm. There is no rabies in Portugal.

Useful Numbers
Ambulance Tel: 112 (emergency number)
INEM (Instituto Nacional de Emergência Médica)
Tel: 213 508 100
Portuguese Red Cross
Tel: 213 913 900
Linha Vida (for information on drug use and abuse)
Tel: 1414

Chemists
When closed, all chemists *(farmácias)* have a list on their doors highlighting the nearest one that is open. Newspapers also publish a list of chemists that stay open late.

Hospitals
Every town has a **centro de saúde** (health centre), some with 24-hour emergency service.

Lisbon
There are half a dozen large hospitals in Lisbon. The following have accident and emergency departments:
Hospital Cruz Vermelha, Rua Duarte Galvão, 54 (situated behind the zoo), tel: 217 714 000.
Hospital de Santa Maria, Avenida Prof. Egas Moniz (in the Cidade Universitária area not far from Sete Rios), tel: 217 805 000 for general enquiries or 217 805 111 for emergencies.
Hospital São Jose, Rua José A. Serrano, tel: 218 841 000.
The British Hospital, Rua Tomas Fonseca, Torres de Lisboa, tel: 217 213 400; or Rua Saraiva de Carvalho, 49 (overlooking the British cemetery near the Jardim de Estrela), tel: 213 943 100. No casualty department, but takes outpatients and may be able to help as all staff speak English.

Porto
Centro Hospitalar do Porto, Largo Prof. Abel Salazar, tel: 222 077 500.

Private Clinics
Lisbon
Clinica de Santo António, Avenida Hospitais Civis Lisboa, 8, Reboleira, 2720 Amadora, tel: 214 999 300.

Porto
Hospital da Ordem Trindade, Rua Da Trindade, tel: 222 075 900.

Internet
Wi-fi is increasingly available in mid-range to top-end hotels. There will generally be at least one internet terminal for guests' free use as well. Wi-fi zones are also on the increase in the larger towns and cities. Internet cafés come and go, but there are generally a healthy number, again in the larger cities. Expect to pay around €2–3 an hour. Public libraries generally provide free internet access, as do post offices, many of which have NetPost terminals, where you pay with a special card.

Media
Newspapers & Magazines
Portugal has several daily newspapers, two of which are dedicated solely to football!
The principal general newspapers are now published in both Lisbon and Porto and tend to have a regional bias, as indicated: *Diário de Notícias* (Lisbon), *Jornal de Notícias* (Porto), *Público* (Lisbon and Porto) and *Diário Económico* (Lisbon and Porto).
Weeklies include the *Expresso* (up to *Sunday Times/Observer* standard).
The *Anglo-Portuguese News* (http://lisbon.angloinfo.com) is a website including news and listings and *The Portugal News* (www.theportugalnews.com) likewiseprovides local and international news, plus listings and classifieds. In the Algarve, *The Resident* (www.algarveresident.com) is a popular weekly English newspaper primarily aimed at the local expat community.

Television
RTP, the state-owned corporation, operates two national television channels (rtp 1 and rtp 2), two regional stations and one international (rtp Madeira, rtp Azores, rtp Internacional). There are also two commercial stations (**SIC** and **TVI**).
Films are transmitted in the language of origin, with subtitles, as are many serials and documentaries. There is a high content of soap operas (many Brazilian) and quiz shows.
Most hotels have satellite/cable TV, which will include Sky News, Eurosport, cnn and CNBC.

Radio
There are four national and five regional **RDP** (state-owned) radio stations as well as more than 300 local radio stations. Among them are Antenna 1, which broadcasts popular music and news, and Antenna 2, a classical music station. There are also commercial radio stations, among them **TSF** and **RR**, which offer a similar mix of news and popular music.

Money Matters
Currency
The euro is the national currency of Portugal. It is divided into 100 cêntimos which is the basic unit of currency. The smallest coin is the 1 cêntimo piece; and the largest is the 2 euro coin. Notes go from 5 to 500 euros. The symbol for the euro is € and is written before the figure, eg €7.50 is 7 euros 50 cêntimos.

Exchange
While you may want to buy a small amount of euros before you leave home, you will get a better exchange rate if you wait until you are in Portugal. Once you have bought euros, however, it may be costly to re-exchange them for foreign currency. The most economical policy is to change money as you require it.
Money is best changed at banks, rather than at hotels or travel agencies. Outside normal banking hours, atms (cash machines), usually called *Multibanco*, are widely available and there are currency exchanges at Lisbon's Santa Apolónia railway station as well as at the airports. Major credit cards are accepted. atms taking all the major cards, including credit cards, are widespread throughout the country.

Exchanging money at a bank or cashpoint works out far cheaper than paying the higher rate of commission on traveller's cheques.

Traveller's Cheques and Credit Cards

Traveller's cheques are accepted in all banks, although, as already mentioned, the commission charge is higher than for changing cash. It is best not to use them in stores, where, if they are accepted at all, you will be charged at a disadvantageous rate. Major credit cards can be used in most hotels, restaurants and shops, but check in advance to avoid embarrassment. Country restaurants and *pensãos* may only accept cash.

Tipping

A tip of 10 percent is sufficient in restaurants and for taxi drivers. Barbers and hairdressers expect to receive the same.

O

Opening Hours

Most stores open for business Monday–Friday 9am–1pm, and from about 3 to 7pm, Saturday 9am–1pm, and are closed Sunday and holidays. Some shops in central Lisbon are open on Saturday afternoon and some malls and supermarkets are open on Sunday and all day during the week.

Major **banks** are open Monday–Friday 8.30am–3pm. **Museums** usually open 10am–12.30pm and 2–5pm, and are closed on Mondays.

P

Postal Services

Postal services, both international and domestic, are generally reliable and efficient. Allow five days for delivery within Europe. For next-day delivery within Portugal, use *correio azul*, an internal express service.

The post office also provides services such as express mail *(expresso)*, postal money orders *(vales)*, general delivery *(poste restante)*, registered mail *(registos)*, insurance on packages *(seguro)*, and telephone and scanning services.

Public Holidays

1 January New Year's Day
February Shrove Tuesday
March/April Good Friday
25 April Anniversary of the Revolution (1974)
1 May Labour Day
10 June Portugal and Camões Day
early/mid-June Corpus Christi
15 August Day of the Assumption
5 October Republic Day
1 November All Saints' Day
1 December Restoration of Independence
8 December Day of the Immaculate Conception
25 December Christmas Day
Local municipal holidays are as follows:

Aveiro – 12 May
Beja – 17 May
Braga – 24 June
Bragança – 22 August
Castelo Branco – 24 April
Coimbra – 4 July
Évora – 29 June
Faro – 7 September
Guarda – 27 November
Leiria – 22 May
Lisbon – 13 June
Porto – 24 June
Portalegre – 23 May
Santarém – 19 March
Setúbal – 15 September
Viana do Castelo – 20 August
Vila Real – 13 June
Viseu – 21 September

Post offices are open Monday–Friday 9am–6pm; smaller branches close for lunch from 12.30–2.30pm. In district capitals, the main branch is usually open on Saturday morning. Mail is delivered Monday to Friday.

To buy stamps, stand in any queue marked *selos* (stamps). To mail or receive packages, you need to go to the queue marked *encomendas*.

Be certain to write Via Aérea on all airmail items. To send large parcels home, if speed is not important, consider the less expensive alternative of surface mail.

R

Religious Services

Portugal is a Catholic country with around half of the more traditional north's population attending Sunday Mass (fewer in Lisbon and the south of the country). Many of the country's festivals have their roots in religion and Fátima attracts some 300,000 pilgrims every May and October, the most important months on this site's calendar. Although around 80 percent of the population is Catholic, the Portuguese are, overall, very tolerant of other religions.

S

Security and Crime

Portugal has a well-deserved reputation for non-violence, and crime rates are low. However, petty theft and muggings can be a problem in some of the more run-down areas of Lisbon and Porto, close to some of the larger shopping centres, and some of the major resorts. Foreign-registered cars or cars obviously rented may be targets for thieves if left unattended in out-of-the-way locations.

Use your common sense and the usual degree of attention, and, as in most places, take special care walking around late at night in resorts and in the larger cities.

Stolen Property

In the event of theft, report it to the police within 24 hours to reclaim insurance. In Lisbon the main Policia de Segurança Pública (PSP) station dealing with foreigners who have been robbed is at the Palacio Foz, in the Praça Restauradores.

Lost Property

All lost property given to the Lisbon police ends up being dealt with at Olivais police station, Praça Cidade Salazar. You will need to wait 24 hours before trying to reclaim your property, tel: 21 853 5403.

T

Telecommunications

All **phones** are equipped for inter-national calls and most accept coins.

A Portugal Telecom phonecard can be bought at kiosks and many shops. Instructions for using the phone are written in English and other major languages. You can also make calls (international and local) from post offices. Go to the window for a cabin assignment and pay when the call is finished. **PT Comunicacãos** is the national communication company. Many of the internet cafés in the larger cities also have several telephone booths. In general they can be found near train stations.

Many village stores and bars in Portugal have metered telephones. Phone first, pay later, but be prepared to pay more than the rate for call-box or post-office calls. As elsewhere, calls made from hotels are higher still.

For US phone credit card holders, the major access numbers are:
AT&T: tel: 800 800 128.
Verizon: tel: 800 800 118.
Sprint: tel: 800 813.

Mobile Phones

Mobile phone (cellphone) use is widespread, with the main local operators being Vodafone, TMN and Optimus. You can buy a pre-paid SIM card to insert in your GSM mobile phone. You can also buy a pay-as-you-go cheap local phone at the airport or numerous mobile phone shops, which is generally cheaper than renting.

Tourist Offices

The national tourist office (ICEP) has offices in Lisbon, Porto and at Faro airports. Most towns have *Turismo* (tourist offices), which are generous with maps and information. Some of the smaller ones close at weekends off season. Regional capitals have separate city and regional offices. Portugal's official website is www. visitportugal.com.
Aveiro
Rua João Mendonça, 8
Tel: 234 420 760
Azores
Rua Ernesto Rebelo, 14
Horta, Faial
Tel: 292 200 500
Beja
Largo Dr. Lima Faleiro
Tel: 284 311 913
Braga
Avenida da Liberdade, 1
Tel: 253 262 550
Bragança
Avenida Cidade de Zamora
Tel: 273 381 273
Castelo Branco
Avenida Nuno Álvares, 30
Tel: 272 330 339
Coimbra
Largo da Portagem

Tel: 239 488 120
www.turismodecoimbra.pt
Estoril
Avenida Clotilde, Edificio Centro de Congressos, 3º A
Tel: 214 647 570
www.estoril-portugal.com
Évora
Praça do Giraldo, 73
Tel: 266 777 071
Faro
City
Rua de Misericórdia, 8
Tel: 289 803 604
www.visitalgarve.pt
Algarve region
Avenida 5 de Outubro
Tel: 289 800 400
Guimarães
Largo Conego José Maria Gomes
Tel: 253 421 221
www.guimaraesturismo.com/
Lagos
Praça Gil Eanes
Tel: 282 763 031
Lisbon
Lisboa Welcome Centre
Rua do Arsenal
Praço do Comercio
Tel: 210 312 700
www.visitlisboa.com
City and National (ICEP)
Palacio Foz, Praça dos Restauradores
Tel: 213 463 314
Madeira
Avenida Arriaga, Funchal 18
Tel: 291 211 902
www.visitmadeira.pt
Porto
City
Rua Clube Fenianos, 25
Tel: 223 393 472
www.portoturismo.pt
Setúbal
Travessa Frei Gaspar, 10
Tel: 265 539 135
Tomar
Rua Serpa Pinto, 1
Tel: 249 322 427
Viana do Castelo
Rua do Hospital Velho
Tel: 258 098 415

Portugese Tourist Offices Abroad

Ireland
Portuguese Trade & Tourism Board, 25/26 Windsor Place, Lower Pembroke Street, Dublin 2
Tel: +353-1-670 91 33/34
Spain
Núñez de Balboa, 33 - 7ª planta,

Time Zone

GMT (summer time March– October GMT +1); the Azores are 1 hour behind continental Portugal.

28001 Madrid
Tel: +34-91 761 72 30
United Kingdom
11 Belgrave Square, London, SW1X 8PP
Tel: +44 20 720 1666
United States
590 Fifth Avenue, 4th Floor, New York, NY 10036-4785
Tel: +1-646 72 30200

Tours

There are numerous travel and tour companies that offer comprehensive packages. Most are booked via the internet, including the following:
Portugal: www.portugal.com. A wide range of accommodation options, including *pousadas*, manor houses and rural stays, as well as packages that include sightseeing, including week-long tours of Lisbon and northern Portugal.
Lisboa Sightseeing: www. lisboasightseeing.com. Offers custom-designed tours of the capital, including boat tours, jeep safaris of the surrounding countryside and sightseeing days in Porto.
Affordable Tours: www. affordabletours.com. A US-based company that offers a variety of reasonably priced tours.
Euro Adventures: www. euroadventures.net. A Spanish-based company offering food and wine tours of Portugal and Spain.
Saranjan Tours: www.saranjan. com. Customised tours including a 7-day cooking school, bicycle tours and market and craft fairs tour.

W

Weights and Measures

Portugal uses the metric system of weights and measures.

Women Travellers

Women travelling alone should take the normal precautions, although, overall, the incidences of sexual assault and other forms of violence are low. Bag snatching is more of a problem and women should avoid carrying a bag late at night in quieter areas of the cities. The north of the country tends to be more conservative, and in smaller villages it may be more prudent for unmarried couples to check in under the same name.

LANGUAGE

UNDERSTANDING THE LANGUAGE

GETTING BY

If you speak Spanish you will be able to read Portuguese and understand some, but certainly not all, of the spoken language. There are also slight similarities with written, but little with spoken, French. For most English-speakers, however, Portuguese, which has many nasal sounds, is not easy to follow.

Many Portuguese speak a second language, and most have the tolerance and courtesy to help resolve problems or queries. At the tourist offices and in virtually all hotels and many restaurants you will find the major European languages are spoken. Yet learning just a few simple words and phrases in Portuguese will certainly enhance your visit.

BASIC COMMUNICATION

yes *sim*
no *não*
thank you *obrigado/a*
many thanks *muito obrigado*
all right/okay *de acordo/está bem*
please *faz favor, por favor*
excuse me *faz favour* (to get attention)
excuse me *com licence* (to get through a crowd)
excuse me *desculpe* (sorry)
wait a minute *espere um momento*
can you help me? *pode ajudar-me?*
certainly *com certeza*
can I help you? *posso ajudálo/a?*
can you show me? *pode mostrar me?*

I need... *preciso...*
I'm lost *estou perdido/a*
I'm sorry *desculpe-me*
I don't know *não sei*
I don't understand *não comprendo*
do you speak... *fala...*
English *inglês*
French *francês*
German *alemão*
please speak slowly *faz favor de falar devagar*
please say that again *diga outra vez, se faz favor*
slowly *devagar*
here/there *aqui/ali*
what? *o quê?*
when/why/where? *quando/porquê/ onde?*
where is the toilet? *onde fica a casa de banho?* (or more politely: *pode-me indicar onde fica a casa de banho?*)

Greetings

hello (good morning) *bom dia*
good afternoon/evening *boa tarde*
good night *boa noite*
see you tomorrow *até amanha*
see you later *até logo*
see you soon *até já*
goodbye *adeus*
Mr/Mrs/young lady/girl *senhor/ senhora/menina*
pleased to meet you *muito prazer em conhecê-lo/lá*
I am English/American *sou Inglês/ Americano (a)*
I'm here on holiday *estou aqui de férias*
how are you? *como está?*
fine, thanks *bem, obrigado*

Telephone Calls

I want to make a telephone call *quero fazer uma chamada*

Questions

where is...? *onde é...?*
when...? *quando...?*
how much...? *quanto custa?*
is there...? *há...?*
do you have...? *tem...?*
at what time...? *a que horas...?*
what time is it? *que horas são?*
do you have a...? *tem um...?*

the area code *o indicativo*
the number *o número*
can you get this number for me? *podia fazer-me uma chamada para este número?*
the line is engaged *está ocupada*
no one replies *ninguém atende*
the operator *a telefonista*
hello? *está lá?*
may I speak to... *posso falar com...*
hold the line please *não desligue, faz favor*
who is that? *quem é?/de onde fala?*
may I leave a message? *posso deixar um recado?*
I will phone later *ligarei mais tarde*

At the Hotel

do you have a room available? *há algum quarto disponível?*
I have a reservation *tenho uma reserva*
single/double room *um quarto individual/duplo*
twin/double bed *camas individuais/ cama casal*
with bathroom *com casa de banho*
for one night *para uma noite*
two nights *para duas noites*
how much is it per night? *qual é o preço por noite?*
with breakfast? *com pequeno almoço incluindo?*
does it have air conditioning?

o quarto tem ar condicionado?
it's expensive é caro
can I see the room? posso ver o quarto?
what time does the hotel close? a que horas fecha o hotel?
dining room sala de jantar
what time is breakfast? a que horas é servido o pequeno-almoço?
please call me at... acorde-me às...
the bill please a conta por favor
can you call a taxi please? chame um táxi por favor?
key a chave
lift elevador
towel toalha
toilet paper papel higiénico
pull/push puxe/empurre

EATING & DRINKING IN A RESTAURANT

can we have lunch/dinner here? podemos almoçar/jantar aqui?
we only want a light meal queremos apenas uma refeição ligeira
a table for two/three... uma mesa para dois/três...
may we have the menu? a ementa se faz favor
we should like... queríamos...
what do you recommend? que recomenda?
what is this? o que é isto?
do you know what this is in English? sabe o que é isto em Inglês?
what wine do you recommend? qual é o vinho que recomenda?
not too expensive não muito caro
I'll have that quero aquilo
is it good? É bom?
well-cooked/rare bem passado/ mal passado
grilled grelhado
fried frito
boiled cozido
vegetables legumes
spoon colher
fork garfo
knife faca
would you like some more? deseja mais?
no thank you – no more obrigado – não desejo mais
yes please sim, mais faz favor

Sopas (Soups)

caldo verde cabbage and potato
canja chicken broth
creme de marisco seafood soup
sopa de coentros coriander, bread, and a poached egg

Drinks

coffee (black and strong) um café
coffee with milk um café com leite
large, weak coffee with milk um meio de leite/galão
tea (lemon) um chá (de limão)
orange juice (bottled) sumo de laranja
orange juice (fresh) sumo de laranja natural
mineral water (still) agua sem gás; (fizzy) agua com gás
chilled/room temperature fresca/natural
red (mature)/white wine ("green") vinho tinto (maduro)/branco (verde)
bottle/half bottle garrafa/meia garrafa
beer cerveja
milk leite
cheers! saúde!

I enjoyed that gostei muito
we have finished acabámos
the bill please a conta se faz favor
toilets (ladies/gents, men/women) casa de banho (senhoras/senhores, homens/mulheres)

MENU DECODER

Entradas (Starters)

amêijoas ao natural clams with butter and parsley
camarão prawn
gambás langoustines
pasteis de bacalhau dried-cod fishcakes
presunto smoked ham
rissois de camarão shrimp pies
santola recheada dressed crab

Peixe (Fish)

arroz de polvo octopus with rice
atum grelhado grilled tuna
bacalhau á Brás fried dried cod with fried potatoes and scrambled eggs (there is an almost endless variety of dishes with dried cod)
caldeirada de peixe fish stew
ensopado de enguias eels with fried bread
lagosta lobster
linguado sole
lampreia lamprey
lulas recheadas stuffed squid
robalo sea bass
rodovalho halibut
salmão salmon
salmonete red mullet
salmonetes á moda de Setubal

grilled red mullet
sardinhas grelhadas com pimentos grilled sardines and peppers
savel shad
truta trout

Carne (Meat)

arroz à moda de Valência kind of paella
arroz de pato duck with rice
cabrito assado roast kid
carne assada roast beef
churrasco pork cooked on a spit
coelho à caçadora rabbit stew
cozido à portuguesa variety of boiled meats and vegetables
feijoada dried beans with rice and various smoked meats
frango de carril roast chicken with a hot sauce
frango na pucara chicken casserole
leitão assado roast sucking pig
peru turkey
porco pork
tripas à moda do Porto tripe with dried beans
vitela veal

Salada (Salad)

alface lettuce
cebola onion
cenoura carrot
pepino cucumber
tomate tomato

Doces (Desserts)

arroz doce sweet rice
fruta fruit
gelado ice cream
laranja orange
leite creme type of custard
maça apple
marmelada quince marmalade
papos de anjo small butter cakes with syrup
pasteis cakes
pera pear
pudim flan crème caramel
queijo cheese
uvas grapes

Basic Commodities

açucar sugar
alho garlic
azeite olive oil
azeitona olive
manteiga butter
pão bread
pão integral wholemeal bread
pimenta pepper
sal salt
vinagre vinegar
sande (fiambre/queijo/misto) sandwich (ham/cheese/mixed)

TRANSPORT
ACCOMMODATION
EATING OUT
ACTIVITIES
A – Z
LANGUAGE

HEALTH

is there a chemist's nearby? *há uma farmácia aqui perto?*
where is the hospital? *onde fica o hospital?*
I feel ill *não me sinto bem*
it hurts here *tenho uma dor aqui*
I have a headache *tenho dor de cabeça*
I have a sore throat *dói-me a garganta*
I have a stomach ache *tenho dores de estômago*
I have a fever (temperature) *tenho febre*
call a doctor *chame um médico*
take this prescription to the chemist *leve esta receita para a farmácia*
take this note to the hospital *leve esta carta para o hospital*
danger! *perigo!*
look out! *cuidado!*
help! *socorro!*
fire! *fogo!*

SIGHTSEEING

what should we see here? *o que podemos ver aqui?*
what is this building? *que edifício é este?*
where is the old part of the city/town? *onde fica a zona antiga da cidade/vila?*
when was it built? *quando foi construída?*
what time is there a Mass? *a que horas se celebra a missa?*
when is the museum open? *qual o horário do museu?*
is it open on Sunday? *está aberto no domingo?*
how much is it to go in? *quanto custa a entrada?*
free admission *entrada gratuita*
can I take pictures? *posso tirar fotografias?*
photographs are prohibited *é proibido tirar fotografias*
follow the guide *siga o guia*
we don't need a guide *não precisamos de guia*
where can I get a plan of the city? *onde posso obter un mapa*

da cidade?
how do I get to...? *como se vai para...?*
can we walk there? *podemos ir a pé?*

SHOPPING

what time do you open/close? *a que hora abre/fecha?*
can I help you? *posso ajudar?*
I'm looking for... *procuro...*
we are just having a look around *queremos ver o que há*
how much does it cost? *quanto custa?*
do you take credit cards? *aceitam cartões de credito?*
have you got...? *tem...?*
can I try it on? *posso experimentá-lo?*
this is not my size *não é a minha medida*
too small/big *é muito pequeno/muito grande*
it's expensive *é caro*
I like it/don't like it *gosto/não gosto*
I'll take this *levo este/a*

Shops

bakery *padaria*
barber *barbearia*
bookshop *livraria*
butcher *talho*
chemist *farmácia*
department store *armazém*
dry cleaner *lavandaria a seco*
fishmonger *peixaria*
grocer *mercearia*
hardware store *drogaria*
optician *oculista*
post office *correios*
shoe shop *sapataria*
shopping centre *centro comercial*
stationer *papelaria*
tobacconist *tabacaria*

TRAVELLING

airport *aeroporto*
arrivals/departures *chegadas/partidas*
boat *barco*
bus *autocarro*
bus station *centro camionagem*

Days of the Week

Sunday domingo
Monday segunda-feira
Tuesday terça-feira
Wednesday quarta-feira
Thursday quinta-feira
Friday sexta-feira
Saturday sábado

bus stop *paragem*
car/hire *carro/a lugar*
customs *alfândega*
driving licence *carta de condução*
flight *voo*
motorway *auto-estrada*
railway station *estação de comboio*
return ticket *bilhete de ida e volta*
single ticket *bilhete de ida*
smokers/non-smokers *fumadores/não fumadores*
ticket office *bilheteria*
toll *portagem*
train *comboio*

NUMBERS

1 *um/uma*
2 *dois/duas*
3 *três*
4 *quatro*
5 *cinco*
6 *seis*
7 *sete*
8 *oito*
9 *nove*
10 *dez*
11 *onze*
12 *doze*
13 *treze*
14 *catorze*
15 *quinze*
16 *dezasseis*
17 *dezassete*
18 *dezoito*
19 *dezanove*
20 *vinte*
30 *trinta*
40 *quarenta*
50 *cinquenta*
60 *sessenta*
70 *setenta*
80 *oitenta*
90 *noventa*
100 *cem*
200 *duzentos*
1,000 *mil*

FURTHER READING

PORTUGUESE WORKS

Luís de Camões Author of Portugal's best-known piece of literature, the epic poem *The Lusiads*, written in 1572 and celebrating the Portuguese Era of Discoveries.

Eça de Queiroz (1845–1900) is one of Portugal's best-known authors. His most popular work is *The Maias*, about a wealthy Lisbon family in the early 20th century. Other titles include *The Tragedy of the Street of Flowers* and *The Crime of Father Amaro*.

Eugénio Lisboa has edited a number of books of poetry and short stories, including *The Anarchist Banker and Other Portuguese Stories*, and *Professor Pfiglzz and His Strange Companion*.

Fernando Pessoa (1888–1935) is second only to Camões in the list of illustrious Portuguese poets. He wrote under other names: Alberto Caeiro, Ricardo Reis and Álvaro de Campos, transforming his style with each. His *Book of Disquiet* contains his disturbing meditations around Chiado.

José Saramago (1922–2010) received the Nobel Prize for Literature in 1998, hastening the translation of his works into English. *Journey to Portugal* is a good place to start, a wonderful travelogue full of detailed insight. *Baltasar and Blimunda* and *The Year of the Death of Ricardo Reis* are also recommended.

Miguel Torga's autobiography, *The Creation of the World*, recalls his Trás-os-Montes childhood, a boyhood in Brazil and return to qualify as a doctor and work in his native village, where *Tales from the Mountain* and *More Tales from the Mountain* are set.

BOOKS ABOUT PORTUGAL

Backwards Out of the Big World: A Voyage into Portugal by Paul Hyland. Following in the steps of Henry Fielding from Lisbon to the Spanish border, Hyland brings a new insight into the country.

Birdwatching Guide to the Algarve by Kevin Carlson. Where to go and what to see.

A Concise History of Portugal by David Birmingham, CUP, 2003. A standard, with many illustrations.

In the Lands of the Enchanted Moorish Maiden, edited by Mandi Gomez. These 11 "exhibition trails" on Moorish Portugal cover "Christianised" mosques, palaces, fortifications and urban settlements between Coimbra and Algarve.

The Last Kabbalist of Lisbon by Richard Zimler. Set in Lisbon in 1506, when "New Christian" Jewish converts were being murdered.

Prince Henry The Navigator: A Life by Peter Russell. A portrait of the king as Renaissance man.

The Portuguese Seaborne Empire 1415–1825 by C.R. Boxer. An

Send Us Your Thoughts

We do our best to ensure the information in our books is as accurate and up-to-date as possible. The books are updated on a regular basis using local contacts, who painstakingly add, amend and correct as required. However, some details (such as telephone numbers and opening times) are liable to change, and we are ultimately reliant on our readers to put us in the picture.

We welcome your feedback, especially your experience of using the book "on the road". Maybe we recommended a hotel that you liked (or another that you didn't), or you came across a great bar or new attraction we missed.

We will acknowledge all contributions, and we'll offer an Insight Guide to the best letters received.

Please write to us at:
Insight Guides
PO Box 7910
London SE1 1WE
Or email us at:
insight@apaguide.co.uk

enthralling work full of awkward truths and compelling anecdotes.

Portugal's Struggle for Liberty by Mário Soares. By Portugal's most eminent political figure – a long-serving president and a key personality in post-revolution events.

The Portuguese: The Land and Its People by Marion Kaplan. A revised and updated edition to the revealing, readable and entertaining portrait.

A Small Death in Lisbon by Robert Wilson. Excellent novel of life in Portugal.

Portuguese Voyages 1498–1663: Tales from the Great Age of Discovery, edited by Charles David Ley. Contemporary accounts of the great sea voyages.

Republican Portugal, a Political History 1910–1926 by Douglas L. Wheeler. A fascinating account of the period between monarchy and dictatorship when Portugal endured 45 successive governments.

The Taste of Portugal by Edite Vieira. Recipes, history and folklore.

Hunting Midnight by Richard Zimler. After the success of *The Last Kabbalist of Lisbon* (see above), Zimler has set this fictional tale of bigotry and betrayal in 18th- and 19th-century Porto.

The Migrant Painter of Birds by Lidia Jorge. A beautifully crafted poetic novel by this feminist novelist about a girl from a Portuguese farming family and her absent father.

OTHER INSIGHT GUIDES

More than 120 **Insight Guides** and **Insight City Guides** cover every continent, providing information on culture and all the top sights, as well as superb photography and detailed maps. In addition, **Insight Fleximaps** highlight all the main tourist sights and provide essential facts about the destination, while being printed on durable paper with a laminated finish – write on the map with a non-permanent marker pen and wipe it off later.

CREDITS

Photo Credits

AKG Images 114L
Alamy 7BL, 37, 68/69, 72, 73, 74, 225B, 261, 309B
Art Archive 40, 41
AWL Images 27, 96, 294/295T, 294BR, 334/335, 338
Biblioteca Nacional, Lisbon 49, 50, 58
Corbis 10/11, 24T, 48, 52, 57, 63, 65, 66, 78, 80L, 80R, 98/99T, 114R, 336, 340B, 343B
Dreamstime 82/83, 86, 118/119, 121, 122, 125, 182, 191, 193B, 195, 196B, 218B, 236B
Farol Design Hotel 351
Fotolia 0/1, 8T, 9BL, 46, 105, 141, 190, 212B, 216B, 218T, 200T, 222, 223B, 224B, 241, 290T
Getty Images 25, 32, 33, 64, 67, 76, 79, 180B
Gil Gavin/Apa Publications 183T, 196T, 332, 343T
Hotel Eva 352
iStockphoto.com 6MR, 7ML, 7BR, 8B, 24B, 88, 209, 328B, 329, 337, 340T, 341B, 379L
Lapa Palace 350B
Lydia Evans/Apa Publications 2/3, 4/5, 6B, 6ML, 7TR, 7MR, 7BL, 9TL, 9MR, 12/13, 14, 15T, 15B, 16, 17, 18, 19, 20, 21, 29, 36, 38, 39, 44, 59, 70, 71, 75, 81, 84, 85, 87, 89, 90, 91, 92, 93, 95, 98BR, 98BL, 99BR, 99ML, 99BL, 102, 103, 107, 109, 112, 116, 117, 120, 123, 124,

126/127, 128/129, 130/131, 132, 133T, 133B, 136/137, 138, 140T, 140B, 143T, 143B, 144B, 145, 146B, 147, 148, 149T, 149B, 150T, 150B, 151, 152, 153B, 154B, 155T, 155B, 156, 157, 160BL, 160BR, 160/161T, 161TR, 161BL, 162/163, 164, 165, 167T, 168, 169B, 169T, 170, 171, 172B, 173, 174B, 176/177, 178, 179, 180T, 181, 183B, 184/185, 186, 187, 189T, 189B, 192B, 192T, 193T, 194/195, 197, 198, 199T, 199B, 200B, 201T, 201B, 202/203, 204, 205, 207, 208, 210B, 211, 212T, 213, 214B, 215B, 224T, 226BL, 226/227T, 226BR, 227BR, 227BL, 227TR, 230, 231, 233B, 233T, 234, 235T, 235B, 237T, 237B, 238B, 238T, 239B, 242/243, 244, 245, 247, 249, 250, 251, 252/253, 254, 255, 257B, 258B, 259, 262/263, 264, 265, 266, 267, 268, 269, 270T, 270B, 271T, 271B, 272/273, 274, 275, 277B, 277T, 278B, 279T, 279B, 280, 281, 282/283, 284, 285, 288B, 290B, 291, 292B, 292T, 293, 294BL, 295ML, 295BR, 295BL, 296/297, 298, 299, 301B, 302B, 303B, 304, 305B, 306, 308B, 308T, 309T, 310/311, 312, 313, 315B, 315T, 316, 317B, 319B, 319T, 320, 344, 346, 347L, 348/349, 350T, 360T, 360B, 363, 365, 367, 370, 371, 376

Mark Read/Apa Publications 99TR, 104, 106, 108R, 153T, 154T, 172T, 174T, 214T, 215T, 216T, 219T, 220, 221T, 227ML, 232, 236T, 240, 246, 248, 257T, 258T, 276, 278T, 286, 288T, 289, 295TR, 301T, 302T, 303T, 305T, 314, 317T, 318, 321
Mary Evans Picture Library 43
Museu da Cidade, Lisbon 28, 31, 54, 55, 56
Museu da Marinha, Belem 45, 61
Museu de Evora, Evora 113R
Museu Militar, Lisbon 22/23, 30, 51, 53
Museu Nacional de Arte Antiga, Lisbon 34, 35, 42, 47, 110, 113L
Phil Wood/Apa Publications 100/101, 108L, 144T, 146T, 161ML, 161BR, 210T, 223T, 239T, 327T, 327B, 328T, 331T, 331B
Press Association Images 62
Reid's Palace, Funchal 359
Rex Features 115
Scala 77, 111
Sheraton Hotel 356
Superstock 26, 94, 97, 217, 330, 342
TopFoto 60
Travel Pictures 6/7T, 139, 219B, 228/229, 260, 307, 322/323, 324, 325, 333, 339
Turismo de Portugal 167B, 175, 221B, 225T, 341T, 369

Cover Credits

Front cover: Castelo de Vide at twilight, *AWL Images*
Back cover: (top) Parque natural da Arrabida, *Lydia Evans/Apa Publications*; (middle) traditional dress, *Lydia Evans/Apa Publications*
Front flap: (from top) Porto as viewed from the Douro River, *Lydia Evans/Apa Publications*; Beira Alta, Idanha-a-Velha *Lydia Evans/Apa Publications*; Faro lit up at night, *Fotolia*; Albefeira, *Lydia Evans/Apa Publications*
Spine: Traditional folk dancing *Lydia Evans/Apa Publications*

Insight Guide Credits

Distribution

UK
Dorling Kindersley Ltd
A Penguin Group company
80 Strand, London, WC2R 0RL
sales@uk.dk.com

United States
Ingram Publisher Services
1 Ingram Boulevard, PO Box 3006,
La Vergne, TN 37086-1986
ips@ingramcontent.com

Australia
Universal Publishers
PO Box 307
St Leonards NSW 1590
sales@universal
publishers.com.au

New Zealand
Brown Knows Publications
11 Artesia Close, Shamrock Park
Auckland, New Zealand 2016
sales@brownknows.co.nz

Worldwide
Apa Publications GmbH & Co. Verlag
KG (Singapore branch)
7030 Ang Mo Kio Avenue 5
08-65 Northstar @ AMK
Singapore 569880
apasin@singnet.com.sg

Printing
CTPS-China

© 2014 Apa Publications (UK) Ltd
All Rights Reserved

First Edition 1992
Sixth Edition 2014

www.insightguides.com

Project Editor
Carine Tracanelli

Series Manager
Carine Tracanelli

Art Editor
Alice Earle

Map Production
Original cartography Colourmap
Scanning, updated by Apa
Cartography Department

Production
Tynan Dean and Rebeka Davies

INDEX

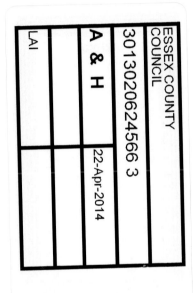

ESSEX COUNTY
COUNCIL

301302062456663 3

A & H

22-Apr-2014

LAI

4273784

Lisbon Metro

Legend:
- Blue Line
- Yellow Line
- Green Line
- Red Line
- ○ Interchange Station
- ○ Station

Odivelas
Senhor Roubado
Ameixoeira
Aeroporto
Moscavide
Encarnação
Oriente
Lumiar
Cabo Ruivo
Quinta das Conchas
Olivais
Alfornelos
Pontinha
Telheiras
Campo Grande
Alvalade
Chelas
Carnide
Colégio Militar/Luz
Amadora Este
Cidade Universitária
Roma
Bela Vista
Alto dos Moinhos
Laranjeiras
Entre Campos
Jardim Zoológico
Campo Pequeno
Areeiro
Olaias
Praça de Espanha
São Sebastião
Saldanha
Alameda
Parque
Picoas
Arroios
Anjos
Marquês de Pombal
Intendente
Rato
Sta Apolónia
Avenida
Martim Moniz
Restauradores
Rossio
Cais do Sodré
Baixa-Chiado
Terreiro do Paço

Map labels:
Estádio do Sport Lisboa e Benfica S.L.B.
Alto dos Moinhos
FURNAS
Cruz da Pedra
Palácio dos Marquêses de Fronteira
ALT SERA

CASELAS
CARAMÃO
Estrada de Queluz
Estrada dos Marcos
PARQUE FLORESTAL DE MONSANTO
Avenida da Ponte
Rua
Est. de Caselas
CEMITÉRIO DA AJUDA
ALTO DA AJUDA
TAPADA DA AJUDA
Avenida da Ilha da Madeira
JARDIM BOTÂNICO DA AJUDA
Palácio Nacional da Ajuda
TAPADA DA AJUDA
Rua do Cruzeiro
Avenida de Ceuta
CEMITÉRIO DOS PRAZERES
Rua G. Zarco
Rua da Ajuda
Estádio do Restelo
Calçada do Galvão
Calçada da Ajuda
Calçada da Tapada
Rua A. Operária
Rua de Camões
Alcântara-Terra
TAPADA DAS NECESSIDADES
BELÉM
Mosteiro dos Jerónimos
JARDIM AGRÍCOLA TROPICAL
Palácio de Belém
Rua Jau
Palácio Necessidades
Museu Nacional de Arqueologia
Museu Nacional dos Coches
SANTO AMARO
ALCÂNTARA
Cascais
Praça do Império
Feira Internacional de Lisboa
Alcântara-Mar
Museu do Oriente
Belém
Rua da Junqueira
Avenida da Índia
Avenida da Ponte
Doca de Alcântara
Padrão dos Descobrimentos
Doca de Santo Amaro
Porto Brandão
← Tejo
Ponte 25 de Abril
Cristo Rei